Opera & Vivaldi

Orlando, played by Marilyn Horne, before the Temple of Infernal Hecate
in act 3 of Vivaldi's *Orlando furioso*, the Dallas Opera, 1980. Photo: Phil
Schexnyder. Frontispiece courtesy the Dallas Opera.

Opera & Vivaldi

Edited by Michael Collins and Elise K. Kirk

 University of Texas Press, Austin

Copyright © 1984 by the University of Texas Press
All rights reserved
Printed in the United States of America
First Edition, 1984

Requests for permission to reproduce material from this work
should be sent to Permissions, University of Texas Press,
Box 7819, Austin, Texas 78712.

Library of Congress Cataloging in Publication Data
Main entry under title:
Opera and Vivaldi.
  Includes index.
   1. Opera—18th century—Congresses.   2. Vivaldi,
Antonio, 1678–1741.   Orlando.   3. Vivaldi, Antonio,
1678–1741.   Operas.   I. Collins, Michael (Michael B.),
1930–   .   II. Kirk, Elise K. (Elise Kuhl), 1932–   .
ML1703.063   1984   782.1'09'033   83-23557
ISBN 0-292-70746-0

Contents

INTRODUCTION. Vivaldi's *Orlando furioso*: The Dallas Opera
Production and Symposium   1
by Elise K. Kirk

PART I. Literary Sources and Their Transformation into Opera
Dramatic Theory and the Italian Baroque Libretto   15
by Michael Collins
Mythological Subjects in Opera Seria   41
by Sven Hansell
Ariosto and the Oral Tradition   54
by C. Peter Brand
Ariosto's *Orlando* and Opera Seria   64
by Gary Schmidgall
Orlando in *Seicento* Venice: The Road Not Taken   87
by Ellen Rosand
Eighteenth-Century Orlando: Hero, Satyr, and Fool   105
by Ellen T. Harris

PART II. Venetian Opera in Its Cultural Milieu
Venetian Theaters during Vivaldi's Era   131
by William C. Holmes
Costume in the Frescoes of Tiepolo and Eighteenth-Century
Italian Opera   149
by William L. Barcham
Baroque Manners and Passions in Modern Performance   170
by Shirley Wynne
Opera Criticism and the Venetian Press   179
by Eleanor Selfridge-Field

PART III. The Practice of Opera Seria
Voice Register as an Index of Age and Status in Opera Seria   193
by Roger Covell

Cadential Structures and Accompanimental Practices
in Eighteenth-Century Italian Recitative   211
by Michael Collins

Declamation and Expressive Singing in Recitative   233
by Mary Cyr

Embellishing Eighteenth-Century Arias: On Cadenzas   258
by Howard Mayer Brown

PART IV. Vivaldi as Dramatic Composer

The Relationship between Text and Music in the
Operas of Vivaldi   279
by Eric Cross

Vivaldi as Self-Borrower   308
by Klaus Kropfinger

Vivaldi's *Orlando*: Sources and Contributing Factors   327
by John Walter Hill

PART V. Baroque Opera Today

Preparing the Critical Edition: An Interview with
Alan Curtis   349
by Marita P. McClymonds

Opera Seria Today: A Credo   358
by Andrew Porter

APPENDIX. Grazio Braccioli's *Orlando furioso*: A History
and Synopsis of the Libretto   367
by Michael Collins

Contributors   379

Index   383

Opera & Vivaldi

Vivaldi's *Orlando furioso*: The Dallas Opera Production and Symposium *by Elise K. Kirk*

In November 1980, the Dallas Opera produced the first fully staged performance in America of Antonio Vivaldi's opera *Orlando furioso*. It was the first time an opera by Vivaldi had ever been staged in this country. *Orlando furioso* had its premiere at the Teatro Sant'Angelo in Venice in 1727, and in 1978 was revived through the research of Claudio Scimone for Verona's Teatro Filarmonico in celebration of the 300th anniversary of Vivaldi's birth. This production, featuring Marilyn Horne with sets and costumes by Pier-Luigi Pizzi, was brought to Dallas and conducted by Nicola Rescigno at Fair Park Music Hall on November 28, December 1, and December 3, 1980. In addition to Miss Horne, who sang the role of Orlando, the cast included Ellen Shade as Angelica, princess of Cathay; Dano Raffanti as the Saracen Medoro; Gwendolyn Killebrew as the sorceress Alcina; James Bowman as the Saracen knight Ruggiero; Rose Taylor as Bradamante, cousin of Orlando; and Nicola Zaccaria as the Christian knight Astolfo.

The opera's libretto by Grazio Braccioli is based loosely upon Lodovico Ariosto's popular epic—a legendary masterpiece that combines tales mainly from Arthurian and Carolingian cycles. The Christian knight Orlando, or Roland as he is called in the Carolingian *Chanson de Roland*, is the nephew of Charlemagne, and his romantic adventures are recounted with wit and capricious imagination in Braccioli's colorful libretto. Braccioli also provided the libretto for Ristori's *Orlando furioso* of 1713, an opera that Vivaldi revised in 1714 to replace his unsuccessful *Orlando finto pazzo* of the same year. It was the 1714 revision, as John Hill details in part IV of this book, that later became the source for Vivaldi's *Orlando* of 1727 (renamed *Orlando furioso* for the Verona and Dallas productions).

An original 1727 libretto is in the possession of the Library of Congress,[1] and its relationship with the Ariosto story is apparent when one considers the synopsis in the appendix to this volume. Braccioli himself offers the following overview of the weaving and melding of events from Ariosto's epic in his preface to the 1713 libretto:

> Only the island of Alcina . . . is the setting in which the action takes place, although in the vast epic the numerous exploits involve half the world, so to speak. Such actions have been limited by us . . . to the love, madness and recovery of Orlando. The loves of Bradamante and Ruggiero, Angelica and diverse passions of Astolfo serve to accompany this action and lead it to its end.[2]

To witness a performance of a Vivaldi opera is a rare experience by any measure. The famed "Prete Rosso," known principally through his instrumental works, claimed toward the end of his life to have written ninety-four operas. While modern scholarship identifies at least forty-nine, texts are extant for only twenty-six of these.[3] Indeed, the Vivaldi tercentenary only recently triggered editions and concert performances of a few of the operas, notably *La fida ninfa* (1732) in Paris, *Griselda* (1735) in London, and *Farnace* (1727) at Alice Tully Hall, Lincoln Center, New York. This last performance, directed by Newell Jenkins, appears to be the first Vivaldi opera produced in America unstaged. The 1978 Verona *Orlando furioso* has been recorded by RCA, and parts of *L'Olimpiade* (1734), edited by Francesco Degrada, were recorded in Milan (RIA). In addition, *L'incoronazione di Dario* (1716), edited and conducted by Newell Jenkins, was staged in Siena, and Franz Gielig's edition of *Tito Manlio* (1720) was produced at Milan's Piccola Scala with Vittorio Negri conducting the orchestra of the Teatro alla Scala.[4]

It is little wonder that the Dallas Opera's *Orlando furioso* generated an enormous amount of interest both here and abroad. Besides being an American premiere of a beautiful work that had slumbered in oblivion for about 250 years, it was a very enjoyable and successful enterprise. Marilyn Horne sang with extraordinary bravura and power. Critic John Ardoin claimed rightfully that "there is no other singer today who could turn with comparable ease from a pathetic, sustained aria such as 'Fonti di pianto' to the virtuoso ragings of Orlando which followed." Other members of

FIGURE 1. The sorceress Alcina (Gwendolyn Killebrew) tries to seduce the knight Ruggiero (James Bowman), who had recently arrived on his flying horse. Act 1, scene 5, from Vivaldi's *Orlando furioso*, the Dallas Opera, 1980. Photos: Phil Schexnyder.

the cast were dramatically and musically convincing as well as vocally compatible. Conducting with vitality and sensitivity, Nicola Rescigno exhibited a special affinity with Vivaldi's warm, lyrical lines and transparent textures. He interpreted the score's brilliant instrumental and vocal passages and constantly shifting expressive moods with an awareness of Vivaldi's dramatic powers.

Pier-Luigi Pizzi's stage designs for the Dallas *Orlando* reminded some viewers of an old-fashioned valentine. They seemed to capture the spirit of eighteenth-century theatricality in a stylish sort of "Baroque fantasy," to use Maestro Pizzi's own phrase. The floor was black marble, and scenes changed deftly, primarily at the rear of the stage, against a background of dark reflecting mirrors. There were cupids, boats, leafy bowers, temples with gleaming white columns, a flying golden horse, an ornate bed for sorceress Alcina, and an array of Baroque contrivances simulating the "machines" that captivated eighteenth-century audiences. Art historian Alessandra Comini observed during the final day of the concurrent symposium that the marvelous, huge mirror, which rose up at the beginning of the opera and descended at the end, allowed the audience to experience genuinely the eighteenth-century *quadratura* painting and perspective of an artist such as Tiepolo. Pizzi's costumes, in turn, had an aura of Tiepolo about them. Except for Marilyn Horne's voluminous black robe, their colors reflected the warmth and richness of the Baroque master's famed frescos.

Howard Mayer Brown, Schevill Distinguished Service Professor at the University of Chicago, spoke of the vitality and charm of the Dallas production in his BBC review delivered in December 1980: "Rescigno and his company had certainly translated 18th-century conventions into modern terms that they thought their audience could better understand. This was the best such production I had ever seen."

"Who could ask for more?" said Andrew Porter, who also found the Dallas *Orlando* a wealth of "beautiful melodies, fine singing and spectacular decor." "But more there was," he claimed.[5] From November 28 through December 1, the Dallas Opera held an international symposium, "Opera and Vivaldi: Reflections of a Changing World," in cooperation with the Meadows School of the Arts, Southern Methodist University. Bringing together twenty-nine noted participants from seven countries, the symposium was the first of its kind to explore the relatively obscure field of opera seria, and with the attendant production attracted press and opera luminaries from all over the world. Held in the university's Caruth Auditorium, the meeting drew excellent reviews. Andrew Porter, for example, called the symposium a "bold venture," and added that "whoever next puts on, takes part in, or, for that matter, attends a Baroque opera should be able to do so with mind, ears, and eyes sharpened by what was revealed at the Dallas symposium."

About 450 persons registered for the symposium, which included scholars, students, performers, and opera lovers. Many of the registrants and participants had come from great distances such as Scotland, England, Germany, Italy, and Australia. The Italian ambassador to the United States, His Excellency Paolo Pansa Cedronio, attended the performance, and brief parts of his address on the opening day of the symposium were televised. Since no one had ever seen a Vivaldi opera before, or knew very much about

FIGURE 2. Alcina causes Ruggiero to drink from her magic fountains, and the knight immediately falls victim to her enchantment. Act 1, scene 5.

Vivaldi's dramatic sensibilities, a decided mood of suspense, apprehension, and excitement was felt everywhere.

Accompanying the production and symposium was an extensive exhibition prepared by Dr. Maria Teresa Muraro of the Istituto Italiano Antonio Vivaldi, Venice. Ninety-eight panels and five theater models had been flown to Dallas by Alitalia and were displayed at the Meadows School of the Arts where the symposium was held. Entitled "The World of Antonio Vivaldi," the exhibition illustrated the life and works of the Venetian composer through reproductions of stage designs, librettos, letters, and other pictorial and iconographical materials. After leaving Dallas the exhibition traveled to Durham, North Carolina, Boston, New York, San Francisco, and various cities in South America.

The present volume is a series of essays derived from the Dallas Opera Vivaldi symposium. My initial concept for the symposium and the book to follow was an exploration of Baroque opera within its social, philosophical, and cultural framework, with the sessions progressing in a carefully planned sequence. Thus the

FIGURE 3. The Saracen Medoro (Dano Raffanti) sings of his love for Angelica, princess of Cathay, to a viola obbligato performed onstage. Act 2, scene 5.

symposium began with the broadest possible perspective—the early theories of drama. It continued with literary sources and their transformation into opera; Venetian culture, caricature, stage architecture, and journalism; performance practices of opera seria; and finally focused on Vivaldi's operas themselves with special attention to *Orlando furioso*. The final afternoon of the three-and-a-half-day meeting consisted of a series of panel discussions: "Opera Seria and the Dance: Stage Gesture and Movement," "Preparing the Modern Edition," and "Baroque Opera Today."

While the symposium's sequence and overall content have been retained in this edition, certain adjustments were made in order to convert the conference into a readable, well-focused book. Panel discussions, therefore, have been omitted. Participants in the three panels included Plato Karayanis, general director, and Nicola Rescigno, artistic director of the Dallas Opera; Ellen Shade and James Bowman from the *Orlando* cast; John Ardoin, music editor with the *Dallas Morning News*; William Ball, founder and director of San Francisco's American Conservatory Theater; Alan Curtis, professor of music from the University of California at Berkeley; and a few of the scholars from the previous sessions.

Other participants, whose papers do not appear in this volume, were Alessandra Comini, professor of art history at Southern Methodist University ("Mirror of Venice"); Louise Cowan, former professor of English at the University of Dallas ("Aristotelian Theories of Drama"); Barry S. Brook, codirector of the Research Center for Musical Iconography ("Iconographical Sources and Operatic Performance"); Philip Gossett, chairman of the Department of Music, University of Chicago ("The Doctrine of Affects and the Meaning of Music"); and Edoardo Farina, harpsichordist in both the Verona and Dallas productions ("Aspects of Text and Music in Vivaldi's *Orlando furioso*"). Three new essays have been added to this volume to provide further perspective and depth within the topic: William Barcham on Tiepolo and costume design, Eric Cross on the Vivaldi operas, and Marita McClymonds on Alan Curtis's views concerning the editing of Baroque opera. This compilation of essays, through its unique approach to an important early art form, should be an invaluable source for performers, conductors, and stage designers as well as music students, scholars, literary critics, and aficionados of Venetian cultural life.

The genre of Baroque opera presents some serious challenges to performers, production personnel, and scholars—challenges very different from those found in the re-creation of operas by Wagner or Verdi, for example. Clearly no single solution is going to please everyone. Most of the symposium participants agreed, however, that they had learned something about opera seria as a "theatrical experience" through the Dallas Opera's production, which was definitely not intended to be an "early music" performance by and for specialists.

To be sure, there were liberties taken with the score, as well as from the vantage point of Baroque performance practice. Extensive cuts were made in act 1, which omitted scenes 1, 2, 3, and 4 and most of 5, 9, and 13, and additional cuts were made in acts 2 and 3. Probably no more than two-thirds of Vivaldi's original score was retained. And to achieve a more modern, palatable balance of voices (four female parts were almost in the same range), the role of Medoro was sung by a tenor rather than an additional woman, or a second countertenor, as would have been more in keeping with the vocal range of Vivaldi's time. "Still, I think our audiences received a rather good idea of what opera seria is all about," Maestro Rescigno felt. "I'm not saying it was definitive in any way, but I do think it presents what was being done in those days, in a theater which is possibly ten times as large as the original one was. There was a great immediacy between the audience and the performers in Vivaldi's day. Our use of the raked stage and little runways which brought the performers out into the audience—as well as placing the solo flautist and violist on stage during the two arias—served the purpose of bringing the performance closer to the audience in the same spirit in which it existed 250 years ago."

Of all the art forms, opera is undoubtedly the most complex. It involves not only visual and auditory elements, but temporal aspects that must be considered. Certainly "authentic" does not mean "autocratic" as the Greek word *authentēs* implies, but rather a healthy, vigorous approach to the way mankind perceives its art. Some critics maintain that until someone discovers a way to re-create a Baroque audience we will never experience a Baroque opera in its fullness and "correctness." Operas at the time of Vivaldi were often five or six hours long. When an intermezzo was interposed between the acts—as in the case of Orlandini's *Il marito*

FIGURE 4. The knight Orlando (Marilyn Horne), having gone mad over the loss of Angelica's love, rages in an extended dramatic recitative. Act 3, scene 6.

giocatore, e la moglie bacchettona within Vivaldi's *Orlando furioso* —the performance lasted even longer. The audiences, however, went to the theater as much to visit, play cards, and dine as to hear the music. As Alessandra Comini noted, "Vivaldi had simply concocted one more musical morsel for the carnival-hungry Venetian public. . . . It was the silver age of a once-mighty maritime Republic now nostalgically charting a course backwards in time, through the Grand Canal of Escapism, toward a titillating world of fantasy inhabited by princesses, knights, Moors, and magicians."[6] Italian audiences of the eighteenth century knew the events of Ariosto's epic intimately. While they may have chatted during the long recitatives, they paid attention to their favorite arias and vehemently applauded the singers.

Modern opera producers, especially those associated with professional opera companies, quite clearly must know their audiences. Plato Karayanis, for example, perceives opera today as an economic venture and an industry as much as an art: "Satisfying the audience is necessary for survival . . . opera seria must be viewed as a living art form, not merely a museum piece." And he is quick to point out that without a preexisting edition and production, there would have been no *Orlando* in Dallas. Nicola Rescigno, who exercised his own sense of theater through editorial decisions within the Vivaldi/Scimone score, considers the practical as well as the historical. Rescigno draws a parallel between his rationale and that of Antonio Vivaldi, who would make additions and adjustments in accordance with the particular cast and instrumental resources that he would find from one city to the next. Rescigno worked on the recitatives (whose texts were written in archaic Italian with numerous references to mythology and situations in Ariosto's epic), endeavoring to make them more understandable to an American audience while preserving their original character. To suit the vocal qualities of the Dallas Opera singers, he wrote cadenzas, embellishments, and variations in the da capo arias that, happily, were left intact. In the continuo, moreover, Rescigno included "as many reproductions of original instruments as existed in Dallas with musicians to play them." A modern orchestra of about fifty players was employed, with lute, harpsichord, and portative organ used variously within the continuo.

A sincere expression of gratitude is extended to the organizations that provided invaluable assistance in the symposium project, and thus have made this book possible. Through grants from the Meadows Foundation and the National Endowment for the Humanities, the symposium not only deepened appreciation for Vivaldi's dramatic output, but it engendered a positive approach through which the humanities can creatively and effectively serve the steadily expanding performing arts community today. A special note of thanks is also offered to my capable deputy chairman, Professor Michael Collins, and to the following individuals whose enthusiasm and encouragement contributed directly to the success of the project: Mr. Plato Karayanis, general director, and Maestro Nicola Rescigno, artistic director, the Dallas Opera; Dr. Eugene Bonelli, dean, Meadows School of the Arts; Mrs. William Winspear, administrative vice-president, the Dallas Opera Guild; Dr. William Hipp, chairman, Division of Music, Meadows School of the Arts; Dr. Marco Miele, director, the Italian Cultural Institute, New York City; and Mr. Philip Miller, president of the Dallas Opera. The Honorable Roger L. Stevens, chairman, John F. Kennedy Center for the Performing Arts, kindly served as honorary chairman. Finally, we recognize with deep appreciation Elsa von Seggern, whose great love of opera and extraordinary generosity made possible the American premiere of Vivaldi's *Orlando furioso*.

Perhaps the most appropriate closing to this brief essay is the commentary of Peter G. Davis from the *New York Times*, Sunday, December 14, 1980:

> . . . in view of what we can do in the commercial operatic arena today, it [*Orlando*] was a serious, thoughtful, consistent and imaginative realization of a beautiful, long-neglected work, one that deserved all the loving attention it received. As such, the production and its attendant symposium made a positive contribution to the cause of Baroque opera, an accomplishment that can only point to even better things to come.

NOTES

1. *Orlando, Drama per musica da rappresentarsi nel Teatro di Sant'Angelo l'autuno dell'anno MDCCXXVLL* (Venice, 1727), 60 pages. Schatz Libretto Collection 10776, Library of Congress. On the libretto's title page is the designation *drammatico divertimento*.

2. As quoted by Claudio Scimone in "Vivaldi and *Orlando furioso*," *The Dallas Civic Opera Magazine* 3, no. 3 (1980): 46. The article was an excerpt from Scimone's essay printed in the program booklet and libretto for the RCA recording (ARL 3-2869). For more on the Dallas version of the story, see Stoddard Lincoln, "Orlando in Full Glory," *Opera News* (November 1980).

3. Peter Ryom, *Verzeichnis der Werke Antonio Vivaldi; kleine Ausgabe* (Leipzig, 1974; suppl. Poiters, 1979). See also the 1981 congress proceedings *Antonio Vivaldi: Teatro musicale, cultura, e società*, ed. Lorenzo Bianconi and Giovanni Morelli (Florence, 1982); and Eric Cross, *The Late Operas of Antonio Vivaldi, 1727–1738* (Ann Arbor, Mich., 1981).

4. E. Garbero, "Drammaturgia Vivaldiana: Regesto e concordanze dei libretti," in *Antonio Vivaldi da Venezia all'Europa* (Milan, 1978). A thirty-volume series of Venetian opera facsimiles, *Drammaturgia musicale veneta*, edited by Giovanni Morelli, Reinhard Strohm, and Thomas Walker, is being produced between 1983 and 1993 and will contain several Vivaldi operas.

5. *New Yorker*, December 15, 1980.

6. Alessandra Comini, "Mirror of Venice: From Titillation to Tiepolo," *Arts Magazine* (June 1980): 80.

PART I

Literary Sources and Their Transformation into Opera

Dramatic Theory and the Italian Baroque Libretto *by Michael Collins*

The fate of the operatic genre seems to be that it periodically become subject to attacks from reformers who believe that it has gone astray from its proper goals, either poetically, dramatically, musically, or some combination of the three. The end of the seventeenth century, only one hundred years after the birth of opera, witnessed the launching of a virulent siege by Roman literati against Italian drama in general and the Venetian opera libretto in particular. The besiegers, who had been frequenters of the Roman salon of the expatriate Queen Christina of Sweden until her death in 1689, founded the Arcadian Academy in 1690 under the leadership of Giovanni Maria Crescimbeni. Seventeenth-century librettists were condemned by Crescimbeni for a multitude of sins, including absurd plots and generic confusion, improper characterization and mixture of serious and comic characters, vulgar poetry and excessive number of arias, extended temporal limits and numerous scenic changes, and three-act rather than five-act division.[1] In fact, Crescimbeni goes so far as to claim that "the person who invented opera would have done better not to have invented it and to have left the world as he found it."[2] His position echoes that of Francesco Fulvio Frugoni, who had written as early as 1675 that "the art of producing dramas has become nothing but the art of ruining human society. Instead of imitating nature for the ethical betterment of mankind, literature, painting, and the theater have become monstrous fantasies which corrupt."[3] In sum, the Arcadians were against everything that was immoderately Baroque in opera, which during the course of its development had become a *drame libre* like that of Lope de Vega in Spain, Shakespeare in England, and Alexandre Hardy in France. They desired a return to the rigid classicism of Aristotelian authority. One recent author has seen this movement correctly as a form of nationalism, an attempt of the Roman literati to redeem Italy for Aristotle and regain from France its hereditary cultural leadership.[4]

Music, too, took its share of criticism. If Claudio Monteverdi, composer of *Orfeo* (1607), which perfectly balances the arts of poesy and music, had for his credo "to make the words the mistress of the harmony and not the servant," then by 1723 Scipione Maffei, the Veronese Arcadian, could write that "until the present variety of music is moderated, it will never be possible to construct operas so that they do not always appear like one form of art distorted for the sake of another—a situation in which the superior miserably serves the inferior,"[5] and Ludovico Muratori in 1730 could agree that "there where music once was the servant and waited on poetry, now poetry is the servant of music."[6]

Blame for the chaotic state of opera fell equally on those poets and musicians who had given the public what it wanted. The Arcadians were totally unaffected by the smashing successes the operas had with the Venetian public, not to mention the thousands of Northern Europeans who crowded Venice at carnival time. They were, after all, learned men, quite unconcerned with public taste. The battle of public versus learned taste had been fought and lost as early as 1637 in France, over Corneille's *Le Cid*. Jean Chapelain, representing the French Academy and Cardinal Richelieu, held that some masters are "too much inclined toward pleasure, holding that delight is the true purpose of dramatic poetry," while others "maintain that its real end is to instruct. But," he continues,

> we should not consider every work of art good if it please the people but fail in the observance of the rules and if the experts, who are the sole judges, did not by their approval confirm that of the multitude. Hence we must not say with the crowd that a poem is good merely because it pleases, unless the learned and the expert are also pleased. . . . We are not here concerned with satisfying the libertine and the vicious man. . . . Nor have we to do with pleasing those who are ignorant and untutored. . . . But, for that matter it is impossible to please anyone with disorder and confusion.[7]

Thus did Chapelain dispose of Corneille's *Le Cid*, judged by history as one of the greatest dramas of any age. In vain did no less than Honoré de Balzac defend Corneille:

> You say that he has dazzled the eyes of the world and you accuse him of charm and enchantment. I know many people who would be vain

of such an accusation: You accuse him of violating the rules of art, whereas he has succeeded better than art itself. He has deceived the public? The deception which extends to so large a number of persons is less a fraud than a conquest.[8]

Likewise in vain apparently was Molière's reassertion of the rule of pleasure in 1663:

I should like to know whether the great rule of all rules is not to please, and whether a play which attains this has not followed a good method? Can the whole public be mistaken in these matters, and cannot everyone judge what pleases him? . . . in short, if pieces according to rule do not please, and those do please which are not according to rule, then the rules must, if necessary, have been badly made. So let us laugh at the sophistry with which they would trammel public taste. . . .[9]

Chapelain champions rules; Molière scoffs at them. But whence came these rules on which was based the hereditary cultural supremacy of Italy, the loss of which to France so troubled the Italian literati? And how had opera come to the point where jaded Venetian audiences dictated "irregular" dramas and broken "rules"?

Before the turn of the sixteenth century, Horace and Cicero were the principal authorities on both comedy and tragedy. It was Donatus, however, in his fourteenth-century commentaries on Terentian comedy who taught the sixteenth century what the structure and function of both comedy and tragedy ought to be: "Tragedy is the treatment of heroic stations in misfortunes. . . . Comedy is the treatment of private and civil stations without danger to life."[10] Donatus further emphasizes the difference in social stations, saying comic characters "live in villages because of moderate circumstances, not in royal palaces as do tragic personages."[11] Cicero, in his treatise *On the Best Style of Orators*, says that "in tragedy anything comic is out of place."[12] Also important for our present purposes is that Horace and Donatus agree that no play should be more or less than five acts.

In 1502, however, printed texts in Greek of Aeschylus, Sophocles, and Euripides began to appear.[13] Latin translations of these works followed in Paris in 1506, in Venice in 1507. Very soon afterward a group of learned Italian poets under the leadership of Giangiorgio Trissino of Vicenza began composing Italian tragedies in neo-Greek style. Such was the fame of Trissino's *Sofonisba* that over two hundred years after its composition in 1515 Voltaire was to state, "Sofonisba . . . is the first regular tragedy that Europe had seen after so many centuries of barbarity."[14]

Following the example of the Greek tragedians, *Sofonisba* is not divided into five acts, but into five episodes enclosed by choruses and preceded by a prologue. Trissino freed the dialogue from medieval ottava rima and terza rima, employing instead blank hendecasyllabic verse, which soon became the normative form for dialogue even into the nineteenth century.[15] Trissino used rhyme, however, for the choruses, since they had presumably been sung in ancient drama. In this respect he followed the medieval practice of employing rhyme for lyrical poetry. Imitating the Greek ode, with its strophe, antistrophe, and epode, he cast most of the choruses in the freely alternating eleven- and seven-syllable verses of Petrarch's canzone. In making these decisions he established the formal pattern of Renaissance tragedy in Italy and also in England: blank verse for most of the dialogue, rhyme for the choruses and for certain lyrical and sententious portions of the dialogue.[16]

Literary criticism received a new and tremendous impetus with the recovery of Aristotle's *Poetics*, a work unknown to the Middle Ages. Although Trissino must have been familiar to some extent with an earlier translation, the most influential was the translation into Latin in 1535 by Alessandro Pazzi.[17] With Aristotle's *Poetics* we come upon the "rules" of dramatic art, or to the concept of a "regular" tragedy. These rules represent a coordination of Aristotle and Horace arising from Italian commentaries in the sixteenth century.

Perhaps the foremost rule is that of decorum, or as Aristotle called it, propriety, the necessity for logic of plot, creating the illusion of reality and suiting the style and poetic dialogue to the age, race, and social station of the character. The sixteenth-century term used in the Italian commentaries is verisimilitude.[18] As to the difference between comedy and tragedy, Aristotle says the former imitates the actions of men worse than the average and the latter those better than the average.[19] As a consequence, the sixteenth-century commentators naturally assumed Aristotle to mean men of noble rank, kings and heroes for tragedy, men of bourgeois or humble rank for comedy, thus according with the definitions of Horace and Donatus.

Most important to the history of the theater are the much-debated unities of action, time, and place. Unity of action is the only one that Aristotle specifically prescribes: "Tragedy is the imitation of a perfect and whole action, and of one which possesses a certain magnitude, [and] a whole is that which has a beginning, middle, and end."[20] But he implies a sense of temporal unity as well: "[Appropriate magnitude] is when the time of its duration is such as to render it probable that there can be a transition from prosperous to adverse, or from adverse to prosperous fortune, according to the necessary or probable order of things as they take place."[21] Now this passage is certainly reasonable, but elsewhere Aristotle makes another statement on time that caused storms of controversy: "For tragedy is especially limited by one circuit of the sun, or admits a small variation from this period."[22]

Giraldi Cinzio, leading dramatist of the mid century, was the first to comment on this statement of Aristotle's in 1543. Cinzio writes that a good playwright "feigns the passage of time in his action as the length of one day or a little more."[23] In his own plays, however, he takes great pains to limit the action to a few hours. Robortellus (1548) believes that Aristotle meant an artificial day consisting of twelve hours of light, because "people sleep at night, during which they neither move nor converse."[24] A naive thought at best, and one quickly countered by Bernardo Segni in 1549, who thinks that a natural day of twenty-four hours is meant, since the business of tragedy—adulteries and murders—and of comedy, too, belong to the night: "For although night may well be a time for repose, intemperate and unjust people use it for their own purpose."[25] Madius (1550) has the novel idea that the action should be limited to the actual duration of theatrical performances, in other words, to just a few hours.[26] Scaliger (1561) and Castelvetro (1570) concur, while a more reasonable Minturno (1559) would restrict the action to a day or two.[27]

> As to the third unity, that of place, Aristotle has only this to say: One cannot [in tragedy] represent an action with a number of parts going on simultaneously [as in an epic poem]; one is limited to the part on the stage and connected with the actors.[28]

This statement is the basis for Castelvetro's unity of place. He actually invented it himself; but he did not invent it without reason. Critics and architects of the sixteenth century undoubtedly knew very little about the Greek stage, which actually did present a single, permanent set, but they knew a great deal about the Roman theater from Vitruvius. Italian theater architects were completely indebted to Vitruvius for his prescriptions for correct scenic design: the tragic, with columns, pediments, and statues and other royal surroundings; the comic, with private dwellings and balconies and windows to imitate reality; and the satyric (or pastoral), with trees, caves, mountains, and other country features designed to imitate landscape.[29] (Palladio's Teatro Olimpico in Vicenza, built in 1585 and still in use today, is a magnificent permanent stage set designed for tragedy.) There is, therefore, basis for Castelvetro's third unity. Normally on the stage, however, this unity was construed to mean a limitation of the action to a single palace or city.

Most Italian dramatists of the sixteenth century, whether writing tragedies or comedies, adhered fairly closely to the rules, although they were never as devoted to the unities as were their literary critics. The neo-Grecian tragedies of Trissino and his circle were meant primarily for private reading rather than for the stage, but the works of Giraldi Cinzio were composed for the pleasure of his audience at the court of Ferrara. With his *Orbecche* of 1541, the first Italian tragedy *regolare e rappresentata*, that is, composed according to neoclassical rules and produced on the stage, he created a new type. *Orbecche* represents a synthesis of the Senecan tradition of violence with the romantic novella of the sixteenth century, presenting for the first time the modern romantic heroine in tragedy. And in his *Altile* (ca. 1541), he invented the romantic tragicomedy, which he called *tragedia mista*, because it concludes tragically for the villain and happily for the heroes. This is the sort of double outcome of which Aristotle did not approve, although he admitted that the audience preferred this type. Tragicomedy is differentiated from the *commedia seria*, which also treats of tragic events and has a double outcome, in that tragicomedy deals with characters of noble station, whereas the station of those of *commedia seria*, as in comedy, is bourgeois. Cinzio introduced the sort of plots that were later to delight opera audiences: feminine heroines in dire circumstances, barbarian peoples, and obscure periods of the lower empire. Oriental themes presented greater opportunity for gruesome horror and spectacular luxury. The prologue to *Altile*, which is laid in Damascus, proclaims, "Behold spectators, behold the royal chambers, the proud and lofty palaces of those rulers whom you will see appear today to give you high delight."[30] Most of Cinzio's plots are drawn from his own novellas, with their themes of love and the romantic adventure of their duels, ambushes, abductions, mistaken identies, and disguises.

Cinzio returns to the Horacian five-act formula partly to give relief to the audience with intervals that renew its attention. To provide relief he imports from the intervals of comedy the music and sumptuous decor of the *intermedii*. These consist of music, dancing, pantomime, and tableaux, the subjects of which are usually mythological or pastoral. In this manner the mechanical and visual extravagances of the medieval *sacre rappresentazioni* were brought to bear upon secular Renaissance drama. The marvels and machinery of the *intermedii* were not to vex literary critics until they were introduced into the plot proper of operas.

Meanwhile a new dramatic genre, highly influential on early opera, was brought to perfection in Torquato Tasso's *Aminta* (1573) and Giambattista Guarini's *Il pastor fido* (ca. 1585). Such works are often called *favole pastorali*, but Guarini preferred the term *tragicommedia*, because the characters are of dignity and rank worthy of tragedy. Most of them are in fact shepherds and nymphs, but it was felt that in the Golden Age of Arcadia, where such pastorals are laid, shepherds were not inferior to nobles, because in those days everyone tended sheep. The fundamental difference between Cinzian *tragedia mista* and the pastoral tragicomedy is that in the latter there is a single comic outcome, in which all the characters emerge in good cheer, while in mixed tragedies not only is virtue rewarded, but vice punished. The subject matter of the pastoral is love, with at least two sets of lovers, much intrigue, and mistaken identity. Guarini wrote that if tragedy is to purge pity and fear, pastoral tragicomedy is to purge the mind of the evil effects of melancholy, since it has a wholly comic and single outcome.[31]

The poetic structure of *Aminta* also sets a new model. It is a free metrical form with a mixture of *settenari* and *endecasillabi*. The choruses rhyme freely, while at lyrical moments in the dialogue, which is normally hendecasyllabic, single lines or passages of *settenari*, with and without rhyme, intermingle. Above all the poetry is lyric rather than rhetorical as it is in tragedy. The same is true of *Pastor fido*, except that two of the choruses have the canzone form. Both dramas are divided into the classical five acts, and at least *Aminta* preserves the unities.

The earliest operas, Rinuccini's *Dafne* (1597) and *Euridice*

(1600) and Striggio's *Orfeo* (1607), derive from the pastoral tradition, except that they are much shorter in length because of their being sung throughout: *Dafne* has 448 verses, *Euridice* 790, and *Orfeo* 592, while Guarini's *Pastor fido* has 5,576.[32] The form of *Euridice* is more like that of *Sofonisba* because it consists of episodes surrounded by choruses. *Orfeo* maintains the standard five-act formula and the unities of action and time are preserved. However, place is not, since Orfeo must descend from the Thracian fields to Tartarus in order to reclaim Euridice.

The dialogue in all three operas, as in *Aminta* and *Pastor fido*, is in freely alternating eleven- and seven-syllable verses, the novelty, of course, being that they are to be sung in the new *stile rappresentativo*. The choruses have the same lyric structure, except that they rhyme. Some of them are in the eight-syllable verses of canzonettas. The soloists also have occasional songs in *ottonari*, and in Striggio's *Orfeo* there is an aria in terza rima. In addition, there are hendecasyllabic solos with rhyming quatrains, sestets, etc. These lyric elements within dialogues of pastoral dramas, derived from the *intermedio*, do not cause problems with critics, for it was thought that in Arcadia, shepherds, though elevated, could sing songs without losing decorum, an impossibility, however, for heroes and kings.[33] The first operas, then, represent a continuation of the *favola pastorale*.

A drastic change, however, was already in the air. Cavalieri, in the preface to his quasi opera *La rappresentazione di Animo e di Corpo* (Rome, 1600), heard in the Oratorio di San Filippo Neri, recommends that a poem for music be filled with verses not only of seven syllables, but also of five and of eight, and at times in *sdruccioli*, that is, with antepenultimate accents; that a graceful effect is made for the music when the rhymes are close together; and that the narratives for a soloist be as brief as possible.[34] Cavalieri's work adheres faithfully to this advice: Almost the entire dialogue is composed of short *settenari* in rhyming couplets. One chorus is set in sestets of mixed *settenari* and *endecasillabi* rhyming *ababbcc*; there is an ensemble of hendecasyllabic ottava rima, a quartet and chorus of five-syllable Adonicos, a hendecasyllabic aria in blank verse, a chorus in blank verse with eight-syllable *sdruccioli*, and the final chorus is in *ottonario* couplets. The text can be described as nothing short of polymetric.

Indeed the same use of polymetrics was entering spoken drama as well. Jacopo Cicognini introduced a notable variety of meters in his *Amor pudico* (1614).[35] Among the choruses are found an eight-syllable *sdrucciola* rhyming *ababbcc*, a mixed stanza composed of three *ottonari*, a *quaternario*, a *quinario*, and four *ottonari* rhyming *aaabbcded*; still another of an *ottonario*, a *settenario sdrucciola*, an *ottonario tronco*, and a *novenario tronco* rhyming *abbcc*; and finally a *sonnetto*. There is an aria of *quaternari* and *ottonari* mixed and another of *ottonari* alone. In addition, six poets are introduced, each singing in his preferred meter: Dante, a *terza rima*; Petrarch, a *sonnetto*; Ariosto and Tasso, each an *ottava*; Sannazzaro, a *terza rima sdrucciola*; and Anguillara, an octave rhyming *abababaa*. Furthermore, *Amor pudico* completely abandons the unities, introducing nine changes of scene.

This sudden effulgence of polymetric lyricism and disregard for the unities in Italian works comes from Spain, where as early as 1577 Italian modes of versification had been introduced into the choruses and dialogues of the five-act tragedies of Jerónimo Bermúdez.[36] Then, between 1579 and 1581, Juan de la Cueva composed a series of highly irregular dramas for the public theaters of Seville. They are in four acts, and take great liberties with the unities of time and place.[37] The dialogues are a continuous mixture of lyric strophes, canzones, hendecasyllabic blank verse, terza rima, ottava rima, sonnets, *quinari*, *lire*, and Spanish *redondillas*. His polymetry surpasses that of any of his predecessors; the plays are almost totally rhymed. De la Cueva, who paved the way for a Spanish national drama, was strongly influenced by the Senecan dramas and romantic novellas of Cinzio, but his polymetrics and disregard of the unities were Spanish.

The greatest boost to popular theater in Spain came with the arrival in 1574 of the commedia dell'arte troupe called *I gelosi* under the leadership of Alberto Naseli, known as Ganassa.[38] The troupe came to Madrid fresh from Paris at the invitation of Philip II. Not only did these Italians create a mass public of all classes for theater, but the style of their three-act *scenari* influenced the budding Spanish *comedia*, a term that refers to all theatrical genres.

The true founder of Spanish national drama, Lope de Vega, whose attendance at commedia dell'arte performances in Madrid is documented,[39] began writing his plays around 1585. As we shall see, his foremost concern was pleasing his audience, if necessary at the expense of all the rules. With Lope, the *comedia* of three acts or *jornadas* became established as more practical than the classical five-act formula. Lope's *comedias* are almost entirely in rhymed verse, and these are not Italian versifications, for a nationalistic reaction against them had set in around the time Lope began to write. Spaniards returned to a variety of native verse drawn from popular song and the *auto sacramentale*. These *romance* measures of eight syllables restrict the Spanish *comedia* to the narrower limits of lyricism and rapid action.

Fortunately, Lope wrote his own *Ars poetica*, called *Arte nuevo de hacer comedias*, read at the Academy of Madrid and published in 1609. In this treatise he advocates mixing the genres of tragedy and comedy, presenting kings together with the lowly and vulgar, the tragic with the comic. He is bold in denying the validity of any rule limiting the duration of time or forbidding a change of scene. The genre is characterized by absolute freedom. Lope admits that no one is more barbarous than himself in defying rules. When it comes to writing a *comedia*, he says, "I lock in the precepts with six keys, I banish Terence and Plautus from my study that they may not cry out at me . . . and I write in accordance with that art which they devised who aspired to the applause of the crowd; for, since the crowd pays for the *comedias*, it is fitting to talk foolishly to it to satisfy its taste."[40] On the unity of time, Lope says,

> Let [the action] take place in as little time as possible. But if some years have to pass, let the character go on some journey during the space between the acts. . . . considering that the wrath of a seated Spaniard is immoderate, when in two hours there is not presented to him everything from Genesis to the Last Judgment, I deem it fitting, if it be for us to please him, for us to adjust everything so that it succeeds.[41]

Elsewhere he declares that he would have obeyed the dictates of the learned theorists if only the public had permitted. He thus throws the blame on the depravity of public taste, declaring cynically, "We who live to please, must please to live."[42]

Lope is in agreement with Aristotle, however, on the decorum of having each character imitate his own rank or estate. For Lope, polymetry is part of decorum, and he advises young playwrights to suit their verses to the subject being treated: eight-syllable *décimas* for complaints, the hendecasyllabic sonnet for soliloquies, eight-syllable *romances* occasionally in the form of the Italian *ottava* for narrations, *tercetos* or terza rima for grave affairs, and the Spanish *redondillas* (octosyllabic quatrains rhyming *abba*) for affairs of love.[43] He also employs blank verse and occasionally prose for short comic interludes between persons of low station. His plays are thus polymetric and full of rhyme.

To understand how the Spanish *comedia* could enter Italy and together with the commedia dell'arte cause the great deviation from the traditions of neoclassical theater, we must remember that a great deal of Italy was under Spanish domination at the turn of the seventeenth century. Spain held Sicily, Sardinia, Naples, and Milan, and such Renaissance courts as the duchies of Parma, Mantua, and Urbino were dependent on and stipended by the Spanish. The influence was particularly strong in Naples, where Spanish was spoken by both the aristocracy and the populace. The Spaniard Don Pietro Fernando de Castro, viceroy from 1610 to 1616, brought in great numbers of Spanish *comedias*;[44] and it was not long before Italian dramatists began imitating the Spanish manner, particularly that of Lope de Vega and Calderón de la Barca. Jacopo Cicognini, whose polymetrics we have already noted, received an exhortation from Lope himself to

> find out for himself the delights of presenting actions which surpass the space not only of a single day, but even months and years, so that one enjoys the incidents of the story not just through the narration of the *antefatto*, but by showing before the eyes those same actions which happened at various times.[45]

In Venice, Gian Francesco Loredan, founder of the Accademia degli Incogniti (1630), gained renown for his translations from Spanish, and his own plays were based on Spanish models. Jacopo Cicognini was the first Italian to write a play (*Il convitato di pietra*) based on Tirso de Molina's *El burlador de Sevilla*, the Don Juan story, and Giulio Rospigliosi's *Dal male il bene* (1654) is a libretto based on a Spanish play by Calderón de la Barca.

Spanish traits mix with Italian early on in opera. Productions at the fabulous Teatro Barberini, opened in Rome in 1632, abandoned the unities and relied heavily on spectacle, with elaborate scene changes accomplished by machinery from *intermedii*. Rospigliosi's *Chi soffre speri* (1637) calls for rain, hail, a tempest, battles, and a fair. Andrea Salvadori's *Regina e Sant'Orsola* (Florence, 1625) encompasses at least a week, with many changes of scene and two battles between the Romans and the Huns. With the opening of the first public opera house, San Cassiano, in 1637, these extravagances were transported to Venice. Francesco Busenello states in the preface of *La Didone* (Venice, 1641), "This opera is influenced by modern opinions. It is not made according to the prescription of the ancient rules, but in accord with Spanish usage it represents years and not hours."[46] And his *Prosperità infelice di Giulio Cesare, dittatore* (Venice, 1644) presents a history of the Mediterranean world from 49 to 44 B.C.[47]

Lope's practice of mixing serious and comic characters begins at Teatro Barberini with Rospigliosi's *Sant'Alessio* (1632), and is even more prevalent in his comic opera *Chi soffre speri* (1637). Although Rospigliosi's comic characters are borrowed from the *maschere* of the commedia dell'arte, their mixture with serious characters is Spanish. It is in Rome, moreover, that operas begin to be called *commedia per musica* after the Spanish *comedia* rather than *favola* or *pastorale*.[48] Giacomo Badoaro's *Il ritorno d'Ulisse* (1640) and Busenello's *L'incoronazione di Poppea* (1642), both set by Monteverdi, employ comic figures within serious plots, frequently in the Spanish manner, for comic relief after scenes of particular dramatic tension.

The reduction from five acts to three in opera could have come from the commedia dell'arte troupes, but they were performing Spanish plays as well as their own *scenari*. When this reduction in acts occurs together with lack of unities, a mixture of serious and comic characters, fast action, and intrigue, the source would seem to be Spanish. One must remember, too, that the *scenari* were played in prose, while the Spanish *comedia*, like opera, is poetic. In his librettos of the 1640s, Giacinto Cicognini set the tone for the rest of the century with his fondness for Spanish dramatic intrigues and flouting of the classical distinctions between comedy and tragedy.

With regard to poetic forms, the concept of polymetrics in a dramatic work is certainly Spanish, but the metrics themselves, as employed by Italians, are not Spanish. Contrary to the Spanish practice of using rhyming *redondillas* for dialogue, the operatic dialogue of the Italians, inherited from Tasso and Guarini, remained a mixture of *endecasillabi* and *settenari*, usually without rhyme. Aria versifications, as we shall see, are not Spanish either. The use of popular poetic forms such as *ottonario* for pastoral or comic characters presents no problem, as already stated, but when used for royal personages and heroes, the classical rule of decorum is transgressed. Even with such Spanish practice well established in Italian opera, Francesco Sbarra felt constrained to explain why he allowed Alexander and Aristotle to sing arias in popular meters in his *Alessandro vincitor di sè stesso* in 1651. He writes in the preface:

> I know that some people will consider the *ariette* sung by Alexander and Aristotle unfit for the dignity of such great characters . . . never-theless it is not only permitted but even accepted with praise. . . . If the recitative style were not mingled with such *scherzi* [*arie*], it would give more annoyance than pleasure. Pardon me this license, which I have taken only in order to make it less tiresome for you.[49]

The use of polymetrics became more prevalent as arias relieved the perceived tedium of recitative. Ottavio Tronsarelli's *La catena d'Adone* (1626), set by composer Domenico Mazzocchi, is the first libretto to mention this: "There are many short arias scattered throughout the opera which break the tedium of the recitatives."[50] And Giovan Battista Doni, certainly the most perceptive of the early writers on opera, tells us in his *Trattato della musica sceneca* (1633–1635) that to continue recitative too long soon brings boredom.[51]

Doni expounds at length on the use of polymetrics. After admitting that most people prefer short verses (*versetti piccoli*) of not more than seven syllables, either because they are better adapted to *canzonette*, which are the rage, or because the rhymes come closer together (compare Cavalieri above), he presents his own opinion. In discourse, eleven-syllable verse should be most prevalent, seven- or eight-syllable verse less frequent, short-syllable verse never used. For choruses, however, long and short verses should be used least, medium length most often. Furthermore, in discourse he does not approve intermixing long and short verse, but writes that after thirty long verses, ten or twelve short of one kind or another make a good effect, adopting seven-syllable for grave or indifferent matters, eight-syllable for light and happy matters.[52] For choruses he approves *arie* or *canzonette* and also *ballate* or *canzoni a ballo*, called by the ancients *hyporchemata*.[53]

With Doni's last statement we have, I believe, come across the origin of the short verses of three, four, five, and six syllables condemned by the Arcadians: they are imitations of Greek *hyporche-mata*. The study of ancient measures was undertaken by Gabriello Chiabrera, a member of the Camerata and composer of several extravagant *intermedii* for the grand duke of Tuscany. The real source of his poetic innovations, however, lay closer at hand; they are found in the short and flexible measures of the French Anacreontics of Ronsard and the *Pléiade*.[54] Anacreontics, for example, provided Chiabrera with the mixture of *ottonari* and *quaternari* found in his *canzonetta* "Damigella, / Tutta bella, / Versa versa quel bel vino."[55] Adonicos, or five-syllable verses, come from the Sapphic ode, one of the earliest Italian examples of such *quinari* being a quartet in Cavalieri's *La rappresentazione*: "O gran stupore! / O grave errore! / C'huomo mortale / D'un tanto male, / Ch'eterno dura / Sì poco cura!" Another is the chorus "Lasciate i monti, / Lasciate i fonti" in Monteverdi's *Orfeo*, and in Stefano Landi's *La morte d'Orfeo* (1620) satyrs, maenads, and a Fury all sing in *quinari*.[56] The *paeon* of the *hyporchemata* may have provided Chiabrera with *quaternari* and the Cretic *ternari*, and perhaps he was also familiar with Meleager's erotic *epigrammata*, which are often in *quaternari* or *ternari*. Giacomo Badoaro's *Le nozze di Enea con Lavinia*, set by Monteverdi in 1641, offers an early *ternario*: "Ch'io porti / Sconforti / Rie sorti / Sì, sì; / Scontenti / Spaventi / Tormenti / Darò."[57] In this libretto Badoaro regularly uses *senari sdruccioli* for low-born persons. Alessandro Striggio's stanzas composed for Monteverdi's ballet *Tirsi e Clori* (1615) are entirely in *quinari*, and in Niccolò Enea Bartolini's *Venere gelosa* (1643) sylvan creatures sing "Correte Naiadi, / Saltate Satiri."[58] References to dancing and musical instruments call forth *quinari sdruccioli* in Giacinto Cicognini's *Orontea* (1649): "Suonisi il cembalo / Tu, alza i mantici / Toccate gli organi / Si senta il piffero / S'accord'il zuffolo / Batti le nacchere / Suoni la cetera / Io vò ballar."[59] In Giovanni Faustini's *Il Titone* (1645), *quinari sdruccioli* are employed for violent images: "Lupi famelici / Cinghiali rabidi / Orsi fierissimi / Lasciate l'horride / Tane, qui pregovi / Venite rapidi / E laceratemi / E divoratemi."[60] Although Chiabrera is rather conservative in the versification of his own works for the theater,[61] it is my opinion that by elevating the popular *canzonetta* of the sixteenth century and fusing it with neo-Greek *hyporchemata*, he created a new type of poetry most suitable for musical setting in the new genre of opera.

While the early operas were relatively conservative with respect to meter—dialogue in seven- and eleven-syllable verses, arias in the same or *ottonario*—the increase in number of popular arias was to bring a bewildering metric variety. For example, in Giovanni Faustini's libretto for Cavalli's *La Calisto* (1651), there are arias in *ternario, quaternario, quinario sdrucciola, senario sdrucciola, settenario,* alternating *ottonario* and *quaternario, ottonario sdrucciola, novenario sdrucciola, ottanario* with occasional *endecasillabi,* and a hendecasyllabic soliloquy for Juno.[62] By 1672, Aurelio Aureli could write in the preface to his *Claudio Cesare,* "I offer you my Claudio richer in songs and airs than incidents. It is enough to say that it is a *dramma per musica;* what can one do? If today the caprices of Venice wish it so, I endeavor to please their taste."[63] Francesco Sbarra, librettist of Cesti's *Alessandro vincitor di sè stesso* (1651), defends the whole concept of setting speech to music on the basis of public taste:

> . . . I know also that it is improper to speak in music, not imitating in this manner natural discourse . . . and yet this defect is not only tolerated in this century, but is received with applause. These days this species of poetry has no other aim than to delight, and therefore one needs to accommodate himself to the usage of the times. . . .[64]

And in the preface to his *Giasone* (1649), Giacinto Cicognini writes:

> I compose for pure caprice, and my caprice has no other aim than to delight. To bring delight for me is nothing else than to please the genius and the taste of him who listens to or reads [my verses].[65]

Not only the audience, but the music itself takes its share of the blame from librettists, who excuse their transgressions against the rules. In 1623, Andrea Salvadori, in the preface of his *Medoro,* writes of the details of his story being described with that *brevità* that music requires.[66] Although *Medoro* has only 959 verses, I take brevity to refer here not to overall length, but to that of individual discourses, which are also very short by comparison with those of spoken drama. In the 1640s, librettist Giulio Strozzi explains, "It is the poet's duty to abandon his own ornaments to make room for those of the musicians."[67] Giacomo Badoaro, in his *Ulisse errante* (1644), attributes to the special demands of music his own failure to observe the ancient rules:

It is normal today for the purpose of increasing the delight of the spectators to introduce improbable situations so long as they do not disturb the main action. . . . Having introduced music into our dramas, we cannot avoid the implausible, namely, that men should carry on their most important transactions in song. . . . It is no wonder, then, that in committing ourselves to pleasing modern taste, we have rightly departed from the ancient rules.[68]

The same sentiments are expressed by Vincenzo Nolfi in his preface to *Bellerofonte* (1642):

You waste your time, O reader, if, with the *Poetics* of the *Stagirita* [that is, Aristotle] in hand you go tracking down the errors in this work, because I freely confess that in composing it I observed no other precepts than the desires of the inventor of the machines, nor had I any other aim than the pleasure of that audience for which it was to be performed.[69]

In the same year, Giovanni Battista Fusconi prefaced his *Amore innamorato* with an ironic statement on the futility of following rules:

Before taking up my pen, I had proposed to write a grand piece to demonstrate that this *favola* has all the good rules taught by the Masters: that it ends within a single day, or a little more; that it has a single action; that it has no incompatible incidents, and that it never transgresses decorum. . . . [But what is the use] since this century . . . believes in no other rules than those of caprice and passion.[70]

For the most part poets of librettos considered libretto writing something to engage in for money and quite apart from their aspirations to poetic fame. In the preface to his *Statira* (1655), Francesco Busenello indicates that he holds writing for the operatic stage the lowest form of poetry:

It is one thing to compose an ode or a sonnet where the poet's enthusiasm and ecstasy of imagination are permitted to delight the ear and inflame the heart with a pleasing and ingenious style. It is something else to compose a [musical] drama where the characters are earthy, speak in common language, and if their tone becomes too elevated lose their decorum and conviction.[71]

And Aurelio Aureli prefaces his *Medoro* (1658) with "you already know that I compose for my own pleasure and not out of aspiration for the title of poet."[72]

In their embarrassment, these poets failed to realize that they had created an inspired and unruly national theater as surely as Lope de Vega had done in Spain and Shakespeare, together with his predecessors, in England. Likewise, neither Lope nor Shakespeare seemed mindful of the glory each had reaped in drama, although both took great pride in other poetic genres. Both wrote lengthy poems in the Italian manner—Shakespeare's *Venus and Adonis* and *The Rape of Lucrece*—and sonnets, which they carefully edited for publication while surrendering their plays to the groundlings.[73] Lope wrote in 1604: "If anyone should cavil about my *comedias* and think that I wrote them for fame, undeceive him and tell him that I wrote them for money."[74] Late in life Lope, realizing his chief fame would lie in his *comedias*, made an attempt to correct his plays for publication, and they were printed under his supervision. Shakespeare, on the other hand, never seemed to have cared about the fate of his plays and never corrected or revised them. Pope, then, was right in his couplet on Shakespeare: "For gain, not glory, wing'd his roving flight, / And grew immortal in his own despite."[75]

No one could truthfully say that any of the seventeenth-century librettists achieved the stature of a Shakespeare. Nevertheless, unruly and outrageous as the seventeenth-century libretto may be, it is a vital drama that characterizes the nature of the people for whom it was written to entertain and presents a gorgeous and enthusiastic panoply of life. At least Giacomo Badoaro had the courage of his convictions when he prefaced his *Ulisse errante* of 1644 with these words:

> The ancients prescribed rules for many things, because they prided themselves that the world would hold to their precepts, and perhaps men of the preceding century were deprived of the faculty of invention. . . . Unhappy century, if the footsteps of the past were to obligate our feet to an unalterable path. . . . The precepts of the *Poetics* [of Aristotle] are not like mathematical proportions, certain and permanent . . . because the changes of the centuries have brought diversity of composition . . . and perhaps in the future the changing of the times will see our posterity introduce new forms. . . . Since in every age the road to invention is open, we have no obligation toward the precepts of the ancients except to know about them. . . . I wanted . . . to beat a path not trod by others, sure that, if Aristotle lived in these days, he would adjust his *Poetics* to the inclinations of this century. . . . The best rule is to satisfy the audience.[76]

The Italians, however, were to succumb to the academicians just as the free drama in France had done earlier under the onslaught of Cardinal Richelieu and French Academicians around 1636. No one of stature came to the defense of the Venetian librettists as did Balzac to Corneille's after the attacks on his *Le Cid* (see above). Just as the Italians were to do, however, Corneille had submitted, as recorded in the abbé d'Aubignac's *Pratique du Théâtre* (1657): "M. de Corneille has confessed several times that in looking over plays that he had given to the public ten or twelve years since with great approbation, he felt shame for himself and pity for his approvers."[77]

Ironically, it was the reformed Corneille, together with Racine, who provided the substance of the Italian submission. Apostolo Zeno and Pietro Metastasio illustrate the ideal code of duty for both princes of the age and their subjects, as Corneille had done in France. "Loyalty and human steadfastness were the moral requirements. . . . Obedience to the law of the land, the renunciation of personal desires for the sake of the common good."[78] Thus Aristotle's "to instruct" rejoins "to delight" and the opera libretto becomes the tool of absolutism. Not surprisingly the reform took place primarily at the Imperial Court of Vienna under two successive court poets: Apostolo Zeno (1718–1729) and Pietro Metastasio (1730–1782). Zeno's better character development and dramatic motivation through extra doses of recitative all but silenced the critics.[79] Metastasio completed the reform by reducing the number of arias and eliminating smaller roles and comic scenes. He legitimized opera as a descendant of classical tragedy by rationalizing recitative as proper for dialogue and arias as substitutes for the chorus, justifying the three-act formula and confining any lapses of time greater than the revolution of one sun to those intervals during which the stage is empty (the last certainly borrowed from Lope de Vega's *New Art of Writing Plays*).[80]

Even so, Metastasio's eighteenth-century libretto failed to achieve the greatness of Shakespeare or Racine just as surely as did the seventeenth-century libretto. Metastasio's rarified lessons in virtue made lyrical poetry eminently suitable for musical setting, but the really vital musical theater in the eighteenth century was opera buffa. The tragic qualities of pity and terror do not come from the gods or a malignant star, but from within the characters themselves. In addition, religious, or at least moral, convictions on good and evil, on justice and injustice are necessary for great drama. Italian drama and opera had none—just the classical trappings, as in Lope's Spain they followed only the code of honor. These convictions are what, together with greatness of poetry, elevate the Elizabethan drama of Shakespeare and that of Racine in France to a position not limited by time or place.[81]

In the final analysis the seventeenth-century libretto is certainly more vital and less conventional than the eighteenth-century one. The problem was, as Worsthorne comments, that "a rule that made 'delight' the criterion could not effectively check bad taste in less tasteful authors."[82] And eighteenth-century librettos were subject to abuses just as great, although of other kinds. In any event, rules do not great drama make, and into the teeth of the academicians should have been thrown the answer of Tirso de Molina to his academic adversary and proponent of the ancient rules:

> And if you argue . . . that we of the same craft owe it to the initiators to guard their principles intact, I answer that . . . it is Genius which, when the fundamental laws fail to help, knows how to change the accidental, improving it with experience. There is this difference between Nature and Art: that which the former began, cannot be changed; thus the pear tree will bear pears to eternity, and the oak the uncouth acorn, and notwithstanding the difference of soil and the varying influences of the atmosphere and climate to which they are subject, she produces them over and over again. Amid other changes, species is constant. Does it matter how much the Drama may modify the laws of its ancestors . . . ?[83]

NOTES

1. Giovanni Maria Crescimbeni, *La bellezza della volgar poesia* (Rome, 1700), pp. 106–108, and *Comentarii intorno alla sua istoria della volgar poesia I* (Rome, 1702), pp. 234ff. Cited in Robert Freeman, "Apostolo Zeno's Reform of the Libretto," *JAMS* 21 (1968): 325, 328.
2. Freeman, "Apostolo Zeno's Reform," p. 325.
3. Ibid., pp. 321–322, from the preface to Frugoni's *Epulone*.
4. Nathaniel Burt, "Opera in Arcadia," *MQ* 41, no. 2 (1955): 151.
5. Scipione Maffei, *Teatro italiano* (Verona, 1723), trans. Freeman, "Apostolo Zeno's Reform," p. 333.
6. Ludovico Muratori, *Della perfetta poesia italiana* (Venice, 1730). Quoted in Simon Towneley Worsthorne, *Venetian Opera in the Seventeenth Century* (London, 1954), p. 48.

7. Jean Chapelain, *Les Sentimens de l'académie françoise sur la tragi-comédie du Cid (1737)*, trans. Barret H. Clark, *European Theories of the Drama* (New York, 1957), pp. 89–90.

8. Balzac to Scudéry, August 27, 1637. Quoted from J. J. Jusserand, *Shakespeare in France under the Ancien Régime*, reprint of 1899 edition (New York, 1966), p. 95.

9. Molière, *La Critique de l'école des femmes* (1663), trans. Clark, *European Theories*, pp. 111–112.

10. Marvin T. Herrick, *Tragicomedy: Its Origins and Development in Italy, France, and England* (Urbana, 1955), p. 2. Rediscovered in 1433, these commentaries are actually two essays—*De Fabula* now ascribed to Evanthius and *De Comoedia*—both of which were combined under the title *De Comoedia et Tragoedia* and ascribed to Donatus.

11. Marvin T. Herrick, *Comic Theory in the Sixteenth Century*, Illinois Studies in Language and Literature, vol. 34, nos. 1–2 (Urbana, 1950), p. 59.

12. Ibid., p. 67.

13. Aldus of Venice published Sophocles in 1502, all of Euripides except *Electra* in 1503, all of Aeschylus except *Choephorae* in 1518.

14. G. Pace-Sanfelice, *Romeo and Juliet* (Cambridge, 1868), p. xlviii, note.

15. This form, modified to iambic pentameter, was introduced into England in 1557, with the posthumous publication of the English translation of Vergil's *Aeneid* of Henry Howard, Earl of Surrey.

16. Marvin T. Herrick, *Italian Tragedy in the Renaissance* (Urbana, 1965), p. 54.

17. Alessandro Pazzi, *Poetica per Alexandrum . . . in Latinum conversa* (Venice, 1536). The earlier translation into Latin appeared in Giorgio Valla's *Logica* (Venice, 1498).

18. Marvin T. Herrick, *The Fusion of Horatian and Aristotelian Literary Criticism* (Urbana, 1946), p. 56.

19. Herrick, *Tragicomedy*, p. 3.

20. Clark, *European Theories*, p. 10.

21. Ibid.

22. Ibid., p. 8.

23. Herrick, *Italian Tragedy*, p. 9. Cinzio's *Discorsi . . . intorno al comporre de i romanzi, delle comedie, e delle tragedie, e di altre maniere di poesie* (Venice, 1554) was actually written at the University of Ferrara in 1543, where he had lectured on Aristotle since 1534.

24. Franciscus Robortellus, *In librum Aristotelis de arte poetica explicationes* (Florence, 1548). Cited in Herrick, *Fusion*, p. 78.

25. Bernardo Segni, *Rettorica de arte poetica d'Aristotele tradotte di*

Greco in lingua vulgare fiorentina (Florence, 1549). Cited in Herrick, *Fusion*, p. 79.

26. V. Madius and Bartholomaeus Lombardus, *In Aristotelis librum de poetica communes explanationes* (Venice, 1550). Cited in Herrick, *Fusion*, p. 79.

27. Julius Caesar Scaliger, *Poetices* (Heidelberg, 1561), Lodovico Castelvetro, *Poetica d'Aristotele vulgarizzata, et sposta* (Basel, 1570), and Antonio Minturno, *De poeta* (Venice, 1559). All cited in Herrick, *Italian Tragedy*, p. 91, and Herrick, *Fusion*, p. 80.

28. Herrick, *Fusion*, p. 81.

29. Herrick, *Tragicomedy*, p. 170.

30. H. B. Charlton, *The Senecan Tradition in Renaissance Tragedy* (Manchester, 1946), p. lxxxix.

31. Giambattista Guarini, *Compendio della poesia tragicomica* (1599–1601). Cited in Herrick, *Tragicomedy*, p. 138.

32. Emilio de' Cavalieri, in his preface "Ai lettore" of *La rappresentazione di Animo e di Corpo* (1600), which has 626 verses, says the poem in such works should not surpass seven hundred verses. Cited in Angelo Solerti, *Le origini del melodramma*, reprint of 1903 edition (Bologna, 1969), p. 8.

33. Note the following dialogue, cited in Herrick, *Tragicomedy*, pp. 170–171, from act 1 of Molière's *Le Bourgeois Gentilhomme* (1670):

    MUSIC MASTER: Come, move forward. You must imagine that they are dressed as shepherds.

    M. JOURDAIN: Why always shepherds? One sees them everywhere.

    MUSIC MASTER: When people have to speak in music it is necessary to use the pastoral in order to secure verisimilitude. Song has always been assigned to shepherds; it is scarcely natural for princes or citizens to sing their passions in dialogue.

34. Solerti, *Le origini*, p. 8: ". . . e conviene, che [il Poema] sia facile, & pieno di versetti, non solamente di sette sillabe, ma di cinque e di otto, & alle volte in sdruccioli; e con le rime vicine, per la vaghezza della Musica, fa gratioso effetto . . . e le narrative d'un solo siano più breve che possano."

35. Ulderico Rolandi, *Il libretto per musica attraverso i tempi* (Rome, 1951), p. 44.

36. Bermúdez's *Nise lastimosa* preserves most of the dialogue in hendecasyllabic blank verse, but the choruses are in seven-syllable verse and a virtuosic six-stanza *sestina* (cf. chorus in act 3 of Cinzio's *Orbecche*). His *Nise laureada* is more complicated. There is a speech in ottava rima, one in terza rima, and the king frequently speaks in freely alternating seven- and eleven-syllable lines. There are choruses

in five-syllable Adonicos, three sonnets, two Italian *lire*, a blank-verse ode, seven-syllable blank verse, eleven-syllable blank verse, and several of mixed lengths.

37. Cueva's contemporary, Cristóbal de Verués, composed a tragedy, *La gran Semiramis*, in which sixteen years elapse between the first and second acts, and six more between the second and third. His admixture of rhymed verse types compares to that of de la Cueva.

38. First mention of this troupe is in 1566 at the Gonzaga Court in Mantova. See Antonio Belloni, *Storia letteraria d'Italia*, vol. 7 (Milano, 1929), p. 366. As is generally known such troupes were the first professional actors in Italy, and their art was an improvised one, based on stock characters and situations. Their scenarios were frequently adaptations or travesties of the ancient comedies of Plautus and Terence or the learned comedy of the Italian courts. They reduced the five acts of serious comedy to three, and the play itself was called a *giornata*, that is, a "day." The term probably comes from the French practice of calling that part of the great mystery cycles that the church allowed to be presented in a given day a *journée*. In sixteenth-century Spain, the term *jornada* became used to mean an act of a play rather than the whole play.

39. Othón Arróniz, *La influenca italiana en el nacimiento de la comedia española* (Madrid, 1969), p. 284.

40. William T. Brewster, *The New Art of Writing Plays of Lope de Vega* (New York, 1914), pp. 34–35.

41. Ibid., pp. 30–31.

42. Ibid., p. 9.

43. Ibid., pp. 34–35.

44. Belloni, *Storia*, p. 353.

45. Ibid., p. 354. The words are quoted in Cicognini's preface to his drama *Il trionfo di David* (Florence, 1628; published 1633): "Lope . . . scrivendogli che conveniva 'far prova del diletto che porta seco il rappresentare azioni che passino lo spazio non solo d'un giorno, ma anco di mesi ed anni, acciochè si goda degli accidenti dell'istoria non con la narrazione dell'antefatto, ma col mostrar presenti all'occhio le azioni stessi in vari tempi avvenute.'"

46. Worsthorne, *Venetian Opera*, p. 125: "Quest'opera sente delle opinioni moderne. Non è fatta al prescritto delle Antiche regole, ma all'usanza Spagnuola rappresenta gl'anni & non le ore."

47. Patrick J. Smith, *The Tenth Muse* (New York, 1970), p. 37.

48. Nino Pirrotta, "Early Opera and Aria," in *New Looks at Italian Opera, Essays in Honor of Donald J. Grout*, ed. William W. Austin (Ithaca, 1968), p. 95.

49. "Sò che l'Ariette cantate da Alessandro, e Aristotele, si stimeranno

contro il decoro di Personaggi sì grandi . . . pur questo difetto non
solo è tolerato dal Secolo corrente, ma ricevuto con applauso. . . . . se
lo stile recitativo non venisse intermezzato con simili scherzi, por-
terebbe più fastidio che diletto; condonami però quell'errore, che
solo hò commesso per meno tetiarti." Cited in William Holmes,
"Giacinto Cicognini's and Antonio Cesti's *Orontea* (1649)," in Austin, *New Looks*, p. 120.

50. Rolandi, *Il libretto*, p. 53: "Vi sono molt'altre mezz'Arie sparse per
l'Opera che rompono il tedio del Recitativo."

51. Solerti, *Le origini*, p. 218: ". . . dico che a continuarlo troppo a di
lungo, presto verrebbe in fastidio."

52. Ibid., p. 206: "Noi vediamo dunque che queste azioni per la maggior
parte si compongono di versetti piccoli, massime settenari, che chia-
mano mezzi versi, o sia per conformarsi con l'opinione dello Speroni,
il quale in tal forma compose la sua *Canace* e con un discorso s'in-
gegnò di provare che tali versi convengono più alla scena de' lunghi, o
pure perchè si adattano meglio alle canzonette, nelle quali molti pen-
sano che consista la perfezione della musica teatrale, o perchè rice-
vono la rima più frequente." "Ogni sorte dunque di versi potrà en-
trare ne' ragionamenti scenici e ne' cori; ma, per avviso, con questa
limitazione, che ne' ragionamenti più frequenti saranno i lunghi, e nel
secondo luogo i mezzani e non mai i versetti piccoli. Ma ne' cori, i
meno frequenti saranno i lunghi e i piccoli (perchè questi vi si po-
tranno ammettere) e più degli altri i mezzani. Quest'altra differenza
ancora si doverebbe osservare, che ne' ragionamenti scenici non si
mescolassero tanto i grandi con i piccoli; ma, verbigrazia, dopo
trenta versi lunghi, staranno bene dieci o dodici mezzani di questa o
quella specie, secondo le materie, massimamente i settenari comuni
nelle cose gravi o indifferenti (come nell'*Aminta* vediamo praticarsi) e
gli ottonari in alcune leggiere e molto allegre."

53. Giovan Battista Doni, *Compendio del trattato de' generi e de' modi
della musica* (1635). Cited in Solerti, *Le origini*, p. 224: ". . . benchè
[le villanelle] s'accostino alquanto più alla semplicità di quelle che
propriamente si dicono arie o canzonette, et anco alle ballate o canzoni a ballo, dagli antichi chiamate *hyporchemata*."

54. The poetry of Anacreon had been brought forth in its first modern
edition by Stephanus (Henri Estienne) in Paris in 1554. Chiabrera
was influenced principally by his friend, the exiled disciple of Ronsard, Marc-Antoine Muret. See B. R. Hanning, "Chiabrera," in *The
New Grove Dictionary* (London, 1980, 6th edition), vol. 4, p. 219.

55. Set by Monteverdi in the *Scherzi musicali* (1607). Chiabrera's most
famous *canzonetta* "Belle rose porporine" was set by Giulio Caccini
in *Le nuove musiche* (1602).

56. Angelo Solerti, *Gli albori del melodramma*, vol. 3, reprint of 1904 edition (Hildesheim, 1969), pp. 297ff.
57. Belloni, *Storia*, p. 428.
58. Anna Maria Monterosso-Vacchelli, "L'opera veneziana nella prima metà del seicento," in *Storia dell'opera*, ed. Alberto Basso (Torino, 1977), vol. i, p. 70.
59. Ariella Lanfranchi, "La librettistica italiana del seicento," in Basso, *Storia dell'opera*, vol. 3, p. 35.
60. Ibid.
61. But see the chorus of Amori in *quinari* in *La veglia delle grazie* (1615) in Solerti, *Gli albori*, p. 196, and alternating *ottonari* and *quaternari* in *La Galatea* (1614), ibid., p. 129.
62. Shakespeare's *Midsummer Night's Dream* comes to mind in this respect, with its human dialogue in ten-syllable blank verse, couplets, and quatrains; fairy dialogue often in seven-syllable couplets and quatrains; Puck in *quaternario*, Bottom's songs in *quaternario* and quatrains of alternating *ottonario* and *quaternario*; Pyramus and Thisbe in tercets of two *quaternari* and a *senario*; and the rustics in prose.
63. Worsthorne, *Venetian Opera*, p. 122: "Ti presento il mio Claudio ricco più di canzoni e d'ariette, che d'accidenti. Basta il dire, che sia Drama per Musica. Che si può fare? S'oggidì i capricci di Venetia così lo vogliono, io procuro d'incontrar il lor gusto."
64. Holmes, "*Orontea* (1649)," in Austin, *New Looks*, p. 120: ". . . sò ancora che'è improprio il recitarsi in Musica, non imitandosi in questa maniera il discorso naturale . . . e pur questo difetto non solo è tolerato dal Secolo corrente, ma ricevuto con applauso; questa specie di Poesia hoggi non hà altro fine che dilettare, onde conviene accomodarsi all'uso de i Tempi. . . ."
65. Ibid., p. 120: "Io compongo per mero capriccio; il mio capriccio non hà altra fine, che dilettare: L'apportar diletto appresso di me, non è altro, che l'incontrare il genio, & il gusto di chi ascolta, ò legge. . . ."
66. Rolandi, *Il libretto*, p. 46: ". . . i particolari (della Favola) . . . descritti con quella brevità che richiede la musica, per la quale è stata composta."
67. Ellen Rosand, "In Defense of the Venetian Libretto." Unpublished paper read at the annual meeting of the AMS, New York, 1979.
68. Basso, *Storia dell'opera*, vol. 1, p. 61: ". . . niente si cura al presente, per accrescer diletto agli spettatori, il dar luogo a qualche inverisimile che non deturpi l'azione . . . abbiamo introdotta la musica, nella quale non possiamo fuggire un inverisimile, che gli uomini trattino i loro più importanti negozii cantando. . . . Non è dunque maraviglia,

se obbligandoci noi al diletto del genio presente, ci siamo con ragione
slontanati dall'antiche regole. . . ."

69. Ibid., p. 60: "Tu perdi il tempo, o lettore, se con la Poetica dello
    Stagirita in mano vai rintracciando gli errori di quest'opera, perch'io
    confesso a la libera, che nel comporla non ho voluto osservare altri
    precetti che i sentimenti dell'inventore degli apparati, nè ho avuto altra
    mira che il genio di quel popolo a cui s'ha ella da rappresentare."

70. Ibid., pp. 60–61: "Prima che prender la penna io m'aveva proposto
    di trattenermi un gran pezzo co'l dimostrarti che questa favola ha
    tutte le buone regole insegnate da Maestri; che termina co'l giro di un
    giorno, o poco più; ch'è un'azione sola; che non ha accidente che sia
    incompatibile, e che non travia punto dal costume. . . . Tanto più,
    ch'essendo al presente il secolo composto d'opinioni e d'interessi non
    crede ad altre regole, che a quelle del capriccio e della passione. . . ."

71. Rosand, "In Defense."

72. Smith, *The Tenth Muse*, p. 26.

73. Hugo Albert Rennert, *The Spanish Stage in the Time of Lope de Vega*
    (New York, 1909), p. 37.

74. Ibid., p. 38.

75. Ibid., p. 39.

76. Basso, *Storia dell'opera*, vol. 1, pp. 61–62: "Hanno gli antichi pre-
    scritte in molte cose le regole, perchè si tenevano a gloria che il
    mondo si fermasse ne i loro precetti, e forse agli uomini del venturo
    secolo restasse levata la facoltà dell'inventare. . . . Infelice secolo, se
    l'orme dei passati obbligassero il nostro piede ad un inalterabil cam-
    mino . . . i precetti della Poetica [di Aristotele] non sono come le pro-
    porzioni matematiche, certi e permanenti . . . perchè le mutazioni de
    secoli fanno nascer le diversità del comporre . . . e forse per l'avvenire
    col cambiare dell'età vedranno i nostri posteri introdotte nuove
    forme. . . . Onde in ogni tempo si è veduta aperta la strada dell'in-
    ventare, non tenendo noi altro obbligo circa i precetti degli antichi,
    che de saperli. . . . ho voluto . . . battere una strada non da altri cal-
    cata, sicuro che, se vivesse Aristotele ne' presenti tempi, regolarebbe
    anch'egli la sua Poetica all'inclinazione del secolo . . . la vera regola è
    soddisfare a chi ascolta."

77. Jusserand, *Shakespeare*, p. 98.

78. Hellmuth Christian Wolff, "Italian Opera from the Later Monteverdi
    to Scarlatti," in *New Oxford History of Music* (London, 1975), vol.
    5, p. 87.

79. Freeman, "Apostolo Zeno's Reform," p. 334.

80. Piero Weiss, "The Rules of Tragedy, The Vagaries of Opera: A Chap-
    ter in Baroque Aesthetics." Unpublished paper read at the annual

meeting of AMS, New York, 1979. Cited from Pietro Metastasio, *Estratto della Poetica d'Aristotele e considerazioni sulla medesima* (1773).
81. Herrick, *Italian Tragedy*, pp. 288–292.
82. Worsthorne, *Venetian Opera*, p. 15.
83. Tirso de Molina, *Cigarrales de Toledo* (1624). Cited in Clark, *European Theories*, pp. 68–69.

Mythological Subjects in Opera Seria
by Sven Hansell

Today when we speak of tales relating fabulous deeds of extraordinary persons, we attempt to classify them according to origin, content, and function by using labels like myth, fable, folktale, saga, and legend. Thus, most twentieth-century writers define myths as narratives that a society (usually of the distant past) not only accepted as true but considered to be primordial revelations and exemplary models of a sacred tradition. Few scholars continue to speak of myths as fictions, even if the Greek term *mythos* originally meant "word" in the sense of a decisive, final pronouncement even about something that could not really exist. The term *mythos* was distinguished from *logos* or "word," denoting order and intelligibility or reason and thus used to designate a truth, the validity of which could be argued, measured, or otherwise demonstrated. However fascinating etymologies may be and however important it is to keep present-day terminology straight, it should be pointed out here that the eighteenth century was rather casual in distinguishing between myth and fable. For example, the article "Fable" written by Louis, chevalier de Jaucourt for the French *Encyclopédie* in 1756 begins by defining myth thus: ". . . a collective noun which includes theological history, mythical or heroic legend [*l'histoire fabuleuse*], poetic story and, to say it in a word, all the *fables* of a country's religion [*la théologie payenne*]." [1] Jaucourt then goes on to speak of historical fables as a mixture of true stories and fictions, such as those telling about the principal gods and heroes: Jupiter, Apollo, Bacchus, Hercules, Jason, and Achilles. In his article, he also mentions *fables inventées à plaisir* that have no other function than to amuse and cites the story of Psyche to serve as an example. Interestingly, he refers to the *Metamorphoses* of Ovid as a fable that relates true facts but to which supernatural circumstances have been added as an embellishment.

On the basis of his comments, one might assume that the Enlightenment did not take mythology very seriously, or at least did not burden itself by regarding supernatural as an essential element. Of course, Jaucourt points out that a general knowledge of mythology, or what he continues to call *la fable*, is widespread:

> Our spectacles, our lyric and dramatic pieces and our poetry in all genres, make perpetual allusions to fable; the prints, paintings and statues which decorate our rooms, our halls, our ceilings, our gardens, are almost always drawn from fable; finally, it is in such common usage in all our writings, our novels, our pamphlets and even in our ordinary conversations, that up to a certain point it is not possible to be unaware of it without having to blush for such a lack of education.[2]

Certainly, reminders of the deities and heroes of ancient times confront us repeatedly not only in France but throughout Italy, and we find the inclusion of mythology in different genres of Italian music composed in the seventeenth and eighteenth centuries. While it may seem ubiquitous to the casual observer, its use actually diminished noticeably in Italian opera seria from about the 1720s until some time in the mid 1760s. Moreover, regional differences may also be noted: mythological subjects disappeared earlier from the *drammi per musica* staged in Naples than from those given in Venice, Vienna, and some other operatic capitals north of the Alps, and their revival in Naples seems also to have preceded their return in operatic performances at Venice.[3]

On the other hand, characters and situations taken from mythology often appeared in the *licenza* of an opera and in the *feste teatrali* usually written to celebrate particular occasions like birthdays or weddings. Although the *festa teatrale* often featured lavish scenery as well as choruses, its performance was not always limited to the opera house. Those *feste teatrali* that we know best, written by the librettist Metastasio and set to music by resident composers in Vienna (Fux, Caldara, Reutter, Predieri, Bonno, Hasse, and Gluck) to celebrate birthdays and weddings of the ruling Hapsburg family, were given in Schönbrunn, the Favorita Palace, and the court residence in Vienna.[4] A group of six elaborate productions performed between 1731 and 1740 were followed by a few modest cantatas with mythological subjects in the 1740s and 1750s and then another set of six grand *feste teatrali* between 1764 and 1767. These two series of occasional works using mythological subjects parallel groups of *feste teatrali* presented at the court in Naples except that fewer were performed there in the 1760s and only one or two staged in the 1730s.[5] During the 1720s, when Metastasio himself was in Naples, occasional works with mythological plots were even rarer; I have found reference to only one written for the *palazzo reale* at the close of the 1720s (L. Vinci's *Peleo* of 1729). Metastasio's three youthful librettos involving mythological figures—*Endimione* of 1720, *Gli orti esperidi* of 1721, and *Galatea* of 1722, which were performed privately in Naples—may well represent a type of modest musical entertainment about which we know very little, librettos or other documentation having eluded researchers to date.

Surveying the years immediately preceding Metastasio's sojourn in Naples, we find a surprising absence of both occasional works as well as full-length serious operas using plots or even characters taken from Greek or Roman mythology. The decade 1710 through 1719 witnessed perhaps only one entertainment staged at Naples' Teatro de' Fiorentini involving a myth (A. Orefice's *Circe delusa* of 1713). An average of three serious operas on mythological subjects was given at Teatro San Bartolomeo and afterward at San Carlo in each of the ensuing decades: the 1720s, 1730s, and 1740s.[6] During the 1750s only one more was staged (A. M. Mazzoni's *Arianna e Teseo*, 1758). It was not until the 1770s and thereafter that an average of eight opere serie per decade began to reflect a renewed appreciation for the serious portrayal of gods and heroes of the mythological past.[7]

Later in my paper I shall touch again upon the rise in popularity of mythology during the 1770s. But first I should like to point out an intriguing difference between Neapolitan and Venetian opere serie as far as their plots are concerned. While the twenty years from 1710 to 1729 produced five mythological operas in Naples,[8] during the same two decades about ten serious operas based on mythology were staged in Venice.[9] In fact, Neapolitan audiences saw only one opera with a mythological plot in the decade 1725 to 1734 while the Venetian public saw eight.[10] Adding *pastorali* and comic works like *scherzi*, as well as the occasional entertainments called *serenate*, *feste*, and *azione teatrali*, I find that Venice staged a grand total of twenty-six or twenty-seven mythological works while Naples had but six between 1710 and 1735.[11] In compiling these statistics I do not include entertainments taken from medieval legends, specifically Ariosto's *Orlando furioso* and Tasso's *Gerusalemme liberata*, despite any supernatural episodes reminding us of the marvel and magic of ancient Greek and Roman tales. Shortly, I shall turn my attention to Vivaldi and other composers who set to music portions of Ariosto's chivalric epic, but for the moment I wish to comment on the apparent lack of interest among Neapolitans for the musical portrayal of mythological events with costumes, scenery, and all the rest.

Their attitude is noteworthy for what it suggests about certain ideas that one generally associates with the Enlightenment. The belief in progress and the attack on superstitions that later came to characterize *Illuminismo* must have been strong in Naples even around the time that the first edition of Giambattista Vico's *Scienza nuova* (Naples, 1725) was published, Vico whom historians have recently begun calling the father of modern approaches to mythology. Although we can assume that Metastasio would have heard of Vico's treatise—Metastasio already referred to Vico in a letter from Naples of December 16, 1721[12]—we may suppose that Metastasio largely ignored Vico's ideas or, what I consider more likely, accepted only those arguments that reinforced his own views on taste and Christian decorum. For example, Vico explains his belief that a truly heroic emotion, an unrestrained, impassioned outburst, does not belong to rational ages in which "democratic republics" have developed, with his observation that every age lives, speaks, acts, thinks, governs, legislates, and reads according to its own psyche, its own dominant temper.[13] Certainly Vico's association of the brutal interactions between heroes and gods with early stages of societies would have strengthened Metastasio's disinclination to incorporate in dramas what were for him the vulgar elements of any idolatrous age. Vico's view of Homer as a minstrel of barbarism may appeal to our anthropological interest in early cultures, but for eighteenth-century Italians it was probably disturbing, given their ignorance or even fear of alien worlds, believed to be crude and repulsive in comparison to their own. The Vichian argument that the Greeks and Romans of relatively late date had imputed sagacity to the heroic and barbarous progenitors of nations—in fact, Vico thought of them as uncouth aborigines[14]—

may well have impressed Metastasio and his intellectual contemporaries considerably. Had Vico claimed, on the other hand, that myths were merely false narratives or allegories, he would have lent support to a perpetuation of the seventeenth-century tradition of presenting fantastic and marvelous events on the stage. Since, however, Vico wrote of myths as expressions of the collective mentality of a bestial age, he essentially issued, however unintentionally, a warning to his contemporaries; to wit, that eighteenth-century man would debase himself if superstitions and witchery of the past were affectively represented in the modern theater.

Of course, we know about Metastasio's sensitivity to the character of dramas and their function as public entertainments, thanks to his commentary on Aristotle's *Poetics*, the *Estratto dell'arte poetica d'Aristotile e considerazioni su la medesima*, which he completed in 1773, but which, he claimed, incorporated the reflections of fifty years of experience. "The duty of the playwright is to employ his talents for the good of society instilling a love of virtue, so necessary to public happiness."[15] Metastasio actually criticized Aristotle's partiality for dreadful actions and goes on to praise

> . . . those poets who, in order to go along with the taste of another day, took a path different from that of Euripides [and] adopted the practice of ending a tragedy with the reconciliation of the cruelest enemies without having anyone killed or having a single drop of blood shed. Thus, what was unsuitable in Aristotle's time, is not in ours, and . . . were Aristotle writing his *Poetics* today, he would adapt his above-mentioned laws to present usages and not to those of 20 centuries ago.[16]

This near echo of Vico's teaching, especially its recognition of links between times and attitudes, is also encountered in Metastasio's private notes on Greek theater, his *Osservazioni sul teatro greco*. Citing a work of Aristophanes, he explains that because it is fouled with coarse manners not only tolerated but applauded by the Athenians, the good taste of the Greek public is cast in doubt.[17] And one may assume that Metastasio also had in mind later seventeenth-century Italian opera with its vulgar antics, fantastic elements, and brutal details often linked to mythological references.

If I have dealt at length with Metastasio, it is only partially because he has come to represent the mainstream of serious opera during the second third of the eighteenth century; it is also because his poetry is rated so highly by modern critics. For example, Walter Binni calls Metastasio the culmination of the Arcadian reforms begun in the late seventeenth century.[18] It is more than a convenience to use Metastasio's texts as a basis for comparing librettos of all other authors of the second and third quarters of the century.

Turning to his *Didone abbandonata*, his first *dramma per musica* and one of only two with a tragic ending,[19] we encounter a libretto that treats the well-known mythological story of Dido and Aeneas in essentially the same way that his later opera texts develop historical characters without recourse to magic linked with fantastic scenic inventions. Aside from the tigers, lions, and other gifts that a procession of guests brings the Carthaginian queen in act 1 and the conflagration of Carthage offstage (or visible at a distance) in act 3, there is no other spectacular action, certainly no implausible events, nothing not also encountered in Metastasio's other opere serie. Juno and Venus never appear in order to command Aeneas to marry Dido, and Mercury never presents Jupiter's wish that Aeneas leave Carthage, as Metastasio's own mythological sources informed him. This libretto was extremely popular throughout the 1730s, 1740s, and 1750s—indeed it was set to music dozens of times during the last third of the eighteenth century and even as late as the 1820s—and yet I did not count its performance in Naples and Venice when I earlier gave statistics on productions of mythological entertainments. Let me therefore point out now that the opera seems to have enjoyed almost twice the popularity in Venice during the 1730s, 1740s, and 1750s that it did in Naples due perhaps to a greater lingering interest in mythology on the part of the Venetians.[20] Two other Metastasian librettos that should be of special interest to us today are *Angelica*, his youthful *serenata* of 1722, and *Ruggiero* of 1771, Metastasio's last opera seria, because both are based on Ariosto's *Orlando furioso*. However, neither resembles in general character the libretto by Grazio Braccioli with which Vivaldi worked in 1714 and reset in 1727.

Orlando, as portrayed by Metastasio in his *serenata*, expresses anger in aristocratic phrases that never transgress reasonable bounds to generate fear or wonder in the audience. He shows no superhuman strength; appropriately, the serenade is set in a flower garden rather than a remote wilderness. But most significant is the lack of dramatic contrast anywhere in the text. For example, when

Orlando learns that Medoro is Angelica's lover, he accepts the news with composure. And when Orlando's madness could erupt following Medoro's and Angelica's departure at the end of the serenade, an ever-present pastoral atmosphere pervades his readiness for reconciliation. He sings: "Torna, torna ad amarmi . . . [Return, return and love me . . .]". Both untamed nature and Arcadian innocence yield here to a sentimental *raffinatezza*.

In Metastasio's *Ruggiero ovvero l'eroica gratitudine*, we confront the same conflict between love and duty that animates the dialogue in *Didone abbandonata*. Here, duty is born of gratitude to a friend to whom the hero, Ruggiero, should surrender his beloved—a situation already known from Metastasio's opera *Olimpiade* of 1733 based on Greek history. Other details remind us of recurring situations in almost all Metastasian operas. Predictably, Ariosto's Melissa and her magical interventions are entirely absent from Metastasio's adaptation. Her function is fulfilled by Clotilde, the *seconda donna*, who makes appropriate identifications to ensure rational decisions on the part of rivals and lovers. In other words, there is no hint of the witchcraft that plays such an important role in Ariosto's epic.[21]

In sharp contrast to this and every other libretto by Metastasio, Grazio Braccioli's text set by Vivaldi is embellished with superhuman powers and extraordinary persons taken from both classical mythology and medieval legend. Although it is not, strictly, a mythological opera and does not present the inexorable force of tragedy that characterizes the most impressive myths, it has unmistakable and recurring elements of the irrational that could well have inspired impassioned acting on the part of Lucia Lancetti, Anna Girò, and others, fantastic scenic effects by Alessandro Mauro possible at the Teatro Sant'Angelo, as well as the unusually fine music of Vivaldi that alone survives.

References to mythological personages in Braccioli's libretto supplement those already in Ariosto's epic. For example, the chorus at the wedding of Angelica and Medoro in act 2 sings, "Great mother Venus, great god Thespius, great father Liberus, hear their vows," to which Angelica responds, "Thou, lovely Cytherea, Thou tender Cupid, Thou loving Liberus, I invoke, drinking this nuptial cup . . ." The chorus continues, "Goddess of Hesperus, youthful Idalius, divine Semeleus . . ." to let us have a catalog of names associated with spring and love from both Greek and Roman mythology. This mix of classical sources is extended by references to Arthurian legend when, in act 3, an urn with the ashes of Merlin as well as a statue of the medieval wizard are displayed within the Temple to Infernal Hecate, who was the chief goddess presiding over magic and spells in Greek religion. Other similar examples serve to remind the listener that the opera, perhaps more than the epic from which it was drawn, lacks a single, cohesive, mythological basis. But the extraneous references that amuse us may have been intended like witty conceits to beguile contemporary audiences. For instance, near the end of the opera, when Alcina loses her magic and Orlando is awakened by a torch, the light they see is probably meant to represent *Illuminismo* (the Enlightenment) or, rather, the awakening of rational faculties—or do we perceive an anachronistic symbol, one that an audience of the 1720s would not yet have known? At any rate, it may be safe to suppose that references to mythology in the opera rarely rise above the level of the humorous or casually didactic.

That some humor was intended, nevertheless, seems likely thanks to the relatively simple, direct style of language that Braccioli uses. In the preface to his original libretto of 1713 he says, ". . . remember that I speak as a playwright; that is to say, that I accommodate myself to the passions and feelings of the characters introduced and converse in their language." [22] But Braccioli's dialogue is far removed from Giulio Rospigliosi's in his *Il palazzo incantato ovvero la guerriera amante*, a text also based on Ariosto's epic (which Luigi Rossi set to music for Rome in 1642); [23] his characters, despite occasional hints of seventeenth-century artificialities, speak more like the aristocrats in Francesco Antonio Tullio's opera buffa *Angelica ed Orlando* (set by Gaetano Latilla and first performed at Naples's Teatro de' Fiorentini in 1735). [24]

What Tullio's comic opera seems to demonstrate especially well is that Ariosto's epic and various mythological tales were probably so well known to the Italian audience that they were easily treated satirically. In fact, Tullio's libretto, like other comic texts on this theme, suggests that the irrational, presented for what it is, produced laughter, which is to say that the serious representation of tragic myths must, at that time, have been very difficult to stage in Naples. It is perhaps no accident that there were as many if not more comic versions of mythological stories in Naples between 1735 and 1745 as serious ones.

Let me cite one example of humor in Tullio's opera buffa. When stage machinery is called for, and it is required only once, it permits a cloud to descend to hide Angelica and Medoro from Orlando; thus, unseen and unmolested, they tease him with a love duet. I assume, of course, that the conventions of earlier opera seria and of the marvelous are parodied, if not also the behavior of the aristocracy.

In light of the inconsequential use to which mythology was put in opera both serious and comic during the *Primo Settecento*, it becomes imperative to find very strong reasons for the return to favor in the 1750s and 1760s of classical myths. Were the excavations in Pompeii and Herculaneum and publications about them in the 1750s important factors in reawakening an appreciation for mythology? Would the collection of eight hundred plates illustrating antiquities that Count de Caylus published in seven volumes between 1752 and 1767 in Paris, as *Receuil d'antiquités égyptiennes, étrusques, grecques, romaines et gauloises* have contributed significantly to its revival? What about Winckelmann's celebrated books of the 1750s and 1760s, beginning with his *Gedanken über die Nachahmung der griechischen Werke* and culminating in his *Monumenti antichi inediti, spiegati ed illustrati* (published in Rome, 1767–1768)?[25] And what about books on Germanic, Egyptian, and Asian myths and religions like Charles DeBrosses's *Du culte des dieux fétiches* of 1760? The possible influence of English enthusiasts and writings besides David Hume's criticism of 1757, *The Natural History of Religion*, might be considered, too. And then, of course much closer to home were the operas on mythological subjects by Tomasso Traetta for Parma on texts of Carlo Frugoni in 1759 and 1760 as well as the collaborations in Vienna of Gluck and Calzabigi shortly thereafter.

But none of these suggest to my mind a greater, more direct impact on the opera seria than that other form of dramatic entertainment staged in the theater with all the conventions of scenery, acting, and music: ballet. Entr'acte ballets were popular in Venice throughout most of the *Settecento*. More precisely, these were divertissements without plots between the acts of serious operas at the beginning of the century or roughly until the early 1720s, then once again between the acts of comic and serious operas during the 1740s and 1750s,[26] and finally as extended entertainments, usually with titles often indicating mythological subjects, in the

1760s and thereafter. Since about half of the ballets with titles using pantomime involved mythological tales, it seems probable that many of the untitled Venetian pantomimes of the 1740s and 1750s could have had mythological subjects as did those we know were produced at Milan.[27] The character of the dance, its appeal to the imagination of the spectator, along with its need to exploit fully the stage and its machinery to achieve marvelous effects further recommends ballet as the genre in which the most fantastic and irrational aspects of mythology found acceptance already in the 1740s and 1750s.

Its importance could well have been greater than that of the cantata for one or two voices, it seems to me, because most cantatas disclosing mythological borrowings maintain an untroubled pastoral tone at the same time that they avoid any reference whatsoever to irrational events. The cantata texts of Metastasio may serve as convenient illustrations of this style.[28]

On the whole, Italian audiences seem not to have been ready in the 1720s for serious contemplation of psychological characterizations often lacking Christian values. Evidently it was not until an awareness of rationalistic principles had penetrated the common mind and convinced the general public of the depth of human irrationality in the past that its sympathies were awakened to accept manifestations of irrationalism in the present. Perhaps one can best describe *Orlando furioso* as an opera truly summing up prevailing Venetian attitudes of the 1710s and 1720s. Its superficial use of mythology may also help explain why Braccioli's text strikes us as particularly attractive. Compared, let us say, to the typical Metastasian plot, Braccioli's libretto is a blend of fantasy and satire that audiences of the present day should enjoy. Mythological references providing a touch of the exotic do much to justify the imaginative plot, scenery, and music of Vivaldi's setting. In other words, the fantastic quality of the art work is itself symbolized by the ever-recurring references to mythology.

NOTES

1. Louis, chevalier de Jaucourt, "Fable," in *Encyclopédie, ou dictionnaire raisonné des sciences, des arts et des métiers* (1756), pp. xvi, 342–349.
2. Ibid., p. 344.
3. Generalizations given in this paper are based on over four hundred

works, the titles of which identify them as mythological in subject. Most are listed in the following published catalogs: "Franz Stieger, *Opernlexikon, Teil I: Titelkatalog,* 3 vols. (Tutzing: Hans Schneider, 1975); Felice de Filippis and R. Arnese, *Cronache del teatro di S. Carlo (1737–1960),* 2 vols. (Naples: Edizioni Politica Popolare, 1961–1963); Franco Mancini, *Scenografia napoletana dell'età barocca* (Naples: Edizioni Scientifiche Italiane, 1964); Taddeo Wiel, *I teatri musicali veneziani del settecento* (Venice: Fratelli Visentini, 1897); Oscar G. T. Sonneck, *Library of Congress: Catalogue of Opera Librettos Printed before 1800,* 2 vols. (Washington, D.C.: Government Printing Office, 1914); Anton Bauer, *Opern und Operetten in Wien* (Graz: Hermann Böhlaus, 1955).

4. The notes by Bruno Brunelli to his edition of Metastasio's works give information on every production (*Tutte le opere di Pietro Metastasio,* 5 vols. [Milan: Mondadori, 1943–1954]).

5. So called *feste teatrali, azioni teatrali,* and *serenate* performed in Naples during the 1760s included T. Traetta, *Armida,* 1763; G. Sigismondi, *Endimione,* 1764; J. A. Hasse, *Partenope,* 1767; and G. Paisiello, *Le nozze di Peleo e Tetide,* 1768.

6. Nine Neopolitan productions from the 1720s through the 1740s: L. Leo, *Arianna e Teseo,* 1721; G. B. Mancini, *Endimione,* 1721; D. Sarri, *Adone in Cipro,* 1724; G. DeMajo, *Erminia,* 1729; D. Sarri, *Le nozze di Teti e Peleo,* 1738; D. Sarri, *La Partenope,* 1739; G. Latilla, *Alceste,* 1740; G. Latilla, *Olimpia nell'isola di Ebuda,* 1741; G. DeMajo, *Arianna e Teseo,* 1747. Sarri's work of 1738 may have been a *festa teatrale* like L. Leo's *Le nozze di Amore e Psiche* of the same year.

7. Eight Neapolitan productions from 1770–1800: G. Insanguine, *Arianna e Teseo,* 1773; W. Gluck, *Orfeo ed Euridice,* 1774; P. Cafaro, *Il natale d'Apollo,* 1775; D. Fischietti, *Arianna e Teseo,* 1776 and 1777; I. Platania; *Bellerofonte,* 1778; J. Schuster, *Amore e Psiche,* 1780; G. Insanguine, *Calipso,* 1782; D. Cimarosa, *Oreste,* 1783; G. Pugnani, *Adone e Venere,* 1784; P. A. Guglielmi, *Enea e Lavinia,* 1785 and 1788; W. Gluck, *Alceste,* 1785; F. Cipolla, *Polifemo,* 1786; A. Priati, *Olimpia,* 1786; G. Paisiello, *Giunone e Lucina,* 1787; G. Paisiello, *Fedra,* 1788; G. Paisiello, *Pirro,* 1790; G. Paisiello, *Apollo e Dafne,* 1790; N. Piccinni, *Ercole al Termedonte,* 1793; G. Andreozzi, *Giasone e Medea,* 1793; F. Paer, *Ero e Leandro,* 1794; F. Piticchio, *La vendetta di Medea,* 1798.

8. In addition to the first four works cited in note 5 is A. Orefice's *Circe delusa* of 1713.

9. Ten operas for Venice of 1710–1729: G. Boniventi, *Circe delusa,* 1711; P. G. Rampini, *La gloria trionfante d'amore,* 1712; F. Chelleri,

Penelope la casta, 1716; T. Albinoni, *Meleagro*, 1718; G. Boniventi, *Arianna abbandonata*, 1719; G. Porta, *Ulisse*, 1725; G. F. Brusa, *Medea e Giasone*, 1726; N. Porpora, *Arianna e Teseo*, 1727; T. Albinoni, *Le duc rivali in amore* (which includes the characters Paride and Elena), 1728; G. B. Pescetti and B. Galuppi, *Gli odi delusi dal sangue*, 1728; A. Pollarolo, *L'abbandono di Armida*, 1729.

10. To the last six works cited in note 9, two later works should be added: T. Albinoni, *Elena*, 1730 and F. Courcelle, *Venere placata*, 1731.

11. Thirteen nonseria works for Venice, 1710–1735: F. Gasparini and A. Lotti, *La ninfa Apollo*, 1709/10; C. F. Pollarolo, *Marsia delusa*, 1714; G. A. Ristori, *La Pallade trionfante in Arcadia*, 1714; B. Marcello, *La morte d'Adone*, 1719; G. M. Buina, *Il Filindo*, 1720; A. Vivaldi, *Dorilla in Tempe*, 1726 and 1734; N. Porpora, *Imeneo in Atene*, 1726; A. Pollarolo, *Nerina*, 1728; G. B. Pescetti and B. Galuppi, *Dorinda*, 1729; B. Cordans, *La Silvia*, 1730; B. Galuppi, *La ninfa Apollo*, 1734. In addition to the serious operas cited in notes 6 and 7 there were two lighter or shorter works performed in Naples between 1710 and 1735: L. Vinci's *La festa di Bacco* of 1722 and his *Peleo* of 1729.

12. Brunelli, *Tutte le opere*, vol. 3, p. 38. In other letters Metastasio refers to persons known to have been acquainted with Vico (e.g., Paolo Mattia Doria).

13. An excellent discussion of Vico's recognition of societies' differing attitudes toward myths is Frank E. Manuel, *The Eighteenth Century Confronts the Gods* (Cambridge: Harvard University, 1959), pp. 151 passim. Among other pertinent studies are David Bidney, "Vico's New Science of Myth," in *Giambattista Vico: An International Symposium*, ed. G. Tagliacozzo and H. V. White (Baltimore: Johns Hopkins, 1969) and Donald P. Verene, *Vico's Science of Imagination* (Ithaca: Cornell University, 1981).

14. Manuel, *The Eighteenth Century*, p. 164.

15. Brunelli, *Tutte le opere*, vol. 2, p. 1089.

16. Ibid., vol. 2, p. 1072.

17. Ibid., vol. 2, p. 1151.

18. *L'Arcadia e il Metastasio* (Florence: La nuova Italia, 1963).

19. The other opera is *Catone in Utica*, premiered in Rome in 1728.

20. In addition to Albinoni's setting of 1725 it was performed in Venice set by D. Sarri, 1730; A. Bernasconi, 1741; A. Adolfati, 1747; F. Bertoni, 1748; G. Manna, 1751; and T. Traetta, 1757. Neapolitan productions after D. Sarri's first version of 1724 included those by J. A. Hasse, 1744 and G. B. Lampugnani, 1753.

21. Good analyses of Metastasio's *serenata* and opera are included in Renate Döring, *Ariostos 'Orlando Furioso' im italienischen Theater des*

seicento und settecento (Hamburg: Hamburg University, 1973), pp. 280–309.

22. The original Italian reads: "... che parlo da Poeta Drammatico; cioé a dire che mi trasformo nella passione e ne' sentimenti delli Attori introdotti, e ragiono con la loro favella."

23. A copy of this work is published in the series of facsimiles *Italian Opera 1640–1770*, ed. H. M. Brown (New York: Garland Publ., 1977).

24. Tullio's libretto, along with Rospigliosi's, is discussed in Döring, *Ariosto's 'Orlando Furioso,'* pp. 141–157, 262–278.

25. Winckelmann's *Geschichte der Kunst des Alterthums* (Dresden, 1764) appeared in Italian translations at Milan, 1779 and at Rome, 1783–1784. Numerous other archaeological studies published in Italy are cited in Giulio Natali, *Il settecento* (in the series *Storia letteraria d'Italia*), 4th ed. (Milan: F. Vallardi, 1955), pp. 407–416 passim.

26. Vocal intermezzi dominated the later 1720s and 1730s.

27. Pantomime ballets are discussed in considerable depth by Kathleen Kuzmick Hansell in the chapter "Ballet at the Regio Ducal Teatro before 1770," in "Opera and Ballet at the Regio Ducal of Milan 1771–1776: A Musical and Social History," Ph.D. dissertation (University of California, Berkeley, 1980), pp. 581–688.

28. Those by Antonio Conti set by Benedetto Marcello are considered by Eleanor Selfridge-Field in "Ancora sul mito della rifondazione stilistica della musica nelle cantate mitologiche di Marcello," in *Mitologie: Convivenze di musica e mitologia; testi e studi*, ed. Giovanni Morelli (Venice: Biennale, 1979), pp. 101–106.

Ariosto and the Oral Tradition
by C. Peter Brand

The adaptation of literary classics to the stage, film, or television screen is often greeted with shouts of protest by the literary purists who, it must be admitted, frequently have good cause to complain that the author's original creation has been violated or disturbed and that an outrage has been committed on his or her memory. The protests have not been quite so loud, I think, in the case of Ariosto's *Orlando furioso* (which, after all, had been a pretty violent transplant of the epic *Chanson de Roland* some four hundred years previously), despite the radical treatment of, for example, Sanguineti's version for the Teatro Stabile di Roma or the recent version by the Italian television studios. Indeed, many of those who saw the Teatro Stabile's adventurous production at the Edinburgh Festival a few years ago were delighted to find that it was the most popular offering of the whole festival. This was true even though it was given in Italian and the audience was threatened, on the open floor of the stadium where the action was taking place, by charging horses, dragons, and hippogriffs. What delighted many of us was to find one of the original dimensions of the chivalrous romance restored; that is, the element of public performance as opposed to private reading and the broad general appeal as opposed to the restricted scholarly study of the present day.

It is true, of course, that already in Ariosto's day the medieval tradition of the *cantastorie* was giving way to the private reading made possible by the comparatively recent introduction of printing. Before printed texts became reasonably numerous, the poems and prose tales of the Carolingian and Arthurian cycles were generally communicated orally by the professional storytellers. With his tattered scripts supported by an incredible memory, the *cantastorie* varied and adapted his tales according to his moods, circumstances, audiences, and even the changing seasons. The same tale told in the piazza to a noisy male crowd must have undergone quite a transformation when taken up into the palace hall among the gentlefolk. Yet it was essentially the same material, as Luigi Pulci insisted of his poem *Il Morgante* (1483): "Materia è da piazza e da sala [There's matter here for the public square *and* for the drawing-room]." The occasional reports we have from contemporary witnesses underline the contrast between the crude texts carried around by the minstrels and the scintillating performances they gave, with their sweeping gestures and thumping drums, their winks and grimaces, witty insertions and subtle innuendos. Each reading was indeed a separate performance and could attract a considerable public interest and involvement. Witness, for example, the report of the man who, on hearing a *cantastorie*'s account of the death of a paladin, went straight home, took to his bed, and could not be persuaded by his wife to eat his supper.

The invention of printing certainly led to a reduction in the *cantastorie*'s role. While the early printed books were expensive, cheap editions soon became available. It has been reckoned that about 25,000 copies of popular editions of *Orlando furioso* appeared in Italy in the sixteenth century,[1] and Ariosto certainly wrote for a reading (rather than a listening) public. Even if the poem must have been read aloud in many households from the single family copy, many professional entertainers continued to engage popular audiences with recitations, songs, and, until quite recently, puppet and other visual shows based on Ariosto's poem. (Nineteenth-century travelers in Italy frequently report their delight at hearing octaves of Ariosto and Tasso sung across the Venetian lagoons, one gondolier taking up the tale where the other left off, and there was at least one itinerant storyteller in Sicily within living memory equipped with his text and a large illustrated board, like a kind of visual aid, which he carried around on a bicycle!)[2] The very popularity of the poem was the target of later sixteenth-century critics in Italy who sneered at "il *Furioso* che piace al popolo [the *Furioso* that is liked by the people]."

This aspect of public performance is then deeply rooted in the tradition of the chivalrous poem, so much so that Ariosto makes no effort to discard it, despite the new sophisticated environment of the Renaissance court. Indeed the dialogue with the reader/audience is meticulously preserved in a careful reformulation of oral techniques: "Se mi domanda alcun chi costui sia / che versa sopra il rio lacrime tante, / io dirò ch'egli è il re di Circassia / quel d'amor travagliato Sacripante: / io dirò ancor che . . . [If any of you should ask me who this is, weeping so profusely, I will tell you that it is the Circassian king, the love-worn Sacripante, I will also tell you that . . .]" (1.45). The tone seems neutral, but we know that the poet is smiling at that earnest *cantastorie* down in the piazza, leading his unlettered audience along by the nose. So too when Ariosto dedicates his poem to the Estensi he maintains the fiction that he is speaking to his patron (ending a canto because his throat is sore) and addresses him directly in the midst of his narrative; for example, when the lovesick Sacripante bewails Angelica's infidelity and seems turned to stone, "Pensoso più d'un ora a capo basso / stette, Signore, il cavallier dolente . . . [Anxiously, for more than an hour, my Lord, that grieving knight stood still . . .]" (1.40). The aside to Ippolito d'Este (*Signore*) is as good as a wink in underlining the heavy irony with which the poet treats this stylized lover. So a long series of nods and winks, of special messages to the ladies or confessions of the poet's own failures, of jibes at court figures and eulogies of the poet's patrons are woven into the text to preserve the illusion of oral narrative and to gain the advantages associated with it: intimacy, vividness, ambiguity of tone, and so on.

The translation of the poem to the opera stage, therefore, might be said to restore something of the element of performance that the text, being "dead" in the Pirandellian sense, has partly lost. For it is not only in these stylistic archaisms that the *Furioso* craves a living audience. Indeed one could argue that, on many occasions, the material is conceived in theatrical terms. Fifty years later, with Tasso's *Gerusalemme liberata*, an incipient Baroque taste translates the action of the Crusade into a succession of theatrical "colpi d'occhio": "Degne d'un chiaro sol, degne d'un pieno / teatro, opre sarian sì memorande . . . [Worthy of a brilliant sun, worthy of a full theater would such memorable deeds be . . .]" (XII.54). This is not Ariosto's taste, but he was nonetheless a man of the theater, one of the earliest and most influential figures in the creation of Italian comedy, a producer and theatrical manager, and his narrative poem is certainly colored by his theatrical experience and inclinations. Braccioli and Vivaldi certainly exploit this Ariostan precedent, sometimes by extension rather than reproduction. In the poem the superbly dramatic encounter of the proud Angelica with the wounded Medoro presents a little haven of love amid the clash of arms and vengeance. The opera transfers this very effectively in the opening scenes to the garden in which Medoro shelters from the violence, not of the battlefield, but of the sea.

Thus the action of the romance tradition is frequently presented as a series of encounters between key figures in which the interplay of conflicting personalities and intentions is represented in a dramatic dialogue form. What happens when the false Odorico, who has attempted to seduce his friend Zerbino's beloved Isabella, is caught and handed over to Zerbino? The scene is vividly presented with the words of both men (XXIV.20–41). The same is true of the scene where Polinesso insists to Ariodante that Ginevra is false to him (V.27–46). These confrontations are carried further in the libretto where characters who never meet in the poem share a rather crowded stage and reveal their varied emotional reactions to each other: Angelica, Alcina, Medoro, and Orlando, for example, make up the improbable fourth scene in act 1, as do Bradamante and Alcina in act 1, scene 6.

We should also note the many eloquent or pathetic monologues —Fiordiligi's lament for the death of Brandimarte, for example (XLIII.160–163), or Olimpia's when she is abandoned by Bireno (X.25–53). Thus there *are* precedents in the poem for the style of Orlando's long lament in the opera. Ariosto, however, gives Orlando only three octaves of monologue in the long and carefully built-up account of his rising frenzy, from which, incidentally, the libretto preserves three famous lines: ". . . Orlando è morto . . . / la sua donna ingratissima l'ha ucciso . . . / Io son lo spirto suo da lui diviso . . . [Orlando is dead . . . his ungrateful lady has killed him . . . I am his spirit, separated from him . . .]" (XXIII.128). We should also remember the conventional *agnizioni*, or revelations of identity, as when Rinaldo discovers Guidon Selvaggio in canto XXXI, and when Marfisa turns out to be Ruggiero's sister in canto XXXVI. Here too the libretto reproduces the poetical precedent but in different contexts. Angelica, for example, passes off Medoro as her brother, which never happens in the poem to these particular characters. (This is borrowed from another scene involving Martano, Grifone, and Orrigille in canto XVI.) Some of the episodes build up to fine dramatic denouements, as, for example, the Dalinda tale with the surprise arrival of Ariodante (canto VI) and the story of Drusilla with its final poisonings (canto XXXVII).

I have tried so far, in very limited space, to indicate how Ariosto's poem contains elements of performance or dramatic presentation that could make it appealing to Vivaldi and his contemporaries as a subject for the operatic stage. Let me now underline how, by the sophistication of essentially narrative techniques, he created a poem that did part company with the living audience and that no theater could ever represent adequately. One could do this in different ways, but I shall concentrate here on the central theme and title subject of poem and opera: Orlando's madness. The jealous love of Orlando for Angelica, which ultimately explodes in an outbreak of violence, has been seen by many readers since the nineteenth century as an uproarious burlesque, but to Ariosto's contemporaries and many seventeenth-century readers it was admired as a perceptive and moving psychological study of the mounting effects of thwarted passion. (See the interest of the Pléiade in France, for example, and Nisiely's confession that he had read this passage a hundred times "and that each time I read I fall in love with this episode. I weep with pity, I am overcome with amazement.")[3] The focusing of Vivaldi's opera on the madness of Orlando, therefore, is both true to the spirit of Ariosto and predictable of an eighteenth-century work—and it might not have happened today. The madness, for example, was certainly not the most memorable feature of Sanguineti's version.

In Ariosto's poem the *furia* of Orlando, set significantly in the precise middle of the poem (overlapping cantos XXIII and XXIV), is the culmination of a long series of events carefully contrived by the poet to give his central crisis the meaning he intended. What precedes it is indeed part of it, and the isolation of this, as of many other crucial scenes in the action, cannot but damage the elaborate structure that supports it. This has not in fact been generally recognized; on the contrary, Ariosto's poem has often been criticized for its haphazard structure, for the seemingly casual accumulation of disparate elements that charm by their fortuitousness, as one of Byron's contemporaries wrote:

> . . . Just like those wand'ring ancient Bards of yore:
> They never laid a plan nor ever reckon'd
> what turning they should take the day before;
> they followed where the lovely Muses beckon'd:
> the Muses led them up to Mount Parnassus,
> and that's the reason that they all surpass us.[4]

Thus while many eighteenth-century readers were particularly attracted by the apparently irrational, almost instinctive creativeness of Ariosto, they felt that his poem could be sampled more or less anywhere, and did not understand the full effects of isolating even so prominent and apparently clear-cut a feature of the poem as the madness of Orlando. His fury is occasioned by the incontrovertible proof he is given that Angelica has indeed gone off with Medoro; that she has, in his eyes at least, betrayed him or "played him false." Yet this potential tragedy has in fact been undercut in the very first canto of the poem, where the chastity of Angelica is called seriously into question and the futility of her suitors' obsession with their primacy is exposed. When Angelica, fleeing from the battlefield, hides in a bush, where she falls asleep, she is awakened by the clanking arms of Sacripante, who breaks into a stylized Petrarchan lament that Angelica, his beautiful flower, must have been plucked by Orlando. The lyric in which he glorifies maidenly virtue was to become, in the seventeenth century, one of the most admired passages in the poem,[5] translated, imitated, and set to music again and again:

La verginella è simile alla rosa
che'in bel giardin su la nativa spina
mentre sola e sicura si riposa,
nè gregge nè pastor se le avicina
. . . .
gioveni vaghi e donne inamorate
amano averne e seni e tempie ornate.

Ma non sì tosto dal materno selo
rimossa viene . . . tutto perde
La vergine ch'l fior . . .
lascia altrui còrre, il pregio ch'avea inanti
perde nel cor di tutti gli altri amanti.

[The virgin is like a rose on its native thorn in a lovely garden: while it rests safe and alone it is untouched by the shepherd or his flock, admired by all, especially by lads and lasses in love who want it to adorn their breasts and brows. But once removed from its stem it loses all its attraction—and so too the virgin, who allows someone to gather her maidenhood, loses her appeal to all her other lovers.]
(1.42, 43)

Isolated from its context, as it so frequently was by composers and anthologizers, this lovely lyric seduces the reader as a moving tribute to female virtue. Yet it is really blatantly false, as a moment's reflection shows: How do lovers deck themselves with roses whose beauty makes everyone respect them and leave them alone? Does a rose lose its appeal when decking a lady's bosom? Won't it fade anyway if it is left on the bush? Sacripante is in fact indulging in a typical piece of male chauvinist pleading, as will soon become patently obvious when Angelica steps out of the bush and insists she still *is* an unplucked rose. Moreover, Sacripante believes her and now turns his lyric the other way around. If Orlando failed to take advantage of all those opportunities when he was alone with Angelica in the past, Sacripante is no such fool now: "Corrò la fresca e matutina rosa, / che, tardando, stagion perder potria [*I will pluck that fresh morning rose which, if I waited, might lose its freshness*]" (1.58). So much for the sincerity of these despairing lovers. As for Angelica's claim of chastity, Ariosto himself seems very sceptical: "Forse era ver, ma non però credibile / a chi del senso suo fosse signore . . . [Perhaps it was true, but it would scarcely have been believed by anyone in possession of his senses!]" (1.56).

So, long before we have reached Orlando's madness, its raison d'être has been heavily undermined, and that touching lyric of the rose, along with that famous scene of jealous fury, acquire an ambivalence we might not have suspected from a reading of them in isolation. In the opera we are given no reason to suspect Angelica's virtue. In his more limited space I assume that Braccioli needed a virtuous Angelica as a foil to Alcina, rather than another Mark 2 seductress, but nonetheless he does provide that scene of almost drawing-room comedy: the audience sees Angelica leading Orlando along by the nose ("Rimira, io fingo," she says. "Watch carefully, I'm pretending!" [act 1, scene 4]) set against the high tragedy of his subsequent madness.

What *is* lost by the isolation of the theatrical moments in the poem is the effect of the patient buildup of ancillary material that is a feature of this long narrative. Commenting on Sacripante's credulous acceptance of Angelica's words, Ariosto wrote, "Quel che l'uom vede, Amor gli fa invisibile / e l'invisibil fa vedere Amore. [What a man *sees* Love makes invisible to him, and Love makes him see what is really invisible]" (1.56).

In a series of subsequent love stories, moreover, he exemplifies precisely that rule that will eventually cause the collapse of the greatest knight in Christendom. The near-suicide of Ariodante in the tale that follows (omitted in the libretto) is caused by his giving excessive credence to his eyes: when his rival in love shows him Ginevra apparently receiving *him* into her chamber, Ariodante is so jealous that he does not stop to question the evidence of his senses. The next episode (which the librettist does feature prominently) is carefully appended to the Ariodante adventure: Ruggiero is so infatuated with sexual longing for Alcina that he fails to *see* that her beauty is false. It is all due to magic and paint, which turn a toothless old hag into a siren. The undertones and overtones of Ariosto's Alcina episode understandably get lost in Braccioli's libretto, where Ruggiero's transgression is attributed exclusively to magic. Alcina, moreover, never turns into the old crone patched up with fine silks and plasters with which Ariosto mocked the Ferrarese court ladies and their cosmetics. This vulnerability to deception is carried a stage further in the episode that follows in the poem, where Olimpia, who has given up everything to follow the man she loves, is deceived by Bireno, who goes off with another young girl, leaving her to reenact the abandonment of Dido. Yet this great romantic passion, which surely might have set us in the mood for Orlando's crisis of rejected love, is defused when Olimpia is persuaded to go off with a much more suitable admirer, King Oberto, whom she marries, thus bringing her romantic story to a prudent conclusion—and this thanks to the kindly intervention of . . . Orlando himself! Thus these tales are no random anthology of amorous adventures but a carefully chosen sequence of illustrations of the effects of passion and thwarted sensual love, each building up the picture a little more until we are ready for the entrée of the deluded hero, Orlando. Then the essential difference between Ariosto's chosen genres, narrative and drama, becomes apparent.

Thus Ariosto's great dramatic moments, which Braccioli so cleverly exploits (the madness of Orlando and the seduction of Ruggiero), may only too easily lead us to misinterpret his overall mood. Such moments are often ironical in the sense that they do not quite mean what they say. We can indeed shed tears with the raving Orlando, the suicidal Isabella, the despairing Olimpia, but we dry them quickly when we stop to reflect on their recent histories or their subsequent actions.

What should perhaps also be noted in a comparison of poem and opera is the loss in the musical version of that fine sensitivity of the *Furioso* to the historical moment of its publication. A feature of the poem, as compared with nearly all its predecessors, is the close association of the traditional material with the events and mood of its age. While employing an essentially medieval subject matter and form, Ariosto is writing at a critical moment in the Renaissance. The classical culture and humanist values of the last hundred years made the chivalrous romance seem anachronistic; but those values themselves were now in question among the Italians who saw their country overrun by French and Spanish armies in a series of wars that were to leave Italy under Spanish domination for many generations. The final version of the poem was prepared in the gloomy years following the sack of Rome (1527), and a new ironical and anxious mood undercuts both the chivalrous idealism and the humanist confidence that preceded Ariosto. None of the later versions and imitations of the poem could recapture this.

Braccioli's ghost, who I am sure hovered over Dallas during the performance of *Orlando furioso*, of course muttered his protests: How *can* you reduce some two hundred thousand words of poem to five thousand words of libretto and achieve the same effects, even with the help of Vivaldi's music? He wasn't, of course, trying to achieve the same effects, and I really think that even an Ariosto fanatic must admit that Braccioli did his job very well. His knowledge of Ariosto's poem and sensitivity to its implications is borne out in the oblique references to areas of the poem not adopted for the libretto: the shipwreck of Medoro, for example, preserves a similar shipwreck of Ariosto's involving Ruggiero (canto XLI); Bradamante's playacting at the end of act I brings in the otherwise omitted story of Olimpia and Bireno (canto X); and Alcina's brief mistaking of Bradamante for a man recalls another episode, otherwise omitted, involving Ricciardetto and Fiordispina (canto XXV). The latter two items were surely intended by Braccioli as compensation to lovers of the *Furioso* for the many much-admired episodes excluded from the opera.

Ultimately, of course, we know that opera is to be judged on its own conventions and its own merits, and this *Orlando furioso* with Braccioli's libretto and Vivaldi's music emerges triumphantly from the test. Ariosto stands at a critical moment in the evolution of the genre, when the oral tradition has given way before the printed text and the resources of the narrative and dramatic genres buttress each other in a unique fashion. As the sixteenth century progresses and writers feel the impact of Counter-Reformation moralizing and neo-Aristotelian theorizing, the delicacy of Ariosto's pattern gets lost, the allegorizers take over, and Tasso eventually produces a great epic fit for a Baroque theater. The reservations we have had about the dramatizing of the *Furioso* would be much muted for the *Liberata*, fifty years later, which provides a series of superb theatrical scenes: Olindo and Sofronia at the stake, Peter the Hermit in prayer, Trancredi baptizing Clorinda, Erminia among the shepherds, etc. These are scenes not undercut by irony but pushed to the limits of pathos by a heavily stylized diction and dramatic setting; thus critics have interpreted the poem as a series of spectacular dramatic scenes connected by rather lifeless and unconvincing narrative passages in a structure reminiscent of aria and recitative.

When Don Quixote discussed with Sancho the question whether he should go mad in the fashion of Orlando or of Amadis of Gaul, he was wise to choose Amadis. No one could really have taken on Orlando's role, and that was really the end of Orlando's long literary career. He survived, of course, but, as I have tried to suggest, only with heavy resuscitation. As a long-standing admirer of Ariosto I applaud the happy act of resuscitation of Braccioli and Vivaldi some two hundred years after Orlando's demise in Renaissance Ferrara. Anyone who doesn't quite recognize the new Orlando should remember that Ariosto himself had had to resort to some pretty strong measures to resuscitate the central hero of the *Chanson de Roland*, and I doubt whether even Charlemagne would have recognized *him*!

NOTES

1. See M. Catalano, *Vita di L. Ariosto* (Geneva, 1930), vol. 2, p. 603.
2. See F. Foffano, "La popolarità dell'*Orlando Furioso*," in *Archivio per lo studio delle tradizioni popolari*, vol. 18 (Palermo, 1899) and G. Pitré, "Le tradizioni cavalleresche popolari in Sicilia," in *Usi e costumi, credenze e pregiudizi del popolo Siciliano* (Palermo, 1899), vol. 1, p. 123.
3. See A. Cioranescu, *L'Arioste en France* (Paris, 1939), p. 44 and M. Chevalier, *L'Arioste en Espagne* (Bourdeaux, 1966).
4. J. H. Frere, *Monks and Giants* (London, 1818). See C. P. Brand, *Italy and the English Romantics* (Cambridge, 1957), p. 81.
5. See Cioranescu, *L'Arioste en France*, p. 215.

Ariosto's *Orlando* and Opera Seria
by Gary Schmidgall

My subject is the aesthetic relationships that exist between Ludovico Ariosto's *Orlando furioso* and the numerous *opere serie* (Vivaldi's especially) based upon this preeminent Italian chivalric poem. But I hope to shine some reflected light on the nature of opera generally. To this end, I open with one of my favorite poems about opera. William Meredith's three-quatrain homage is called "About Opera," and its tone is at once wry, passionate, and witty. What surprised me as I reread this splendid *apologia pro opera* during a rest from a recent march through Ariosto's 4,842 stanzas was how well this poem might serve as a concise prolegomenon to the peculiarly similar natures of Ariosto's and Vivaldi's *Orlando furioso*s. Here it is:

ABOUT OPERA

It's not the tunes, although as I get older
Arias are what I hum and whistle.
It's not the plots—they continue to bewilder
In the tongues I speak and in several that I wrestle.

An image of articulateness is what it is:
Isn't this how we've always longed to talk?
Words as they fall are monotone and bloodless
But they yearn to take the risk these noises take.

What dancing is to the slightly spastic way
Most of us teeter through our bodily life
Are these measured cries to the clumsy things we say,
In the heart's duresses, on the heart's behalf.[1]

We do not put down Ariosto humming the "tunes" of the poet; that is, we do not delight in the tropes and *topoi* that he uses time and again with magnificent comic deadpan. After Aurora rises from her weary bed to kiss the sky for the third time, after we meet yet another maiden whose composure is spoiled by a stream or, better, a river of tears, after the umpteenth sorry warrior is cleaved by a heroic sword from bald spot to belly button, we cease to distinguish among them and perhaps we even begin to cease to care. Likewise with opera seria: it's not their tunes we are apt to hum or whistle or—after a longish evening—be able to distinguish one from another. Even the most famous arias of the period do not exactly cry for exultant amateur re-creation on the way to the car. Try humming or whistling "Ombra mai fu" or "Verdi Prati"; it just does not work.

As for Meredith's second qualification, it is not the *Orlando*'s plot that holds its attraction. Part of the supremely good humor of this work is the way Ariosto conveys to us a sense that he too knows what an unwieldy, Rube Goldbergian literary contraption he is creating. Often he must stop to wonder (out loud) what he has already told us, assure us that he has not "lost the thread" of his elaborate "tapestry" (XIII.81), or jog our memory by adding, for instance, "I do not know if you remember him / From the last lines of Canto Thirty-four?" (XXXV.11).[2] The *Orlando* is too much for the mere human mind to comprehend, and Ariosto sharpens his wit on this fact. He will remark parenthetically in one stanza, "You will recall why this is necessary." Of course we do not, so in the next stanza he tells us (adding, also parenthetically, with perfect insouciance, "as I many times have said" [XL.58–59]). In short, one cannot hope to grasp systematically Ariosto's grandiose, complex, and whimsical plotting.

The *Orlando* has 38,736 lines; the average opera seria libretto contains perhaps 1,600. But some would say that opera seria is, in spite of what would appear by comparison to be enormous concision, quite capable of more exquisitely bewildering plot. I alphabetized the plot of Handel's *Alcina* in *Literature as Opera*; here is a similar version for Vivaldi's opera: A (Orlando) loves B (Angelica); B loves C (Medoro); C amazingly loves B; D (Astolfo) loves E (Alcina); F (Bradamante) loves G (Ruggiero); E loves G. No, it is not the plot of opera seria that recommends our interest.

If opera is not the tunes or the plots, Meredith suggests it is "an image of articulateness." In other words, opera is about ideal utterance. Most of us are, in our quotidian lives, merely capable of a boring recitativo secco. Our words fall out, as Meredith writes, "monotone and bloodless." Most of us are no more capable of rising to our true emotional power than we are of rising to the full physiological capacity of our brains (about 3 percent, we are told, is the best we can hope for). I would suggest that both Ariosto's epic and Vivaldi's opera are engaging because they express, through techniques of exaggeration and expansion, the kind of heroic emotional perfectionism that Meredith is thinking of. Ariosto begins his epic, following Vergil: "Of ladies, cavaliers, of love and war, / Of courtesies and of brave deeds *I sing*." The "brave deeds" in the *Orlando* that interest us most—and that interested librettists most—are feats of volition that put one's self-image, one's psyche, one's peace of mind, or (less important), one's body in jeopardy. The *Orlando* is quintessentially hyperbolic, and much of Ariosto's hyperbole can be traced back to his fascination with the "brave deeds" performed by characters who are not afraid of the consequences of their emotions. "Moderation," Ariosto tells us, "is not nature's plan" (XXVII.120); nor is it the plan of opera seria. There is something wonderful in a personage who, instead of shedding the few tears we are all capable of, can cry a river of tears; or a distraught lover who can sigh a tempest of sighs from the depths of his heart; or the man who, out of jealousy, can not only literally lose his wits but also tear off his clothes and run naked and dreadful through the countryside.

The real bravery in the epic is not that of the interminable jousting, traveling, and military mayhem, but the bravery of characters who confront eloquently and head-on the emotions that they cannot resist. They are, like Grifone in canto XVI, passion's slaves: "His error he perceives but cannot break" (XVI.4). The poet apostrophizes of cruel Love (*ingiustissimo Amor*): "Into the darkest, blindest depths must I / Be drawn, when I might ford a limpid pond?" (II.1). For the poet and for his characters, the answer to this question is yes. Rarely do they choose the easy way out. Most of the memorable passages in the *Orlando* occur because characters wittingly or unwittingly take the most difficult path—a path that usually runs into a dark, terrifying, treacherous, labyrinthine forest. This is the Dantean *selva oscura* of human passion. For these characters life without risk is nothing. They prefer tempestuous seas to limpid ponds.

For most memorable operatic characters life without risk is also nothing. I speak not merely of the laryngeal risk taken by the singer attempting a high C before three thousand people rather than before a consummately uncritical shower nozzle. More important, the "risk these noises take," as Meredith describes it, is almost always called for when an operatic character is risking something more profound. W. H. Auden expressed this view when he wrote, "Opera in particular is an imitation of human willfulness; it is rooted in the fact that we not only have feelings but insist upon having them at whatever cost to ourselves . . . The quality common to all great operatic roles . . . is that each is a passionate and willful state of being."[3] The great characters in Ariosto can be described in exactly this way. They all exist primarily in passionate and willful states of being, as figures who know what they want but—fate and Ariosto's art work in strange and wonderful ways— who do not usually get what they want when they want it. It is little wonder that such characters would prove so attractive during an epoch in operatic history devoted to the affective representation of human experience. Ariosto's characters are always risking ideal utterance, whether of lamentation, joy, jealousy, or despair. This may seem to us moderns embarrassingly simplistic or farfetched, but it was grist for the opera seria librettist's mill.

Meredith raises another important point of contact in his last quatrain. It is that both the *Orlando* and *Orlando furioso* are written "on the heart's behalf" and achieve their most marvelous effects because of the "heart's duresses." The recent translator of Ariosto's poem wrote in her introduction, "The constant, the norm to which everything is ultimately linked, remains the human heart. It is the aspirations, the love, the despair, the rage, the grief of the characters which matter."[4] Here is the real interest of the epic; our hearts too are involved here, as Ariosto himself suggests, referring to "the longing we all harbor in our heart / To learn about another man's affairs" (II.36). And love presents the central affair of the *Orlando*. The fate of two minor characters in canto XXXVII is typical for most of Ariosto's lovers:

> . . . they both fell prey
> To that desire we dignify as love;
> And from the straight path wandering astray,
> Through labyrinths of error now they move. (XXXVII.47)

The consequence of loving is a plethora of dark journeys—some large, some small—into "the forest's heart of darkness" (XXIII.124).[5]

The point here, of course, is that these journeys—hippogriffs, magic rings, miraculous books, and manipulative magi and sorceresses notwithstanding—are journeys of the heart made by characters with whom we can humanly identify. That is why John Hoole, an eighteenth-century translator of Ariosto, preferred the characters in the *Orlando* to those in Spenser's *Faerie Queene*: "For what sympathy can we experience, as men, for the misfortunes of [Spenser's] imaginary beings?"[6] The sympathy of Ariosto's characters is, for me, one of real human beings in extraordinary imaginative environments. This is very nearly the aesthetic crux of opera.

The "heart's duresses" are similarly the centerpiece of most opere serie. In 1958 Delmore Schwartz published in the *New Yorker* a poem titled "Vivaldi."[7] It includes these lines:

> Love is the dark secret of everything,
> Love is the open secret of everything,
> An open secret as useless as the blue!

I suspect that Schwartz, in this poem, had Vivaldi's sacred music in mind, but these lines happily express not only the centrality of love in Vivaldi's opera, but also the paradoxical secretness and openness and uselessness of love that this work is about. There is a truth in the whimsy of these lines that one can find reflected frequently in the *Orlando*. For instance, at the very center of the poem, Ariosto pauses for his famous warning:

> Who in Love's snares has stepped, let him recoil
> Ere round his wings the cunning meshes close;
> For what is love but madness after all,
> As every wise man in the wide world knows?
>
> . . . It is a wood of error, menacing,
> Where travellers perforce must lose their way;
> One here, one there, it comes to the same thing. (XXIV.1–2)

Ariosto is constantly illuminating the "dark secret" of love, but, because we are mortal fools, the opened secret does not do us much good. Our knowledge of the secret is as useless as the blue.[8]

In the very first words of Vivaldi's opera, we will hear of "the depths of this dark world" ("el profondo cieco mondo") through which we all labor. The dark world is of course the world of passion and desire. For some the labors of love are won, for others lost, as the force of destiny decrees. The arias of the ensuing three acts are simply the "measured cries" of laboring lovers. Be aware of Meredith's play on words in the phrase "measured cries." These cries are measured only insofar as the musical staff is divided into measures; nothing is more anathematic to opera than the measured or moderated emotica of Aristotle. Opera is an art of epiphany, not lucidity.

I want finally to comment on Meredith's tone of humane bemusement, a tone that reminds me of the *Essays* of Michel de Montaigne. Those references to "the slightly spastic way / Most of us teeter through our bodily life" and to "the clumsy things we say" remind me of Montaigne's countless deprecations of human vanity and of our inveterate tendency to assume that we really can think straight. Meredith's idea that opera's fascination derives ultimately from a Montaignesque sense of our own human frailty and our desire to transcend it sits very comfortably with Ariosto's own view of the way of the world. Though the *Orlando* takes place in the eighth century A.D., Ariosto often "prophesies" about European history up to and including his own time; unwittingly, he also happened to "prophesy" many of the ideas for which Montaigne was to become famous. (Montaigne was born the year after the definitive edition of the *Orlando* appeared in 1532.) The passages that lead me to this comparison are, for example, his expostulation at the beginning of canto XXIX: "How vacillating is the mind of man! / How rapid are the changes which it makes! / How quickly jettisoned is every plan!"; or his remark in canto XLI: "How fallible are the beliefs of men!" And there is something of the bittersweet Frenchman in Ariosto's observation that *one* thing will never be lost from this world only to be retrieved from the moon, as are Orlando's wits:

> Every event in life, every affair
> Is found, with one exception, on the moon:
> Never will madness from the earth be gone. (XXXIV.81)

Orlando—e tutti altri—furiosi. The idea has echoed through the centuries. "Lord, what fools these mortals be." "Così fan tutti." Or, as Giuseppe Verdi left the operatic stage singing, "Tutto nel mondo è burla." All the world is at once a laugh, joke, and hoax.

The frailty, the short emotional attention span, the vacillation of human intentions are the givens behind the complexity of most opera seria plots. The characters in these plots, also teetering in a slightly (or extravagantly) spastic way through their emotional lives, are redeemed by their "measured cries." It is, to return to my initial point, their ideal utterance in the event that separates them from us and makes them more interesting. Delmore Schwartz, in closing his poem on Vivaldi, offered a marvelous paraphrase of this concept of ideal, resounding utterance:

> The vivid world has been barred,
> The press of desire shut out.
> This is the dark city of the innermost wish,
> The motion beyond emotion,
> The power beyond and free of power.
> This is the dark city of the hidden innermost wish,
> This is the immortality of mortality, this
> Is supreme consciousness, the grasped reality of reality, moving
> forward,
> Now and forever.

Schwartz, I think, is suggesting here that the vivid, real world and the ordinary, daily press of desire are shut out by the transcending vocalism of the singer. A "supreme consciousness" is achieved because music is Meredith's "image of articulateness" specially available to the singing human being. The power and the paradox of this most self-conscious of art forms is that it always inclines, where genius is at work, toward a level of "supreme consciousness." Paradoxically, this most "unreal" of art forms can most powerfully achieve what Schwartz calls "the grasped reality of reality."[9]

I would like now to temper the dithyrambic force of my preceding comments by turning to the more practical and circumstantial reasons why Ariosto's poem proved such an agreeable quarry for librettists and composers. This, I find, can be done conveniently by referring to an important dialogue on opera written by one of Vivaldi's Italian contemporaries, Pier Jacopo Martello (1665–1727). The "fifth session" of Martello's *Della tragedia antica e moderna* (1715) is devoted to opera seria and has recently become available in an annotated English translation by Piero Weiss.[10] Martello's comments on opera are in the droll, trenchant style not only of William Meredith but also of Marcello's more familiar *Teatro alla moda* of 1720. The work is cast in the form of a Socratic dialogue between an "imposter" Aristotle and his neophyte, Martello. This

Aristotle is distinctly not rulebound as Renaissance Aristotelians were; rather he is pragmatic, modern-minded, and amusingly acerbic. He is of course saying what Martello himself thought. Martello gives us a lively description of the state of opera at the time Vivaldi was flourishing, but I would like to pass through his pages with a particular view to their relevance to Ariosto. Weiss asserts that Martello describes "pretty accurately the standardized form of late Baroque opera";[11] the question I wish to pursue, though, is to what extent was the *Orlando* amenable to this standardized form?

It should be stated at the outset that a constant theme of Martello's is that an opera seria librettist's life was not a happy one. "The profession of writing *melodrammi* . . . teaches Poets how to conquer themselves and renounce their own wishes," and the pseudo-Aristotle adds sarcastically that librettos are "the only kind of poetry meant to be written for pay" (p. 398). Martello's dialogue ends with one of the loveliest attempts to place literature in the operatic context. Here is a part of this passage: "Only one thing is condemnable, and that is your judgment and the judgment of all those who go to opera under the mistaken assumption that poetry is to play the chief part in it. She is a supernumerary of higher rank than painting, of lower rank than singing, and has her appointed place in the train of a greater personage, the music" (p. 401).[12]

It is in this context, then, that the mentor explains the first matter of business for the versifying poetaster (*il poetastro verseggiatore*) who is preparing a libretto: the choice of subject. "Let these happy dramatists [this is sarcasm: opera dramatists were by definition unhappy] derive their plots not from history but from fable" (p. 387). He explains that it would be cruel to historians to distort actual fact while making the changes inevitably imposed upon librettists by singers, designers, and impresarios. He continues, "It will anyway be difficult but not impossible to satisfy [these people] in a plot based on fable, since the versifier will have the same freedom as did our ancestors to palm off absurdities and to pile Italian fibs upon Greek ones." One of the ancestors to which Martello refers is obviously Ariosto. In Ariosto's echoing of Virgil and countless other classical, Carolingian, and Arthurian precursors, he was laminating fable upon fable with the most extraordinary artistic license. The *Orlando* is perhaps one of the most elastic monuments of Western literature, and by its very structure—or lack of structure—it must have proved attractive to librettists who were burdened by numerous priorities other than that of maintaining fidelity to their literary source.

Indeed, the *Orlando* presented perhaps the most famous and the richest *florilegium* from which opera seria poets might pick their operatic bouquets. A description of the popularity of the *Orlando* in the sixteenth, seventeenth, and eighteenth centuries need hardly detain us here, so clearly was the work perceived as a universal or at least a pan-European achievement (some say the first such romance to reach this status).[13] The work's notable characters, confrontations, miraculous events, and poetic setpieces were ingrained in the culture and literary consciousness of the time. The libretto for Vivaldi's opera is but one example of how successfully (and, when one thinks about it, how easily) the massive work could be culled for its "highlights." Here we have all the important personages but Rodomonte and Rinaldo; we have too the magic ring, the hippogriff, the two magic fountains, and Alcina's glorious but evil island; and we have Bradamante's famous pants role, Orlando's furious jealousy and mad scene, and his salvation by Astolfo. And we also have many changes both subtle and obvious from the original, and these too would provoke interest in an audience intimate with Ariosto's poem. The "recognition factor"—to use some Madison Avenue cant—would in the eighteenth century have been very high.

The mentor also observes that "fables, too, are more capable of machines and spectacle" (p. 387). The aesthetic of opera seria and the chivalric epic was fundamentally escapist. "This type of entertainment," says "Aristotle," is "such that it can lift people's spirits above all cares and absorb them in restful forgetfulness" (p. 383). And he says a few pages later, with a certain sarcasm, "behold, then, our entertainment, delightful enough in itself, enhanced by scenery, personal beauty, and costumes. See how insatiable we are, especially when wallowing in pleasure" (p. 385).[14] The variety, dexterity, visual splendor, and number of scenes and scene changes (*mutazioni*) were therefore an important part of the success of a new opera seria. Martello in fact warns the librettist to run away from any impresario who "wishes to present the public with an opera containing little in the way of glitter, properties, changes of scenery" (p. 390). The original printed libretto for Vivaldi's opera has a separate description of its *mutazioni* following the dramatis personae. This description is reflected with uncanny accuracy in Martello's paragraph devoted to scenery:

> The scenery must be various and imposing. Not too many forests . . . [compare, in act 2 of the opera, the "boschetto delizioso con ritiri di verdura" and the "ritiro ameno in delizioso Boschetto"]. Much architecture, from various angles, and let it display width and depth far beyond the truth [i.e., scenery drawn in perspective; compare act 1's "Cortile nel Palazzo di Alcina" and the act 3 "Vestibulo avanti il Tempio d'Ecate Inferna con muro d'acciaro in prospetto"]. Gardens with real fountains contrived ingeniously upon the stage [the "Giardino delizioso di Alcina contiguo all'incantato Palazzo della stessa, nel Giardino vi sono le due Fonti" in act 1]. A view of the sea, with frothy waves twisting and turning [the "Mare Tempestoso in lontano" behind Alcina's garden in act 1 and the "Mare in lontano con Navi da imbarco" at the end of the opera]. And let us not forget some Gothic shrine, or perhaps a dungeon built of rustic masonry [the "Tempio d'Ecate Inferna" in act 3].[15]

It need hardly be added that Ariosto's poem—with its pleasure palaces, various *loci amoeni*, numerous voyages to exotic places, its vast geography of purling, crystal streams and verdant dells—was a rich source for pleasantly varied stage scenery.

"Aristotle" in the course of his argument makes a number of stipulations worth noting here even though they do not relate directly to Ariosto. They represent hallmarks of the Baroque operatic aesthetic. "Custom," he says, "requires that your opera be divided into three acts" (p. 390). He warns that the principal singers must have an equal share in the action ("else what endless squabbles between those fearless maidens and those bold castratos" [p. 392]); the arias in Vivaldi's opera are in fact divided more or less evenly (though not in the recorded version or the Dallas version). And Vivaldi also follows with care the warning that "exit arias must close every scene, and no singer may exit without first warbling a canzonetta. Whether it is verisimilar is not material. It is much too pleasant to hear a scene end with spirit and vivacity" (p. 394). The opera must be made of recitatives and arias, and every scene must contain one, the other, or more usually both. For recitatives Martello lays down perhaps the one great and simple rule: "The recitative we prefer to have short enough so that it will not put us to sleep with tediousness, and long enough so that we will understand what is happening" (p. 393).

Martello then urges his librettist to insist that each act of his op-era contain at least one *scena di forza*, which he describes as a scene involving "some violent or unusual opposition of contrary passions, or some untoward event unexpected by the audience" (p. 393). Vivaldi and his librettist appear to have followed this ad-vice to the letter, and for each of their *scene di forza* a famous event from the *Orlando* was chosen:

Act 1, scene 5 of the recorded version (original libretto 1.11): Al-cina's magic fountain has its effect on Ruggiero.

Act 2, scene 10 (11.13): Orlando's jealous fury, based on perhaps the most famous passage in Ariosto (XXIII.108–133).

Act 3, scene 3 (III.3): Alcina causes the Temple of Hecate to be revealed; this temple, the statue of Merlin, and Arontes are not in Ariosto. They were probably invented to escape the theatrical difficulties of the original's trip by Astolfo to the moon.

Act 3, scenes 4 and 5 (III.4–5): Orlando's mad scene and contin-uation.

Act 3, scene 6 (III.10): Orlando's second mad scene.

Martello also recommends that in the *scena di forza* "the recitative must predominate at the expense of the arias, since it is better able to convey the pulse of the action and place it in the foreground" (p. 393). As originally performed, *Orlando furioso* generally fol-lowed this pattern, but on two occasions in the recording it is up-set. Ruggiero's aria "Sol da te" is moved from a later scene into the position of an exit aria (act 1, scene 5), and at the beginning of act 3, scene 6 the producers of the recording have interpolated an aria from a Vivaldi cantata. (I feel this insertion has precisely the effect that Martello warns against: it stops the pulse of the action.)

In Martello's discussion of arias lies the most interesting aspect of the aesthetic relation between Ariosto and opera seria. I do not refer to Martello's bemused suggestion "to use similes involving little butterflies, little ships, a little bird, a little brook," though there is clear evidence in the opera that this suggestion is followed. After all, there was in Ariosto a vast stock of poetic commonplaces involving metaphoric brooks, birds, and ships. More interesting, rather, is Martello's admonition to "fix it in your mind that the more general the sentiments in an aria, the more pleasing they will be to the public" (p. 397). The implication here is that the passions expressed must be the kind the audience can identify with. The audience, finding these arias "verisimilar or true . . . will store them up to make honest use of with their ladies and to sing them as daily occasion arises between lovers for jealousy, indignation, mutual promises, absences, and the like." Behind Martello's obvious facetiousness is the serious point that these emotions must be common, orthodox, human emotions. In this Martello is true not only to the doctrine of affects that dominated Baroque opera, but also to the great generalizing urge of the eighteenth century. "Great thoughts," wrote Samuel Johnson, "are always general." This belief was carried over into musical theory, for instance by James Beattie in *Essays on Poetry and Music*: "The ideas of Poetry are rather general than singular; rather collected from the examination of a species or a class of things, than copied from an individual." [16] The age of Vivaldi avoided the eccentric, idiosyncratic, and the curious. So in large part did the librettists of the age in their choice of emotions for musical expansion. Their strength lay in the main line of human experience: filial devotion, jealousy, melancholy enervation, dalliance, connubial bliss, courage, and so on. Ariosto's poem is rife with emotional set pieces of this kind. Of them Barbara Reynolds says in the introduction to her translation, "In many ways such set pieces seem to anticipate the appeal of an operatic aria." [17] Some of Ariosto's best moments are indeed expansions. On one page a running head is "Fiordispina's laments," and on the next page it is "laments continued." This is an operatic text!

In two dominant and ubiquitous techniques, Ariosto reflects the structure of opera seria; that is, the movement during the recitative to a moment of emotional crisis when "the pulse of the action" stops and there is a slow-motion expansion and delectation of whatever emotion is aroused by this crisis. The first Ariostan technique is simply to bring a character to the edge of an emotional precipice and then allow this character a grand outcry. For example, in canto x Olimpia, not unlike Ariadne, is suddenly and mysteriously abandoned by her lover, Bireno. Ariosto brings her to her tent, where, "lying prone, confiding to her bed, / Drenching her pillow, she began to mourn." Here follows a poetic "aria" lasting sixty lines, during which outburst the plot and action stop.

Olimpia's lamentation is in fact an exit aria, for in the next stanza Ariosto vanishes to pick up another plot thread. This event is typical of the *Orlando*.

Similar to this "emotional interruption" is the other common Ariostan technique of bringing a character to a critical moment and then in effect stopping for a poetic "commercial interruption" in the form of an elaborate simile. Here, from Orlando's incitement to jealousy (XXIII.112−114), is one famous example of a simile stopping "the pulse of the action" in the manner of a da capo aria:

> He stands dejected, brow and chin held low,
> His grief obstructs his words, no tears can flow.
>
> A flood of sorrow in his bosom stays,
> And by its very impetus is checked:
> As we may sometimes notice in a vase,
> Broad-bellied in its shape and narrow-necked,
> When someone has too fast upturned the base,
> The liquid in the outlet will collect,
> And there, in too great haste to issue, stop,
> With difficulty dripping, drop by drop.
>
> He comes then to himself, and thinks again
> How he might prove the truth to be untrue.

Like an operatic character, Orlando "comes to himself" again, and the act of thinking and the pulse of the action recommence. One example will show how naturally the method of Ariosto came to the opera seria librettist. In canto XL the poet wishes to emphasize how the soldiers of Orlando flow into the besieged city of Biserta:

> With the same rage as when the stately king
> Of Rivers [the Po] banks and margins overtops
> And, on the fields of Ocnus trespassing,
> Rich ploughlands sweeps along and fruitful crops . . .
> With that same rage the impetuous soldiery
> Rushed through the spaces in the broken wall. (XL.31−32)

In scene 4 of act 2 the librettist wishes to portray Bradamante's overflowing joy at regaining her beloved Ruggiero:

> When a stream swells to a troubled flood and breaks its banks,
> proudly its waters pour into the fields knowing no restraint.
> So great is the joy I feel . . . ("Se cresce un torrente")

Nor should I overlook the many affecting Ariostan moments that prefigure countless scenes in the history of (especially Italian) opera. One of my favorite examples is the death of Zerbino, cradled in the arms of Isabella (xxiv.78ff.). How many lyric death scenes are prefigured in this stanza:

"My only grief, dear heart," Zerbino said,
"Is that I leave you helpless and alone.
If you will love me after I am dead,
I'll have no vain regrets when I am gone.
If in some safer place my life were shed,
These few moments had serenely flown:
Contented, happy and entirely blest
That, dying, in your loving arms I rest." [18]

Compare this with the sentiment of Ruggiero's aria in act 2, scene 4:

How beautiful to die
in your embrace, my sweet,
beloved joy of my soul.

Love, as I have already had occasion to note, makes Ariosto's world go round, and it was therefore easy for the librettist of an *Orlando* opera to follow another Martello recommendation on the making of aria texts: "Let the passions be various and opposing. If possible let hatred be opposed to love, love by hatred. Anger, too, must play a part. But the amorous passion must triumph over all: let the others merely serve to bring love to the fore, which, being common to all mankind, is seen with the greatest pleasure" (pp. 391–392).[19] This is precisely what Vivaldi's librettist does. In the very first speech in the recorded version of the opera we hear Orlando announce that inexorable destiny decrees that "the strongest love will conquer with the help of valor."

One more theme of Martello's essay is worth remarking on, and this is his repeated emphasis that the librettist's artistry must inevitably serve what he calls "the musical symmetry of the moment" (p. 386). Ideally, he suggests, the "verse-weaver" (*testor de' versi*) should be the composer himself, but failing this the librettist should at least "know something of notes and music, so that he may fit his invention and verses as much as possible to the composer's idea" (p. 387). But finally the words must suffer the exigencies of music.

"I have known some of these note-stuffers [*caricatori di note*] and they are the most versatile fellows in the world. Sitting at the harpsichord, they find facile words, abundant in vowels (which you need if the vocal passages are to succeed) and having little or no meaning at all" (p. 387). This last remark is one commonly heard from eighteenth-century Englishmen who were exasperated by the London fad for Italian opera,[20] but it is refreshing to hear an Italian say the same thing!

Martello's ultimate point, though, is that operatic verses "in their own place, and sung," can still "delight whole droves of literati." The real challenge to the librettist is to know his place, as Martello charmingly explains: "poetry is one of those gentlemen who have fallen upon evil days and are obliged to serve for a living. He still remembers the pride of commanding [the spoken stage] and is but ill-accustomed to his present condition. But who serves is a servant; and as such poetry behaves honorably, never commanding, and obeying only the music, the mistress of the theater" (pp. 401–402). Martello ends by warning a dramatic poet never to allow his librettos to be printed as part of his oeuvre, "for you should be doing music an injustice by separating a mere accessory from it, while you should reap your punishment in being mocked by your readers" (p. 403).

By way of leaving Martello I would like to return to perhaps his most fundamental admonition, an admonition that has to do with the distinction between the verisimilar and the marvelous in opera seria. This distinction has also to do with the mixture of the human and the fantastic in Ariosto that I have already discussed. Martello writes:

> I do not mean . . . that you are to drop all verisimilitude from your incidents, but let this precious verisimilitude of yours not prevent you from preferring the marvelous. Let the means by which the events take place lack verisimilitude, too, if you like; but then *let the events themselves be plausible*, and you will provoke the astonishment and applause of your audience. (p. 391, emphasis added)

Martello is paraphrasing here the dominant modern critical view of Ariosto's *Orlando*, namely that, marvelous though the writer's narrative and poetic techniques are, the emotional events and psychology of his characters are in themselves humanly plausible. Ariosto's audience can recognize themselves in his pages. Martello is here urging the librettist to seek the same sympathy. He is urging a focus upon what is "common to all mankind" and what will therefore be seen "with the greatest pleasure" (p. 392). Baroque composers were not the last to succeed in combining humane verisimilitude with the greatest imaginative fantasy, as witness Mozart's *Die Zauberflöte*, Wagner's *Der Ring des Nibelungen*, and Strauss's *Die Frau ohne Schatten*.

I would like now to proceed even further in my transit from generalities to specifics and devote attention to the undertaking of producing Vivaldi's *Orlando furioso* in this day and age and country. It is hard to avoid sensing a certain futility in the enterprise, and I would like to mention here some of my reasons for this feeling.

Most obviously, with a reading of the complete *Orlando* recently behind me, I have a lively awareness of just how much any *Orlando* opera depends for its dramatic engagement upon the audience's intimacy with the full Ariostan panoply. I do not mean merely the ability of the cognoscenti to pick up immediately the important references to Logistilla, Merlin, Melissa, Bireno, or Olimpia, but also the consistently intriguing ability to catch the sometimes subtle, sometimes blatant alterations in the original story. An awareness of Ariosto also provides the kind of heightened expectation of notorious scenes that any *Orlando* setting would promise. The cognoscenti can wait interestedly for *this* new version of Alcina's wanton two-timing, or *this* new presentation of Orlando's madness, rather as an English-speaking audience attends *Hamlet* and awaits "to be or not to be." And even in England, in the early eighteenth century, an audience for an Italian *Orlando* opera could be expected to bring considerable familiarity with Ariosto to bear. In the 1732 libretto containing the English translation of Handel's *Orlando*, Ariosto's "incomparable Poem" is described as "being universally known." Alas, at least outside Italy, the poem is today little known, even less actually read. This is the first problem.

The second problem is that the Renaissance epic and the opera seria were both superb art forms for killing time, and they existed for social classes that had much time to kill. When Ariosto finally, in his forty-sixth canto, reaches the home port of a denouement, the friends he sees waving to him from the dockside are the cream of the Italian aristocracy and the Italian intelligentsia, and he spends nineteen stanzas identifying them. It has been a long, long journey, and one of the continuing interests of the poem has been Ariosto's sometimes frantic, sometimes suave, and (alas) sometimes unsuccessful attempts to avoid boring the reader. He tries as best he can to stay one step or more ahead of ennui. He ends canto xxviii by saying, "I end this canto lest I too incur / The anger which loquacity can stir." We moderns, it would appear, no longer have the patience with loquacity that Renaissance readers possessed. The *Orlando*, I say here, is too long by a great deal and contains many exceedingly tedious passages. It would not pain me to see the best passages (of which there are to be sure a very high number) selected and anthologized.

The typical opera seria was also by modern standards enormously long, usually five or six hours and consisting of approximately forty-five scenes and forty-two arias.[21] Even at the time of its vogue some in the audiences were affected by it as are we, who always hear opera seria in radically cut form. Sir Isaac Newton's response to Handel's *Radamisto* in 1720—"The first Act he heard with pleasure, the 2d stretch'd his patience, at the 3d he ran away" —typifies the response to opera seria of many otherwise enthusiastic opera-goers. Of course, in contemporary Italian performances, there was no expectation that the audience would pay the kind of more or less rapt attention accorded opera nowadays. There was then plenty of time—during "sherbet arias," for example—to gossip, eat, and socialize.[22] Unfortunately, it is impossible to sustain great attention for five hours. Cutting is unavoidable. There has been even in the last few decades, I believe, a withering of the audience's attention span. The only well-made, three-act, three-hour plays I have seen on Broadways in recent years have either been classics or plays written prior to 1950. The ninety-minute play performed without intermission is becoming increasingly modish. This trend puts the producer of opera seria under great pressure to prune and lop off, as can be seen in the recent commercial recording. For this recording about sixteen pages or 30 percent of the text was cut. The Dallas Opera's performing version takes away a further 5 percent. That is 35 percent gone.

Now I do not want to take a purist's maestro-spare-that-text stance. I hunger to experience in one fell evening a complete opera seria no more than the average sensible person with but one lifetime to spare. But, once one begins making such wholesale cuts like those in the recording, the comprehensibility of the complex plot (and the libretto *is* comprehensible if read through whole) truly evanesces. In the recording and the Dallas performances, the first four-and-a-half scenes are cut. Consider what information is thus lost: We learn that Angelica loves Medoro, Orlando loves Angelica, Bradamante loves Ruggiero, and Astolfo loves Alcina; Merlin's urn is explained; we are told who Aronte is; we find out who Melissa is and learn about her magic ring; and Orlando explains Merlin's prophecy. The poor audience hoping to make sense of what follows is thus placed squarely behind the eight ball. This is the third problem.

Of course, these cuts are being made in Dallas with the knowledge that the audience will be almost completely non–Italian speaking. This additional fact that the audience will not be aware of what precisely is being said at every moment, particularly during the recitative, gives strenuous cutting an unanswerable raison d'être. Martello refers to recitative as "in itself a dead thing," and Italian recitative to an English-speaking audience is, as Shakespeare puts it, "dead as nail in door." The less of it the better. Here cynicism and common sense meet and embrace. Of course, these two met and embraced often in the period itself, as witness the wholesale sharing, borrowing, and interpolating of libretto texts and arias. Vivaldi's 1727 version of *Orlando furioso* was quite popular, so he used ten of its arias in the following year's masterpiece. And, too, if all of one's characters are lovers (Angelica could have been called the Princess of Cathay, Orlando the nephew of Charlemagne, but the 1727 libretto refers to everyone as *amante* or *inamorata*) and if these characters *never* venture upon heterodox or kinky emotions, then it does not matter very much who sings what. In *Orlando furioso* I can find only one aria that is character-specific: Alcina's "Vorresti amor da me?" (freely translated: "my cheatin' heart"). All the rest could be given to someone else and no one would, I suspect, be the wiser. This remarkable aesthetic detachment is perhaps the fourth problem: it is hard to identify with characters who do not seem concerned to identify themselves. Maybe the only resolution to this problem really lies in the performance of opera seria in translation.

Being reluctant to close on such negative notes, I will hasten to add that there is, as always with opera, one thunderingly irresistible riposte to such cavils as I have just uttered. And that is: If, amid all the inimitable unreality of the operatic event, the singers are gifted of voice and possess sufficient genius for the stage and physical charisma, then an audience can be made to believe anything. If the vocalist is a true artist, the audience will be able to grasp "the reality of reality" and achieve the particular triumph toward which opera should always be directed, the triumph of ear over matter.

I can strengthen this point by returning to the poet William Meredith. (I hope the da capo construction of this paper is lost on no one.) For he has written another splendid poem that makes precisely my point that the "reality of reality" is immanent in the unreality of opera. Meredith's poem is called "At the Opera," and it is a fitting conclusion to my observations and a perfect prologue to the Dallas performances of *Orlando furioso*:

AT THE OPERA

This queen, caught up in error,
Who cries so sweetly out
Against her own hard laws,
Might put all grief in doubt
By her repetitious furor,
Her rallies to applause.

But no one minds her sawing
The air and looking perfectly unreal,
Or remembers what he's *seen*
In the foolhardy ordeal
We are brought through by her being
Every decibel a queen.[23]

NOTES

1. William Meredith, *Earth Walk* (1970), p. 14.
2. For the sake of clarity, I will refer to Ariosto's work as the *Orlando* and to Vivaldi's opera as *Orlando furioso*. All Ariostan quotations will be cited in the text by canto and stanza number and will be made from the Penguin paperback edition (1975–1977) of the translation by Barbara Reynolds.
3. W. H. Auden, "Some Reflections on Music and Opera," *Partisan Review* 39 (1952). This article is reprinted in Ulrich Weisstein's *The Essence of Opera* (1964).
4. Barbara Reynolds, *Orlando Furioso*, vol. 1, p. 26.

5. The reader may wish to refer to other important passages on love in the *Orlando*: I.56, II.40–41, X.38, XVI.1, XLII.46, XLV.92.
6. John Hoole, trans., *Orlando Furioso* (1783), vol. 1, p. xxxi.
7. The complete poem can be found in *The New Yorker Book of Poems* (1969), pp. 768–770.
8. The uselessness of the knowledge of love's ill effects is wittily expressed by Ariosto in canto XXIV, where he has the reader object that the author of the *Orlando* should not cast the first stone:

> You might well say: "My friend, you indicate
> The faults of others; yours you do not see."
> But I reply: "I see the matter straight
> In this brief moment of lucidity,
> And I intend (if it is not too late)
> To quit the dance and seek tranquillity.
> And yet I fear my vow I cannot keep:
> In me the malady has gone too deep." (XXIV.3)

9. There is a wonderful passage in Saint Augustine's *Soliloquia* that defends the unreality of plays in very much the same way. Since it can apply as well to opera, I quote it here:

> The fact that [some things] are false in one sense helps them towards their truth. Hence they cannot in any way arrive where they would be or should be if they shrink from being false. For how could the actor I mentioned be a true tragic actor if he were not willing to be a false Hector, a false Andromache, a false Hercules . . . ? Or how could a picture of a horse be a true picture unless it were a false horse? or an image of a man in a mirror be a true image unless it were a false man? So if the fact that they are false in one respect helps certain things to be true in another respect, why do we fear falseness so much and seek truth as such a great good? . . . Will we not admit that these things make up truth itself, and that truth is so to speak put together from them?

I quote this passage from Donald Howard's translation in *The Idea of the Canterbury Tales* ([1976], p. 196). Howard introduces this passage with a thought pregnant for any discussion of operatic unreality: "the test of truth [is] not in its correspondence with reality, but in the intentions of the artist."

10. Piero Weiss, "Pier Jacopo Martello on Opera (1715): An Annotated Translation," *The Musical Quarterly* 66 (July 1980): 378–403. Quotations from this essay will be cited by page number in the text.
11. Weiss writes, "It is full of oddities and quirks; yet in several respects it is undoubtedly important as a pioneering effort" (p. 379). In his Princeton doctoral dissertation "Opera without Drama: Currents in

Italian Opera, 1675 to 1725" (1967), Robert Freeman describes Martello's essay as "longer and more thoughtfully considered" than had ever appeared in Italy (p. 51).

12. Martello continues with attractive imagery:

> The musical composition is the very substance of operas, and all the other parts are incidental, poetry among them; or if it is substance, then it is akin to color, which is but a luminous substance (to borrow another man's expression) applied to a surface, which, as it reflects light variously, so it appears variously hued. Light itself is colorless; but when it stoops to the obedience of solids, it clothes itself differently according to the greater or lesser roughness of their surface and, although deformed, still pleases; but it pleases because color, dependent on extraneous matter for its effect, is not mistaken for a substance. Here, then, is a way for you to view the operatic poem, reduced to a mere accessory, without altogether disliking it; indeed that accessory, such as it is, may even please you. (p. 401)

13. A 1732 English libretto for Handel's *Orlando* refers to the *Orlando* as "being universally known."

14. It is not too farfetched to compare the effect of Italian opera on its listeners with the enervating effect of Alcina's island and all its sensual pleasures on Ariosto's heroes. An eighteenth-century Englishman asserted that in listening to Italian opera "the whole Man is dissolv'd in the Wantonness of effeminate Airs." And the same person warned that the "Pleasure of Sense being too much indulged, makes Reason cease to be a Pleasure." This was of course precisely Ariosto's point in creating the island. See, generally, John Dennis, *An Essay on the Operas after the Italian Manner, which are about to be Established on the English Stage: With some Reflections on the Damage which They may Bring to the Public* (1706), in *The Critical Works of John Dennis*, ed. Edward Hooker (1939), vol. 1, pp. 382–393. Dennis elsewhere carried his argument to its logical conclusion: "The Ladies, with humblest Submission, seem to mistake their interest a little in encouraging Operas; for the more the Men are enervated and emasculated by the Softness of the *Italian* Musick, the less will they care for them, and the more for one another."

15. Joseph Addison has a witty time discussing scenery for the Italian opera in his *Spectator No. 5* of March 6, 1711. He reports a "project of bringing the New River into the house, to be employed in jetteaus and waterworks. This project, as I have since heard, is postponed until the summer season; when it is thought the coolness that proceeds from fountains and cascades will be more acceptable and refreshing to people of quality." In the meantime, "to find out a more agreeable entertainment for the winter season, the opera 'Rinaldo' is filled with

thunder and lightning, illuminations and fireworks; which the audience may look upon without catching cold, and, indeed, without much danger of being burnt; for there are several engines filled with water, and ready to play at a minute's warning, in case any such accident should happen."

16. James Beattie, *Essays on Poetry and Music, as They Affect the Mind* (3rd ed., 1779), p. 56.

17. Introduction in Reynolds, *Orlando Furioso*, vol. 2, p. 12.

18. Another scene played time beyond number on the opera stage is caught in Brandimarte's last words:

These words he uttered just before the end:
"Remember me, Orlando, when you pray";
And he continued, "To you I commend
My Fiordi . . ." but the "ligi" could not say.
On high, angelic voices sweetly blend
With the celestial instruments which play,
As from the mortal veil his soul, set free,
Is wafted heavenwards in melody. (XLII.14)

19. The brief explanation of the plot of Handel's *Orlando* that appeared in 1735 serves easily for Vivaldi's opera too: "[The story] tends to demonstrate the imperious Manner in which Love insinuates its Impressions into the Hearts of Persons of all Ranks, and likewise how a wise Man should be ever ready with his best Endeavours to reconduct into the Right Way, those who have been misguided from it by the Illusion of their Passions." Nicholas Boileau made the same point (maliciously) in one of his verse satires: "With what Air dost thou think she [your wife] will listen to a Discourse that rolls upon Love alone, to those mad *Orlandos*, and those melting *Rinaldos*, hearing from them that we ought to sacrifice all, nay, even Virtue it self, to Love, as to the only supreme Deity?" (quoted by Dennis, *An Essay*, p. 384).

20. Richard Steele in 1720 wrote a "Lyric for Italian Music" that he claimed was designed to give "no manner of disturbance to the head" (*Occasional Verse*, p. 59):

I

So notwithstanding heretofore
Strait forward by and by
Now everlastingly therefore
Too low and eke too high.

II

Then for almost and also why
Not thus when less so near

> Oh! for hereafter quite so nigh
> But greatly ever here.

21. These figures are taken from the statistics compiled by Robert Freeman at pp. 27–29 of the work cited in note 11.

22. A century later, the situation had probably not changed much. Hector Berlioz describes it amusingly in his *Memoirs* (translated by David Cairns [1969], p. 208):

The noise of the audience was such that no sound penetrated except the bass drum. People were gambling, eating supper in their boxes, etcetera, etcetera. Consequently, perceiving it was useless to expect to hear anything of the score, which was then new to me, I left. It appears that the Italians do sometimes listen. I have been assured by several people that it is so.

23. William Meredith, *The Wreck of the Thresher and Other Poems* (1964), p. 32.

Orlando in *Seicento* Venice: The Road Not Taken *by Ellen Rosand*

Ariosto's *Orlando furioso* offers a wealth of material for an opera librettist in search of a story: adventures, magic, transformations, love tangles, and laments are its stock in trade. But it also poses a serious challenge: how can an epic romance of forty-six cantos be reduced to the size of a single evening's entertainment? Which, if any, of its myriad episodes can be unfastened from the whole without collapsing? How can a librettist render the effect of a text filled with narrative description in a drama of recitative dialogue and arias? How can he limit the dizzying multitude of geographical settings to those that can be presented on the stage of a theater, and reduce the characters to something less than an army? These questions obviously concerned librettists who attempted to use Ariosto's work, and they responded to them differently, according to the theatrical poetics of their time.

In seventeenth-century Venice, *Orlando furioso* is conspicuously absent from the operatic stage. Among the close to four hundred operas performed there between 1637 and 1700, by far the largest number (some 250) are based on episodes from ancient or early medieval history, while most of the others have mythological sources. Only four, by virtue of their titles, claim a relationship to Ariosto's epic-romance: two are by Pietro Paolo Bissari (*Bradamante* [1650] and *Angelica in India* [1656])[1] and the other two are by Aurelio Aureli (*Medoro* [1658] and, much later, *Olimpia vendicata* [1681]). None of these works was ever successful enough to be revived in Venice after its initial season; and only two of them, each only once, found their way to other Italian cities. *Bradamante* was performed in Milan in 1658 and *Medoro* in Palermo in 1667.[2]

At the beginning of the eighteenth century, however, Orlando's Venetian fortune took a sudden turn for the better. Indeed, in the first half of the century Ariosto's text provided the subject matter for some twenty operas. The reversal of fortune is instantly apparent from the overwhelming reception accorded the hero on his arrival in Venice in 1713 in the libretto by Grazio Braccioli.[3] The impact of this libretto, which was to become one of the most successful of its time, was immediate. In addition to the unusual number of close to fifty performances during its inaugural season in a setting by the Bolognese composer Alberto Ristori, it enjoyed a revival the very next year with the same music freshened up somewhat by a few arias composed by an operatic neophyte, Antonio Vivaldi.[4]

Braccioli was obviously buoyed by the success of *Orlando*, for both of his new works for the following season were inspired by it. One of them, *Rodomonte sdegnato*, derives directly from Ariosto. As the librettist explains in his preface to the reader: "The universal and continued appreciation that my *Orlando furioso* received as a result of your kindness, which lasted for the period of more than forty performances, encouraged me to present to you a new drama drawn from the same celebrated poem of Ariosto."[5] And Braccioli's other new opera, *Orlando finto pazzo*, is a spin-off that utilizes material from Ariosto as well as Boiardo in a rather free manner. To quote the librettist again: ". . . and having recognized a distinct partiality in the approval that my *Orlando furioso* received last year, honored so overwhelmingly for the extended period of nearly fifty performances, I was motivated to serve the taste of my audience by staging *Orlando finto pazzo*."[6] This latter work, of course, is the one that made its mark in retrospect as Vivaldi's first Venetian opera and the beginning of his highly successful impresarial relationship with the Teatro Sant'Angelo.

All three operas performed during the 1714 season at the Teatro Sant'Angelo, then—the revival of *Orlando furioso*, *Rodomonte sdegnato*, and *Orlando finto pazzo*—were based on Ariosto. While such a level of saturation was not reached again, Orlando continued to make his presence felt on the stage, in Venice as well as elsewhere. Braccioli's original libretto underwent two later *rifacimenti*, in 1727 with music entirely by Vivaldi (our opera) and in 1746 in a setting by Pollaroli. And these, in addition to settings of Braccioli's other *Furioso* librettos, enjoyed numerous revivals outside Venice.[7] Moreover, Ariosto's text inspired other librettists as well, and eighteenth-century Venetian opera houses became hosts to a long list of Alcinas, Angelicas, Ruggieros, Ariodantes, and Ginevras.[8]

Measured against his overwhelming presence in Venice after 1713, the infrequency of Orlando's appearance there during the preceding century is especially striking. Moreover, when the four seventeenth-century librettos allegedly "based on Ariosto" are examined more closely, the situation becomes even further unbalanced, for only one of them—*Bradamante*—actually draws upon Ariosto for its plot.

Bradamante, by the Vicentine academician Bissari, is the earliest of the seventeenth-century examples. It was first performed at the Grimani Theater of Santissimi Giovanni e Paolo in 1650 (probably set to music by Francesco Cavalli).[9] The librettist's choice of Ariosto as a source was deliberate and self-conscious. He was evidently quite aware that he was breaking new ground, that his was the first Ariosto-based libretto to be heard in seventeenth-century Venice.[10] Indeed, novelty was his chief aim, as he explains in his preface to the reader:

> The fact that the city of Venice has enjoyed some fifty operas in only a few years has rendered the creators sterile and nauseated the listeners; it has become increasingly difficult to find things that have not been seen, or to produce them with greater pomp and splendor than ever before. . . . and so I decided to take a very well-known story and convert some of its less necessary narrative passages into new dramatic actions.[11]

In describing his adaptation of Ariosto, Bissari explains that he has followed the precepts of the ancients regarding unity of action and of time: he has focused on a single relationship, that between Bradamante and Ruggiero, reducing the numerous difficulties and various episodes of their courtship (interlaced with the many other adventures of the epic) to the single, final confrontation toward the end (in canto XLIV) between Leone, son of Charlemagne, who wishes to marry Bradamante, and Ruggiero, the only knight capable of fulfilling Bradamante's condition for marriage; that is, of defeating her in combat. As Bissari puts it, "The day of this combat will be the one designated by the rules for this drama."[12]

But, although he claims to have imposed unity on Ariosto's

complex plot, in fact he has not done so. For his cast of twenty-three includes only two or three characters not found in the *Furioso*, and he lards his drama with material taken directly from a variety of cantos of the epic, although in an order different from the original. I summarize the succession of borrowed episodes as they occur in the libretto: Angelica is saved from the Orc by Ruggiero (canto X); she evades Orlando's advances by disappearing with the help of the magic ring (XXIX); Fiordespina falls in love with Bradamante, who is disguised as a man (XXII); Angelica cures Medoro's wounds and falls in love with him (XIX); Orlando comes across their names on trees and goes mad (XXIII); Alcina seduces and loses Ruggiero (VII, VIII); Leone asks Ruggiero to fight for him (XLV); Rodomonte guards the bridge (XXIX); and Astolfo restores Orlando's wits (XXXIX).

Despite his prefatory claim to unity, then, Bissari has in fact opted to compete with the original with regard to size of cast and complication of action. But beyond this, the librettist also manages to impose material of his own, gathered from the storehouse of Venetian operatic convention. This includes a parenthetical bow to Venetian military might (in the prologue)[13] and the introduction of a selection of stock comic characters: the frustrated hag who laments the contrast between her icy old corpse and the fiery young heart, and the blacksmith who stutters so badly that he cannot finish explaining to Orlando where Angelica was, and with whom, when he last saw her.

Such characters, immigrants from the pastoral and commedia dell'arte, were commonplace in Venetian opera of the period. Indeed, the stuttering servant had only recently arrived, having been introduced by Bissari himself, in a libretto two years earlier, but used with special and lasting effect in that hit of the immediately preceding season, *Giasone*.[14]

In addition to these characters, several of the most outstanding scenes in Bissari's libretto can boast standard Venetian operatic pedigrees. Ruggiero's sleep scene, for example, traces its operatic heritage as far back as *Poppea* of 1643, although it is more closely modelled on a more recent sleep scene, again in *Giasone* from the previous season.[15] The inadvertent transvestite seduction of Fiordespina by Bradamante, too, has an operatic forebear, although not in *Giasone*. Such seductions in drag were one of the most frequent means of plot complication in early Venetian opera.[16] Finally, Orlando's mad scene claims a specifically Venetian heritage in such operas of the early 1740s as *La finta pazza.*[17]

What is striking here, of course, is the fact that all three of these scenes—sleep, seduction, and madness—quintessentially operatic as they are, figure prominently in *Orlando furioso* itself, which raises the whole issue of the general indebtedness of Venetian opera to the model of Ariosto. This issue, to which we will return, is central to our understanding of the dilemma posed by *Orlando furioso* for seventeenth-century librettists.

Bissari's *Bradamante*, then, despite its rather close adherence to the *Furioso* for its plot, is a thoroughly characteristic Venetian opera. We might describe it as a kind of "pasticcio furioso alla veneziana," with slices of *Orlando* seasoned by a few other, more typically Venetian ingredients. The smooth blending of these ingredients brings out the essential compatibility between Venetian opera and Ariosto. Bissari's libretto has no trouble being Ariostan and conventionally Venetian at the same time.

Bradamante was the first Venetian opera of the seventeenth century to incorporate material from *Orlando furioso* in its plot; it was also the last, for Bissari's other "Ariosto" opera, *Angelica in India* (1656) as well as Aureli's nearly contemporaneous *Medoro* (1658) take a completely different turn. The mixture of ingredients is different and the result is not a blending with Ariosto but a smothering of him. The balance between source and invention has been completely upset.

Both works ostensibly treat the Angelica-Medoro relationship, but only a few of the characters and none of the action derive from Ariosto. Besides Angelica and Medoro, both Bissari's cast of eleven and Aureli's of twelve include only Sacripante and Astolfo from Ariosto's constellation. The other characters—various jealous and betrayed lovers and the usual complement of comic servants—are invented. Still, an Ariosto-like atmosphere pervades these librettos, providing an ambience in which features borrowed from Ariosto (such as the magical apparition of a castle, illusions of voice and appearance, a magic ring, and the complications of mistaken identity) are entirely appropriate.

Although both of these librettos feature Angelica and Medoro, their plots are completely different from one another. Yet both exploit the *Furioso* in the same way: they both build on the same *antefatti.* Here, finally, is where Ariosto comes in. The action of both of these librettos presupposes the events in the *Furioso* that have led up to the marriage of Medoro and Angelica, and it occurs in a crack left open by Ariosto in canto xxx (stanza 16).

Both librettists are careful to excuse their departure from Ariosto by citing permission from the poet himself, and they do so in strikingly similar terms. First Bissari:

> Angelica, according to Ariosto, hereditary queen of Cathay . . . wishing to travel the earth, landed with Orlando in Europe. . . . She covered many countries and experienced many incidents; she finally ran into Medoro, healed him of some wounds with herbs, fell in love with him, made him her husband, and returned with him to India to set him upon the throne and to assume, with him, the scepter of great Cathay. . . . But what happened to them there, and what kinds of adventures they had before they reached their empire, that poet didn't tell us; because he, not foreseeing that a weak lyre might play the rest of the story, concluded by saying [and he quotes the passage directly from Ariosto]: As to what became of Angelica, my Lord, after her narrow escape from the madman, and how she found a good ship and better weather to return to her own country, and how she gave Medoro the scepter of the Indies, perhaps another will sing with a new lyre.[18]

Aureli's preamble is somewhat shorter-winded and more direct. It reads like a gloss on Bissari's:

> Angelica, after having healed the wounds of Medoro, and making him privately her husband, returned with him to Cathay, her kingdom in India: but the kinds of adventures she experienced in love before setting him upon the throne were left by Ariosto to be written by another pen; which provides the material for this drama. So, let us imagine that . . .[19]

Both librettists have used Ariosto merely as a pretext for their action, to supply the (solid) "historical" background, "quello che si ha da l'historia," on which they can build "quello che si finge," by exercising to the full their "fantasia."[20]

If Bissari's imagination needed additional stimulation (and justification) from a variety of sources other than Ariosto—sources he dutifully lists at the end of his preface[21]—Aureli's was sparked by the desire to please his audience. He too knows Aristotle's rules but the rules that count are the ones established by the Venetian public.[22] These he obeys by mixing, in the proper proportion, novelty (a new twist to an old story) with familiarity (elements that had already proved their operatic success, that had become conventions). Indeed, his libretto includes a number of scenes whose use in opera can be traced back to its earliest Venetian years: a confrontation between two male characters representing morality and licentiousness (which resembles the scenes between Nero and Seneca in *Poppea*); an invocation of spirits of the underworld written in *senari sdruccioli* (as in *Giasone* and other, earlier operas); and a deliberately occasioned singing scene.[23] It also uses such standard theatrical props as the portrait dropped by mistake and the letter misdelivered and misunderstood, as well as stock comic characters such as the fearful soldier and the lascivious old nurse.[24]

In Bissari's *Angelica* and Aureli's *Medoro* Ariosto has become thoroughly domesticated to the Venetian stage in the same way that Venetian opera had subjugated Ovid, Vergil, or Livy. Venetian librettists mistreated all their sources equally, using them as springboards for inventions of their own, in order to maintain the precarious balance, the dialectic, between novelty and convention that characterized the mid seventeenth-century operatic aesthetic. But as the century wore on, new operas proliferated and conventions accumulated, forcing librettists in their quest for novelty to rely more and more on their own increasingly bizarre imaginations. The sheer weight of conventions finally submerged all plot sources, reducing the differences between them beyond perception.[25]

If Bissari's *Angelica* and Aureli's *Medoro* still maintain a tangential relationship to *Orlando furioso*, using it in the conventional way as a source (and for ambience), twenty years later the separation is complete. In his twenty-second libretto *Olimpia vendicata* of 1681, the last Ariosto-inspired libretto of the seventeenth century, Aureli, without bothering to excuse himself, without recourse to any convenient opening in the *Furioso*, and armed only with the sword of operatic success, plunges right into his plot—a completely invented one—without displaying even the minimum respect for his alleged source. As he puts it:

> Bireno's betrayal of Olympia in love was the invention of the famous Ariosto. Olympia's revenge against her faithless lover is a caprice of my weak pen. . . . If the former is so pleasing to those who read it in the *canti* of that agreeable poem, I hope that the latter will not displease you when you see it represented in *canto*.[26]

Aureli has boldly set himself up as an equal of Ariosto, an equation that exemplifies the literary crisis of late seventeenth-century Italy and the crisis of opera.

In comparison to the Venetian operatic violence perpetrated on Ariosto during the seventeenth century, Braccioli's libretto of 1713 seems a model of "classical" restraint and decorum. Respect for Ariosto is evident in his commitment to the original material. All of the characters and much of the action come directly from the *Furioso*. Much of it, but not all. A number of relationships, emotions, and situations are superimposed by the librettist. For example, Braccioli expands upon the love relationship, with attendant jealousy, between Astolfo and Alcina, and he develops Alcina's character, exaggerating her fickleness by showing her in serial pursuit of all the male characters of the cast as well as Bradamante in disguise. And his Medoro displays some feelings of jealousy, an emotion foreign to Ariosto's Medoro but hardly implausible. These "inventions," however, occur fully within the realm of Ariostan possibility; they are merely slight embellishments. One of Braccioli's elaborations even borrows Ariosto's own arms: the librettist emphasizes Bradamante's suffering when Ruggiero has abandoned her under the spell of Alcina by having her pretend to be Olimpia in search of her faithless Bireno. This rather ingenious conflation of two very separate episodes from *Orlando furioso* adds poignancy to Bradamante's complaint here.

The differences between Ariosto and Braccioli's libretto are essentially dictated by the conventions of opera seria requiring that a certain number and variety of arias be allotted according to *le convenienze*. The plot had to be both telescoped and embellished in order to accommodate the spreading out of the emotional action and the equitable distribution of arias among the characters.

But the comparatively decorous impression of Braccioli's libretto derives, I think, from more than just its greater fidelity to Ariosto. The librettist had made a distinct effort to impose unity of place and action upon the promiscuous narrative of the epic-romance. He explains it this way:

> Alcina's island alone provides the setting for the action of this drama, reduced by me from the many that encumber the vast poem to one: whose beginning, middle, and end are the love, the madness, and the healing of Orlando. Secondary plots, that is, the love stories of

Bradamante and Ruggiero, and Angelica and Medoro, the various inclinations of Alcina, and the passions of Astolfo, will serve to conduct the main one to its conclusion.[27]

Braccioli has created a unified libretto, which was also geared to the conventions of opera seria. No wonder it was so successful.

But Orlando's operatic conquest of *Settecento* Venice is symptomatic of a larger phenomenon, of a general revival of interest in and appreciation of Ariosto. This is borne out by the publication history of the epic during the seventeenth and early eighteenth centuries. After having been reprinted nearly every year from 1600 to 1630, and at least once a decade until 1679, *Orlando furioso* saw no new edition for more than thirty years until 1713 (in Venice!), the same year as Braccioli's libretto. After this it was regularly reprinted every few years until the end of the century. The interruption between 1679 and 1713 was by far the longest since the work was originally published in 1532.[28]

The revival of interest in Ariosto can be observed among the most influential literary critics of the period, the Arcadians, especially Giovanni Maria Crescimbeni and Gian Vincenzo Gravina. While acknowledging with earlier critics the shortcomings of *Orlando furioso*[29]—its indecorous mixture of comic and serious elements, its incoherent profusion of unconnected episodes and improbable incidents, and its emphatic lack of unity of time, place, and action—the Arcadians were fairly unanimous in dismissing them in the face of the poem's strengths. Citing it as a prime example of "natural and rational poetry,"[30] they carefully attributed most of its so-called defects either to the genre of the work or to the influence of Boiardo, or else they turned them into positive features. Gravina, for example, praised the mixture of characters for its resemblance to life.[31]

Such a revaluation of Ariosto conforms to the primary Arcadian goal, that of reaffirming the traditions and the excellence of Italian literature, particularly in the face of French criticism. But the Arcadians' involvement in Ariosto went well beyond mere revaluation. They invoked his poem explicitly as a means of restoring literary quality to Italian opera: the Arcadians were directly responsible for placing *Orlando* on the operatic stage after a long absence.

The author of the first eighteenth-century *Orlando* libretto, which was performed in Rome in 1711 in a setting by Domenico

Scarlatti, was Carlo Sigismondo Capeci, a founding member of the original Arcadian academy in Rome;[32] and our own Braccioli, whose Orlando followed Capeci's by only two years, was a founding member of the Arcadian colony of Ferrara.[33] Capeci's libretto, which displays, according to the author, unity of time and action that is more characteristic of tragedy than of an epic,[34] elicits high praise from Crescimbeni, who especially appreciated the way in which the poet "knew how to transpose not only the principal action of Ariosto's poem, that is Orlando's madness, but also some of the most beautiful secondary episodes."[35] We should recall in this connection Braccioli's prefatory description of his libretto quoted earlier: his focus on the story of Orlando as the central action of his drama. In fact, the isolation of Orlando as operatic hero is new to the eighteenth century. In not one of the *Seicento* librettos related to Ariosto does Orlando assume a leading role, and his name never appears in a title.[36]

It is the Arcadians' revaluation of Ariosto, their new understanding and defense of the genre of the *Furioso*, and their emphasis on the centrality of Orlando himself within the epic that are ultimately responsible for Ariosto's conquest of the *Settecento* operatic stage. The requirement of order and decorum, of adherence to the unities set down by the Arcadians, is fulfilled by the emphasis on Orlando as hero. But the Arcadians' *Orlando furioso* had many potential heroes; many of the characters of Ariosto's epic could—and did—become the focus of coherent, unified opera librettos (Alcina, Ruggiero, Ariodante) and many episodes could be—and were—detached to form the central one. By appreciating the seriousness of the work, the Arcadians demonstrated its potential for supplying heroes for the librettos of opera seria. It is the compatibility of this critical view, this seriousness, with the ideals of operatic reform that gives *Orlando furioso* its special place in the history of early eighteenth-century opera.

Contrary to the sixteenth-century view of Ariosto's epic-romance that saw its lack of unity, its mixture of characters and places, and its extended range of emotions as flaws, the early eighteenth century saw in *Orlando furioso* a world richly varied and inflected, a reality worthy of imitation, and thus a specially appropriate source for a libretto. The confounding of character types and emotions, the "humanity" that could only pollute conventional historical plots were already integrated within Ariosto's poem. Thus it provided, legitimately, within itself, the possibility of greater emotional range than the more strictly historical sources. This was surely what Gravina meant when he praised the work for its proximity to life.

This kind of critical perspective—and distance—was not available to librettists of the seventeenth century. Their works, so self-consciously and exaggeratedly inventive, were essentially too close to *Orlando furioso*. To them Ariosto's poem was a model for the tricks of their trade. His devices, transformations, contrasts, and surprises were theirs, too, too familiar, too much a part of the very fabric of *Seicento* opera. In its mixture of comic and serious elements, unconnected episodes, and improbable incidents, with its lack of respect for the dramatic unities, Venetian opera, in becoming a genre itself, had already absorbed too much of the spirit and the letter of *Orlando furioso*.[37] For all its variety, its rich inventory of adventures, probable and improbable (rather, precisely for all that), the poem could be only a most problematic plot source for Venetian librettists; it left little space (except between the cracks) for those bards of the commercial theater to give full rein to that sine qua non of operatic success in the *Seicento*, their own *invenzione*.

NOTES

1. *Angelica in India, Istoria favoleggiata con drama musicale del Co. Pietro Paolo Bissari in Vicenza, 1656*, should perhaps not even be included in this group since it was probably never performed as an opera. Neither composer nor theater is named in the libretto, which was not printed separately but only in a publication of miscellaneous works by Bissari, *Le scorse olimpiche, Trattenimenti academici* (Venice, 1656).

2. Since most Venetian operas of this period eventually found their way to a variety of Italian cities, the *Furioso* librettos are somewhat atypical as a group. Musical settings for two of these works have survived: Francesco Luccio's setting of *Medoro* and Domenica Freschi's setting of *Olimpia vendicata*. The lost music of *Bradamante* was attributed to Cavalli by the first chronicler of Venetian opera, Cristoforo Ivanovich, in *Minerva al tavolino, Memorie teatrali di Venezia* (Venice, 1681). His Cavalli attributions, however, have been called into ques-

tion by Thomas Walker, "Gli errori di 'Minerva al tavolino,'" in *Venezia e il melodramma nel seicento*, ed. Maria Teresa Muraro (Florence, 1976), pp. 7–16.

3. "ORLANDO FURIOSO / Drama per Musica / Da rappresentarsi nel Teatro di S. Angelo L'Autunno del 1713 / Del Dotto GRAZIO BRACCIOLI . . ." (Venice, 1713). In the preface to his libretto Braccioli expresses some trepidation (possibly a manifestation of that chronic librettist's ailment, false modesty) about using Ariosto's poem as his source: it is too vast, too well known, too great. In any case, Braccioli's words are worth quoting as they give some insight into the real problems presented by *Orlando furioso* for a librettist.

La pazzi di Orlando, per l'Amore di Angelica; gli amori di Ruggiero con Bradamante; le fatucchierie, e gli Incanti d'Alcina sono così celebri nell'incomparabile Poema di *Lodovico Ariosto*, Principe fra tutti i Poeti; che ad ogni straniero Clima, non che alla nostra Italia, sono notissimi. Di loro ho dovuto formare un Drama, e per dire la verità non senza grande apprensione, ho impreso a scriverlo; da una parte mi si è parata avanti la difficoltà di accozzare insieme, in una sola azzione, ed in un suol luogo, azzioni appunto, e luoghi tanto fra di loro lontani. Dall'altra ho veduto che lo stare appuntino attacato alle invenzioni, che nel *Celebre libro del gran Poeta* sono maravigliose saria in un Dramma cosi riuscito in quella guisa, che apparirebbero le statue da valente Architetto poste su gli altri archi di qualche Gran Palagio Reale, se di la si trasportassero su le basse volte di una fabbrica benchè Principesca ma di vastita e mole minore.

Pure fattomi corraggio ho creduto potere dall'Essemplare del così grande, e maestoso Edificio, tirare una copia di altro meno vasto, e grandioso; servendomi di quello nelle parti, che ho stimato dicevoli a questo, aggiungendo, levando, variando secondo ho giudicato apportuno alli due giudicij troppo diferenti, che del primo forma l'orecchio nel solo udir raccontare, e del secondo forma l'occhio nel vedere rappresentare.

4. In the libretto of the 1714 revival ("Da rappresentarsi la seconda volta nel Teatro di Sant'Angelo") Braccioli refers several times to the success of the work in the preceding season. His dedication to Angelo and Annibale Marsigli Rossi mentions its "solenne approvazione l'anno scorso su questo Teatro," and his preface assures the reader that "sono li stessi [as last year] li Nobilissimi non men che virtuosi e discreti Spettatori, e Lettori; ed è la stessa questa povera mia fatica, ch'ebbe l'onorata fortuna d'incontrare felicemente la sublimità della loro Idea." On Vivaldi's contribution to this revival see Peter Ryom, *Les Manuscrits de Vivaldi* (Copenhagen, 1977), p. 35 and Reinhard

Strohm, "Zu Vivaldis Opernschaffen," in *Venezia e il melodramma nel settecento,* ed. Maria Teresa Muraro (Florence, 1978), p. 241.

5. *Rodomonte sdegnato* (Venice: Rossetti, 1714), preface: "L'Universale continuato aggradimento che ha riportato dalla tua amorevolezza per lo spazio di oltre quaranta recite il mio Orlando furioso me ha incoraggito a presentarti un nuovo Dramma tratto dallo stesso Celebre Poema dell'Ariosto."

6. *Orlando finto pazzo* (Venice, 1714), preface: "Ed avendo conosciuto una distinta parzialità nell'approvazione ch'ebbe l'anno scorso il mio *Orlando furioso,* onorato di così abbondevole concorso per il lungo tratto di presso cinquanta [!] recite, ho voluto servire al genio de'miei spettatori col mettere su il teatro *l'Orlando finto pazzo.*"

7. Revivals of this libretto, with Vivaldi's music as well as that of various other composers, can be culled from the libretto catalog of Claudio Sartori (*Italian Librettos to 1800*), which, though as yet incomplete and unpublished, exists in photocopy form in various research libraries in the United States and in Italy. They include performances in Brunswick (1722), Prague (1724), Mantua (1725), Bruna (1735), Bergamo and Vicenza (1738), Este (1740), Bassano (1741), and Venice (1746).

8. In addition to the various versions of Braccioli's libretto, these include such works as Antonio Salvo's *Ariodante* (1716, 1718; called *Ginevra* when Vivaldi set it in 1736), Antonio Marchi's *Avenimenti di Ruggiero* (1732), and Carlo Vedova's *Angelica* (1738). For others, see Sartori, *Italian Librettos,* passim.

9. "LA / BRADAMANTE / DEL / CO. PIETRO PAOLO / BISSARI. / DRAMA PER MUSICA / Nel Teatro Grimano" (Venice: Valvasense, 1650). Although it is all we have, the attribution of the lost music to Cavalli is insecure. See note 2.

10. It should be emphasized that Ariosto's poem was used as a source for several early seventeenth-century librettos but not in Venice. These include Andrea Salvadori's *Medoro,* set by Marco da Gagliano, possibly with the collaboration of Jacopo Peri (Florence, 1619, 1623); Ferdinando Saracinelli's *Liberazione di Ruggiero dall'isola di Alcina,* set by Francesca Caccini (Florence, 1625); and Giulio Rospigliosi's *Palazzo incantato di Atlanta,* set by Luigi Rossi (Rome, 1642).

11. Bissari, *Bradamante,* Argomento:

L'haver goduto la Citta di Venetia in pochi anni circa cinquanta Opere Regie . . . hà insterilito chi compone, e nauseato chi ascolta: riuscendo difficile il trovar cose non vedute, o il farle così ben comparire, che con pompa, & apparenze maggiore son siano per avanti comparse. . . . mà comandato di nuova Rappresentanza senza potermene con alcuna scusa sottrare, mi fu necessario l'applicarmi à più nuovi, e stravaganti pensieri, che non diversi da i buoni precetti, nascendo da una favola *ex notissimis* convertissero in moltiplicità d'accidenti quelle narative, & informationi, di che la chiarezza delle cose non ha bisogno.

12. "Il giorno destinato all'abbatimento sara quello, ch'è destinato da i precetti a questo Drama" (Bissari, *Bradamante*, Argomento).

13. In the prologue, set in Merlin's cave, the ghost of the magician summarizes the conflict between himself and Atlas that lies at the root of the following drama, thus providing it with a reasonable context. Just before his explanation, however, he refers pointedly, and punningly, to the Lion of Venice (Leone-Lion):

> . . . Vedo non ancor nati Ispani Abetti / Carchi d'armi, e guerrieri / Crescer i Mondi, & discipar gl'Imperi? / Vedo Leon, che già da l'onde è sorto / Di Leon coronato aprirsi il vanto, / E premer di Bisanto / con la Zampa regal le navi, e'l Porto: / Vedo contro di lui volger la Luna i duri influssi, e rei: / Ma stringa a sue ruine / Sotto quall'alte Insegne Arabo, e Moro, / Ch'erger lui vedo al fine / Su le Corna d'argento un Corno d'oro: / E pur a me, cui fine il tempo cede, / A me non cede Atlante. . . .

Clearly irrelevant to Ariosto's tale, this parenthetical bow in the direction of Venetian military might—especially against the Turk, because these were the years of Candia—was obligatory in operas of the period. On Venetian politics and Venetian opera see Ellen Rosand, *Opera in Seicento Venice* (forthcoming), chap. 3.

14. Although common in commedia dell'arte, the first operatic stutterer seems to have been the servant Nuto in Bissari's *Torilda* (1648). Stuttering servants, incidentally, were among the operatic abuses singled out for excision by the Arcadians early in the eighteenth century.

15. Venetian librettists found sleep scenes—either pretended or actual—useful for many purposes, dramatic as well as musical, to extend the limits of verisimilitude. Often sleep scenes were preceded by lullabies, which thus assume a specific realistic function as music. These scenes, too, were considered ridiculous and highly expendable by the Arcadians.

16. Transvestite disguise and sexual confusion figure prominently in many Venetian librettos of the 1640s. See, for example, such works as Giulio Strozzi's *La finta pazza* (1641), Giovanni Faustini's *La virtù de' strali d'Amore* (1642), and *Doriclea* (1645), and Maiolino Bissacioni's *Ercole in Lidia* (1645).

17. The operatic mad scene became something of a cliché during the 1640s. Following Giulio Strozzi's *La finta pazza* (1641), there are mad scenes in Giovanni Francesco Busenello's *Didone* (1641), Bene-

detto Ferrari's *La ninfa avara* (1643), and Giovanni Faustini's *Egisto* (1643), among others.

18. Pietro Paolo Bissari, *Angelica in India*, Argomento:

Angelica, secondo l'Ariosto, Regina hereditaria del Cataio . . . vaga di girar la Terra passò con Orlando in Europa. . . . Scorse Angelica molti paesi, molti accidenti; abbatutasi finalmente in Medoro lo risanò con erbe d'alcune ferite . . . se ne invaghì, lo fè suo sposo, e se ne ritornò con esso in India per ergerlo al Trono, & imprender insieme lo Scettro del gran Cataio. . . . mà ciò ch'in quelle parti loro avenisse, e con qual varietà d'accidenti si riportassero a i loro Imperii, non s'ha da quel Poeta; perch'egli, non prevedendo, che dovesse un debolissimo Plettro cantarne il resto, così termina a dir di loro [direct quote from Ariosto]: Quanta Signor ad'Angelica accada / Doppo, che usci di man del Pazzo a tempo, / E come, a ritornare in sua contrada, / Trovasse e buon naviglio, e miglior tempo / E dell'India a Medor dasse lo Scettro, / Fors'altri canterà con miglior plettro.

19. Aurelio Aureli, *Medoro* (Venice, 1658), preface: "Angelica dopo aver risanato le ferite a Medoro, e fattolo privatamente suo sposo, se ne ritornò con esso al Cataio suo Regno nell'India: mà qual varietà d'accidenti passasse in Amore prima d'ergerlo al Trono, fù dall'Ariosto lasciato in libertà di scriverlo ad altra penna; il che da materia alla tessitura di questo DRAMA, mentre con supposti d'accidenti verisimili si finge . . ."

20. Most Venetian librettists in works published after 1650 divide their material into two categories to distinguish what is borrowed from what is their own. Predictably, the proportion of "poetic invention" to "historical source" increases geometrically as the century progresses.

21. Bissari, *Angelica in India*, preface: "I successi tutti, che dan forma all'Opera sono Istorie registrate nel fine, che se ben disgiunte, concatenate però in Angelica fanno historica la sua Favola, e la Favola qual la prefisse lo Stagirita al secondo della Metafisica, Rappresentatione di cose meravigliose simili al vero; diversa solo in quello, che porta la diversità de'tempi correnti." And his list of sources includes various Italian humanists and Latin authors.

22. Aureli, *Medoro*, preface: "Già tu sai, che compono per mero capriccio, e non per ambitione d'acquistarmi titolo di Poeta. So anch'io le regole d'Aristotile, mà studio quelle d'aggradire al Veneto genio, e di compiacere a chi spende."

23. The singing scene in *Medoro*, for one of the main characters, is completely unnecessary to the plot. Initially, when opera was new and

verisimilitude less easily breached, such scenes served to provide extra opportunities for songs, for actual music. The convention would persist, however, to the end of the century, long after opera had become overwhelmed with arias.

24. The "floating" portrait and misdelivered letter, like the overheard and misunderstood conversation, were all familiar from commedia dell'arte and from the pastoral. Likewise, the fearful soldier and lascivious old nurse were descended from the *maschere* of commedia dell'arte; see Nino Pirrotta, "*Commedia dell'arte* and Opera," *Musical Quarterly* 41 (1955): 305–324.

25. By the last quarter of the seventeenth century, all Venetian librettos, whether mythological, historical, or freely invented, were virtually indistinguishable as far as the attributes and behavior of their characters and the peripatetics of their plots were concerned. For the "Venetianization" of mythology during this period, see Ellen Rosand, "*L'Orfeo*: The Metamorphosis of a Musical Myth," *Israel Studies in Musicology* 2 (1980): 101–120.

26. Aurelio Aureli, *Olimpia vendicata* (Venice, 1681), preface: "Il tradimento fatto da Bireno in amore ad Olimpia, fù inventione del famoso Ariosto. La vendetta fatta da la medesima contro il traditore suo amante è capriccio della mia debole penna. . . . Se quella tanto diletta a chi lo legge nei canti di quel gradito Poema, spero, che questi non sia per dispiacerti se vedrai a rappresentarla in canto. . . ."

27. Braccioli, *Orlando furioso* (Venice, 1713), preface: "La sola Isola di Alcina nelle vicinanze del di lei Palazzo, forma il luogo in cui l'azzione si rappresenta; quantunque nel vasto Poema ingombrino per così dire mezzo Mondo le molte azzioni da me restrette nel Drama ad un solo; il cui principio, mezzo, e fine sono l'Amore, la Pazzia, ed il risanimento d'Orlando. A questa servono di scorta, e di strada per condurla a fine, gli amori di Bradamante, e Ruggiero, di Angelica e di Medoro, le varie inclinazioni di Alcina, e le diverse passioni di Astolfo."

28. For a chronology of reprints of Ariosto's poem, see Giuseppe Agnelli and Giuseppe Ravegnan, *Annali delle edizione ariostee*, 2 vols. (Bologna, 1933).

29. For a summary of Ariosto criticism in the sixteenth century, see Bernard Weinberg, *A History of Literary Criticism in the Italian Renaissance* (Chicago, 1961), chaps. 19, 20.

30. ". . . poesia razionale, verosimile, e naturale" (Gregorio Caloprese, *Lettura sopra la concione di Marfisa* [1690]; quoted in Raffaello Ramat, *La critica ariostesca dal secolo XVI ad oggi* [Florence, 1954], p. 48).

31. Gian Vincenzo Gravina, *Della ragion poetica*, 2 vols. (Rome, 1708), vol. 2, p. 209: "Tale mescolanza artistica di persone rassomiglia le produzioni naturali, che non mai semplici, ma sempre di vario genere composte sono." This appreciation of Ariosto comes at the end of Gravina's lengthy critique of the *Furioso*, in which he lists many of the shortcomings of the work, most of them to be forgiven because they were "attacatigli addosso . . . dall'imitazione del Boiardo. Tal'è il nojoso ed importuno interrompimento delle narrazioni, la scurrilità sparsa alle volte anche il più serio, le sconvenevolezze delle parole, e di quando in quando anche de'sentimenti, l'esaggerationi troppo eccidenti, e troppo spesse, le forme plebee, ed abbiette. . . ." But Gravina concludes with a blanket pardon: "Più piacciono le sue negligenze che gli artefizi altrui."

The other chief Arcadian supporter of Ariosto is Giovanni Maria Crescimbini. In *La bellezza della volgar poesia* ([Rome, 1700], p. 137), for example, he defends the lack of unity in *Orlando furioso* as a necessary function of its genre: "non hà unità di favola perchè e Romanzo: ma anche Romanzi sono spezie di moderna Poesia all'Epopeia appartenente." And his conclusion leaves no doubt as to his opinion of the work: ". . . ancor che non abbia quella esattissima unità di favola, che si richiederebbe, lo stimo, lodo, e reputo degno, non pur tra i Poemi Romanzeschi, ma d'onorato luogo appresso l'Epopeia."

32. "L'ORLANDO, / OVERO / LA GELOSA PAZZIA. / DRAMMA / Da rappresentarsi nel Teatro Domestico / DELLA REGINA / MARIA CASIMIRA / DI POLLONIA. / COMPOSTO, E DEDICATO / AL SERENISSIMO PRINCIPE / GIACOMO / DI POLLONIA / DA CARLO SIGISMONDO CAPECI / Segretario di SUA MAESTA' / *Fra gli Arcadi* METISTO OLBIANO, / E posto in Musica / DAL SIG. DOMENICO SCARLATTI, / *Mastro di Cappella* di SUA MAESTA'" (Rome, 1711).

33. The Ferrarese colony was founded in 1699. Braccioli's Arcadian name was Nigello Preteo. For biographical information on Braccioli, see Giovanni Maria Mazzuchelli, *Gli scrittori d'Italia*, 2 vols. in 6 parts (Brescia, 1753–1763), vol. 2, p. 1954.

34. Capeci, *Orlando*, preface: ". . . si è procurato non discostarsi da un così celebre Autore, se non quanto ha portato l'obligo delle unità del tempo, & azzione, richieste più strettamente nel Tragico, che nell'Epico; e perciò si fa risanare Orlando dal furore, non con l'ampolla portata da Astolfo, ma con l'Anello di Angelica, col quale un'altra volta, narra il Boiardo, che ritornò in se stesso, quando per la forza di un'incanto havea perduto, e memoria, e senno: Onde non è

inverisimile questo nuovo avvenimento appoggiato sul primo, con gli altri, che si fingono per maggior vaghezza dell'Opera, non contrarii a quelli del sopradetto Poema."

35. Crescimbeni's remarks on Capeci are quoted from Giovanni Maria Crescimbeni, *L'istoria della volgar poesia*, 3rd edition, 6 vols. (Venice, 1730–1731), vol. 2, p. 352: "seppe . . . trasportare non solo l'azzione principale del Poema dell'Ariosto, cioè la pazzia d'Orlando; ma anche alcuni de' più begli episodi."

36. There is one significant seventeenth-century exception to this generalization that I know of, *Roland* by Quinault and Lully, first performed in Paris in 1685. In fact, the specific inspiration for Orlando as operatic hero may have come from this work. At least one *tragédie lyrique* by Quinault and Lully (*Armide*, in Italian translation) is known to have been performed in Rome in 1690; and the translator of that work claimed to have made similar translations of Lully's last six operas, which included *Roland*. (See Robert S. Freeman, "Opera without Drama: Currents of Change in Italian Opera 1675 to 1725, and the Roles Played Therein by Zeno, Caldara, and Others," Ph.D. dissertation [Princeton University, 1967], pp. 9–10.) The possible French influence on Arcadian interest in *Orlando furioso* as a libretto source and, indeed the whole question of French influence on the operatic reforms of the early eighteenth century await thorough investigation. A superficial comparison of Quinault's text with those of Capeci and Braccioli, however, reveals few striking similarities.

37. It is hardly coincidental that the faults sixteenth-century critics found with Ariosto's poem—exaggeration, breach of verisimilitude, lapse of decorum, mixing of genres—are the very same faults cited by early eighteenth-century critics of Italian opera, particularly Crescimbeni and Gravina. Translations of many of the relevant passages criticizing opera are given in Freeman, "Opera without Drama," chap. 1.

For an overview of the characteristics of the Italian pastoral in the sixteenth century, many of which are absorbed within seventeenth-century opera, see Louise George Clubb, "The Making of the Pastoral Play," in *Petrarch to Pirandello, Studies in Honor of Beatrice Corrigan*, ed. Julius A. Molinaro (Toronto, 1973), pp. 45–72. Many of the operatic conventions discussed in notes 15–17 (sleep scenes, transvestite jokes) are inherited from the pastoral.

Eighteenth-Century Orlando: Hero, Satyr, and Fool   *by Ellen T. Harris*

Those who think that all these [operatic] categories have their differences only in the circumstances, incidental matters, and the arrangement of the words, not the musical art of composition, err greatly.
Though the whole, speaking roughly, consists of recitatives and arias
for the most part, these latter also have their essential difference in
the main traits or characteristics. . . . It is probably true that very few
among the present-day musical scholars observe such distinguishing
characteristics. . . . They insist that an aria is an aria and a recitative
is a recitative, as if one would want to say that all books are nothing
but letters. Indeed, [since] they all consist of the alphabet, a book is a
book.[1]

Although this passage by Johann Mattheson first appeared in
1739, its arguments have yet to be accepted by many scholars of
the Baroque opera. Nevertheless, as Mattheson was quick to point
out, distinctions between types of operas play an important role in
the composition of eighteenth-century librettos and scores. A true
recognition of these can only help to enhance our knowledge and
appreciation of Baroque opera. For example, the *Orlando furioso*
of Ariosto became a popular source for operatic librettos mainly
as a result of such distinctions. By studying its adaptations in the
context of operatic genre, we will be able to identify three different
eighteenth-century Orlandos: the hero, the satyr, and the fool.

Because the story of *Orlando furioso* tells "Of Loves and Ladies, Knights and Arms, . . . Of Courtesies, and many a Daring
Feat,"[2] its fabric naturally mixes heroic, pastoral, and comic elements. Although this diffusion of content and atmosphere seems
closely related to many seventeenth-century librettos, the epic was
far too long and elaborate to be distilled into an evening's entertainment. Thus, it was little used.[3] With the operatic reforms at

the end of the century, however, librettos became more focused. Comic elements were eliminated from serious plots, and heroic and pastoral stories were clearly delineated even though each could contain elements of the other. Until the redevelopment of mixed types at the end of the century (primarily through the medium of comic opera, for example, the *dramma giocoso*), the three categories—the heroic, pastoral, and comic—remained the dominant genres of eighteenth-century opera.[4] Furthermore, this separation of genres propelled the rapid rise of *Orlando furioso* as a major source for eighteenth-century librettos—not in its entirety, but in segments separated from the main story line and divested of their mixed heroic-pastoral-comic character. Stories of Ruggiero and Bradamante in Alcina's pleasure garden, of Ariodante and Genevra, and of Orlando with Angelica and Medoro became particularly popular. By studying their adaptation we can learn a great deal about eighteenth-century operatic practice and aesthetics. This is particularly true when the excerpted segment contains diverse elements that can be presented in different ways.

There are three possible ways of looking at the story of Orlando, Angelica, and Medoro. The first depicts an episode in the life of the heroic figure of Orlando, during which he conquers his own emotions; in the familiar words of many Baroque operas, "vincer se stessa è la maggior vittoria." The second emphasizes the pastoral element; that is, it tells the story of the young lovers and reduces Orlando's role to that of "fly in the ointment." The third possibility focuses on the comic element in Orlando's madness, turning him into a Don Quixote figure—the central character once again, but divested of his heroic qualities. Ariosto, of course, manages all three vantage points simultaneously, weaving into a single strand the images of the pastoral landscape with the hidden grotto of Angelica and Medoro; the warrior so fierce he can uproot trees with his bare hands; and the demented madman who rides his lover's horse to exhaustion, then carries it on his shoulders, and finally drags its dead and broken body behind him like a child's broken toy.[5] As has been said, these contrasts were not in the nature of late Baroque opera. Thus in eighteenth-century librettos, the story of Orlando's madness was treated as heroic, comic, or pastoral, but never as a mixture.

The pastoral versions prospered best, probably because the simplification of character eased the difficulties of excerpting from

Ariosto's rich and complicated epic. Of the many librettos that explore this aspect of the story, Metastasio's *Angelica e Medoro* appears most often, stretching over much of the century, from 1720 to the 1790s. The comic versions, which also simplify the characters, begin to appear only during the rise of comic opera in the middle third of the century. The most important of these, *Orlando paladino* (1775) by Nunziato Porta, was ultimately set by Haydn in 1782.[6] Heroic treatment of this episode is more rare, for the necessity of showing a warrior hero acting demented in a pastoral environment severely taxed the creative powers of the eighteenth-century librettist. Grazio Braccioli's libretto for Vivaldi's *Orlando furioso* exists as the outstanding example. The crucial distinction between these various adaptations lies in the roles played by the principal characters.

As a pastoral story the love triangle of Angelica, Medoro, and Orlando functions as a simple variation on the nymph-shepherd-satyr prototype. The mythological story of Acis, Galatea, and Polyphemus offers a familiar example. Here the Cyclops replaces the anonymous and lustful satyr and becomes a real object of terror. His passion for Galatea is grotesque, and his jealousy of Acis sparks a fearsome revenge. Orlando in his raving madness behaves just as monstrously, and the parallels between his role and that of Polyphemus (or any neighborhood satyr) should be clear at a glance. Thus, although it meant demeaning Orlando's stature, the pastoral adaptation of this story was obvious and easy; it fit naturally into the traditional pastoral mold.

It is no surprise, then, that pastoral librettos based on this subject tend to be titled *Angelica*, or *Angelica e Medoro*, or *Medoro*. Orlando has lost the leading role. In Metastasio's *serenata*, *Angelica e Medoro*, Orlando's madness does not even serve to heighten the knight's power but to render him impotent and incapable of action, thus saving the lovers. Although feared by the lovers, he is almost more to be pitied.[7]

The comic adaptations of Orlando's madness tend also to occur in pastoral environments. Pastoral drama itself had derived from low comic origins in the mid sixteenth century,[8] but these roots had been buried for almost 150 years as operatic librettos tended toward the semitragic by following the models of Tasso and Guarini or by adapting the Graeco-Roman myths. As the comic mode regained its popularity, the pastoral came to be used more and more in that way even though the upper-class, tragicomic pastoral maintained its position as well.

Haydn's opera *Orlando paladino* changes Orlando from satyr to buffoon. A model for this kind of change can be found once again in the character of Polyphemus. For example, in Handel's first setting of the Acis legend (his Italian *serenata* of 1708), Polifemo is a terrifying monster with no redeeming features. By Handel's English masque of 1718, however, he has become something of a blustering giant who is forbidding only on account of his size; when he sits down with his pipe to sing "Ruddier than the cherry" he seems an amiable, if awkward, peasant.

In Haydn's comedy the transformation goes further, as the character of Orlando shifts from villain to victim. In his madness he thinks the shepherdess Eurilla is Medoro and that his squire Pasquale, a clear throwback to the Don Quixote model, is Angelica. Furthermore, his madness puts him in danger of assault by his mortal enemy Rodomonte—the true villain of this opera, as of Ariosto's epic. Alcina, contrary to her evil function in the original, serves here as the benevolent goddess who defends the lovers against Rodomonte and Orlando, protects Orlando from his own madness, and ultimately cures him of his debilitating passion. She sings at the end, "Let everyone then be content and rejoice in quiet and peace; through the power of magic everyone will live in happiness."[9]

Orlando's madness can easily be viewed as fearsome or foolish, but depicting an insane person as a hero, as in the heroic versions of this story, creates certain difficulties. Braccioli overcomes these in his libretto by surrounding Orlando with his friends, Ruggiero and Astolfo, who know and honor his past (III.i), and by showing him in the performance of heroic deeds demanding extraordinary strength (II.vii).[10] His madness is not made central to the portrayal of his character, as it is when Orlando becomes a quixotic figure in the comic versions, and the demented hero is met with compassion, instead of the fear that greets the Polyphemus-like figure of the pastorals. The villain of the heroic version is none other than Angelica. She is "that deceiver, who lured Orlando to the cliff; because of her, he wanders insane."[11] Astolfo even demands that she be arrested, but the restored Orlando, with knightly courtesy, forgives the lady and wishes her well.

The identity of the villain in any adaptation of the Orlando story gives the greatest assistance in the determination of its genre. In the pastoral, Orlando is the villain who victimizes the lovers. In heroic librettos, Orlando is victimized by the lovers' and especially Angelica's deceit. In the comic versions, both the lovers and Orlando are victimized, usually by some outside source.

Braccioli's libretto differs from the others that have been mentioned in that it combines the story of Ruggiero and Bradamante in Alcina's pleasure garden with the story of Orlando and Angelica. This creates two opposing poles in Alcina and Orlando, both of whom are victims of their own passion. But whereas Alcina maintains control over an evil magical power, Orlando, through the deceit of his loved one, loses all control over his powers for good. Orlando's restoration, however, completes the destruction of Alcina: "Orlando returns to his senses and the last of my magic has no power."[12] Since Alcina's increased power was due to Orlando's madness, and this in turn was due to Angelica's deceit, an interesting and complicated dramatic texture results. The only truly evil person is Alcina, but she and Orlando both are feared, and Angelica also causes evil by rather innocently trying to protect her Medoro. Because he maintains Orlando in his full heroic garb throughout the many turns of plot, Braccioli must grapple with the complexities of Ariosto's original poem, and he comes closer than any other librettist to reproducing them successfully. This is especially obvious when his libretto is compared with other eighteenth-century attempts.

The use of a double plot, for example, was not unique to Braccioli nor to the heroic mode. It could also be found in comedy and was traditional to the pastoral, as can be seen in Guarini's *Il pastor fido*. In Nicola Porpora's *Polifemo*, an operatic example of a pastoral, the heroic story of Ulysses and the Cyclops is successfully grafted onto that of Acis and Galatea.[13] In blinding the Cyclops (i.e., Polyphemus), Ulysses rescues his men and releases Acis and Galatea from their constant terror.

The stories of Angelica and Alcina, combined by Braccioli in a heroic libretto, also coexisted in a pastoral adaptation. The opera, *Angelica vincitrice di Alcina*, was written by Pietro Pariati and set by J. J. Fux in 1718.[14] Comparing these two adaptations of the same stories helps confirm our generic operatic distinctions, for in order to maintain his pastoral world Pariati leaves out Orlando altogether—the ultimate in the reduction of his stature. He overcomes the potential difficulties with the plot by disguising the magician Atlante as Orlando, of whom the lovers can be afraid. In most pastorals Orlando is demoted from hero to villain. With Pariati's libretto he is reduced still further to a nonentity. This expedient secures the pastoral atmosphere; there remains no heroic conflict to overcome.

Although heroic adaptations of the Orlando story are rare, one libretto that precedes Braccioli's deserves special attention: *Orlando* (Rome, 1711) by C. S. Capeci. Like Braccioli, Capeci indicates a heroic focus in a title that points to the hero rather than the lovers, and in both librettos Orlando's madness is a temporary condition from which the hero reemerges at the end. Capeci's libretto, however, is not as clearly focused as Braccioli's. The inclusion of the Isabella-Zerbino story from Ariosto's epic shows Orlando in his heroic guise, as he has rescued each from life-threatening situations, but a new character, the shepherdess, Dorinda, points the libretto in another direction. This lean toward the pastoral is reinforced by the character of Angelica, who is not the feigning and deceitful woman of Braccioli's libretto but the true and constant "nymph" of the pastoral versions. Far from being blamed for Orlando's madness, she saves the hero from suicide. As in the pastoral adaptations, Orlando is the villain, although as much to himself as to others. The libretto ends, however, with Orlando's recognition of his true self, not simply with the safety of the lovers, and includes also Orlando's decision to don his arms once again; that is, to leave Arcadia. "He who conquered enchantments and did battle with fierce monsters, today is victorious over himself and love [Vinse incanti, battaglie, e fieri mostri: di se stesso, e d'amor oggi ha vittoria]."[15]

Although the original setting of this libretto by Domenico Scarlatti is lost, a later one by George Frideric Handel (London, 1733) shows interesting textual changes, some of which may well have been made by the composer himself.[16] The opening scenes are completely altered and revolve around the added character of the magician Zoroastro (perhaps suggested by Ariosto's Atlante), who gives Orlando the choice between glory and love, strongly advising the former against the indulgence of the latter: "Leave love and follow Mars, go! Fight for glory! [Lascia Amor, e siegui Marte, và! combatti per la gloria!]." In spite of these urgings from "the guardian of his glory," and in spite of the pictures of slothfulness conjured by the magician, Orlando decides to leave the heroic life behind and enter the realm of love: "No, I leave! and bend my glory to the service of love [Nò! parto! e fia mia gloria più servir ad amor]." In Capeci's original libretto, the first scene takes place on a field of battle. Orlando tells Zerbino to go to a nearby village where he will meet him the next day. Against this pastoral backdrop the action spontaneously unfolds. In Handel's version, on the other hand, Orlando makes a conscious decision to enter Arcadia as a lover, leaving his heroic nature behind. This new beginning clarifies the ambiguity of Capeci's libretto by setting up the story of the opera as Orlando's unsuccessful bid to live the idyllic pastoral life.

Another adjustment that helps solidify the new pastoral focus is the omission of Isabella and her lover, Zerbino, from the libretto, thus greatly reducing the evidence of Orlando's heroic virtues (Isabella's rescue is maintained anonymously in a stage direction). Although Handel's Orlando does not thereby become a lowly neighborhood satyr, he voluntarily submits himself to Arcadia and leaves heroic exploits behind. It is possible that Braccioli knew Capeci's libretto, printed only two years before his own, and recognized the ambiguities that ultimately led to a pastoral transformation; his own heroic libretto avoids all such pitfalls.

Although comic operas were still few (they flourished later in the Classical period), the earliest comic adaptation of the Orlando story that I have found (Francesco Antonio Tullio's *Angelica ed Orlando* [Naples, 1735], set by Gaetano Latilla)[17] shows many of the earmarks of later comic opera both musically and dramatically.[18] Nevertheless, musical distinctions between heroic and pastoral modes were far more prevalent, and Mattheson's arguments about operatic categories (from his discussion of the musical pastoral) probably refer to these. By looking at the scores of the pastoral and heroic operas under discussion we may be able to identify the kinds of musical distinctions that were made and judge more completely the achievements of Braccioli and Vivaldi in their faithfulness to Ariosto's mixed genre.

Nicola Porpora's setting of Metastasio's *Angelica e Medoro* was written in 1720 to celebrate the birthday of the Empress Elizabeth of Austria, wife of Charles VI.[19] This little opera follows all the precepts set down for Italian pastoral opera. The text in two parts is short and avoids any striking dramatic effects. The six characters also follow the norm: they include two pairs of lovers (Angelica and Medoro, Licori and Tirsi), the satyr (Orlando), and the older advisor (Tityrus). The arias are all da capo, with ten in each part, and Porpora's musical settings carefully follow the tone of the text. The Italian pastoral idiom is particularly expressed in music by a predilection for the monothematic da capo form.

Examples 1 and 2 give the vocal lines of two arias from the opera. The first, "Dal mio bel sol lontano," is sung by Orlando and shows all the earmarks of a typical five-part da capo. After the opening instrumental ritornello the voice sings through all of the A text, cadencing on the dominant (C major), then comes a ritornello fragment, after which the A text is repeated, returning to the tonic. This second setting differs from the first and, as is usual, is expanded, here by melisma as well as word repetition. A concluding ritornello in the tonic closes the A section. The B section also begins with new material. Here the entire B text is given but once —sometimes it too is repeated—and the setting is, like A2, extended by melisma and word repetition. The differences between A1, A2, and B, although obvious, are not as marked as is true of some da capos. Nevertheless, the noticeable similarities are also few. Arias with B sections strikingly different from the main part, although often well known, are rare and generally saved for highly dramatic situations in heroic operas.[20] On the other hand, arias with distinct parallels between the two vocal sections tend to reflect the simplicity of the pastoral world.

One such aria is sung by Medoro, "Quel umidetto ciglio" (example 2). Here A2, although expanded as usual, derives clearly from A1. Furthermore, the B section is nothing more than another variant, expanding now on A2 and thus including the closing melisma. In all three cases, the head and secondary motives (labeled *a* and *b*) are clearly defined, as is the cadential motive (labeled *x*); all mark important structural points. In contrast to the more vague and general similarities of the typical da capo, this is an example of a monothematic or pastoral da capo aria.

Many late seventeenth- and eighteenth-century composers made use of this form to depict the simplicity of pastoral life, and it seems likely that Mattheson referred to just such stylistic features when he argued that one aria be distinguished from another "in the main traits or characteristics." Of course, the pastoral use of this form was neither absolute nor systematic, but that the monothematic da capo aria was generally associated with the pastoral world there can be no doubt. For example, in a pastoral opera by Carlo Francesco Pollaroli, *La fede riconosciuta*, this musical technique is especially emphasized for descriptive nature texts.[21] Handel, when borrowing a da capo aria from a nonpastoral for a pastoral opera, sometimes altered or completely rewrote the B section to emphasize a melodic relation with the A section, and, when borrowing in the other direction, he did the opposite, recomposing the B section to make it independent.[22] In Porpora's *Angelica*, the treatment of the monothematic da capo is clearest of all; it musically distinguishes the pastoral from the nonpastoral characters.

Each composer tends to use the monothematic device in a special way. Porpora emphasizes the frequent use of matching melismas to close the A and B sections. This happens in example 2, and example 3 illustrates other cases. In fact, Orlando's aria, already discussed, plays with this convention and tells us of his character. In the closing melisma of B it takes Orlando until the last measure to discover any similarity with A, and then the long held note comes after the melisma rather than at its head (see motives marked x, y, and z in example 1). It seems that as hard as he tries, Orlando cannot fully adopt the pastoral garb. In fact, Orlando is the only character never to sing in the monothematic da capo form at all. Of the first eight arias in act 2, the two sung by Orlando are the only ones not in this form. When Orlando goes mad, he loses the ability to sing in the da capo form at all. Interestingly, his mad scene ends the opera, after which there is only an epilogue, or *licenza*, in honor of the Empress Elizabeth. Apparently Orlando succumbs to his grief; no recovery is depicted.

Of the twenty arias in Porpora's opera, eight use the full monothematic form. Four more use just the melisma pairing. Of the eight left, four are sung by Orlando, and the remaining tend to occur in special situations. One, sung by Licori, is interrupted before she can finish. Another shows Angelica feigning love to Orlando, and one presents Licori declaring that she cannot pretend what she does not feel. By making these distinctions the monothematic aria becomes a dramatic tool in Porpora's hands. Orlando's arias illustrate the difficulty of acquiring a simple, Arcadian spirit, while the ladies' experiments with subterfuge show how easily such innocence can be lost. Through his music Porpora reveals the fragility of the pastoral world.

EXAMPLE 1. "Dal mio bel sol lontano" (Orlando), from Porpora, *Angelica e Medoro* (Lbm add. 14120)

EXAMPLE 2. "Quel umidetto ciglio" (Medoro), from Porpora, *Angelica e Medoro* (Lbm add. 14120)

a. "La tortora innocente" (Medoro)

b. "Folle chi sa sperar" (Titiro)

c. "Io dico all'antro" (Angelica)

EXAMPLE 3. Paired melismas, from Porpora, *Angelica e Medoro* (Lbm add. 14120)

In the 1730s Porpora was Handel's primary rival on the English operatic stage, although the energetic revival of English opera under the direction of Thomas Arne also added to the prevailing spirit of competition. Pastoral opera played a critical role in the repertoire of every theater, and direct confrontation was not unusual. Thus Arne's production of Handel's English *Acis* in 1732 brought immediate retaliation from Handel's pen in the form of a totally "new" *Acis* (performed in 1732, 1733, 1736, and so on), and the success of this production led to Porpora's own *Polifemo* in 1735. Because Handel's highly successful Ariosto trilogy—*Orlando* (1733), *Ariodante* (1735), and *Alcina* (1735)—also belongs to this period, it is not surprising that two of the operas by Porpora's immediate successor, Giovanni Battista Pescetti, derive from this same source: *Angelica e Medoro* (1739) and *Olimpia in Ebuda* (1740). Rival composers, however, sought not to duplicate their competitors' efforts, but to distinguish their own works from all others. It is not known whether Porpora's *Angelica* was produced in London, but some of the singers mentioned in the score could not have sung in 1720 (being then under the age of ten), and many can be associated with the London operatic companies of the 1730s.[23] In any case, Pescetti was certainly aware of Porpora's failure in London; he also could have witnessed the growing strength of the English operatic movement against Handel. Thus he countered with an extensively altered version of the Metastasian text and a setting that differed greatly from his predecessor's.

In his *Angelica* Pescetti was following an alternative type of pastoral libretto that derived from the English court masque. Handel's *Acis and Galatea*, written by John Gay, is a prime eighteenth-century example: it is courtly in manner, short, and molded into perfectly symmetrical parts framed by boundary choruses. The changes to the Metastasian libretto make *Angelica* fit this scheme as well. First, choruses were added to the beginning of part 1 and to the beginning and end of part 2. Like the Italian pastoral, however, the English masque was a miniature. Thus, to compensate for the choral additions there were also cuts. In the first act three arias were omitted; in the second act Orlando's entire mad scene was deleted. This last might be deemed an odd choice for the cutting room floor, but retaining even this amount of drama would have undermined the refined nature of the final product. Instead of ending with Orlando's madness (implying his destruction and thus the lovers' freedom), Pescetti's version ends with the lovers' decision to flee, which we are to assume they do safely. Orlando thus becomes even more the anonymous satyr than he had been in Metastasio's original text.[24]

Little of the music from this production survives, but the transformation of the libretto from Italian to English pastoral style is clear enough without the score. However, six arias published by Walsh shortly after the opera's production verify the English predilection. Pescetti has avoided an exclusive dependence on the da capo; of the six arias printed only three are in that form, and none of these use the monothematic technique. Two are in repeated binary form—perhaps a reference to the dance origin of the masque and the close association of dance with things pastoral—and another is in rondo form. They warrant no close attention in themselves, but in the context of Handel's *Orlando* take on added importance.

Unlike English and Italian pastoral traditions, represented respectively by the *Angelica* operas of Pescetti and Porpora, the German pastoral had maintained a large format that depended on the integrated use of ensemble and choral singing—qualities that also distinguish it from contemporary Baroque heroic opera. The general structure was actually borrowed from the Venetian pastoral of the 1630s and 1640s that had become antiquated in its own country. Perhaps because of its older heritage, the German pastoral also placed little emphasis on the use of the da capo. For a time, in fact, French influence created a strong preference for the repeated binary form as a pastoral aria—a fact that makes its use in Pescetti's opera particularly interesting. Indeed, the growing trend toward a synthesis of the various pastoral traditions during the middle years of the eighteenth century is evident in a number of works and may well have led ultimately to Gluck's *Orfeo*. Handel's contributions to this genre are especially important. Perhaps it was his predilection for the pastoral, or perhaps only his association of the Orlando and Angelica story with the pastoral tradition, that led him to set Capeci's semiheroic version in the pastoral vein. The adaptation, however, involved more compromise than synthesis.

Handel had no chorus at his disposal and, not writing an Italian pastoral, he made no use of the monothematic aria. The binary form aria of the English pastoral is also absent. Nevertheless, the opera exhibits certain stylistic eccentricities that distinguish it as a pastoral opera from a typical heroic opera seria. By the end of the fifth scene, there have been three accompanied recitatives (Orlando, two; Zoroastro, one), three ariosos (or, really, through-composed arias, sung by Orlando, Dorinda, and including a duet sung by Angelica and Medoro), and three da capo arias (Zoroastro, Orlando, and Dorinda). This proportion among solo styles is quite different from what one would expect in a contemporary heroic opera and was in contrast to all of Handel's previous works. As the opera continues the da capo becomes more regular and takes on the trappings of normalcy. Once again, therefore, Orlando's madness is expressed by his inability to sing in this form. What is remarkable about this musical freedom, however, is that it contradicts not only the text in Capeci's original libretto but also that of the altered printed version. One can argue that Handel was here making the adaptations, apparently to suit his own musical conception of the text.

In Orlando's act 2 mad scene, three separate texts are given in Handel's printed libretto as da capo arias.[25] In the score, without any omission of text, they all become part of the fabric of a sustained musical scena in which there are no da capos ("Amor, caro Amore," scene 10, recitative; "Già latra Cerbero," scene 11, arioso; "Vaghe pupille," scene 11, rondo). In act 3, Orlando's aria "Unisca amor" is interrupted before its completion; in the libretto the text is given without interruption. At the end of act 3, Orlando's duet with Angelica, "Finchè prendi," and his aria "Già l'ebro mio ciglio" are both indicated as da capo in the libretto; neither is da capo in the score although no text is deleted. Similar changes also help to create the structural freedom of the opening scenes, where two more da capo texts are set as through-composed ariosos ("Stimulato dalla gloria" and "Ritornava al suo bel viso"). In all, Handel sets aside eight da capo indications from the revised libretto. He also raises seven sections of recitative text to accompanied recitative or arioso. This deliberate molding of a striking formal flexibility throughout the opera indicates an attempt on Handel's part to depict an atmosphere quite different from that found in the contemporary heroic opera seria.[26]

The *Orlando* by Vivaldi and Braccioli differs greatly from all three of the pastoral adaptations already discussed. The opera is clearly not diminutive in size—the number of cuts necessary to create a three-hour opera makes that obvious. As in many heroic

operas there are pastoral scenes—here involving the young lovers
—but the opera's nonpastoral nature is clarified by the general
lack of the monothematic da capo, of chorus, of ensemble, or of
forms other than the da capo. As in the settings of Handel and
Porpora (some conventions never change) the use of the da capo
reflects Orlando's mental state, for after he goes mad he sings only
in arioso (act 2, scene 8; act 3, scenes 4, 5, and 10). But this is not
a special characteristic of the pastoral, and Vivaldi's opera remains
outside Arcadia's realm. That Vivaldi was aware of the musical
distinctions between pastoral and heroic opera, however, can be
verified by other more monolithic works.

In his pastoral *serenata Eurilla e Alcindo*,[27] Vivaldi draws on the
Italian tradition of diminution and simplicity. The eight arias in
each of the two parts are exclusively da capo. Some make use of
the monothematic form; some, interestingly, use the repeated binary form in their A sections. Throughout, the goal of simplicity is
always evident. On the other hand, Vivaldi's pastoral opera, *La
fida ninfa* (1732)[28] calls upon the pageantry of the German (that is,
antiquated Italian) tradition. As with Handel's *Orlando*, the score
shows a lessened dependence on the da capo coupled with an increased use of ensemble. There are two duets, a trio and a quartet,
and an integrated solo-chorus finale. There are important ballets
as well. Also like Handel's *Orlando*, *La fida ninfa* includes no
monothematic or binary arias, but through-composed arias, totally
lacking in the *serenata*, often appear ("Selve annose," "Dimmi
amore," "Egli è vano," etc.). These two pastorals by Vivaldi differ,
then, in their approaches, but the scores of both may be clearly
distinguished from the contemporary heroic model of da capo and
secco recitative alternation.

Vivaldi and Braccioli avoided the pervasive pastoral language in
Orlando because it did not belong. Still they had to cope with pastoral images. Thus the one clear example of a monothematic aria,
"Qual candido fiore" in act 2, is sung by Medoro, the shepherd, in
a scene depicting not only Angelica and Medoro's love, but Medoro's innocence and faith (example 4). The melodic relationships
in this aria are much clearer and more extended than the kind of
motivic similarity typical of all Baroque music. Take, for example,
Orlando's first aria in act 1, "Nel profondo." The two sections begin with themes that are quite similar rhythmically, but a deliberate variation has been introduced melodically (example 5). This is

EXAMPLE 4. "Qual candido fiore" (Medoro), from Vivaldi, *Orlando furioso* (Biblioteca Nazionale di Torino)

also the case in Alcina's second aria in act 1, "Amorose à i rai del sole" (example 6). These arias are not monothematic. Indeed their very general motivic stock can be illustrated by comparing the A section of Orlando's aria to the B section of Alcina's; these melodies relate more closely than either section does to its own mate. In a glance one can see that the situation in Medoro's aria is of quite another type. Vivaldi reserves it for that moment.

In the only other arias where Vivaldi plays with the mono-thematic convention, he moderates its effect. In Alcina's "Alza in quegl'occhi," A2 differs substantially from A1; B then plays on a variant of A1 (example 7). Similarly, in Ruggiero's "Sol dà te mio dolce amore," A1 and A2 differ; B then derives from A2 (example

EXAMPLE 5. "Nel profondo" (Orlando), from Vivaldi, *Orlando furioso* (Turin manuscript)

EXAMPLE 6. "Amorose à i rai del sole" (Alcina), from Vivaldi, *Orlando furioso* (Turin manuscript)

EXAMPLE 7. "Alza in quegl'occhi" (Alcina) from Vivaldi, *Orlando furioso* (Turin manuscript)

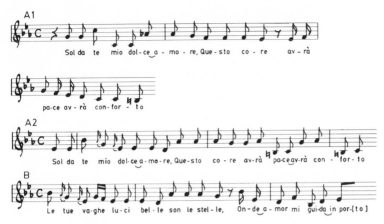

EXAMPLE 8. "Sol dà te mio dolce amore" (Ruggiero), from Vivaldi, *Orlando furioso* (Turin manuscript)

EXAMPLE 9. "Tu sei degl'occhi miei" (Angelica), from Vivaldi, *Orlando furioso* (Turin manuscript)

8). Angelica's "Tu sei degl'occhi miei" comes closer to monothematic form (example 9). A1 and A2 are similarly structured and the head motive of B bears a strong relation to their opening motive, yet the similarities are not pointed; neither do they continue beyond the first measures. Here Angelica is feigning love for Orlando while giving assurances to Medoro. Perhaps she fails to achieve the "true" pastoral aria form on account of her deceit. Such was the case in Porpora's *Angelica*.

Just as Vivaldi reserves the monothematic aria for his shepherd, he reserves the use of chorus for his most pastoral scene: the wedding of Angelica and Medoro (act 2, scene 11). Here, for the only time in the opera, a chorus is used, framing the exchanges of the young lovers. Not until Alcina sings the final aria of the scene does the da capo, conspicuously absent before, reassert itself. The continuing scene (act 2, scene 12) closes with the only duet of the opera. Thus these consecutive scenes follow the same pastoral conventions as Vivaldi's pastoral opera *La fida ninfa* and Handel's *Orlando*. Surely their use here helps to reinforce the pastoral characters of Angelica and Medoro, but they do not compromise Orlando's heroic stature. In fact, Orlando's restriction to bravura arias has been mistakenly "corrected" in the modern performances of this work by the addition of a cantabile aria from a Vivaldi cantata (as at the Dallas Civic Opera production and on the recording), but Vivaldi's own careful blending of the pastoral scenes within a heroic libretto more accurately reflects Braccioli's libretto and Ariosto's poem. A place is even found for the ironic by having Orlando quote from the well-known Baroque bass, *La follia*, when speaking of the "folly of Orlando." By compartmentalizing these musical elements, however, Vivaldi satisfies the demands of the text while retaining the heroic thrust of the adaptation.[29]

In spite of the success of this particular version, and undoubtedly because of the difficult problems it presents, the heroic adaptation of Orlando was seldom attempted. The pastoral portrayal was easier and more popular, and the comic adaptations at the end of the century were really an outgrowth of this type. Nevertheless, the librettos and scores of *Orlando* in the eighteenth century illustrate the importance of genre distinctions in Baroque opera. Just as single arias were meant to focus on one affect, whole librettos also fell into single categories, and these in turn determined the course of the entire musical setting, even though approaches could differ.

Thus Porpora's *Angelica e Medoro* sustains a pastoral atmosphere musically as well as dramatically. Pescetti's setting of an adaptation of the Metastasian text is also pastoral, while Handel moves Capeci's libretto away from the heroic toward the pastoral both in revisions to the text and in the musical setting. Haydn's *Orlando* explores the comic realm perhaps first opened by Latilla. In Braccioli and Vivaldi's collaboration, however, the warrior hero is revealed perhaps for the only time. Eighteenth century operatic conventions dictated that Orlando's heroic, pastoral, and comic qualities be separated, and thus three different operatic Orlandos lived side by side—the hero, the satyr, and the fool.

NOTES

1. Johann Mattheson, *Der vollkommene Capellmeister* (Hamburg, 1739), facsimile edition, ed. Margarete Riemann (Kassel, 1954), p. 218:

   Diejenigen, so da meinen, all diese Gattungen hätten nur in den Umstanden, zufälligen Dingen und in der wörtlichen Einrichtung ihren Unterschied, nicht aber in der musicalischen Setz-Kunst, irren sich sehr: Denn, ob es zwar alles, grössesten Theils, und auf das gröbste zu reden, aus Recitativen und Arien bestehet; so haben doch auch diese ihren wesentlichen Unterschied in den Haupt-Abzeichen oder Characteren. . . . Zwar ist es freilich wol an dem, dass die wenigsten unter den heutigen Ton-Gelehrten solche abstechende Eigenschafften beobachten. . . . Denn sie halten fest dafür, eine Arie sey eine Arie, ein Recitativ ein Recitativ, als wenn einer sagen wollte, alle Bücher wären nichts, als nur lauter Buchstaben; Sie bestünden ja alle aus dem Alphabet; ein Buch sey ein Buch.

   English translation by Ernest Harris, Ph.D. dissertation (George Peabody College for Teachers, 1969), pp. 703–704.

2. Ludovico Ariosto, *Orlando furioso*, canto I, 1–2, translated by William Steward Rose, in the edition by Stewart A. Baker and A. Bartlett Giamatti (New York, 1968), p. 3.

3. See the contribution to this volume by Ellen Rosand, "Orlando in Seicento Venice." Of the four seventeenth-century Venetian librettos related to Ariosto's epic, the first, *Bradamante* (1650), attempts to impose the unities of time and of action on all the major stories of the poem. The next two, *Angelica in India* (1656) and *Medoro* (1658), both take *Orlando* as a jumping-off point, but relate the story of the return of Angelica and Medoro to Cathay, unsung by Ariosto. The fourth, *Olimpia vendicata* (1681), uses the characters of Ariosto to weave a totally new episode. Thus only one libretto is derived directly from the content of Ariosto's poem. This and other matters of importance are discussed in detail in Professor Rosand's article.

4. Other categories have been suggested in modern literature, but these seem often to correspond to twentieth-century sensibilities. For example, Winton Dean uses the terms heroic, antiheroic, and magical (see *Handel and the Opera Seria* [Berkeley, California, 1969] and the article "Handel" in *The New Grove Dictionary*), but these create almost insurmountable problems. The conventions of eighteenth-century opera make it difficult for a twentieth-century critic to know when, if ever, a Baroque librettist is satirizing the traditions within which he works, and the antiheroic category risks our making fun of

an entirely serious effort. True operatic satires such as *The Beggar's Opera* or *The Dragon of Wantley* were rarely subtle. The magical category also cannot stand up under scrutiny, for magic was a stock-in-trade of many types, used, for example, in both heroic poems and pastoral drama. No one, however, could consider these literary types as belonging to the same genre (see my *Handel and the Pastoral Tradition* [London, 1980], to which the reader should refer for further explanation of the topics discussed here).

5. This image is given by A. Bartlett Giamatti in the introduction to *Orlando furioso* (see note 2), p. xliv.

6. For the history of this libretto see the notes by Karl Geiringer provided with the recording of the opera, Philips 6707 029.

7. See the discussion of this libretto by Sven Hansell, "Mythological Subjects in Opera Seria" in this volume.

8. For the origin of the pastoral see especially Louise George Clubb, "The Making of the Pastoral Play: Italian Experiments between 1573 and 1590," in *Petrarch to Pirandello: Studies in Italian Literature in Honour of Beatrice Corrigan*, ed. Julius A. Molinaro (Toronto, 1973).

9. Translated by Carl Zytowski in the notes with the recording of the opera, Philips 6707 029, final scene: "Dunque ognun contento sia / di goder tranquillo in pace, / e in virtù della magia / ciascun lieto sen vivrà."

10. All scene references to Braccioli's *Orlando* derive from the complete libretto preserved at the University of California at Berkeley, Libretto 295. These scene numbers do not correspond to the modern adaptation by Claudio Simone performed in Dallas.

11. Translated by Edward Houghton in the notes with the recording of the opera, RCA ARL 32869. In Braccioli, act 3, scene 12: "Che ingannatrice / Trasse alla Rupe Orlando / Per lei va folle errando."

12. Translation in ibid. In Braccioli, act 3, ultima: "Torna il senno ad'Orlando / E senza forza è in sin la mia Maggia."

13. The score of this opera is preserved in the British Library, RM 23 a. 7–9.

14. This libretto is preserved in the Herzog August Bibliothek Wolfenbüttel, Libretto 131. See the *Kataloge . . . : Libretti* (Frankfurt am Main, 1970).

15. This and the following quotations from *Orlando* are translated from the text in Handel's opera, *Händels Werke*, ed. Friedrich Chrysander, vol. 82.

16. See Reinhard Strohm, "Händel und seine italienischen Operntexte," *Händel Jahrbuch* (1975/76), p. 134. The original Capeci libretto survives in the Civico Museo Bibliografico Musicale di Bologna. Al-

though Handel's libretto was previously thought to be an adaptation of the Braccioli text, there is no connection between the two librettos.

17. The score is preserved at the British Library, add. 14205.

18. Hansell, "Mythological Subjects," also mentions this libretto. The musical qualities that connect this opera with later comic operas include such things as folklike melodies with uncomplicated harmonies, restricted use of coloratura, and simple melodic repetitions.

19. The autograph manuscript is preserved in the British Library, add. 14120; the ends of part 1 and part 2 are dated August 7, 1720 and August 19, 1720, respectively. The empress's birthday was regularly celebrated on August 28. Most secondary sources for Metastasio date this work in 1722, based on the first publication of the libretto, but in light of the manuscript evidence this can no longer be considered the date of composition.

20. For example, Handel's "Piangerò" from *Giulio Cesare* is an aria with strongly contrasting sections. It should be remembered, however, that every da capo includes a built-in conflict between continuity and contrast. The majority reach a compromise. Both the strongly contrasted and monothematic types are special exceptions.

21. See Harris, *Handel and the Pastoral Tradition*, p. 49.

22. See ibid., pp. 183, 176.

23. Of the five singers mentioned, three can be traced to London during the 1737 season: Gioacchino Conti, detto Gizziello (1714–1761), in London 1736/37; Carlo Brosco [Broschi], detto Farinelli (1705–1784), in London 1734–1736 and 1736/37; and La March[esi]na, known as La Lucchesina, in London from 1737–1739. The other singers have not been traced: Sig[a] Marianna and La Rom[agnin]a (Marianna Bulgarelli?). Although it is possible that Farinelli sang this opera in 1720 at age fifteen, and indeed all biographies of Farinelli agree that he did (although the evidence, which may simply be Porpora's manuscript score, is not given), it is impossible to assume Gizziello also performed at that time when he was only six years old. The preservation of this manuscript in London with a cast list giving singers known to have been together in London when Porpora was a leading composer there argues for a contemporary performance of this work in that city; it throws into doubt the relevance of the cast list for performances in 1720 or 1722.

24. Only in Pariati's libretto, mentioned above, is the ultimate step in this direction taken and Orlando absent altogether.

25. A copy of the original printed libretto for Handel's *Orlando* (London: T. Wood, 1732) is preserved in Special Collections, Regenstein Library, University of Chicago.

26. There are comparisons to be made, of course, with Capeci's original

text. Of the arias mentioned, "Amor, caro amore" appears with a slightly different text; it is not marked da capo but is set off as an aria. "Già latro Cerbero" has a longer text, making the da capo more reasonable. "Vaghe pupille" is given as da capo in both written sources; only Handel's score ignores this marking. Similarly, "Finchè prendi" is also da capo in Capeci's text, but no da capo is given there for "Già l'ebro mia ciglio." "Unisca amor" and the text for the new opening scenes are all newly written and have no parallel in Handel's printed libretto. Thus although two da capo indications may be errors in the revised libretto ("Amore, caro amore" and "Già l'ebro mia ciglio"), it is still quite clear that one can speak of three distinct versions of this text: Capeci's, the anonymous adaptor's, and Handel's.

27. Also called by the incipit of its first aria, "Mio cor, povero cor," this serenata is of unknown author, date, and occasion. A modern edition exists edited by Luciano Bettarini (Milan, 1976).

28. Edited by Raffaello Monterosso (Cremona, 1964).

29. John Hill, in "Vivaldi's *Orlando*: Sources and Contributing Factors," this volume, discusses the possibility that in this score Vivaldi did not set single arias to reflect successively different affects, as was typical, but arranged the arias in groups of single affects. This may have been part of a solution to the problem of setting a libretto with such a complexity of idiom.

PART II
Venetian Opera in Its Cultural Milieu

Venetian Theaters during Vivaldi's Era   *by William C. Holmes*

Although opera continued to flourish in Venice during the eighteenth century, operatic production in that city no longer enjoyed the international preeminence it had had during the previous seventy-five years. Such master designers as Giacomo Torelli were long since dead, and the Venetian stage could claim few men whose work matched his in quality and invention.[1] However, even though Venetian theaters at this time imported many of their impresarios, singers, dancers, and stage designers, they managed to keep current with the latest trends and to stage operas in elaborate, if not opulent, productions. My purpose here is to give an overview, with appropriate background, of the state of Italian theaters, particularly in Venice, during the period of Vivaldi's activity there.[2]

In 1714, the first year an opera by Vivaldi was heard on a Venetian stage, there were six major theaters producing opera in Venice.[3] Three of these—San Cassiano, San Moisè, and San Giovanni Grisostomo—had seasons consisting entirely of musical works. The other three—San Salvador, Sant'Angelo, and San Samuele—produced both spoken drama and opera. Although the number of productions varied from theater to theater, all of them adhered to a normal schedule of three seasons annually: one during Carnival, one in the weeks following Easter, and one in autumn, usually beginning in September.

Vivaldi's operas were performed in three of the major theaters: Sant'Angelo, San Moisè, and San Samuele. Sant'Angelo was by far the composer's favorite theater. Twenty-four productions of his works (including an intermezzo and two revivals) were staged there between 1714 and 1739.[4] It was also at this theater that Vivaldi sometimes assumed an unusual role for a composer of operas: he acted as impresario, performing all the duties that such a position entailed.

Sant'Angelo was operated in the traditional manner of all Venetian theaters. A noble family or a group of nobles would buy or build a theater and then would enter into a contract with an impresario,who would be in charge of all aspects of the administration of the theater such as choosing the repertoire, contracting the singers and other musicians, setting the price of tickets for the public, and renting boxes for the season. Profits would then be divided among the principals according to previous agreements. Profitable as the arrangement often was, it nevertheless caused enough financial problems that eventually a state governing body had to intervene. For example, on January 11, 1753, the Council of Ten passed a law requiring the impresario to deposit three thousand ducats before the season began in order to assure that composers, musicians, and set designers received their contracted fees,[5] and on November 10, 1756, the amount of that deposit was increased to four thousand ducats.[6]

By the time Vivaldi's operas were first heard in Venice, the type of theater known as the *teatro all'italiana* had been in vogue for more than seventy-five years, not only in Italy but also in other operatic centers throughout Europe. The interior of this type of theater was in the shape of a U, a horseshoe, or a bell. The auditorium was surrounded by tiers of boxes reaching to the stage proscenium, and sometimes boxes were placed beyond the proscenium arch and above the front part of the stage proper.

One of the best extant views of the interior of an eighteenth-century *teatro all'italiana* is an engraving of the auditorium and stage of San Giovanni Grisostomo in 1709 (figure 1).[7] The auditorium is U-shaped and has five tiers of boxes in addition to ten stage boxes. Above the proscenium is the coat of arms of the Grimani family, owners of the theater. On the stage, in a garden setting with central perspective, are two singers. As is often the case in extant views, the singers are depicted smaller than life size, perhaps to lend more importance to the sets. Below the stage, in the orchestra pit, are twelve musicians.

Another informative view is that of the interior of an imaginary Venetian theater appearing in Zaccaria Seriman's satirical book, *I viaggi di Enrico Wanton* (figure 2). The set is only partially visible. Part of the orchestra can be seen in the pit, and there are peo-

FIGURE 1. Teatro San Giovanni Grisostomo (1709), from *Venezia festeggiante* (1709)

FIGURE 2. Interior of a Venetian theater, from *I viaggi di Enrico Wanton* (1749)

ple standing and seated in the auditorium and in the boxes.[8] This
view offers visual confirmation of the charges of many eighteenth-
century reformers and satirists, depicting as it does many members
of the audience, particularly those in the boxes, visiting among
themselves and not paying the slightest attention to what is happening on the stage.

Venetian theaters ranged in size from quite large, seating more
than one thousand people, to quite small, seating only a few hundred. Some were equipped with large and elaborately furnished
stages, while others were modest and unable to mount complicated settings with stage machines. Plans for seventeenth- and
eighteenth-century Venetian theaters are relatively rare, but enough
of them survive to give us a good idea of how they were designed
and how their stages could be put to use.

One such plan is the well-known and detailed one of Santissimi
Giovanni e Paolo, one of the largest of the theaters in seventeenth-
century Venice (figure 3).[9] It probably shows the theater as it was
in 1678. For more than sixty years, Santissimi Giovanni e Paolo

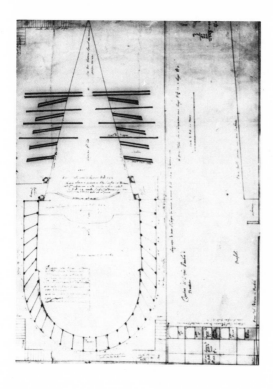

FIGURE 3. Plan of Tea-
tro Santissimi Giovanni
e Paolo (ca. 1678, Sir
John Soane Museum,
London)

produced operas almost uninterruptedly. However, in 1699 operatic productions were suspended, and the theater closed its doors forever in 1715.

The overall length of the theater was about 128½ feet, and its overall breadth about thirty-six feet.[10] There were five tiers, each containing twenty-nine boxes. The boxes ranged in breadth between 4½ and 5½ feet, and the encircling corridor that allowed access to them was little more than 3½ feet wide. The orchestra pit was more than nine feet wide and 4½ feet deep at the center. This pit and the stage were separated from the auditorium by a narrow corridor running more or less parallel to the proscenium. The raked stage was seventy-two feet deep and thirty-two feet wide at the proscenium arch.

The layout of the stage is interesting and typical of its time. There are five pairs of tracks on either side at oblique angles, on which to mount and move the wings (called *telari* in the eighteenth century and *telaii* in modern Italian). There are also three tracks on either side and two pairs of tracks toward the back of the stage, all parallel with the proscenium. These parallel tracks could support and move flats that functioned in the same way as modern backdrops. For example, the parallel tracks toward the middle of the stage might support flats with cutouts representing arches, whereas the ones at the rear acted as supports for a true backcloth. (Drops descending from the ceiling did not come into general use until after the middle of the eighteenth century.) The great number of tracks permitted scene changes (which always took place in view of the spectators) in a minimal amount of time. One can explain further with hypothetical examples. The opening scene of an opera might be designed as a *scena corta* (short scene), i.e., it would not have much depth, and would use perhaps the first of the first two sets of oblique tracks on both sides as wings. The first set of parallel tracks would support the backdrop. At a change of scene to a *scena lunga* (long scene), one of greater depth, the flats of the backdrop would be drawn out of sight on both sides of the stage, allowing the next three sets of oblique wings and a new parallel backdrop to appear. Meanwhile the forward oblique wings would be substituted with others, allowing for a full change of scene in a relatively short period of time.

The Teatro San Moisè was much smaller than Santissimi Giovanni e Paolo; in fact, San Moisè was the smallest of all eighteenth-century Venetian theaters (figure 4). Four of Vivaldi's operas were presented there during the seasons of 1716, 1717, and 1718. No plan of this theater was known to exist until this one was recently discovered by Maria Teresa Muraro. It is one of a number of such plans drawn by J. Gabriel Martin Dumont during a visit to Italy in 1742, and was apparently intended to be included in his *Parallèle des plus belles salles de spectacle d'Italie et de France . . .* (Paris, 1764).[11] For unknown reasons, however, this plan never appeared. San Moisè had only four tiers of boxes, and its stage was fewer than thirty-five feet deep, less than half the depth of the stage of Santissimi Giovanni e Paolo. On the stage there are only three double sets of tracks for wings. Thus, perforce, the stage settings at San Moisè were limited to *scene corte*, and elaborate stage machinery was out of the question. As a matter of fact, not one of the librettos of the four operas by Vivaldi presented at San Moisè calls for stage machines.

Unfortunately, no plan exists for Vivaldi's favorite theater at Sant'Angelo. Perhaps this is because there was no compelling rea-

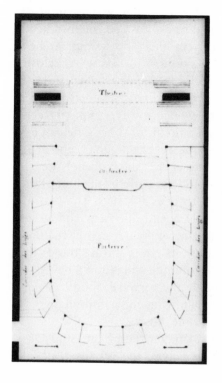

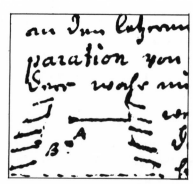

FIGURE 4. Plan of Teatro San Moisè, drawn by J. Gabriel Martin Dumont (1742, Bibliothèque de l'Opéra, Paris)

FIGURE 5. (*above*) Sketch of the stage of Teatro Sant'Angelo, from the diary of Nicodemus Tessin (1688)

son to make one during the theater's long history. Sant'Angelo is unusual among Venetian theaters, for from the time it opened its doors in 1676 until its final performances in 1803, it did not burn, it underwent few structural modifications, and it presented its seasons of spoken drama and opera uninterruptedly. From surviving descriptions and other documents, however, it is possible to gain an idea of the size of Sant'Angelo. For example, an extant plan of the boxes, found in the Museo Correr in Venice, shows that the theater was much smaller than Santissimi Giovanni e Paolo and somewhat larger than San Moisè. Another important source of information is the manuscript diary kept by the Swedish scientist Nicodemus Tessin, who traveled to Venice in the spring of 1688.[12] Tessin describes Sant'Angelo as being rather small (he had not seen San Moisè) and pleasantly decorated. He also says there were five tiers of boxes in addition to three stage boxes in each tier, making a total of 150. (If the extant plan of the boxes is correct, Tessin's arithmetic was wrong.)

In his diary Tessin also hastily sketched a stage plan for a scene from an opera he had witnessed at Sant'Angelo (figure 5). In this sketch are drawn five wings on each side of the stage, which means that there were probably five pairs of tracks. There is also, above the letter A, a free-standing flat with an open space to the left of center stage. As Tessin points out, a character can enter either from a wing, at letter B, or from the opening at the left of letter A, that is, from a point that forms an asymmetrical line of perspective, a practice that was little known and not often employed at that time. The importance of this little sketch, with its stage set that does not employ the standard central perspective, will become apparent later.

Fortunately, the librettos of many of Vivaldi's operas for Sant'Angelo list the names of the set designers for these works; there are in fact twelve mentioned, the best known among them being Bernardo Canal and Antonio Mauro.[13] Canal designed sets for Vivaldi's operas at Sant'Angelo between 1714 and 1717. In the librettos he is sometimes cited alone, but in two cases the librettos refer to Canal "e suoi figli" (*L'incoronazione di Dario*, Carnival, 1717) and "i Signori Canali" (*Il vinto trionfante del vincitore*, autumn, 1717). One of Canal's sons, who collaborated with him on these occasions, was the celebrated painter Antonio Canaletto (1697–1768). Apparently, then, he began his long career in the theater. It was Antonio Mauro (1669–1751), one of a long line of scenic designers active in Venice, who was most closely associated with Vivaldi in Venice, indeed anywhere. Between 1726 and 1734 he designed sets for seven of Vivaldi's operas. Mauro and Vivaldi at one time were also business associates, acting as joint impresarios of Sant'Angelo during the seasons of 1738 and 1739. Unfortunately, this venture ended badly, with both men heaping recriminations upon each other.[14]

Although we know the names of seventeen set designers connected with performances of Vivaldi's operas in various cities (some of them more than once),[15] we as yet have no extant iconographical documentation for any of Vivaldi's operas staged in Venice. However, by looking at the great mass of iconographical materials connected with stage design before and during Vivaldi's time, it is possible for us to gain a reasonably accurate impression of the kinds of stage settings used in his operas.

Ferdinando Galli-Bibiena (1656–1743) had the greatest single influence on the development of scenic design during the late seventeenth and early eighteenth centuries.[16] Aside from heading a clan of internationally admired designers, it was he who first codified the radical innovations in stage design that had begun to take place during the last three decades of the seventeenth century. Bibiena's monumental book *L'architettura civile* was first published at Parma in 1711. The work is devoted primarily to the use of perspective in architecture, but also contains sections concerned exclusively with scenic design. In these sections the creation of visual illusion by use of complicated perspective is singled out for special treatment. In order to appreciate Galli-Bibiena's achievement one must first look at the state of scenic design before his time.

Beginning early in the sixteenth century, stage settings had been conceived symmetrically with the point of perspective centered in the distance beyond the stage. Among the most familiar examples of this sixteenth-century practice are the often-published sets for the Florentine *intermedii* of 1589. Although architectural and decorative styles changed, this basic conception of the stage set remained the model for all stage design for the greater part of the seventeenth century. Two sets from Giacomo Torelli's designs for F. Sacrati's *Il Bellerofonte*, performed at the Teatro Novissimo in Venice in 1642, will serve as examples of stage settings with central perspective.[17] Torelli was the most famous designer of the first

FIGURE 6. Set by Giacomo Torelli for F. Sacrati's *Il Bellerofonte* (1642)

half of the seventeenth century and worked both in Venice and in Paris.

The first of these sets (act 3, scene 8) is a *sala regia* (royal hall), a stock setting that appears in most serious opera librettos until well after the mid eighteenth century (figure 6). There are five wings on either side of the stage. Beyond these are two flats jointed at the middle of the stage with cutout spaces for arches (*spezzati trafo-rati*) and, finally, a painted backdrop. The illusion of a ceiling is achieved by stretching pieces of painted canvas across the upper part of the stage between the wings. As was customary, the central perspective neatly divides the stage into halves. Because of the number of wings and flats utilized, this is clearly a *scena lunga* and is quite deep.

Act 3, scene 7 from the same opera is another matter (figure 7).

FIGURE 7. Set by Giacomo Torelli for F. Sacrati's *Il Bellerofonte* (1642)

This is a *boschetto del giardino* (grove in the garden), also a stock set, sometimes with a fountain and sometimes, as here, without. This is a *scena corta*, with only three wings, a flat with cutouts, and a backdrop.

These two sets from *Il Bellerofonte* illustrate graphically the hypothetical situation referred to earlier when I discussed the plan of the Teatro Santissimi Giovanni e Paolo. Act 3, scene 7 is a *scena corta* using three wings, and act 3, scene 8 is a *scena lunga* with five wings. It is a comparatively simple matter to effect a quick change from one scene to the other: The three forward wings were replaced, the drop at the middle depth of the stage was removed, and the *sala regia* appeared with a minimum of effort, thanks to manpower and a complicated combination of ropes and pulleys.

These archetypal sets with a single central vanishing point were the principal, if not the sole, choice available until the late seventeenth century. With the changes spearheaded and codified by Galli-Bibiena, other more sophisticated possibilities were introduced. It must be emphasized, however, that the symmetrical set was not abandoned; it merely became one of a number of ways to design a scene.

Bibiena's principal innovation was the introduction of asymmetrical settings with the point of perspective not in the center of the stage but to one side or above center. This, in Bibiena's words, is the *scena per angolo* (scene with angular perspective).[18]

Figure 8, a scene from Sabadini's *Didio Giuliano*, performed at the Piacenza in 1687, is a typical *scena per angolo*.[19] This set, designed by Ferdinando Galli-Bibiena, has ten sets of wings with cloth stretched between to simulate a ceiling. At the back is a platform with a throne, in this case a freestanding piece of furniture. Behind this is the painted backdrop. On the right side of the stage the flats are placed one behind the other in the usual manner, but on the left they follow one another diagonally, thus leading the spectator's eye to the throne at right stage back.

FIGURE 8. Set by Ferdinando Galli-Bibiena for B. Sabadini's *Didio Giuliano* (1687)

Another type of set cultivated by Bibiena and widely dispersed by him in his many travels was the *scena a fuochi multipli*, i.e., a set with not one but many vanishing points often going into different directions. Benedetto Marcello, in his noted satire on the operas of his time (*Il teatro alla moda* [ca. 1720]), refers specifically to such sets.

> The modern stage designer or painter should not understand perspective, architecture, drawing, chiaroscuro, and so forth; he should see to it that architectural scenes should never have one or two vanishing points, but that each wing should contain four or six . . . because from such variety the eye of the spectator will be better satisfied.[20]

The *scena a fuochi multipli* was not unknown before Bibiena's time, and indeed there are sporadic examples dating back to the Florentine *intermedii* of 1589. However, it was Bibiena, his family, and his followers who were responsible for its enormous vogue.

An unidentified scene by Giuseppe Galli-Bibiena, one of Ferdinando's sons, illustrates admirably the principles of the *scena a fuochi multipli* (figure 9).[21] This is a garden scene with vanishing points in the center and on both sides of the stage. Note, however, that the stage is still divided symmetrically into halves, a point that has caused some confusion in the past for writers discussing this kind of set. Indeed, the true *scena a fuochi multipli* is fundamentally symmetrical.

Important and far-reaching as the Galli-Bibienas' innovations were, they presented certain inherent problems that were never really solved in a satisfactory manner. Perhaps the greatest defect of the *scena per angolo* and the *scena a fuochi multipli* was that, in order to achieve their desired effect, they had to be viewed from a specific point in the auditorium. That point would naturally be the royal box or the most important box in the theater situated usually in the first tier at the back center. Seen from any other point in the theater, the elaborate effects achieved in the perspective would be distorted. This situation perplexed many contemporary commentators and led to a number of proposed remedies. One of the more improbable suggestions was that all spectators should enter the theater through a door placed at ground level in the center of the back of the auditorium. In this way, everybody would have at least one chance to gaze upon the set as it had been intended to be seen.

Here I should like to mention the only known illustration that

FIGURE 9. An unidentified scene by Giuseppe Galli-Bibiena (1695–1757)

FIGURE 10. Interior of Teatro Filarmonico in Verona with a set by Francesco Galli-Bibiena for Vivaldi's *La fida ninfa* (ca. 1730)

FIGURE 11. Detail of figure 10

can definitely be connected with a specific opera by Vivaldi, although this opera was not performed in Venice. The drawing, by either Francesco Galli-Bibiena or by his student and colleague Joseph Chamant, is part of the collection of the Royal Library at Windsor Castle (figure 10).[22] It depicts the interior of the Teatro Filarmonico in Verona during a rehearsal of the opera *La fida ninfa*. The interior of the theater itself is shown as if it were a *scena per angolo*, with the stage, singers, and orchestra left of center. The whole is viewed as from a first-tier box at the back left curve of the auditorium. It can be seen that the boxes in each tier descend slightly as they come nearer to the stage. This architectural innovation, meant to improve the line of vision from the boxes, was employed by the Galli-Bibiena family in a number of theaters they designed.

In a detail of this drawing (figure 11), one can get a clearer view of the set, a *deliziosa* (delightful garden) with columns that carry the motif of the proscenium columns to the stage proper. Below the proscenium is the very elaborately decorated orchestra pit. Three men in chairs sit watching the stage, and in front of them is another man sitting alone, with yet another man standing at his left. Some of the boxes also contain spectators. The man sitting alone in a chair can definitely be identified as Francesco Galli-Bibiena, who designed both the theater and the sets for *La fida ninfa*.[23] Originally, Maria Teresa Muraro and Elena Povoledo thought that the man standing to his left might be Vivaldi, but recently they have revised their conclusions.[24]

The Teatro Filarmonico was to have been inaugurated in 1729 with performances of *La fida ninfa*, set to music by the Bolognese composer Giuseppe Orlandini. For various reasons the opening of the theater was postponed until 1732; in the meantime Orlandini had withdrawn and Vivaldi received the commission to compose the opera. In his study on the Teatro Filarmonico, Rigoli found documents describing small architectural changes made in the theater in 1730. These changes do not appear in the present drawing, thus the drawing must show the theater auditorium as it was in 1730 or 1729, the year of its planned opening. It is, in all probability, a drawing made to commemorate the planned inauguration of the theater. Since Vivaldi had not yet been asked to set the work, the standing figure cannot be him. Even if Vivaldi has been lost,

Francesco Galli-Bibiena remains, as does the *deliziosa fiorita* from *La fida ninfa,* which in the libretto of Vivaldi's opera is listed as the second change of scene.

In summary, then, the Venice in which Vivaldi's operas were performed was no longer the important musical center that it had been in the seventeenth century. Even though there were still six active theaters staging opera in Vivaldi's time, this number was less than half of what it had been forty years earlier. Hand in hand with the decline in the number of active theaters went a decline in the elaborateness of operatic productions. For example, we should never assume that each new operatic production had completely new sets. Because of the omnipresence in librettos of stock scenes such as the *deliziosa* and the *sala regia,* it was possible to incorporate these sets in any number of operatic productions. To be sure, such giants as the members of the Galli-Bibiena family and others continued to design magnificent sets for theaters throughout Italy and the rest of Europe, but there were many theaters that did not have the resources to commission these designs. However, the theaters of Venice and other cities could, on occasion, still enjoy splendid examples of the scenic designer's art because of the widespread practice of a designer's sketching a set and then sending it to a theater where it would be realized by local craftsmen. Perhaps much of the luster was gone, but opera continued to thrive on Venetian stages, so much so that the Venetians kept their theaters open even as the republic fell in 1797.

NOTES

1. Giacomo Torelli (1608–1678). The standard study on Torelli and his stage sets is P. Bjurström, *Giacomo Torelli and Baroque Stage Design* (Stockholm, 1961, revised 1962). In 1641, Torelli designed the Teatro Novissimo, Venice's fourth opera house.

2. For many illustrations, see M. T. Muraro, "Il secolo di Vivaldi e il melodramma: i teatri, le scene," in *Antonio Vivaldi da Venezia all'Europa,* ed. F. Degrada and M. T. Muraro (Milan, 1978), pp. 50–65. I wish to thank both the Vivaldi Institute and the Cini Foundation in Venice for their help and encouragement. Above all, Maria Teresa Muraro, director of the Institute of Letters, Theater, and Music at the Cini Foundation, has been very generous over the years, putting materials at my disposal and discussing many points with me.

3. The most recent study of theaters in seventeenth- and eighteenth-

century Venice is N. Mangini, *I teatri di Venezia* (Milan, 1974). See also the catalog *I teatri pubblici di Venezia (secoli XVII–XVIII)* (Venice, 1971).

4. For a list of Vivaldi's works performed at Sant'Angelo, see the catalog *Venezia Vivaldi* (Venice, 1978). See also E. Garbero, "Drammaturgia vivaldiana: Regesto e concordanze dei libretti," in *Antonio Vivaldi da Venezia all'Europa*, ed. F. Degrada and M. T. Muraro (Milan, 1978), pp. 111–150. Peter Ryom lists Vivaldi's operas in "Vivaldi," *The New Grove Dictionary*, vol. 20, p. 44.

5. Venice, Archivio di Stato, Compilazione leggi, b. 363, fol. 36.

6. Venice, Archivio di Stato, Consiglio de' dieci, reg. 206, fols. 273v–274.

7. From the commemorative volume *Venezia festeggiante per la creazione del Serenissimo Doge Giovanni II Cornaro* (Venice, 1709). Engraving by A. Coronelli. Venice, Museo Correr, M. 10263, P.D. 3505.

8. Zaccaria Seriman, *I viaggi di Enrico Wanton alle terre incognite australi . . .* (Bern [but Treviso], 1764). An earlier edition was published in Venice in 1749. The onlookers are masked, as was the custom during the pre-Lenten Carnival season. These masks, descendants of those worn by actors in the classical theater, were meant, literally, to mask the true identity of the wearer. In Venice and other cities laws were enacted that forbade citizens to attend theater performances during Carnival season without masks, even though there were often strong objections to the practice. Anonymity encouraged licentiousness.

9. London, Sir John Soane Museum. For further details of this plan, see S. T. Worsthorne, *Venetian Opera in the Seventeenth Century* (Oxford, 1954), pp. 29–31.

10. These figures are from ibid., pp. 30–31.

11. Paris, Bibliothèque de l'Opéra, D 342. Dumont's is a floor plan only. A plan of the tiers of boxes is found in the Museo Correr, Venice.

12. See P. Bjurström, "Uneröffentlichtes von Nicodemus Tessin d. J.," *Kleine Schriften der Gesellschaft für Theatergeschichte* 21 (1966).

13. Garbero, "Drammaturgia Vivaldiana," reproduces the front matter from all of Vivaldi's librettos, including the names of set designers when they appear.

14. See L. Moretti, "Dopo l'insuccesso di Ferrara: diverbio tra Vivaldi e Antonio Mauro," in *Vivaldi Veneziano Europeo*, ed. F. Degrada (Florence, 1980), pp. 89–99.

15. Garbero, "Drammaturgia Vivaldiana."

16. The standard work on the Galli-Bibienas is A. H. Mayor, *The Bibiena Family* (New York, 1945). For more on the Bibiena family and many illustrations, see the exhibition catalogs *Disegni teatrali dei Bibiena*, ed. M. T. Muraro and E. Povoledo (Venice, 1970) and *Illu-*

sione e pratica teatrale, ed. F. Mancini, M. T. Muraro, and E. Povoledo (Venice, 1975).

17. These sets and many others are illustrated and discussed in Bjurström, *Giacomo Torelli*, passim.

18. See the catalog *Illusione e pratica teatrale*, pp. 79–83.

19. Vittorio Tremante Collection, Venice.

20. "Non dovrà l'ingegnere, o pittor moderno intendere *prospettiva, architettura, disegno, chiaroscuro*, etc., procurando pertanto che le *scene d'architettura* non vadano mai ad uno o due punti, ma bensì ch'ogni *telaro* n'abbia quattro o sei . . . perchè da tal varietà resti maggiormente appagato l'occhio de' spettatori" (Benedetto Marcello, *Il teatro alla moda* [ca. 1720?], preface and notes by Andrea d'Angeli [Milan, 1956], pp. 54–55).

21. Museo teatrale alla Scala, Milan.

22. Windsor Castle, Royal Library Inv. 10766. See M. T. Muraro and E. Povoledo, "Le scene della *Fida ninfa*: Maffei, Vivaldi, e Francesco Bibiena," in *Vivaldi Veneziano Europeo*, ed. F. Degrada (Florence, 1980), pp. 235–252.

23. Ibid., p. 238, note. This same drawing of Galli-Bibiena appears on a plan of the Teatro Filarmonico located at the Cooper Hewitt Museum, New York City.

24. See note 22. All documents concerning the Teatro Filarmonico can be found in P. Rigoli, "Il teatro filarmonico di Verona nel settecento," Ph.D. dissertation (Bologna, 1976).

Costume in the Frescoes of Tiepolo and Eighteenth-Century Italian Opera *by William L. Barcham*

Colorful plumes bobbing on gold and silver helmets, embroidered skirts swaying under trains of rich and heavy brocade, and brilliant jewels sparkling on headdresses and around necks—such was the spectacular wardrobe that heroes and heroines in the eighteenth century wore on the operatic stage. Vivaldi's *Orlando furioso* surely must have offered its audiences a similar vestiary pageant when it was first performed in Venice in 1727. But when we in the twentieth century attempt to envision how actors were costumed in the early eighteenth century, we find ourselves in a historical quandary, for drawings or prints that show us precisely how performers were dressed are rare. We do not know, for example, how Orlando was equipped as he went into mortal combat with Arontes or how Alcina was adorned when she tried to ensnare Ruggiero. What kinds of garments and what types of personal furnishings were generally worn by operatic singers in the heroic musical theater of the first half of the eighteenth century in Venice?

Among the sources available in which to find answers to such a question are contemporaneous images of the eighteenth-century stage. Drawings and prints, as well as a number of paintings showing theatrical productions, provide a wide range of pictorial information. Another important reference source is the art of the period, because the themes that Vivaldi took up in *Orlando furioso* are the very same in much of the history painting of the Venetian *Settecento*: personal sacrifice, knightly battle, and romantic love. Giambattista Tiepolo, the foremost Venetian artist of the century, said in fact that the painter's mind should be concerned "with the Sublime, with the Heroic, and with Perfection," those ideals that most moved the audiences of the contemporary operatic theater.[1] This similarity in concept certainly united the fine arts with the

FIGURE 1. Giambattista Tiepolo, *Sacrifice of Iphigenia*, entrance hall, Villa Valmarana, Vicenza

musical theater, and it often brought them to draw upon the same stories from the Italian literary tradition. In fact, Tiepolo, like Vivaldi, also represented Ariosto's great epic, *Orlando furioso*, and during his artistic maturity he sought, as had Vivaldi, to express its deep passions and brilliant heroics.

In 1757, Tiepolo was commissioned by Gaetano Valmarana to fresco several rooms in the Villa Valmarana, the family villa situated outside Vicenza. Tiepolo decorated the *palazzina* with scenes from four different literary masterpieces, two of them ancient and two modern.[2] Homer's *Iliad* and Vergil's *Aeneid* represent classical Greek and Latin poetry, whereas Tasso's *Gerusalemme liberata* and Ariosto's *Orlando furioso*, both composed in the sixteenth century, recount stories made popular by medieval legend.[3]

As Michael Levey explained several years ago, Tiepolo presented episodes from these four epics in an undeniably operatic fashion.[4] The most obvious theatrical element, of course, is the scenographic architecture. The lateral entranceways and classical

FIGURE 2. Giambattista Tiepolo, *Briseis Led to Agamemnon*, room of the *Iliad*, Villa Valmarana, Vicenza

porticoes in the *Sacrifice of Iphigenia* (figure 1) and *Briseis Led to Agamemnon* (figure 2), for example, are reminiscent of stage constructions like the one we find in a contemporary print by Giovanni Carlo Galli-Bibiena, a member of the famous theater family from Bologna (figure 3). Moreover, in the painting in figure 2, as in fact in several others of the Valmarana commission, Tiepolo emphasized a pictorial and physical break between the foreground and the background, which also can be clearly noted in Bibiena's design. There the dramatic action freely develops in the front whereas the painted drop behind functions as a description of a precise geographical or topographical setting (a Roman temple complex in this case). Different from Bibiena's grandiosity, however, is the small size of Tiepolo's stages; the artist clearly wished to create an intimacy between the historical personages represented on the walls and the actual inhabitants of the villa. This intimate relationship between actor and audience recalls another aspect of the contemporary stage: the court theater, where privileged

FIGURE 3. Giovanni Carlo Galli-Bibiena, setting for act 1, scene 5 of *La Clemenza di Tito*, music by A. Mazzoni, presented at the Teatro del Tejo, Lisbon in 1755 (St. Cecilia, Rome)

FIGURE 4. Print by A. Aveline, based on design by F. Juvarra for *Ricimero*, presented at the Teatro a Corte, Turin in 1722 (Biblioteca Reale, Turin)

nobility attended to the plights of the heroic figures onstage. A print of 1722 records just such a performance, as presented at the Teatro a Corte, Turin, during the wedding festivities of Carlo Emmanuele of Savoy and Anna Cristina of Bavaria (figure 4).

Another aspect of the contemporary theater that Tiepolo incorporated into his paintings was the *tableau vivant*, or the freezing of the plot's action during moments of high emotional intensity. This device, essential to Baroque opera by the middle of the eighteenth century, interrupted narrative complication; singers, standing still, expressed their deepest feelings directly to their listeners in long recitatives and dramatic arias. In the Villa Valmarana, Tiepolo transformed this convention into a pictorial formula. He portrayed Iphigenia facing death (figure 1) and Armida about to be abandoned by Rinaldo (figure 5) as two heroines who, overcome by their tragic situations, lament their awful fates in *canti patetici*.[5]

The most shining example in the Villa Valmarana of Tiepolo's realization of a dramatic dilemma through scenic conventions is a fresco illustrating an episode from canto X of the *Orlando furioso* itself (figure 6). Stanza 94 describes how Angelica, chained to a rock in the sea, is about to be devoured by a monster from the deep. Ruggiero descends on a fantastic griffin, kills the monster, and liberates Angelica. This episode, unfortunately not included in Vivaldi's opera, was conceived by Tiepolo in terms of both operatic declamation and stage mechanics: Angelica, like Iphigenia and Armida, shifts her position and gives vent to her despair, and Ruggiero maneuvers toward his deadly opponent as if perched on a theater machine.

But lacking from the scenes we have examined is the visual opulence we associate with eighteenth-century theatrical costume. Where are the brocades, jewels, golden helmets, and billowing plumes, the brilliant colors and the sparkling embellishments that were characteristic of operatic finery?[6] They are, in fact, nearly missing in Tiepolo's Valmarana paintings. Indeed, costume itself is missing from the ample bosoms of the several ladies we have looked at. Tiepolo reveals each of his heroines in various degrees of undress, from Armida's partial baring of her breast to Angelica's complete exposure. Surely eighteenth-century *dive* did not present themselves to their public in such states of *déshabillé*. Would any soprano of the time have forgotten her personal mod-

FIGURE 5. Giambattista Tiepolo, *Armida Abandoned by Rinaldo*, room of the *Gerusalemme Liberata*, Villa Valmarana, Vicenza

FIGURE 6. Giambattista Tiepolo, *Angelica Saved from a Sea Monster by Ruggiero*, room of the *Orlando furioso*, Villa Valmarana, Vicenza

esty or have shunned the rules of public decorum?[7] Tiepolo's frescoes in the Villa Valmarana, although similar in thematic material to Vivaldi's opera and tied in several aspects to theatrical conventions, are not completely representative of practice on the contemporary operatic stage. To understand how singers were dressed in the musical theater of the period, we must turn to images of the stage itself.

No drawings or sketches dated from before 1760 have been preserved from the costume ateliers in Italy. Therefore, prints and paintings enlivened with staffage and showing actual performances are a major source of information about dress on the early eighteenth-century operatic stage. There is, moreover, another source, a work remarkable for its humor: *Il teatro alla moda*, a satirical remonstrance of the contemporary theater written in the early years of the century by the composer Benedetto Marcello.

The musical theater that Marcello satirized was a result of the development of the public theater in Italy during the middle of the seventeenth century.[8] The shift from private court spectacle to performances for the paying populace affected costume design as well as altering the artistic and administrative organization of the theater world. In the sixteenth and early seventeenth centuries, performers had provided their own clothing and furnishings; if the members of the nobility at the court were generous, they gave the singers money for their clothing or, perhaps, even donated parts of their own wardrobe for theatrical use. Rarely was a designer called in and, then, it would have been either the court artist or architect who was responsible for the scene design of the performance at hand.[9] During the second half of the seventeenth century, as public theaters grew in size and scene design itself came to be more ambitious and complicated,[10] costumes necessarily had to be more lavish and fantastical; sparkling jewels, tiny, reflecting sequins, feathery headdresses, and yards of flowing drapery were, by 1700, the rule rather than the exception. Moreover, the Baroque performer was allowed to present him- or herself in garments that had little relationship either to the historical time period in which the opera was set or to the geographical location of its action.[11] Bejeweled opulence and splendor were the principal criteria by the turn of the century, and they dominated the Italian operatic scene until about 1760 to 1770.

Because of the growth in both the number and size of the theaters in Italy,[12] and because of the shift from court spectacle to public performance, a new figure entered the scene of the operatic world in the eighteenth century: the impresario. His presence, as well as the spectacular scenography of the new century,[13] affected costume design and practice by the 1720s, when Vivaldi's *Orlando furioso* was first presented. In order to juggle many different aspects of theatrical production at once and at the same time turn a profit, the impresario needed specialists; as a result, *sartorie*, or tailoring shops, grew up, and they handled the needs of the various impresarios from season to season. The most famous in Venice, and indeed in all of Italy, was that of Natal Canziani.[14] His shop furnished costumes to theaters not only in Venice but as far afield as Turin. Specialists like Canziani, however, did not reduce the richness of stage dress, nor did they aim for a greater truth in historical representation. In fact, their presence in the operatic world reinforced those trends that were already operative. All pretension to correct chronological costuming disappeared altogether, for Canziani and his colleagues aimed at as extravagant a spectacle as possible for as large a commercial market as possible. Their scheme was to create a wardrobe that could move from theater to theater, even from city to city. For example, at the end of the run of an opera in Venice, Canziani would send the costumes (for a high rental fee) to Turin to be used there during the following season for another opera, even though the two operas had entirely different subjects.[15] As a result, costume design became more and more bizarre (figure 7), so that the clothing could fit into any geographical or historical setting whatsoever. The forms of the costumes changed not at all, even if one subject were Persian and the other Greek. In the hands of the new *sartorie*, therefore, the costumes became more magnificent and the accessories more extravagant.

By studying further those paintings of the Turinese and Neapolitan theaters, we can understand both general and specific aspects of costume design and practice of the period. Perhaps the fundamental element that all designers had to remember was the role of gesture. Whether the body was tightly fitted or cloaked in loosely falling drapery, arms had to be free for sweeping movements.[16] Marcello, in his advice to singers in *Il teatro alla moda*, ironically notes that the male performer, in particular, should go onstage with his "sword and very long chains flashing, striking

FIGURE 7. D. Olivero and assistant, *Interior of the Teatro Regio, Turin* (detail), showing a performance of *Arsace*, music by F. Feo, presented on December 26, 1740 (Museo Civico, Turin)

and restriking them frequently so as to move the public to compassion." [17] Women, on the other hand, could attract the public's attention, suggested Marcello, by carrying fans or by using handkerchiefs (see figures 4 and 7). [18] These large-scale gestures demanded a dramatic and even oversized figural silhouette. Long, flowing trains and feathered helmets and headdresses increased the size of singers. These appurtenances eventually came to be regarded onstage as signs of rank, so that the leading singers (male and female) [19] often demanded the longest train in the company or the very highest plumage.[20] And, as can be seen in figure 4, the materials of the costumes, for men as well as for women, were richly embroidered.[21]

Many features in costume design differed, however, between the two sexes. Women were more simply dressed than men; apart from their long trains and the feathery arrangements on their heads, women's gowns most usually followed contemporary fashion. Bodices were tightly fitted, and skirts were pear- or bell-shaped.[22] Thus, the arms moved freely from the shoulders and the singers could easily cross the stage. Making extensive use of fans or handkerchiefs, they brought the audience's attention to their faces, where beauty marks abounded.[23] The comical quality of these polka-dotted faces was caught by Anton Maria Zanetti in a caricature of Faustina Bordoni Hasse (figure 8), dressed for a 1716 performance of *Ariodante* in Venice.[24] Taken together, Zanetti's drawing and the Turinese painting of 1740 (figure 7) show us the typical female performer of the first half of the century; both images emphasize the rich embroidery of the fabrics and the full sil-

FIGURE 8. A. M. Zanetti, Faustina Bordoni Hasse in *Ariodante*, presented at the Teatro San Giovanni Grisostomo, Venice in 1716 (Fondazione Giorgio Cini, Venice)

houette of the skirts contrasted with closely fitting bodices and deep décolletage.

Male costumes were far more complicated than those of the women. The basis of all dress, whether the figure was a soldier or not, was ancient Roman armor; that is, a tightly fitted cuirass above a loose "skirt" falling to the knees. But the elaborations were so many and so extravagant that the male hero on the operatic stage hardly looked able to face the horrors of war. Needless to say, the fabrics were neither leather nor buckskin, but rather the same rich brocades worn by the women, fabulously embroidered with luxurious floral patterns or swelling arabesques, as can be seen again in figure 7 or in two designs of 1749 from Berlin (figure 9). Below the waist, the Roman *lorico* metamorphosed into a *tonnelet*, an oval hoopskirt developed in France during the seventeenth century. The function of both the length and the width of this *tonnelet* was to exhibit, indeed to emphasize and frame, the singer's legs. Marcello laughingly recommended the costumers to provide the *virtuosi* with clothing that would show off "their

FIGURE 9. Designs for Achilles and Arcas, for *Iphegenie in Aulis*, music by Graun, presented at the Königliche Oper, Berlin in 1749

FIGURE 10. A. M. Zanetti, Gaetano Valletta (Fondazione Giorgio Cini, Venice)

beautiful calves so that they [the *virtuosi*] can earn a gratuity."[25]

The vanity of the *virtuosi* hardly began or stopped at their legs, however. Somewhat hampered in movement by extraordinarily long trains (see figures 4, 7, and 10) and vying for the audience's attention against the fluttering handkerchiefs and fans of the female cast, the male singers sought to attract the spectators by adding such piquant details as jewels glistening at button holes, mops of plumage undulating on the heads, and white gloves that emphasized hand gestures. Zanetti caricatured such a figure in a humorous sketch of Gaetano Valletta, a popular singer in Venice during the 1730s, as he assumed a "significant" pose (figure 10).[26]

Having seen how singers were dressed on the operatic stage, we can easily understand that Tiepolo, despite any theatrical device he may have employed in his frescoes, never conceived of his figures as stage performers. The obvious differences between his deeply feeling hero and the self-indulgent male soprano are evident if we compare, for example, his Aeneas (figure 11), moved by Venus's leavetaking, with another Zanetti caricature (figure 12).[27] The

FIGURE 11. Giambattista Tiepolo, *Aeneas Left by Venus* (detail), room of the *Aeneid*, Villa Valmarana, Vicenza

comparison is striking. To be sure, Aeneas uses broad gesture, he also dons plumes and colorful finery, and his mouth is open as if to sing a plaintive farewell. Nevertheless, he cannot be mistaken for an operatic protagonist. His musculature is too well pronounced, his costume is historically evocative, and, most important, his gesturing and stance respond simply and directly to the dramatic situation. Pasi's declamation, on the other hand, is bombastic, his clothing absurd, and his plumage as energetic as his puffing cheeks and mouth.[28] The basis of all the Villa Valmarana figures is, very plainly, a dramatic naturalism, but the fundamental requirement in the early eighteenth-century theater was visible artifice, both for costume as well as performance.

There did exist, however, two forms of theatrical presentation where artifice did not rule, where narrative action, although interpreted dramatically, was shown in a straightforward manner. It is here that we can find direct relationships between historical painting such as Tiepolo's frescoes at the Villa Valmarana and the contemporary stage. Most theater pieces in the eighteenth century

FIGURE 12. A. M. Zanetti, Antonio Pasi (Fondazione Giorgio Cini, Venice)

were preceded either in actual performance or in the printed version by a pictorial *avant-propos*; that is, a painted front curtain in the theater or a frontispiece to a printed script or libretto. Not enough is known about either of these artistic genres, but quick study reveals that the types of figures and the kinds of settings found stand somewhere between mythological/heroic painting of the era and stage performance. Giambattista Crosato and Bernardino Galliari, two of Tiepolo's contemporaries, executed several sketches for drop curtains that would have been lowered during the opening sinfonie or during scene changes.[29] The figures depicted there emote, they move dramatically, but they are dressed neither according to contemporary styles nor in a bizarre fashion. There is, in sum, an effort to create a dramatic mood in a historical ambience.

The same generalizations can be made of printed frontispieces. One such by Pierre-Quentin Chedel (1705–1763) was used for a 1745 edition of Scipione Maffei's *La Merope* of 1713. The play, whose sources lie in Pausanias, Apollodorus, and Hyginus and whose subject matter is tied to a lost tragedy by Euripides, tells a story of usurpation, familial recognition, and murder of an illegitimate ruler. Elements in the play are obviously similar to several in the Orestes legend, but Merope herself is unlike the treacherous Clytemnestra, for she welcomes her son's return and his eventual rescue of her from a forced marriage with the cruel Polifonte. Polifonte's death at the hands of Cresfonte, Merope's son and the rightful heir to the throne, takes place offstage but is related onstage, in typical Greek fashion, to an amazed group of listeners. Chedel's frontispiece (figure 13) illustrates these horrific events as they are recounted in act 5, scene 6. Details in Chedel's print, such

FIGURE 13. Pierre-Quentin Chedel, frontispiece to Scipione Maffei's *La Merope*, ed. D. Ramazzini (1745)

FIGURE 14. Leonardo Marini, design for Ubaldo, for *Armida* (1770, Biblioteca Reale, Turin)

as the classical portico, the high priest officiating at the altar, the clearly designated murderous ax, and the soldiers dressed *all'antica*, remind us of specific elements in Tiepolo's *Sacrifice of Iphigenia* in the Villa Valmarana of a decade later (figure 1).[30] But beyond the individual components, what relates the fresco to the print is that both differ, for the very same reasons, from contemporary theatrical imagery. That is, the intensity of the dramatic action, its response in the secondary performers, the simplicity of the architectural surround, and the relative austerity of costume all make these images manifestly distinct from those that represent actual operatic performances (figures 3 and 7). In sum, although theatrical conventions influenced the pictorial arts, costume design in the first half of the eighteenth century was either too exaggerated or too little concerned with historical veracity to be of any artistic use outside the very limited sphere of the theater itself.

During the 1760s and 1770s, reaction set in against the extravagances of theater costume. Influenced by contemporary critical judgment and, perhaps, by trends abroad, costume designers in Italy sought greater historical accuracy. Reform had already begun in England during the second quarter of the century, and from there it had spread to France.[31] Soon after mid century, Francesco Algarotti, an important Italian literary figure with ties in both England and France, published his *Saggio sopra l'opera in musica*. In it Algarotti complains about opera impresarios, and he censures costume designers ("nostri Canziani" in particular) for the vagaries of stage dress. Aeneas should not be shown with a cap nor should he be wearing "pantaloons in the Dutch manner."[32] Rather, costume must approach as nearly as possible "the customs of the times and of the countries that are represented in the scene [onstage]."[33] Above all, Algarotti hopes that those who oversee theater wardrobes will look to the genius of such erudite craftsmen as Giulio Romano and Niccolò Tribolo.[34]

By 1770, the search for historical verisimilitude in Italian costume design became a reality. A first tenor in Turin signed a contract with the Teatro a Corte there, wherein he agreed to provide his own shoes, stockings, gloves, and headdress, "the ensemble suitable to my character."[35] In 1771, Leonardo Marini, Turin's foremost *sarto* of the period, published a tract entitled *Abiti antichi di diverse nazioni*. Marini argues for exactly those aspects of costume design that had been missing during the previous one hundred years. He notes that stage clothing must conform to the requirements of time and place, that it must appear logical and possible, that reason must always guide fantasy, and that the "designer must read history" before setting out to create a wardrobe. Marini blames the singers themselves for the preposterous designs and the poor taste that had earlier governed theatrical fashion.[36] To show correct usage, Marini describes his creations for a theater piece on Armida, noting that reading Tasso had been of important help to him. In his design for Ubaldo (figure 14), we immediately discern that a fundamental change has taken place in stage attire since Valletta and Pasi strode the boards (figures 10 and 12), or since Achilles was conceived more as a bakery confection than as a heroic warrior (figure 9). To be sure, flamboyant plumes are still present on Ubaldo, and the patterns on his fabric are as rich and colorful as ever.[37] But the total image is altogether new, for the forms are now historically relevant and the shapes restrained. The *bizzaria* that had formerly characterized costume design was, by 1775, suppressed.

Listening to Vivaldi's *Orlando furioso* today, to Angelica's sweet laments and Orlando's frenzied rages, we find it difficult to believe that in 1727 it was sung by performers dressed like Valletta or Bordoni Hasse. But most members of the Venetian audience fully accepted the passions of Ariosto's drama as presented by figures and in circumstances similar to what we see in Olivero's painting (figure 7). Modern sensibility, however, finds that the expressiveness of Vivaldi's music and the excesses of early eighteenth-century singers create a strange union indeed. It is partly for this bizarre juxtaposition, perhaps, that Tiepolo's silver-toned frescoes in the Villa Valmarana have seemed like a more faithful guide to the appearance of operatic production in the middle of the eighteenth century; they savor of a tempered theatricality that we, an audience of film-goers and TV watchers, have come to expect of our opera singers. But, as an accurate mirroring of the musical stage in the first half of the century, Tiepolo is "archaeologically" incorrect. His figures are too restrained and his costuming not flamboyant enough. The miraculous world of Orlando and Alcina was conceived by Vivaldi during a period when the artifice of theatrical forms was still openly exposed.

NOTES

I would like to thank both Maria Teresa Muraro and Margherita Antonelli of the Istituto Internazionale per la Ricerca Teatrale, Fondazione Giorgio Cini, Venice, for their generous help to me in my research.

1. The heroic theater was certainly the most popular in early eighteenth-century Italy. For an account of which subjects were most often produced, see Lione Allacci, *Drammaturgia* (Venice, 1755); for Tiepolo's statement on a painter's goals, see the *Nuova Veneta Gazzetta*, dated March 20, 1762. This material is reported by Francis Haskell in *Patrons and Painters* (London, 1963), p. 253.

2. Following is the principal bibliography on the *palazzina* and its adjacent *foresteria*, both of which together comprise the Villa Valmarana: P. Molmenti, *Les Fresques de Tiepolo dans la Villa Valmarana* (Venice, 1880); A. Morassi, *Tiepolo e la villa Valmarana* (Milan, 1945); R. Pallucchini, *Gli affreschi di Giambattista e Giandomenico Tiepolo alla Villa Valmarana di Vicenza* (Bergamo, 1945); M. Levey, "Tiepolo's Treatment of a Classical Story at Villa Valmarana, a Study in Eighteenth-Century Iconography and Aesthetics," *Journal of the Warburg and Courtauld Institutes* 20 (1957): 298–317; and G. Knox, "The Tasso Cycles of Giambattista Tiepolo and Giannantonio Guardi," *Museum Studies* 9 (1978): 49–95.

3. Levey points out that Tiepolo's frescoes date from the same year as the Comte de Caylus's publication, *Tableaux tirés de l'Iliade, de l'Odyssée d'Homère et de l'Eneide de Virgile, avec des observations générales sur le costume* (Paris, 1757), which was in Consul Joseph Smith's library in Venice. Caylus's instructions on how to dress figures *à l'antique* were possibly known by Tiepolo; cf. Levey, "Tiepolo's Treatment," p. 302.

4. Levey notes that the episodes Tiepolo chose to depict in the villa were often the very same as those found in operatic versions of the same stories. He also describes some of the devices Tiepolo used in his paintings that correspond to conventions of the operatic theater.

5. Tiepolo's Iphigenia seems closely related, as Levey points out, to the heroine in *Iphigénie en Aulide*, a libretto written by Francesco Algarotti, a literary friend of Tiepolo's; Algarotti's Iphigénie offers herself to the high priest, reciting "Je me devoue volontiers pour votre gloire, et pour la Grèce." A moment later Diana descends. See Algarotti, *Iphigénie en Aulide*, act 5, scene 2, in "Saggio sopra l'opera in musica," in *Opere* (Livorno, 1764), vol. 2.

6. While the coloring is often vivid in the Valmarana paintings, Tiepolo presents, as he often does in his mature frescoes, a generalized tonality of neutral beiges and grays against which he juxtaposes primaries and complementaries. Color is never lavishly splurged on the walls; rather, it functions to pull figures together or to set them apart against the neutral stage set.

7. While leading sopranos would not have bared their breasts, women representing allegories, personifications, or deities—particularly those associated with the classical past—often went nude to the waist. As prints of theater productions and court pageants from as far back as the sixteenth century show, these women were seated on chariots or appeared on flying machines that descended from above the stage. I am indebted to Kathleen Weil-Garris for having reminded me of this "topless" aspect of Italian theater production.

8. The first operatic theater actually to open its doors to a paying public, starting in 1637, was the Teatro San Cassiano in Venice.

9. "Costume," *Enciclopedia dello spettacolo* (Rome, 1956), vol. 3, p. 1597.

10. For seventeenth-century scenography, see "Scenografia," *Enciclopedia*, vol. 8, pp. 1595–1598 and P. Bjurström, *Giacomo Torelli and Baroque Stage Design* (Stockholm, 1961).

11. "Costume," *Enciclopedia*, vol. 3, p. 1594.

12. By the mid eighteenth century there were over one hundred theaters operating in Italy. In Venice alone there were about twenty by 1700; the number was reduced somewhat in the following years. See T.

Wiel, *I teatri musicali veneziani del Settecento* (Venice, 1897); *I teatri pubblici di Venezia (secoli XVII–XVIII)*, ed. L. Zorzi, M. T. Muraro, G. Prato, and E. Zorzi (Venice, 1971); and H. Kindermann, *Theatergeschichte Europas, von der Aufklärung zur Romantik* (Salzburg, 1976), vol. 5, part 2.

13. For the *scena per angolo*, see in particular "Scenografia," *Enciclopedia*, vol. 8, pp. 1595–1598; Mercedes Viale Ferrero, *La scenografia del '700 e i fratelli Galliari* (Turin, 1963), pp. 1ff.; and the chapter by William C. Holmes in this volume.

14. "Costume," *Enciclopedia*, vol. 3, p. 1595.

15. Mercedes Viale Ferrero, *La scenografia, dalle origini al 1936*, vol. 3, *Storia del Teatro Regio di Torino* (Turin, 1980), p. 114.

16. Hans Tintelnot, *Barocktheater und barocke Kunst* (Berlin, 1939), pp. 71–72.

17. "spada e catene ben lunghe, e rilucenti, battendole e ribattendole frequentemente, per indurre il popolo a compassione." In Benedetto Marcello, *Il teatro alla moda*, ed. Enrico Fondi (Lanciano, 1913), p. 39.

18. Ibid., pp. 50–51.

19. In the era of castratos, the leading "lady" was occasionally male and, of course, the leading male role was frequently sung by a woman.

20. See another edition of Marcello's *Il teatro alla moda* with notes by Andrea d'Angeli (1927), p. 168.

21. Tintelnot, *Barocktheater*, p. 71.

22. Ibid.; Edw. Burney, *Royal Festivals and Romantic Ballerinas, 1600–1850* (Washington, D.C., 1971), n.p. and A. Blunt and Edw. Croft-Murray, *Venetian Drawings of the XVII and XVIII Centuries in the Collection of Her Majesty the Queen at Windsor Castle* (London, 1957), p. 152.

23. Marcello, *Il teatro*, ed. Fondi, p. 63.

24. The music for *Ariodante* was written by C. F. Pollarolo, the libretto by A. Salvi, and the opera was presented in Venice at the Teatro San Giovanni Grisostomo. Faustina Bordoni was born in 1693 and died in 1781; she was married to the composer Johann-Adolph Hasse (died 1783). In 1739, Charles de Brosses wrote that, although she was a singer of great taste, she no longer had "une voix neuve," and that despite her charm, "ce n'est pas la meilleure chanteuse." Cf. Charles de Brosses, *Lettres familières écrites d'Italie en 1739 et 1740* (Paris, 1929), p. 187. For Zanetti's caricatures, see *Caricature di Anton Maria Zanetti*, ed. A. Bettagno (Vicenza, 1969); the drawing of Bordoni Hasse is cat. no. 26.

25. "L'abito sarà di più pezzi, di roba frusta, etc., dovendo bastare ai

sarti di provvedere . . . i Virtuosi di belle polpe di gambe, per gua-
dagnarsi la mancia." In Marcello, *Il teatro*, ed. Fondi, p. 85.

26. Many male singers dressed this way, even if they took "una parte di
prigionero, [oppure] di schiavo." Cf. Marcello, *Il teatro*, ed. Fondi,
p. 39. For Valletta, see Bettagno, *Caricature*, cat. no. 292.

27. The scene in which Aeneas, soon to part for Carthage, is left by
Venus, comes from book 1, vs. 655ff. of the *Aeneid*. Antonio Pasi,
the subject of Zanetti's drawing, was active between 1704 and 1730;
see Bettagno, *Caricature*, cat. no. 111.

28. Marcello's *Il teatro alla moda* and the caricatures by Zanetti and
Marco Ricci are sure testimony that the absurdities of the time were
recognized and condemned by critical members of the audience.
Zanetti's caricatures date from 1707 to 1746 and Ricci's date from
1719; see Blunt and Croft-Murray, *Venetian Drawings*, pp. 137ff.

29. See Viale Ferrero, *La scenografia del '700*, plates 11 and 23.

30. It should be kept in mind that Maffei and Tiepolo knew each other
since at least the 1730s, when the artist had produced drawings for
the writer's guide *Verona illustrata*. Maffei, in fact, praised Tiepolo
there for his "gusto antico." See *Verona illustrata* (Verona, 1732),
vol. 3, p. 397.

31. "Costume," *Enciclopedia*, vol. 3, p. 1595.

32. Algarotti's words are "braconi alla foggia Olandese." Cf. "Saggio
sopra l'opera in musica," *Opere*, vol. 2, pp. 300–301.

33. Ibid.

34. Ibid.

35. Marie-Thérèse Bouquet, *Il Teatro di Corte, dalle origini al 1788
(Storia del Teatro Regio di Torino)* (Turin, 1976), p. 226.

36. Leonardo Marini, "Ragionamento intorno alla foggia degli abiti teatrali," from *Abiti antichi di diverse nazioni* (1771), reprinted in Viale
Ferrero, *La scenografia, dalle origini al 1936*, pp. 567–570.

37. Marini describes Ubaldo's costume as "armor the color of darkened
steel, chain mail of scarlet satin embroidered in silver with clusters of
jewels, with a white drapery striped in silver. A cloak with a collar of
gold, and with scarlet and black flowers." In Viale Ferrero, *La scenografia dalle origini al 1936*, p. 570.

Baroque Manners and Passions in Modern Performance   *by Shirley Wynne*

From graphic sources we can learn how performers dressed and postured onstage during the early eighteenth century in the important cultural centers in Europe. Although there were regional and individual differences, most conventions were held in common. However, movement, the essential element in any dramatic action, is obviously missing from the iconography.

There are two kinds of sources that can supply these signs of life: (1) descriptive manuals on deportment, dance, and rhetorical and theatrical gesture and (2) dance-notation manuals and scores. The first give specific rules and a staggering array of examples of social rights and wrongs, expressive gestures within the bounds of propriety, and voluminous advice on good taste and the quality of manner and bearing in well-brought-up society. Professor Dene Barnett from the University of Flinders in Australia is the leading expert today on the literature and practice of theatrical gesture in the Baroque period taken from this first type of source.[1] The second type gives information of another sort. Notation manuals describe the significance and usage of a system of signs that represent the dance during the period from approximately 1680 to the last quarter of the eighteenth century. One would not be surprised to note that the system grew out of the French passion for codifying and classifying knowledge in the late seventeenth century, and, indeed, the first volume, *Chorégraphie* (dance writing) was written and published in Paris by Raoul-Auger Feuillet in 1700.[2] The system is extraordinarily rich. A glance at a figure from a ballet score for two men choreographed by Louis Pecour for Campra's *opéra-ballet L'Europe galante*, notated and published in 1704 by Feuillet, will impress one with its ornate filigree of mysterious signs (figure

FIGURE 1. A ballet from the opera *L'Europe galante*, from Raoul-Auger Feuillet (1704)

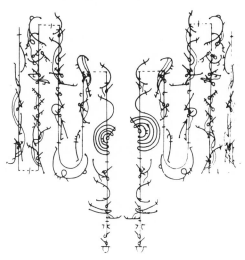

1).³ These signs give, first of all, rather precise correlations between dance steps and music without which one could not reconstruct the dances today. They indicate direction along the figure or floor design (usually a complex symmetrical pattern); body-facing as it travels along the figure (the body can move backward or sideways or turn along the path); level, including aerial steps; arm and hand correlations to steps; movements of the non-weight-bearing or gesture leg (the leg that performs the major ornaments to the step); and relationships among the dancers. Most scores are for one or two dancers, although some exist for four and six and there is one for nine male dancers.

Many hundreds of dance scores using this system were written and published all over Europe, and they record both ballroom dances and ballets for the theater. Those for the ballet contain sequences that were far more difficult technically: multiple entrechats, battements, pirouettes, and virtuosic ornamentation were common in theatrical pieces, particularly those for the men.

Feuillet's publication of 1700 set off a chain of translations, interpretations, and revisions of the system during the next seventy years and, because of widespread acceptance and usage, we may conclude that the steps, dances, and their governing rules of practice represent an international dance language.[4]

The system was brought out in an Italian version in Naples in 1728 by Giambattista (that is, Jean-Baptiste) Dufort entitled *Trattato del ballo nobile*. He credits the great choreographers of the Paris Opéra, Pierre Beauchamps and Louis Pécour, with being the leading masters of the day, and goes on to discuss the minuet and describe Feuillet's notation system. Unlike that of Feuillet, Dufort's first manual did not spark the publication of scores in Italy; in 1739, however, the Italian-trained Barbara Campanini, known as La Barbarina, first appeared at the Paris Opéra in Rameau's *Fêtes d'Hébé*. Rameau, in fact, wrote some special pieces for her in that work. Her training must have been from a tradition held in common with the French since she was at home immediately in their professional dance milieu. Her brio, however, may have been a special Italian trait. In 1779 Gennaro Magri published, again in Naples, a treatise on dance techniques for the theater and ballroom (*Trattato teorico-pratico di ballo*). He records the same steps current in France at the time, but with the invaluable addition of bravura techniques that may have been a distinguishing feature of Italian ballet, perhaps seen as early as 1739 in France in Barbarina's performance.

French uses of this style were different, however, from Italian. In Italy ballet was a frequent entertainment at the end of each operatic act, but did not figure strongly within the acts of an opera as it did in France.[5] Neither was there the same concern for relating the dance to the main dramatic plot.

From the fifteenth to the mid eighteenth century in western Europe, the educated person danced steps and dances that were fundamentally the same as those to be seen in the court theaters. Further, these dances were taught along with movement deportment and courtesy: how to hold a fan, a book, gloves, a hat; how and where to stand, walk, and sit at every occasion; and rule upon rule of movement proprieties. These formed an educated western European behavioral language. The manners of daily life were carried

FIGURE 2. Antoine Watteau, *L'Indifferent* (1707, Louvre, Paris)

to the stage, just as were the dances. We can only imagine the immediate pleasure audiences of those days would have experienced at seeing their very own behavior either brilliantly and ideally represented, artfully mocked by a jokester, or painfully distorted, as with Orlando gone mad.

We are far from this kind of rich, commonly held experience of movement these days. Performers in the theater, particularly opera, are given little or no training in movement, and certainly no attention is given to proprieties of movement or dance training for those of us who move, often with timidity and constraint, through our daily lives. We do indeed see ourselves mirrored onstage in the lack of confident and imaginative use of movement, in the lack of variety in shapes, directions, and rhythms or the range of expressive dynamics. Dancers, actors, but more especially singers usually represent only their uninformed (and unformed) selves over and over again, from one so-called characterization to another. Their movement repertoire is one of personal habit all too often limited, sadly, by incorrect usage as well as lack of movement experience. Would not opera today be more persuasive if singers moved with

FIGURE 3. Antoine Watteau, *Les Bergers* (1717, Charlottenburg, Berlin)

the forces, contrasts, tensions, and ambiguities present in the texts and music? Have we not lost something vital and can we not learn from the eighteenth century?

The underlying ideal for all movement was that of "the presence." This included how one stood, sat, and presented oneself to the public, and in what qualitative manner. Watteau's small painting, *L'Indifferent*, is an example of a "correct" look (figure 2).[6] The young man's posture demonstrates the principle of contrast, or the placement of body parts with multiple facings on a base of turned-out legs. Compare a standing figure facing directly front, arms at the sides, feet pointing forward with a figure whose face looks somewhat to the right at a slight tilt, shoulders twisting a shade to the left, right elbow reaching back to the right with the hand placed just below the right waistline, the left forearm crossing the body, hand just below the waist, left leg toward the back, foot pointed toward the left, right leg crossing the front of the body, foot pointed toward the right. The front-facing figure is typical of a bumpkin; the figure with multiple facings, like that of Watteau, is well bred. Class distinctions are less marked now than in

FIGURE 4. Antoine Watteau, *La Vraie Gaieté* (ca. 1702, National Gallery, London)

those days, but the difference between elegance and gaucheness is still easily discernible to an observant eye, and the signs descend from the older "classical" principles. Compare, for example, Watteau's *Les Bergers* (figure 3),[7] in which a couple is engaged in a well-schooled dance with every attitude of courtly elegance, with the peasants in his *La Vraie Gaieté* (figure 4),[8] who dance with unrefined abandon, their bodies following freely the ungainly thrust of the arms and legs. That which completes the effect of elegance in figure 3 is the air of ease with which all movement, even the smallest and most delicate, is undertaken. The manner of nonchalance that prohibits showing effort or stress has been given lengthy airing in the manuals on good behavior that appeared from the early fifteenth through the nineteenth centuries. In the early sixteenth century, Castiglione (*Il cortegiano* [1516]), to whom we owe the popularity of the concept of *sprezzatura* later taken up by Giulio Caccini, calls the look of the courtier one of *disinvoltura* or "uninvolvement." The young gentleman in Watteau's *L'Indifferent*, his arms and hands in a proper dance position, has a look of sublime confidence and airy nonchalance. Watteau gives more than just a hint of caricature, however, and his title suggests that his subject has reached the outer limits of a tasteful display of these admirable attributes. Overindulgence was as offensive as ineptitude and, like excessive ornamentation in music and dance, was deplored and properly scorned by those who knew moderation. John Weaver, a dancing master and scholar writing in 1712, describes this fine line of taste as an "artful carelessness, as if it were a natural motion, without a too curious and painful practising. To dance too exquisitely is, I must own, too laborious a vanity." [9]

Ideals in behavioral movement were perfected by performers so that audiences could see exemplary models on stage. Actors, dancers, and singers were, moreover, trained in a representational gesture language that was to imitate what John Weaver called "the motions of mankind." [10] The test of good performance, according to the theorists, lay not in technical bravado but in expressive capabilities and range. Dancing was particularly vulnerable to abuse by exhibitionists, and Weaver, like Michel DePure before him (*Idée des spectacles* [Paris, 1668]) and afterward Louis de Cahusac (*La Danse ancienne et moderne* [Paris, 1754]), chastised those who performed or applauded empty virtuosity. Weaver believed that the dancer should above all communicate in such a manner that "without the help of an interpreter, a spectator shall at a distance, by the lively representation of a just character, be capable of understanding the subject of the story represented, and be able to distinguish the several passions, manners, or actions; as of love, anger or the like." [11] The passions derived from what he called "natural" and "primitive" practices: "When men are struck with joy they leap. . . . Thus, when grief assaulted them they cast down their heads; anger and admiration lifted up their hands." [12] A master in dance had to be able to imitate all thoughts and emotions and transform into action any classical fable, which he would have memorized thoroughly in the course of his training.

Many texts in this period described the range of passions and how they were to be represented. They advised repeatedly that actors and singers study the gestures of heroic figures in paintings and use them as their models. Charles LeBrun's *Conférence . . . sur l'expression générale et particulière*, written much earlier but published posthumously in 1698 with engravings of the passions by Picart, was one of the most widely read of these texts, and not only in France, but throughout Europe.[13]

Even with an examination of the instructions and models available in this large and little-touched literature, we have yet to supply an image of the movement itself, without which restoration of the range and flow of gestures and dances is impossible. The key to movement is, of course, the transition from one position to another, not the position itself. Only in the transition can the performer create tension, and it is here that character is formed and interest excited. To discover (or rediscover) these passions of flesh and blood, one must pore over the sources, immerse oneself in the artifacts of the art and culture of the time, believe in them, take them seriously, then set them aside. Only then can one begin to move with confidence, if ever so respectfully, through the many little units and signs, piecing them slowly together into thoughts, like making sense of a forgotten language. After a time, with much performance and thought, a logic emerges, the steps dance, the gestures embody feelings. Possibilities for interpretation finally begin.

Clearly, a dance sequence or gesture can carry a wide range of dynamic tension. No particular affect underlies a movement or series of movements; however, context and general characteristics of particular dance types make for predictable associations. For example, a sarabande can be noble, distant, cool, and ornate; dark, enigmatic, full of binding tensions; soft and light, playful and free—it has a broad range of character. A tambourin, by contrast, will call up another spectrum of images from rustic and broad to bright and tender, perhaps even melancholy.

People in Vivaldi's day valued their choreographies of dance and gesture sufficiently to write them down. Through them we learn that the movements are wedded to their own music as no others can be. They matured together and share common traits. The notations tell better than I can imagine or invent how the dances looked and felt with their own music. By putting them into action, not only the music but the whole physical presence of performance can be brought together in the larger context of opera, where beauty and honor, wickedness and misery still stir us.

Holding fast to principles and rules must be balanced with the sense of what makes for dramatic tension in performance. Decisions must be made as to how immediate the characters and their purposes can become in an authentic setting for a modern audience, and the choices are made by directors and performers now. We should not mistake the current of energy that enlivens a performance today for one that moved an audience then. We cannot be completely "authentic," but we can be believable within the rules of any style if we know it thoroughly and, more important, love it and have something to say of ourselves within its boundaries.

NOTES

1. See Dene Barnett, "Finding the Appropriate Attitude: Dene Barnett in Conversation with Ian Parker," *Early Music* vol. 8, no. 1 (January 1980): 65–69.
2. Raoul-Auger Feuillet, *Chorégraphie, ou l'art de décrire la dance, par caractères, figures, et signes démonstratifs* (Paris, 1700).
3. Raoul-Auger Feuillet, *Recüeil de dances* (Paris, 1704), p. 164.
4. For comprehensive treatment of Feuillet's system see Wendy Hilton, *Dance of Court & Theater, The French Noble Style 1690–1725* (Princeton: Princeton Book Company, 1981).
5. On balletic *intermedii* in Italian opera see Charles E. Troy, *The Comic Intermezzo: A Study in the History of 18th Century Italian Opera* (Ann Arbor: UMI Research Press, 1979).
6. Antoine Watteau, *L'Indifferent* (1707, Louvre, Paris).
7. Antoine Watteau, *Les Bergers,* (1717, Charlottenburg, Berlin).
8. Antoine Watteau, *La Vraie Gaieté* (1702, National Gallery, London).
9. John Weaver, *An Essay towards an History of Dancing* (London, 1712), p. 65.
10. Ibid., p. 90.
11. Ibid., p. 160.
12. Ibid., p. 90.
13. LeBrun (Paris: E. Picart, 1698). Editions were published in Amsterdam in 1698 and 1713, English translations in London in 1701, 1734, etc., and a French-Italian edition in Verona in 1751, among others.

Opera Criticism and the Venetian Press by *Eleanor Selfridge-Field*

Criticism of the arts in the modern sense did not exist at the time Vivaldi was born. However, some commentaries on musical performance do survive. They are preserved in two kinds of sources that are markedly dissimilar: monthly journals and chronicles that are roughly analogous to the files of the Central Intelligence Agency. The link between these two kinds of sources is explained simply by the fact that the Venetian government was highly censorial and rigorously bureaucratic; what news was not fit to print was nevertheless worth retaining, if for no other reason than to demonstrate that the censors were no rubber-stamp outfit. Needless to say, music was not a politically sensitive subject, at least not on the surface level at which censorship operated. Musical commentary, however, tended to surface among material that touched on religion or politics. It was common practice, for example, to report both on the substance of the homily and on the beauty of the mass at San Marco, or to say that the prince of a neighboring domain greatly enjoyed the opera. It is thus because musical commentary was so often an adjunct to religious or political discussion that it was vulnerable to suppression.

A link between government intelligence and public "news" was broadly established in the sixteenth and seventeenth centuries. The secret agents that every major city dispatched to every other major city in Europe were required to submit a report of the week's public and state events each Saturday night. Their reports, or *avvisi*, were in most cases not widely circulated, although in a few places in Italy (including for a time Venice) they were printed and sold publicly. Modern newspapers find some antecedents in these originally secret reports. This lineage is recognized by the modern word "gazette": Venetian *avvisi* were sold for two *soldi,* and the coin that was worth two *soldi* was the *gazzetta.*

Discussions of religion and politics, expressing complete support for the views of the sponsor, were a staple part of *avvisi,* but after perfunctory satisfaction of this requirement the reporter seems to have considered himself free to discuss anything he thought might interest his reader. Besides church services and opera productions he might give accounts of bull fights, processions, visits by foreign dignitaries, and important private entertainments. The approach was a broad-brush one that encouraged less formality in content than in style. *Avvisi* contained variable amounts of common gossip and, given that they were intended for a socially prominent and intellectually astute audience, they were also generous in the amount of commentary they devoted to the pursuits of ordinary people.

Among published models for the news monthly there were two principal types: the literary review and the court calendar. The literary review that emerged in Italy in the middle of the seventeenth century served as an annotated catalog of new books.[1] There was little or no criticism in the modern sense, but there was endless reiteration of facts that might emerge from a careful reading of the item in question. Music found virtually no mention in such periodicals because books about music were published at very rare intervals.

The best-known court review was the French *Mercure galant,* which combined elements of both the *avvisi* and the literary monthly.[2] Also published monthly, it offered numerous details about events at court, visits of foreign noblemen, and public spectacles together with the occasional report on a new book or a recent scientific discovery. Starting in 1677 it began to give commentaries on Italian opera. When in 1687 there appeared in Venice a broad-spectrum periodical named *Pallade veneta,*[3] there can be no question but that it was modeled quite consciously on the *Mercure galant.*

The year 1688 was one in which freedom of the press was dramatically decreased and extreme measures were taken to regulate the book trade. *Pallade veneta,* probably in response to these measures, ceased publication seventeen months after it began.[4] Despite the brevity of its existence as a printed periodical, *Pallade veneta* is a journal of great significance for modern historians of Venetian culture. In it are preserved some of the most detailed commentaries on opera and oratorio productions that survive from the Venetian Baroque, as well as similarly detailed accounts of many other kinds of music. These accounts were written, apparently, by someone named Francesco Coli, a gentleman from Lucca who served as a book censor for the Roman Inquisition.

It was common for journals of the seventeenth century to meet an early demise, but *Pallade veneta* was actually less typical than it at first seems: weekly manuscripts following the format of *avvisi* but all bearing the label "Pallade veneta" survive in fragmentary batches dating from 1698 to 1751. These manuscripts, many of which are preserved in the archive of the Venetian *inquisitori di stato*, are of anonymous authorship.[5] Following a trend noted in Roman and Neapolitan *avvisi*, these documents are progressively less informative with time. Yet they too are of interest for recording certain events that are otherwise recorded imprecisely or not at all. Clerical interests remain quite marked.

In the period of Vivaldi's youth, criticism was adulation. The commentary that survives is not simply positive, it is absolutely glowing. By some interpretations, the reasons for this may have been political. Journals such as *Pallade veneta*, it is held, were intended to flatter certain patrons, sometimes through flattering the employees or friends of the patrons. Certainly with regard to opera it must always be kept in mind that each Venetian theater was owned by an aristocratic family, and these families often had their own informal alliances with foreign princes who patronized one production over another. The superlative praise heaped on certain individuals in *Pallade veneta* may be understood to have existed within the confines of such intentions. It also served to reinforce the values of the Counter-Reformation and the Holy League by supporting friendly rulers.

Apart from being adulatory, criticism was ordinarily mere description. The most commonly described aspect of an opera production was its scenery. Carlo Pallavicino's *Elmiro*, which was given at the Teatro San Giovanni Grisostomo in 1687, was described in a scene-by-scene commentary of thirty pages in the inaugural issue of *Pallade veneta*. The correspondent was particularly impressed by an early scene that recreated a subterranean grotto. The grotto appeared to be very weathered. It was dimly lit at the far end and undoubtedly created just the right degree of

mysteriousness to suit the plot. Outside the grotto night was represented by a single "star" with a serrated edge. The "star" was
raised and lowered mechanically. Similarly impressive was the final
scene, a forest. Tapestries were hung from the boughs of the trees,
and there were statues, fountains, and broad pathways in this forest. A toad (undoubtedly also operated by a machine) hopped
from place to place. In a typically triumphal appearance, Peace
was seated among the clouds overhead.[6]

Other than the scenery, the libretto is the topic that occupies the
balance of the commentary on *Elmiro*. As in other cases, the plot
summary provided by *Pallade veneta* is a verbatim reproduction of
the synopsis found in the libretto. The scene-by-scene descriptions
of the action also incorporate the stage instructions found in the
libretto. The texts of arias that the commentator found especially
pleasing were given in the early volumes of the journal. In the first
number only, he provided a musical supplement (another trait copied from the *Mercure galant*) containing four arias from that
month's productions. One aria was from Pallavicino's *Elmiro* and
another from the same composer's *Gierusalemme liberata*. The
other two, which are not specifically identified in the source, were
from Domenico Gabrielli's *Maurizio*.[7] The *Pallade veneta* correspondent was moved to praise the merits of one of *Maurizio*'s singers, Barbara Riccioni, in a sonnet:

> Bella ceder convien, eccoti il core
> A quel musico labro, omai soggetto,
> Ragion già vuol, che in così vago oggetto
> Bandisca la barbarie, e abbracci amore.
>
> Allor'che canti, incanti, e con stupore
> Regna in Barbara voce ogni diletto
> Alla cui soavità cede ogni affetto
> Rapisce ogn'alma in estasi d'amore.
>
> Io dal tuo dir la mia speranza apprendo
> Che se non può ingannar un vago viso
> Il mio destin nel volto tuo discerno.
>
> Or la sorte variabile ravviso
> Non trasse il suon' un'alma dall'Inferno?
> Il tuo canto dà a molte il Paradiso.

The anagram of the singer's name—shortened from fifteen to four-
teen letters to suit the format of the sonnet—formed by the first

letter of each line was printed vertically, from top to bottom, in the journal. The sonnet was used repeatedly in *Pallade veneta* as a vehicle for praise. This one might be loosely paraphrased as follows:

In something as beautiful as your splendid voice
Barbarism is vanquished and love embraced.
When you sing you enchant.
Every delight reigns, every affect yields to the suavity of your voice.
Some say that voices such as yours can lure the damned out of Hell;
Your song may lead them all the way to Paradise.

Barbara Riccioni was a well-known singer at the end of the seventeenth century. She sang the role of Maurizio's sister Placilla. One aria by her that Coli takes pains to mention is a simple one in binary form, "Che m'inganni quel bel volto," for which he also gives the music. Despite Coli's enthusiasm for it, "Che m'inganni quel bel volto" was eliminated from the work in a February 1687 revision.[8]

The first number in the musical supplement for January is a moving da capo aria, "Venticelli," sung by Maurizio's father, Tiberio, as a soliloquy on abdication. Its vigorous basso continuo part, which calls to mind the fact that Gabrielli was prominent in the development of the violoncello literature, was allocated to the theorbo in a subsequent Modenese production of the work. All three surviving librettos for *Maurizio* show "Venticelli" to have been an interrupted aria, although it is reproduced without the interrupting recitative in *Pallade veneta*. All four arias of the January supplement are unusual in having been printed at all, for operas were performed from manuscript scores that were prepared in such haste that such details as second violin and viola parts were sometimes omitted.

If the journalist was not discussing the scenery or the singers, he was likely to be discussing the audience. Comments such as "the volume of listeners stupefied both the creators and the cast" (which was said in reference to *Gierusalemme liberata*) were fairly common. More conspicuous is a lengthy account of the social ineptitude of a foreign visitor, a pasha of Turkish Rumania. Of his visit to an unidentified opera *Pallade veneta* reported:

He occupied a box with various other dignitaries, and seeing the chandelier that lights the theater lowered and then stilled, he called out, "Well done, well done" and asked if the opera was over already.

He was impressed when the curtain went up, for a scene full of pomp was presented and there was a very noble dance. Asked if this pleased him, he said that there was dancing in his court but it was not so well done.

When he heard the voices of the singers, he was completely enchanted and asked his hosts [either] to bring the musicians to his lodgings or to take him to the theater every evening.

At the end of the work he saw a battle [scene] that was awesomely represented, and he yelled out "Brave soldiers!" One of his companions retorted that they were brave at pretending but that the [Venetian] Republic had [real soldiers] who were genuinely brave.

Finally, when he marveled at the abundance of the audience, it was pointed out to him that this was not the only theater [in town] but that there were five [others] for music drama and two for comedy, all of which were always filled to capacity, not to mention the people who listen[ed] from certain windows and from the gaming casino. He showed surprise at this and then uttered this exclamation of marvel, "In Constantinople war, disease, and famine make life perpetually miserable. There is never any joy. God alone knows why He bestows all his benefits on Christians!"[9]

This last remark on the pasha's behavior was undoubtedly provided for the benefit of the censors.

Pallade veneta was in fact aggressive enough to report on the "Off Broadway" equivalent of the opera circuit in Venice. Here is one example:

> There is in the parish of the Holy Apostles a private theater in which six young singers recite in music an opera called *Oronte* with such grace and composure that they should be promoted to the more famous theaters. . . . They appear with a richness of costume and beauty of scenery and in sum bring unusual consolation to those who hear them.[10]

Still more memorable is a commentary on an improvised theatrical production—perhaps a commedia dell'arte—given on Giovedì Grasso, the last feast day of Carnival:

> Before the fine palace [of the doge] of this Most Serene Republic on Giovedì Grasso there was erected a theater with two orders of columns, with statues and fireworks to be seen by His Serenity with the council and senators, and when the piazza was full of people and the sea was full of boats, this theater was opened with a very noble ball. . . .

A very fat and disproportional flying eagle with a daring and gallant youth astride him came out of the theater. It "flew" along a rope that was stretched from the theater structure to the top of the campanile. . . . When the "eagle" was about half way up [the rope], he [the youth] tossed into the air an infinite number of folios on which were written a beautiful madrigal.[11]

This extract gives a brief glimpse of the occasional recreations that occurred during Carnival season, when most new operas had their premieres.

Commentary concerning the Teatro Sant'Angelo, where most of Vivaldi's operas were produced, is not extensive in *Pallade veneta*. It had only been in existence for eleven years when the journal was started and was not quite so well established as such theaters as San Giovanni Grisostomo. Its singers and scenery did warrant some measure of acclaim. Angelica Vittaloni, "a singer so able that she deserves every praise," succeeded in "ravish[ing] the audience" as Fulvia (apparently in Orgiani's opera *Dioclete* of 1687).[12] The arietta "O quanto voglio ridere" was "sung with grace and ease," and her accomplishments inspired a sonnet that was published in the journal.[13] Nicolin Paris and Signora Volsechi were metaphorically complimented as the "two poles on which the machine of delight revolves"[14] for their roles in Antonio Gianettini's *Virginio consolo*, which was given at Sant'Angelo in 1704. *Artaserse*, also by Gianettini, was presented the following year and was anticipated by the correspondent with great enthusiasm (his report on its performance does not survive).[15]

If there is one element of the production that stands out in the commentaries on Sant'Angelo, it is the treatment of light in the overall stage scheme. This is especially noted in a description of Paolo Biego's opera *La Fortuna tra le disgratie*, where in the final scene there was a light that was "more luminous than the sun." The whole narrative,[16] which is too long to quote here, prompts the question of whether visual symbolism was consciously used in these productions.

The scenery for *La Fortuna* was apparently executed with the greatest precision. There were leaves on the trees, flowers in the gardens, and reefs and precipices at the seashore. There were numerous columns on the galleries, apartments, and palaces. There was running water in the fountains and there were storms on the sea. Jove created lightning and thunder. Boats bobbed on the waves.

The live swans brought great delight to the audience, and the bands of hunters and archers received great applause. Only at the conclusion of this commentary do we find passing mention of the leading man, Bernardo da Rimini.

As for commentary on Vivaldi himself, there is very little in *Pallade veneta* and all of it is by inference. This is owing partly to the poverty of source survival. Of Vivaldi's working years as an opera composer (1713–1739), only 1716, 1717, and 1739 are covered in the surviving *Pallade veneta* manuscripts, and even these years are not preserved completely on a week-by-week basis. In January 1717 "the magnificent *Incoronazione di Dario* opened with great applause,"[17] and in September of the same year Vivaldi's *Tieteberga* also "met with great applause" at the Teatro San Moisè.[18] "The ideas of the poet and those of the composer" were equally important, according to the correspondent, and this was high praise indeed, for in general the librettist was still considered to be chiefly responsible for the success or failure of an opera. The final reference to a work by Vivaldi is this one from November 1739:

> Saturday evening the Teatro Sant'Angelo was opened, and the production of a musical drama entitled *Feraspe* had its premiere. Great was the attendance and the applause merited by the *virtuosi* who sang in it, as well [as] all the other things that [must] coincide [in order to] make [opera] plausible.[19]

This last remark is striking and apt: to the critical mind of Vivaldi's time there was a great deal in addition to the quality of the musical performance that was of interest to the opera-goer, and however contrived and artificial the taste of that time may seem today, the aim was to make the lives that were depicted on the stage seem "plausible."

Pallade veneta sheds some implicit light on what this word "plausible" meant: oratorio, which is discussed at great length in other passages of this journal, was thought most successful when it "carried its hearers to paradise" or brought about some other but similarly celestial effect, whereas opera was accepted as a representation of earthly life that thrived on depicting worldly riches and could at best bring temporal pleasure to its hearers. In contrast to oratorio, opera was intended more to delight the senses than to elevate the soul.

When we fail to take into account this discrepancy in values of

Vivaldi's time, we are likely to misunderstand the composer's approach to his music. There is very little difference stylistically between Vivaldi's operas and his one surviving oratorio, *Juditha triumphans*, but similarity in style between works of different species was not a point of reference in his time. Opera was a preeminently empirical art, and this is really what countless descriptions of elaborate stage effects and sumptuous scenes should serve to remind us of. *Pallade veneta* would lead us to believe that the audience for operas and oratorios in Venice was essentially the same audience, and the composers were by and large the same as well. Yet *Pallade veneta* consistently asserts how lavishly operas were *staged*, while on the other hand it is always at pains to describe how lavishly oratorios were *sung*. There are numerous lengthy accounts of ornaments, fugues, chromaticism, accompaniment, and other purely musical details of oratorio performances. Yet in the great bulk of opera commentary there is rarely more than a perfunctory reference to "sweet canzonettes" or "disingenuous arias." Why? The oratorio was of course given during periods of religious introspection, such as Lent, and church doctrine forbade stimulation of the senses whenever there was any likelihood of distraction from religious contemplation. In some sense opera was a device to counterbalance that Counter-Reformation doctrine, an acceptable reaction to piety as long as it was confined to those parts of the liturgical year during which spiritual devotion was not held to be the only activity appropriate for the faithful. Thus for opera-goers who had been carried to paradise by the last oratorio they had seen, it was essential that they be reminded in every possible way that they were now back on terra firma. Undoubtedly producers did exult in this liberty to make life "plausible."

Flimsy as this opera criticism is, its progress over Vivaldi's lifetime is a noteworthy one. In 1687, when Vivaldi was nine years old, the music was sufficiently important that arias were quoted whole and singers praised in almost ingratiating sonnets. As time passed, music was increasingly only one element in an opera production, and by the time Vivaldi died it appears to have been a lesser one at that.

NOTES

1. Literary reviews were started in Rome (1668), Ferrara (1688), and Modena (1696). The earliest literary journal in Venice was the *Gior-*

nale veneto de' letterati (1671–1690); the bulk of its issues appeared within its first year of publication. Despite its title, the later *Giornale de' letterati d'Italia* (1710–1740) was a largely Venetian enterprise.

2. Disregarding name changes and publishing lapses, the *Mercure galant* (or *Mercure de France*) can be said to have commenced publication in the form in which it was known in the later seventeenth century in 1672. Cricitism of Venetian opera first appeared in 1677.

3. The full title of the first number reads: "PALLADE / VENETA, / Raccolta di fiorite e bizzarre / galanterie ne' Giardini / dell'Adria. / In cui di Mese in Mese si daranno gl'avvisi / de successi del Campo Cesareo, & / Polacco, e dell'Armata Veneta / in Levante. / Con altre virtuose Compositioni, Sonetti, / Amori, Ariette, con la Musica, / e vaghi accidenti occorsi in / questa Dominante." All the printed fascicles except that of February 1687 are in the Biblioteca Estense, Modena, shelf mark 90.d.39–42. The June 1687 fascicle is also found in the Biblioteca Nazionale Marciana, Venice. The author possesses fascicles for January and February 1687. Quotations from *Pallade veneta* in this commentary have been edited to conform with modern practice in regard to capitalization and punctuation, but the spelling, which is standard literary Italian of the time, is unaltered.

4. The publishing history of the second series of the *Giornale veneto* is not dissimilar. There were monthly issues from September 1687 through May 1688. Three further issues were published without any indication of the month (two in 1689 and one in 1690).

5. There are three sources for the *Pallade veneta* manuscripts: (1) Biblioteca Marciana, Cod. It. VII-1834 (= 7622), miscellaneous dates between 1698 and 1705; (2) Museo Correr, Venice, Cod. Cicognia 2071, fascicle "Notizie del Mondo," 1700; and (3) Archivio de Stato Veneto, Venice, Inquisitori di Stato, Busta 713, fascicle "Pallade veneta," random dates between 1702 and 1751. There are no folio numbers on any of these manuscripts; retrieval is by date.

An edition of the musical extracts (and music) from both the printed and the manuscript portions of the journal appears in Eleanor Selfridge-Field, *Pallade Veneta: Writings about Music in Venetian Society, 1650–1750* (Venice, 1984), while a brief résumé of extracts concerning painting, "Fragments of Art Criticism from a Forgotten Venetian Journal," appears in *Arte veneta* (1980).

6. *Pallade veneta*, January 1687, pp. 16–48 passim.

7. Ibid., pp. 67–70 contain the commentary on *Maurizio*; the sonnet appears on p. 71. The title of the work being described can be determined by comparing the aria texts and cast given in the journal with those in the libretto of *Maurizio*.

8. In addition to many source locations for one or other of these libret-

tos, both are preserved in the Music Library at the University of California, Los Angeles.

9. *Pallade veneta*, January 1687, pp. 79–82:

> Stavasi questo accompagnato da diversi nobili in un palchetto, e vedendo scender da alto la lumiera, che doveva render chiaro il teatro, come la vidde ferma, disse, "Bene, bene," e dimandò se l'opera era per anco finita. All'alzarsi della tela restò ammirato, rappresentandoseli all'occhio scena pomposa, ed un intreccio di nobilissimo ballo; richiesto se li piaceva, disse che anco davanti al Gran Sig[nor] si balla, mà non così bene.
>
> Al sentire le voci de' cantanti pareva incantato, e pregò quei signori a condurre ogni sera i musici in sua casa, o lui al teatro.
>
> Sul fine dell'opera vidde un'abbattimento terribilmente rappresentato, e disse, "Bravi soldati." Li fu risposto che quelli erano bravi da burla, ma che ne haveva la Repub[b]lica de' bravi da vero.
>
> In fine essendosi maravigliato del numeroso concorso, li fu detto che non era solo quel teatro, ma che ve n'erano cinque d'opere musicali, e dui di com[m]edie, sempre pieni, e oltre la gente che si porta a festini particolari, ed al ridutto del gioco. Parve a questo dire che restasse sorpreso, e dopo diede in questa esclamatione di meraviglia, "Oh! in Co[n]stantinopoli guerra, peste, e fame far sempre digiuni, sempre piangere, mai far allegrezza; e pure Dio non ci vede perchè vuol tutto il Suo bene a Cristiani."

10. Ibid., November, 1687, pp. 104–105: "Hanno nella parrocchia de' Santi Apostoli scoperto un privato trattenimenta dove sei virtuose giovani cantanti recitano in musica un'opera intitolata *L'Oronte*, con tanta gratia e disinvoltura che paiono allevate su più famosi teatri. . . . Compariscono con ricchezza d'habiti, con vaghezza di scene, ed in somma portano una non ordinaria consolatione a chi le sente."

11. Ibid., February 1687, pp. 24–26:

> Il Giovedì Grasso, davanti l'Eccelso Palazzo di questa Serenissima Repub[b]lica, s'innalza un teatro con doppio ordine di colonne, con statue e fuochi artificiali . . . al comparire di Sua Serenità con l'Eccelso Consiglio e Senatori, ed essendo ripiena la gran piazza di popoli, ed il mare di barche, apertosi questo nobil teatro. . . . Si serrò il teatro con un nobilissimo ballo. . . .
>
> Si vidde dal teatro uscir fuori una grossa e smisurata aquila volante sopra la quale sedea un'ardito e generoso giovine, quale sopra d'una corda che dal palco era tirata alla sommità dell'alto campanile di San Marco, se ne volò alla cima. . . . Alla metà del volo fece anch'egli volar per l'aria quantità infinità di fogli in cui si leggeva un bellissimo madrigale.

12. Ibid., February 1687, p. 65. *Dioclete* is not identified by name, but it is the only opera that was given at the Teatro Sant'Angelo in that season.

13. Ibid., February 1687, p. 66:

Fulvia dai pene all'alme, e fan le pene
Soavi ancor le voci tue canore,
E con le luci fulgide, e serene
Susciti negl'amanti immenso ardore.

Tu sola avvezza ad emular Sirene
Con dolce tirannia tormenti il core,
E spirando beltà puoi su le scene,
Il torto vendicar fatto ad amore.

Perchè se i lumi tuoi rimiro intanto,
E se la voce, oh Dio! stupido ascolto
Hai di canora, ed hai di bella il vanto.

Non sia dunque d'amore alcun disciolto,
Che a far perder il cor basta il tuo canto
Che a far perder il cor basta il tuo volto.

14. Ibid., November 8–15, 1704, p. 1: "Lunedì sera . . . furon[o] poste sul labro del Sig[no]re Nicolin Paris e della Sig[no]ra Volsechi, due poli su quali gira la machina del diletto, comparir p[er] la p[rim]a volta su le scene di S. Angiolo *Virginio consolo*."

15. Ibid., January 3–10, 1704/05, p. 1: "Uscirà venerdì sera su la scene di S. Angiolo il famoso *Artaserse*, che reso poetico del S[igno]r Pariati e armonioso anche nell'idea del suo regnare della musica del S[igno]r Gianet[t]ini, sperassi sarà di molto contento."

16. Ibid., January 1688, pp. 64–71.

17. Ibid., January 23–30, 1716/17, p. 2: "Sabbato pure scorso nel Teatro di Sant'Angelo hebbe principio il nuovo drama musicale in cui rappresentasi con magnificenza *L'incoronazione di Dario*, che riesce con applauso."

18. Ibid., October 16–23, 1717, pp. 2–3: "La sera del scaduto sabb[at]o . . . fu aperto il Teatro di S. Moisè, e su quelle scene cominciò la recita musicale del drama intitolato *Tie[te]berga*, in cui spicano egualm[en]te l'idee del poeta e del compositore della musica, a quali viene fatto grande applauso."

19. Ibid., November 7–14, 1739, pp. 3–4: "Sabbato sera si è aperto il Teatro a Sant'Angelo, e si cominciò la recita d'un drama musicale intitolato *Feraspe*, e fu tale il concorso e l'applauso quale meritano li virtuosi che lo recitano, e tutte le altre cose che concorrono a renderlo plausibile."

PART III

The Practice of Opera Seria

Voice Register as an Index of Age and Status in Opera Seria *by Roger Covell*

The apparent relationship of voice register to status and character-ization in opera continues in our own time to maintain or develop certain conventions. The falsetto voice, or countertenor voice as it is often called, seems to have grown or regrown two consistent associations in twentieth-century opera: first, with real or feigned madness, second, with supernatural beings who have something sexless or at least enigmatic in their identity. In the second (super-natural) category we can cite Britten's Oberon in *A Midsummer Night's Dream* and the voice of Apollo in *Death in Venice*; in the first, the flights into falsetto of the captain in *Wozzeck* and, in Rei-mann's *Lear*, the choice of a tenor (Edgar) who becomes a counter-tenor during his feigned madness as Poor Tom. So potent is the convention, as exemplified in Reimann's opera, that the character of Lear himself, played by a baritone, sings pointedly in falsetto in part I of the work at the word *Wahnsinn* in the line "Auf dem Weg liegt Wahnsinn [That way madness lies]." The prevalence of British countertenors at present, incidentally, is a tiny echo and parallel in our century of the assumption in the seventeenth and eighteenth centuries that castratos were usually Italians, though the twentieth-century phenomenon might be attributed to spontaneous affinity (as well as to the legacy of the English cathedral choir tradition) in a way that cannot be applied to the earlier circumstance.

Such matters are not without relevance to the performance of Vivaldi's *Orlando furioso* by the Dallas Opera: a distinguished British countertenor, James Bowman, was asked, in Dallas, as in Verona, to take the part of Ruggiero in Vivaldi's opera in default of (I say this with no disrespect to Mr. Bowman) a castrato singer. Furthermore, it is pertinent to note that operatic treatment of Or-lando's madness by another great composer—Handel in his *Or-*

lando (1733)—contains a role for a person gifted with the powers of an enchanter, Zoroastro, who sings in the bass register. We may sense here, momentarily, a possible contrast between the idea of supernatural being as countertenor in our own time and magician as bass in the time of Vivaldi and Handel.[1] I am not sure the contrast is an exact one, even if it is conceded that the notion of attaining magical powers through a voluntary loss of virility is widely circulated in some of the stories relating to the Arthurian enchanter Merlin and, more topically, in the character of Klingsor in Wagner's *Parsifal*. Klingsor, in fact, is a bass, a circumstance explicable through the fact that his castration has taken place in adulthood.[2]

In discussing Baroque opera, as it happens, we need to discard the notion of voice register related to virility. As will become apparent from some of the instances mentioned in this paper, this does not seem to have been a relevant consideration in the period of opera seria. The tradition, I believe, that Handel and, in his own way, Wagner were following was related to the conjunction of age with power of a certain kind. Age keyed to knowledge and to what may pass for wisdom, or age viewed as the accumulation of experience or the successful negotiation of degrees of initiation is an aspect of the tribal part of our inheritance and is just as significant when we rebel against it as when we accept it. The notion seems to have been particularized and limited, fundamentally, through the influence of the Old Testament and then stabilized in the powerful imagery of Renaissance art in a God who was not only male but white-bearded. A boy's voice changes and deepens during puberty, so (the argument goes) a society dominated by the male ethos, most tellingly revealed in its idea of a supreme godhead, will have inbuilt associations of voice register with age and initiated wisdom.[3] To put it briefly: the older the deeper, with its corollary, the deeper the wiser. Hence we may hope to identify a generally logical basis for the allotment of the bass register in Baroque opera to male gods and to magicians, enchanters, and similar personages. When there is no bass voice, the tenor voice, as we shall note later, may take over some of this symbolic function.

The figure of the magician (or supernatural controller) is far from being peripheral in the history of opera. Even if we assess the stories of the earliest surviving operas by Peri, Caccini, and Monteverdi as tributes to the extraordinary power of music rather than to the accumulated craft of an enchanterlike figure,[4] we cannot fail to notice that the authority of a godhead is apt to be expressed through voices in the bass register. Persuasiveness may belong to the tenor-baritone of an Orfeo; a determining power like that of Plutone adheres to the bass or deeper baritone register. The controlling deity of much of Monteverdi's *Il ritorno d'Ulisse* is the god Nettuno, whose powers keep Ulisse from his homecoming as long as possible. Nettuno's bass register prohibitions are voided only through the active support of Ulisse by Minerva.[5] In this case, Minerva's sex determines her vocal register, the high register that belongs, as will be apparent from later examples in this paper, to youth and love. The music of Ulisse himself falls comfortably into the high baritone or low tenor range. The contrasts of vocal register typical of the later period of opera seria are already apparent, however, in Monteverdi's final opera, *L'incoronazione di Poppea*. The elder magician-figure of Seneca, if we may so describe him, is an enchanter whose power has departed. Valletto explicitly mocks his lack of potency.[6] Wisdom has been reduced to sententiousness, authority to a hoary-headed posturing. The winners—and the term is appropriate to the plot and ethos of *L'incoronazione*—are the young lovers, both of them singing in a high register, and Nerone, sung by a male soprano, has the higher voice of the two. At least as early as 1642, in other words, we are able to discern a characteristic antagonism in opera between precept-ridden age, represented in the bass register, and willful but heaven-approved youth, fulfilled in the soprano register.

In Peri's *Euridice* of 1600 the part of Orfeo, originally sung by the composer himself, fits the same kind of high baritone or low tenor voice as Monteverdi's Ulisse. We must assume that there was no convention related to voice register in 1600 to discourage Peri, a renowned singer, from taking the leading part. As late as 1639 to 1640, as noted above, the voice register assigned to the eponym of *Il ritorno d'Ulisse* matches the specifications of the *Euridice* of Peri in terms of heroic voice register. Three years later, however, the demands of a paying public and the conventions of regular performance had been sufficiently well established, it seems, for a pattern to be set that would predominate through what is sometimes identified as the period (in approximate terms, of course) of opera seria, i.e., the end of the seventeenth century and at least the first half of the eighteenth century: the hero of *L'incoronazione* is a soprano.

It is noteworthy that the librettist Sbarra apologizes in 1651 for putting little ditties (ariettas) in the mouths of Alexander the Great and other heroes.[7] He does not call for any indulgence for the fact that these ditties are likely to be sung by a castrated singer in an "unnatural" vocal register. The implications of this are worth some thought. We are familiar with the existence of a body of opinion in England and France in the seventeenth century that could not accept the notion of a wholly sung drama. Hence the conventions adopted in the so-called semi-opera in England, in which only certain types of character were licensed to sing: namely, supernatural beings, servants or subsidiary characters, and those whose states of mind (such as being drunk, mad, or in love) sanctioned the idea of their bursting into song.[8] It is less generally known that a body of opinion in Italy, embodying literary opinion in particular, was also troubled by the aesthetics of a wholly sung drama. Concessions to this feeling are to be found in the election of gods or semidivine mythical personages as principal singing characters and in the early insistence on dramatic recitative as the principal medium of expression and communication for major characters. Arias in triple meter and extended coloratura were mainly reserved in the early Venetian period for gods, pastoral characters, musicians by vocation, and servants (more or less comic) or subordinate characters. The apology for Alexander's ditties cited above testifies to the persistence of these qualms well into the professional and public period of opera. (It is still being echoed by an Italian writer, Francesco Algarotti, in his study of opera published in 1755, in which he makes the same kind of complaint about the arias sung by a Julius Caesar or a Cato.)[9] In negative terms it also indicates that the appropriateness of voice register to historical characters of heroic stature is of lesser significance than the notion that they should sing at all.

In one sense the conventions settled upon in opera seria for the relationship between voice register and characterization represent a process of impoverishment, partly owing to the banishment of farcical characters. The fruity tenors and contraltos who played the comic, lecherous nurses of Venetian operatic tradition have disappeared from the list of *interlocutori*,[10] and so have the comically stuttering tenors of subordinate degree. The baritonal tenor heroes who were reasonably well represented in opera until the early 1640s have largely (though certainly not completely) gone; the bass voices of enchanters are heard much less frequently, except in magic operas (and notably in Handel's *Orlando*); and a contralto or soprano enchantress may be heard in Vivaldi's *Orlando furioso* or Handel's *Alcina*. But some voices gain new opportunities. The contralto as prima donna becomes increasingly acceptable in the early years of Alessandro Scarlatti; and the contralto donna is more frequently employed as the young male hero or the principal antagonist.[11]

It is at least possible that the strong personality and identity of those comic and exotic characters who sang in the tenor and bass registers may have helped to widen the gap in status and association between upper voices (male or female) and lower voices (male) in the casting of opera seria once the members of the Arcadian Academy had succeeded in banishing conventional comic characters from that genre. The comic associations of some tenor and bass voices may have reinforced any general preference for upper voices because of the unwelcome laughter that the associations of male voices might evoke in serious characterizations.

The only secure basis for an estimate of the correspondences between voice types and roles in opera seria is an accurate knowledge of which categories of singers sang which parts. This is not always as easy to determine as might at first appear and is not consistent in its application from one operatic center to another. A number of considerations have to be taken into account in trying to decide what conventions may be taken as representative or customary. Among them are the special law that prohibited the appearance of women on the stage in Rome during the eighteenth century and that therefore entailed the use of all-male casts, with (in some cases) a consequent adjustment in voice register to allow for the generally lower ranges of artificial sopranos taking women's roles; the particular shortages of castratos which appear to have influenced operatic casting from time to time (for example, in London in the 1750s), thereby resulting in an unusually generous allotment of nominally male roles to women; not to mention the local and temporary unavailability of certain singers and certain types of singers who might have been favored by composers in ideal circumstances.[12]

Our access to a manuscript score of an opera seria may give us an accurate idea of the voice registers that the composer or, in some cases, the local arranger or copyist intended to allot to each character. This is not, of course, proof that the singers used in the relevant performances actually sang in those registers: they may have engaged in transposition, perhaps with the approval of the composer or the local arranger or musical director. The practice of including the names of singers for each principal part in printed librettos, a practice that developed rapidly in the first quarter of the eighteenth century, is one of the best means we have of determining the voice registers actually used in specific performances, provided we know the classification and characteristics of the voices of the singers concerned. Other singers may have been called in to substitute for the named singers in case of sickness or other disability, and parts may have been (and no doubt were) transposed to suit them when this was necessary. The incidence of these cases, however, is not likely to have been enormous and, in any case, does not affect the significance of the *intentions* of composers and entrepreneurs, as revealed at the moment when it was considered prudent and timely to print the libretto for the performances concerned.

In order to determine the voice register of a given singer we may have to rely on a mixture of contemporary testimony and the inspection of scores in certain cases. Although relatively rare, cases do exist where we can be quite certain that a surviving manuscript score of a particular opera was the one used for the particular performances commemorated in a printed libretto and in which the singers were those named in the libretto. There are such instances: scores dated to coincide with a known series of performances and where the arias in the scores themselves bear the names of some or all of the principal singers who are named in the corresponding libretto.[13] Where we rely on contemporary descriptions of singers we must expect to find, and do find, some disagreement. Singers may be variously described as a *sopranista* or a *contraltista*; and in some cases there may be no history of a loss of upper notes with increasing age (as is the case for the great soprano Faustina Bordoni) to account for an apparent diminution or shift of compass. We surmise that in such cases the continued use of, say, the soprano clef may be based on convention or on personal status and vanity, and Tosi confirms that we are not being uncharitable in our supposition.[14]

Even when we are able to establish that the part for any given singer is written in a particular clef, whether soprano, mezzo-soprano, alto, tenor, or bass, that does not mean that we are automatically entitled to call the singer in question a soprano, a contralto, a tenor, or whatever. Inspection of many parts written in the tenor clef in this period discloses that their actual range is closer to high- or even medium-range baritone by today's reckoning. Some soprano clefs seem to have been allotted out of the courtesy due to a singer playing one of the young lovers' roles rather than as a result of rational choice of the most suitable clef for the compass of the voice. Some parts, whether through deliberate policy or as the result of copyists' inconsistencies, are written in different clefs in different acts or scenes.

It is a rare piece of good fortune when we come across a libretto that not only lists the singers but classifies them in the way we should do today (approximately, if not exactly) as soprano, tenor, contralto, or whatever. Out of the 1,274 librettos from the period 1701 to 1800 whose basic details of performance are summarized by Taddeo Wiel in his invaluable publication of 1897, *I teatri musicali veneziani del settecento*,[15] three, and only three, print voice classifications alongside the singers' names. These are (1) *Cimene* of 1721, set by Girolamo Bassani and Marco Zucchini; (2) *Giulio Flavio Crispo*, set by Giammaria Capelli in 1722; and (3) *Mitridate, re di Ponto* of 1723, also set by Capelli.

It is certainly not an accident that each of these three instances involves a libretto by Benedetto Pasqualigo. Pasqualigo, one of many Venetians of noble rank who practiced the trade of librettist from the earliest years of Venetian opera onward, deserves special attention in the history of the libretto for more reasons than can be detailed here. It is enough to say that at a time when the librettist liked to have his printed text regarded as a tragedy or drama or comedy that merely happened to be set to music by this or that composer, Pasqualigo almost aggressively emphasized that the sole purpose of his text was to furnish the verbal materials for singing. His habitual description of his serious works as *tragedie da cantarsi* is refreshing, a contrast to the practice even of such a complete professional as Metastasio, who liked to think that his dramas were even more successful when spoken than when sung. Where Zeno, in the manner of a dramatist for the spoken theater, is apt to describe his list of characters as "those who speak," Pasqualigo emphatically spells out the implications of the enterprise in which he is engaged by using the parallel phrase, "those who sing." [16] His prefaces are not addressed, as are those of most of his colleagues, to his readers but to his listeners (*agli uditori*).

Pasqualigo's punctiliousness in providing accurate descriptions of everyone engaged in the operatic enterprise extended to a rare scrupulousness in editing and proofreading. My impression is that the casting of operas for which he wrote the texts is consistently better than average. Some of the singers classified by voice type in the three librettos I have cited are not, I believe, identified so unequivocally elsewhere. Pasqualigo's helpful explication through titling and labeling extends in some of his cast lists to providing a succinct cluster of adjectives to characterize the personages to be portrayed. Some examples: "superstitious and passionate," "a friend of heroic virtue," "of a nature sympathetic, amorous, and less than barbarous," "hospitable and amorous" (this of a royal princess), "constant, quarrelsome, and heroically amorous," "fierce, deceitful, and jealous." [17] In addition to the conventional descriptions of rank and relationship that we find in most librettos we are able here to pair the author's own opinion of the character he has imagined with the type of voice allotted to that character. We might well arrive at a similarly pithy summary of the character from our reading of the text, but we might not be quite sure that this was how an early eighteenth-century librettist would have viewed such a personage; and it may be that we have here an important additional tool in arriving at a comprehensive inventory of character types as conceived at the time of the original presentations of the works concerned.

For the purpose of this paper I have consulted scores and librettos in a number of European centers, notably London, Munich, Vienna, Florence, and Venice. I certainly cannot pretend, however, to have examined every document that might have helped my task. My plan has been to use the basic tool provided by Wiel's summary of eighteenth-century Venetian operatic events to furnish a systematic or at least consistently focused supplement to the random correspondences and lucky finds that any researcher is likely to come across.

I have also devoted most of my attention to some of the major texts of Metastasio, the most influential librettist of his time and whose texts were set most frequently to music—up to 102 times in the case of his libretto for *Artaserse*.[18] From some points of view the most advantageous period in which to establish original and subsequent practice in the setting of a single text is in Metastasio's earlier years as court poet in Vienna, in the relatively short but fruitful period in which his texts were first set by Antonio Caldara, *vice-maestro di cappella* of the imperial court. In those years Metastasio was working at the height of his powers in close, if admittedly not always ideally sympathetic, proximity with a brilliant composer. He also was working in a milieu in which casting at the highest levels of accomplishment, without compromise, was possible financially and strategically. The choices of Metastasio and Caldara in these works are of unusual interest in being the product of a theoretically ideal situation (in practice Metastasio felt much less kinship with Caldara than he felt later with Hasse). The task is made easier by the fact that there are still to be seen in Vienna both Caldara's original scores and the official commemorative copies made of them, together with representative copies of the instrumental parts for the operas concerned. We can rarely be as sure as we are here that we know how the creative wishes of composer and librettist were translated through an allocation of voices to parts.

The subsequent settings of these Metastasian texts, often staged in circumstances and under pressures widely divergent from those characterizing the imperial court in Vienna, furnish a comparison more acceptable, I believe, than an attempt to equate the nature and function of characters in texts of differing subject matter. In such circumstances, often drastically changed as they were, without the personal presence of the librettist as a factor in the composer's planning, the likelihood of major changes in the conception of roles is considerable. Any persistent casting of these roles in terms of particular voice registers, if that casting is not to be taken as virtually automatic (as it might be in the case of the allotment of a soprano voice to the role of the prima donna), may be of some significance. It gives, I repeat, a better basis for comparison than the attempt to classify characters of different names in different stories as essentially the same, and the examples we find in Wiel's chronological lists are numerous: approximately one-eighth of all the operas represented in Venice between 1725 and 1798 were settings of Metastasian texts. I have thought it reasonable to include some non-Venetian works and performances in my tabulations, if only as a check on the possibility that we might be unwittingly establishing the coherence of a Venetian, rather than a pan-European, tradition.

The consistencies in casting by voice register are impressive, sometimes to the point of being startling, especially in settings of the same (or nominally the same) text extending across considerable periods of time. Caldara allots the role of the scheming Aquilio in Metastasio's *Adriano in Siria* to a bass; yet all the immediately subsequent settings give the part to a female singer—not because she is female but, I believe, because a female will have the appropriate voice range. In this case we seem to have—and I deliberately cite it first as involving a contradiction between the first setting and later ones—an attempt at innovation or perhaps a bow to expediency on the part of the original composer, followed by a restoration of an older convention by the composers who succeeded him. The point about Aquilio is that he secretly hopes to win the hand of the princess that Adriano also favors. He is not merely treacherous, he is a rival in love. The hypothesis we can state here is twofold: Aquilio is allotted a high voice because he is a lover, however unworthy and dishonorable. Yet he is not a principal of the highest rank and is therefore not endowed with the kind of male voice (the castrato soprano or contralto) that belongs to that rank. There is a complementary consideration of a practical and circumstantial kind. When the number of people involved in love approaches the total of the principals normally to be found in operatic casting of the period—that is, six or seven—it follows that less important male parts will have to be given to voices other than those belonging to the limited number of skillful castratos available at any one time. There is a similar divergence from convention on Caldara's part in *L'Olimpiade* and, it seems, an immediate restoration of conventional principles among composers who came after him chronologically. Caldara provided Clistene, the king in *L'Olimpiade*, with a part written in the alto clef. His successors, beginning in this case with Vivaldi, showed great unanimity in reallocating the part to a bass or a tenor: Clistene has no involvement in love, only in justice.

Marcello, in his satirical *Il teatro alla moda*, makes a characteristically sweeping but significant remark to the effect that "the parts of fathers or tyrants (when these are principal roles) will always be reserved for the castratos, leaving tenors and basses to make do with being captains of the guard, *confidenti* of the king, shepherds, messengers, etc."[19] The truth is not exactly like that. Fathers and tyrants, whose names often furnish the opera with its title (and so are not to be thought of as merely incidental to the action), are as likely to be tenors as to be castrato sopranos and contraltos. Marcello's reference (in his parenthetical phrase) to the special case of fathers and tyrants being principal roles may require a speculative explanation. My guess is that their status as principals in Marcello's usage, as distinct from being merely prominent figures, would depend on their being in love. The preference for a castrato voice in such a role will be based, it seems, largely on the circumstance of whether the father or tyrant is in love or, to refine the definition a stage further, whether he is successful in the love that he feels. If he is not in love or is not successful in love then, in certain periods and places, he is more likely to be a tenor than a castrato singer. The principle at work is simply that reciprocated love inhabits the highest vocal registers available.

General confirmation of Marcello's opinion can be found even in the career of a bass who had some outstanding opportunities in eighteenth-century London. Antonio Montagnana, within four years in London in the 1730s, had roles as apparently various as an enchanter, a high priest, an ancient and loyal retainer, and a general (not merely a captain) of the army. Yet an English journal of the day, in the process of making what appears to have been a satirical point about the British government, took Montagnana's operatic employment as its cue for observing that the Italian singer "was always obliged to act (except an angry, rumbling song or two) the most insignificant parts of the whole drama."[20] It is true that Montagnana had his angry, rumbling songs (angry rumbling being one of the ways in which florid bass virtuosity expresses itself), but to equate them always with insignificant roles is not appropriate to their size and scope in particular operas. In Handel's *Orlando*, for example, Montagnana's tally of opportunities in the part of the enchanter Zoroastro included two extraordinarily effective pieces of accompanied recitative and arioso (invocations both). One of them is the number that opens the opera, the other the prelude to the resolution of the story. Together with three arias

of the most splendid and forceful kind, they were sumptuously in-
strumented, grand and swaggering affairs by any standards. His
dramatic status as puppet-master in this work is clear. He sets up
the framework for the action and his office as mentor and con-
science to Orlando involves turning the entire story into a kind of
painful moral lesson for the young hero, a sort of *Bildungsoper*.
As the eponym of Handel's opera, Orlando was allotted to a *contraltista*, the celebrated Senesino. However puppetlike Orlando's
relationship to Zoroastro was, there is no denying that his vocal
opportunities proclaim his right to be considered the leading performer. In the *Angelica ed Orlando* of Gaetano Latilla (1735), on
the other hand, the role of Orlando has been shifted so far from
centrality, has become so incidental to the love story of Angelica
and Medoro, that we are not entirely surprised to find that he is a
tenor.[21] In Pescetti's *Angelica e Medoro*, as performed in London
in 1739, in which Orlando reads the inscriptions of true love but
has no mad scene and in which Angelica and Medoro make their
way from the scene before Orlando can catch up with them, he
has dropped further in register (and, surely, in status) to become
a bass.[22]

Individual cases of consistent status or changed status as apparently exemplified in the allotment of voice register could only be
pursued further in this paper at the expense of more space than is
available. The additional generalizations I am about to list sev-
erally require more documentation and discussion than they can
now receive. Further, some of them undoubtedly require continued testing and modification. They are offered as working principles, not as universal laws, in unavoidably summary form.
Although the relevant notes list specific cases where these generalizations seem to apply, the phrase "mostly, but not always" can be
taken to qualify most or all of the following assertions:

1. If the heir to a kingdom in opera seria is portrayed by a castrato soprano, his brother (sometimes discovered later to be the
real heir) will often be played by a woman. The brother in such a
case will usually be a younger brother.[23]

2. The role of male *confidente* is often taken by a woman. If the
confidente is secretly in love with one of the *primi amorosi* this
makes the employment of a woman singer apparently more likely.
If the trusted adviser is the secret enemy of the person who trusts
him the choice of a woman for the role becomes, it appears, more

likely still. The explanation I offer tentatively is this: jealousy and enmity are usually based in the operas on the workings of love (including, of course, rejected love). Love's domain is that of the high or highish voice. If, as is usually the case, there is no castrato soprano or contralto available to portray the *confidente*, a voice provided by a woman singer is the obvious answer to the need.[24]

3. A transsexual disguise, as has often been noted, increases the possibility that a castrato will be asked to take a female role or a woman a male role. In other circumstances, leaving aside the special case of Rome, the use of women in male roles was more common than the reverse. Some women in eighteenth-century opera seria, as in the seventeenth century, specialized in playing male roles, but this did not prevent their alternating such parts with female characterizations. Lucia Lancetti, Vivaldi's original Orlando in 1727, played in eleven operas in Venice between 1722 and 1737. Two of her roles were female, the last nine all male.[25]

4. If any doubt exists as to which two characters have supremacy in an opera seria (and if that doubt is not resolved by the relative prowess of the singers employed or by the number and placing of solo arias), they can be infallibly identified by their singing of the work's (usually) solitary duet. This duet, though often placed in a third and final act, is also found elsewhere. In Metastasio's text for *L'Olimpiade*, for example, the duet occurs at the end of act 1. This duet, unlike its third-act counterparts in other works, does not represent resolution and reconciliation but is the first strong premonition of possible disaster. The denouement of *L'Olimpiade* is designed to be too swift to allow time for a duet.[26]

5. The temporary deepening of tessitura to represent strong emotion, such as occurs in Cavalli,[27] or the reverse shift in the work of some later composers is not relevant to the initial creative decision allying a certain part to a certain voice register. The classification of register for this purpose is always relative. A highish range in Porpora will be low by the later standards of, say, Traetta.[28]

6. Even if the *primo uomo* is assigned a higher solo tessitura than the prima donna their duet together will be formalized by her taking the upper line and him the lower in a relationship largely defined, except for exchanged phrases (imitation or echo), by the closest possible intervals of normally consonant harmony.[29]

7. One of the most effective antagonists in the Metastasian op-

era is the unappeasably hostile barbarian king and warrior, whose rough integrity and implacable opposition demand a kind of admiration. Examples are Osroa in *Adriano in Siria* and Iarba in *Didone abbandonata*. Such antagonists are almost invariably tenors (a tradition that goes back at least to the practice of Cavalli), the "almost" in this case being so little short of standardization as to suggest that the exceptions were due to the expedients of day-to-day casting. The more ferocious the barbarian-warrior type the more likely he is to be a tenor and the more florid will be his vocal line. Floridity, and not relative height of tessitura will be one of the characteristics of the force and potency of his opposition.[30] If, however, his ferocity softens sufficiently to allow him to be involved in passionate love, even if this love is expressed mainly as jealousy, then almost as certainly he will not be a tenor but a soprano or contralto.

8. The difference between soprano and mezzo-soprano registers is not critical in a generic sense[31] though it may have meaning within the practice of an individual composer.

NOTES

1. Vivaldi's *Orlando furioso* contains no male enchanter but a mezzo-soprano enchantress, Alcina, as does Haydn's *Orlando paladino*, a considerably later work.

2. Gurnemanz tells the story of Klingsor's self-castration in act 1: "Ohnmächtig, in sich selbst die Sünde zu ertöten, / an sich legt' er die Frevlerhand . . .Darob die Wut nun Klingsorn unterwies, / wie seines and Klingsor confirms it in act 2: "Ungebändigten Sehnens Pein, / . . . den ich zum Todesschweigen mir zwang. . . ." It is said that Wagner heard castratos in Roman church music and toyed with the idea of using one of them to take the part of Klingsor at Bayreuth, transposing the music suitably. Obviously, and prudently, he did not do this (Angus Heriot, *The Castrati in Opera* [London, 1956], p. 21, note 1).

3. A lesser but analogous association may attach itself to female voice registers, based on the observable fact that some women's voices deepen in middle to old age, though for different physiological reasons.

4. This type of personage becomes relatively prominent in the earliest operas performed in the public opera seasons presented in Venice from 1637, e.g., Astarco Mago in the first opera of the Ferrari-Manelli troupe, *L'Andromeda*. The dedication of a laudatory sonnet

in the published libretto tells us that Manelli himself doubled the parts of Astarco and Nettuno.

5. Ultimately this support has to be ratified through intercession with a tenor, Giove, much more remote as a governing influence in this opera than the bass, Nettuno.

6. Cf. the Valletto's characterization of Seneca as "Il gabba Giove." *L'incoronazione* act 1, scene 6.

7. Francesco Sbarra, preface to *L'Alessandro vincitor di se stesso* (Venezia, 1651): "Sò che l'Ariette cantate da Alessandro, e Aristotele, si stimeranno contro il decoro di Personaggi si grandi; ma sò ancora, ch'è improprio il recitarsi in Musica, non imitandosi in questa maniera il discorso naturale, e togliendosi l'anima al componimento Drammatico, che non deve esser altro, che un imitatione dell'attioni humane, e pur questo difetto non solo è tolerato dal secolo corrente: ma ricevuto con applauso . . ."

8. Categories already defined in the assignment of songs in Elizabethan-Jacobean theater.

9. Francesco Algarotti, *Saggio sopra l'opera in musica* (Livorno, 1763), quoted in translation in Oliver Strunk, *Source Readings in Music History* (New York, 1950), pp. 660–661: ". . . the subjects taken from history are liable to the objection of their not being so well adapted to music, which seems to exclude them from all plea of probability. This impleaded error may be observed every day upon the Italian stage. For who can be brought to think that the trillings of an air flow as justifiably from the mouth of a Julius Caesar or a Cato as from the lips of a Venus or Apollo?"

10. They went on in comic opera. Simone de Falco was a tenor who acted the aged female roles in Neapolitan opera from ca. 1717 to ca. 1738. Cf. Michael Robinson, *Naples and Neapolitan Opera* (Oxford: Clarendon Press), p. 203. Some examples of operas in which we find the *vecchia nutrice* part played by a tenor are Cesti's *L'Argia*, Boretti's *Claudio Cesare*, Pallavicino's *Galieno*, P. A. Ziani's *L'Heraclio* and *La Semiramide*, Zanettini's *Medea in Atene*, and Sartori's *Seleuca*. Freschi's *Sardanapolo* contains an instance of a *vecchia nutrice* part in the alto clef. So do Cesti's *La Dori*, Cavalli's *Giasone*, Stradella's *Corispero*, and Provenzale's *Lo schiavo di sua moglie*.

11. There are no fewer than four male roles taken by women in Scarlatti's *Pompeo* of 1684 in Naples: Cf. Rolando Celletti, "La vocalità," in *La storia della opera* (Torino, 1977), vol. 3, p. 52.

12. As implied in the foregoing paragraph, the practical consequences of the availability or unavailability of certain singers (or certain types of singers) for a particular opera must be taken into account in any study of preferences in casting. Affluent centers, or at least those with

the readiest access to a wide range of singers, will probably be a better guide to principles and ideals than those theaters, cities, or courts where some types of singers were in chronically short supply and where compromises were necessary for much of the time. London's limited access to castratos (a few celebrated soloists excepted) must tend to make it a special case in the matching of roles and voice registers. Winton Dean, in *Handel and the Opera Seria* (London: Oxford University Press, 1970), pp. 14–15, points out that Handel's operas, almost all of them written for London, contain at least twenty-six male roles composed for women and eight or nine others, originally written for castratos, that he assigned to women in revivals. On the other hand, my impression is that the patterns are remarkably consistent in view of the exigencies and emergencies that are the lot of all opera productions.

13. One example is a manuscript score apparently associated with performances of Hasse's *Demofoonte* at Dresden in 1748 (GB-Lbl Add. Ms 32,025), in which the names of "Sig^r Annibali," "Sig^{ra} Faustina," "Sig^r Amorevoli," Sig^r Carestini," "Sig^r Bindi," and Sig^{ra} Mingotta" are written at the head of arias sung by them in the opera. Here the names may be correlated with the clefs (alto, soprano, tenor, alto, soprano, and soprano, respectively) and, no less important, with the actual ranges specified in the score. Faustina (Bordoni), for example, does not go above an F-sharp while Bindi, written for in the same clef, is asked to take his soprano voice as high as D in alt. Another example of a manuscript score containing indications of arias assigned to two castratos, "Farfallino" (Giacinto Fontana detto Farfallino) and (Giovanni) "Carestini," is presumably related to the 1730 performances in Rome of Vinci's *Artaserse*. This score bears the date and the name of the theater. The singers mentioned belonged to the Roman cast of that year (Lbl Add. ms 22,106).

14. P. F. Tosi, *Opinioni de' cantori antichi e moderni o sieno osservazioni sopra il canto figurato*, 1723, in *La scuola di canto dall'epoca d'oro (secolo XVII): Con note ed esempi di Luigi Leonesi* (Napoli: Di Gennaro e Morano, 1904), p. 44: "Il maestro se ne sovvenga, poichè crescendo l'età, la voce declina, e in progresso di tempo o canterà il contralto o, pretendo per vanità insulta il nome di soprano, gli converrà di raccomandarsi ad ogni compositore, affinchè le note per lui, non passino il quarto spazio, non vi si fermino."

15. T. Wiel, *I teatri musicali veneziani del settecento* (Venezia, 1897); reprinted Bologna: (Forni, 1978).

16. For example, "Persone, che cantano" in Pasqualigo's *Ifigenia in Tauride, tragedia da cantarsi* (Venezia: Marino Rossetti, 1719) or in *Cimene* (Venezia, 1721), "Li virtuosi cantanti nella tragedia."

17. The originals are as follows: "superstiziosa e passionata" (Ifigenia in *Ifigenia in Tauride*); "amico d'eroica virtù" (Pilade in *Ifigenia*); "d'animo condiscendente, amatorio, e meno che barbaro" (Toante in *Ifigenia*); "costante, rissentita, ed eroicamente amorosa" (Ismene, Vergine Greca, in *Mitridate, re di Ponto*); "feroce, dissimulatore, e geloso" (Mitridate in *Mitridate, re di Ponto*).

18. Franz Stieger, *Opernlexicon I* (Tutzing: Schneider, 1975).

19. B. Marcello, *Il teatro alla moda* (Venezia, 1720), p. 12: "La *Parte* di *Padre*, o di *Tiranno* (quando sia la principale) dovrà sempre appoggiarsi a CASTRATI; riserbando *Tenori*, e *Bassi* per gli *Capitani di Guardia, Confidenti del Re, Pastori, Messaggieri*, ecc."

20. Letter published in *The Craftsman*, April 7, 1733, quoted in Sesto Fassini, *Il Melodramma italiano a Londra nella prima metà del settecento* (Torino: Fratelli Bocca, 1940), p. 165.

21. Lbl Add. Ms 14,205.

22. Gio. Battista Pescetti's *Angelica e Medoro* (1739) has this bass Orlando "impazzito per l'amor eccessivo" that he has for Angelica.

23. This applies particularly to casting practice in early eighteenth-century London. Some examples: Don Fernando (brother of the designated heir) in Galuppi's *Enrico* (1743); Fraarte, brother of Tiridate, in Handel's *Radamisto* (1720); Domiziano in Ariosti's *Vespasiano* (1724); Medarse in the *Siroe* of Hasse (1736) and Lampugnani (1755); Mirteo, unknown brother of Semiramide and in love with Tamiri, in Hasse's *Semiramide* (1748).

24. Some examples of the roles of *confidente* and confederate allotted to female singers: Clitarco, confederate of Tamiri and her lover in *Farnace* (1723); Efestione, agent of a happy ending but temporarily misunderstood, in the Hasse-Leo-D. Scarlatti pasticcio *Alessandro in Persia* (1741); Araspe, *confidente* of Iarba, in love with Selene, in Hasse's *Didone* (1748); Aquilio, *confidente* of Adriano and secretly in love with Sabina, in Giuseppe Scarlatti's *Adriano in Siria* (1752); Timagene, *confidente* of Alessandro and his secret enemy, in G. Scarlatti's *Alessandro nell'Indie* (1753); Osmida, *confidente* of Didone, in *Didone abbandonata* (1753).

25. Wiel, *I teatri musicali veneziani*, pp. 64–125, for entries given in the period specified. Dean, *Handel*, p. 208, suggests that for Handel, working in the special conditions of London, the castrato contralto voice was interchangeable with the equivalent female voice in revivals. It is possible that Handel was by this time simply resigned to necessity but that at an earlier stage of his career the difference between using one voice or the other may have had dramatic significance.

26. For confirmation that this kind of duet was suitably prominent in the audience's reception of an opera, see Stendhal, "Letter on Meta-

stasio," in *The Lives of Haydn and Mozart, with Observations on Metastasio etc.*, trans. L. A. C. Bunker (London: John Murray, 1818), p. 446 and Josse de Villeneuve, *Lettre sur le méchanisme de l'opéra italien* . . . (Naples and Paris: Duchesne/Lambert, 1761), p. 23.

27. Celletti, "La vocalità," p. 29.

28. A rise in soprano tessitura occurs throughout the eighteenth century. Traetta, similarly, is outdistanced in this respect by Cimarosa. Aristea in Traetta's *L'Olimpiade* (I-Fc 344 [D.II 5–7]) goes up to B in alt. Cimarosa's Aristea (Vnm Cod. It. IV 855–6 [= 10261–2]) reaches E in alt.

29. There are exceptions. One is to be found in the score of David Perez's 1753 Lisbon *L'Olimpiade* (Vnm Cod. It. IV 217–219 [= 9788–90]), in which Megacle, whose part is slightly higher in tessitura than Aristea's, also takes the upper line in their principal duet.

30. Osroa is a tenor in, for example, Caldara (1732), Pergolesi (1734), Giuseppe Scarlatti (1752–1754), and Mysliveček (1778?). Iarba is a tenor in, for example, Vinci (1726), Hasse (1748), and in Florence at Teatro di via della Pergola (1753), but a soprano in a Marciana manuscript (Vnm Cod. It. IV 266 [= 9837]).

31. See, for an example of the factors that may be involved here, note 14.

Cadential Structures and Accompanimental Practices in Eighteenth-Century Italian Recitative *by Michael Collins*

Recitative in Italian opera of the seventeenth century enjoys a great variety of full cadences used in both intermediate and final positions. Before the mid 1680s, the old *anticipazione della sillaba* (examples 1a and 1b) and *anticipazione della nota* (example 1c) predominate in the works of Giovanni Antonio Boretti, Francesco Provenzale, Jacopo Melani, Antonio Sartorio, Giovanni Legrenzi, Alessandro Stradella, Bernardo Pasquini, and Pietro Andrea Ziani. Between the mid 1680s and 1700 all types seen in example 1 are still found, but predominance in the works of Carlo Pallavicino, Agostino Steffani, Carlo Francesco Pollarolo, Giovanni Bononcini, and the early operas of Alessandro Scarlatti is given to those seen in examples 1d and 1e. After 1700, in the works of Johann Joseph Fux, Francesco Mancini, Francesco Gasparini, Giuseppe Porsile, Alessandro Scarlatti, and George Frideric Handel those two cadences become stereotypical and all the others virtually disappear. Once this stereotyping of cadence occurs, the recitatives themselves are confined to common time and to the rhythms of speech patterns. No longer do we find passages of $\frac{3}{2}$ or $\frac{3}{4}$ in arioso style interspersed.[1]

The name for these two cadences seems to have appeared in print for the first time in Pier Francesco Tosi's *Opinioni de' cantori antichi e moderni* (Bologna, 1723), where he calls them *cadenze tronche* or truncated cadences, complaining of the thousands that appear in every opera.[2] The term was current, for Fux uses *cadenza truncata* in his *Gradus ad Parnassum* (Vienna, 1725).[3] Tosi's translators, John Ernest Galliard (London, 1743)[4] and Johann Friedrich Agricola (Berlin, 1757)[5] render *cadenza tronca* as "broken cadence" and *abgebrochene Cadenz*, respectively, a quite unfortunate translation as we shall see later.

a.

b.   c.

d.   e.

EXAMPLE 1.

As to the vocal performance of the *cadenza tronca*, the use of appoggiaturas is too well known to warrant discussion here; Alessandro Scarlatti and a few of his contemporaries in fact write out the falling-fourth appoggiatura.[6] No one, however, writes out the appoggiatura on the descending third, probably because it represents a nonharmonic tone. A performance problem arises with the question of the timing of the accompaniment, and Sven Hansell has shown that at least in the first half of the eighteenth century the final dominant-tonic chords were not delayed until after the singer had finished, as is commonly practiced today (example 2).[7] Some of Hansell's findings, however, bear reexamination.

With reference to example 3a, Johann David Heinichen, in his *Der General-Bass in der Composition* (Dresden, 1728), writes, "The voice gives the fourth [above the bass], whereupon a cadence in B minor follows."[8] But what does Heinichen mean by "cadence"? If he means both dominant and tonic chords, then we

a. As written

b. As played today

EXAMPLE 2.

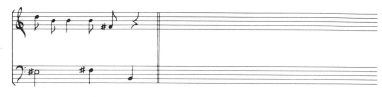

a.

b.

c.

EXAMPLE 3. Heinichen, *Der General-Bass in der Composition*

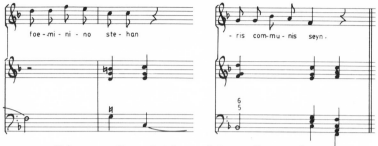

EXAMPLE 4. Telemann, *Sing-, Spiele- und Generalbass-Uebungen*

have a cadence delayed until after the singer finishes. Alessandro Scarlatti, in his manuscript treatise *Per sonare il Cembalo* (1715), defines cadence as the penultimate consonance with which every composition terminates.[9] If we apply this definition to Heinichen's example, the dominant chord will come after the vocal part terminates, thus giving a delayed cadence. In fact, Heinichen does give just such an example of a delayed cadence (example 3b). He is speaking of the irregular resolution of the bass note *d* in example 3c, saying, "Naturally this recitative cadence should always, I say always be resolved in the following manner [example 3b], as one now and then finds in practice. Since, however, this would be wearisome to hear, particularly in theatrical works where it recurs continually and would unnecessarily delay the singer, too, it may be that one has shortened the cadence as in [example 3c] . . . in order to go directly to the cadence."[10] Heinichen then seems to be saying that the cadence is not delayed.

With the Heinichen quotation another concept has been introduced: that there is a difference in the performance of theatrical recitative. Georg Philipp Telemann elaborates on this in his *Sing-, Spiele- und Generalbass-Uebungen* of 1733/34. At the two cadences seen in example 4, Telemann refers the reader to a footnote, where we find the following comment: "The cadences are played in this manner in operas, when the singer speaks the last syllables, in cantatas, however, one is obliged to play them afterward."[11]

Johann Joachim Quantz emphasizes this point in his section on Italian recitative in his treatise of 1752:

Sometimes the accompaniment is interrupted to give the singer freedom to recite at will, and the accompanying parts enter only from time to time, namely at the caesuras when the singer has completed a phrase. Here the accompanists must not wait till the singer has uttered the final syllable, but must enter at the penultimate or preceding note, in order to maintain constant animation. . . . In general the bass in all cadences of theatrical recitatives, whether accompanied with violins or plain, must begin its two notes, usually forming a descending leap of a fifth, during the last syllable; these notes must be performed in a lively manner, and must not be too slow. . . . If in a lively recitative the accompanying parts at the caesuras have quick notes which must be played precipitately following a rest on the downbeat (see [example 5]), the accompanists again must not wait until the singer has fully articulated the last syllable, but must begin during the penultimate note, so that the fire of the expression is constantly maintained.[12]

EXAMPLE 5. Quantz, *On Playing the Flute*

C. P. E. Bach takes a somewhat ambiguous stand on the matter in 1762. In the following excerpt he agrees with Quantz in advocating that the harpsichordist should anticipate the dominant chord even when the rest is indicated:

> These fiery recitatives often occur in operas where the orchestra has a wide range with basses playing *divisi*, while the singer declaims upstage, far removed from his accompaniment. Such being the case, the first harpsichordist, when there are two, does not await the termination of the singer's cadences, but strikes on the final syllable the chord which should rightly be played later. This is done so that the remaining basses or other instruments will be prepared to enter on time.

Just three paragraphs later, Bach contradicts this statement:

a.   b.

EXAMPLE 6. C. P. E. Bach, *Essay on the True Art of Playing Keyboard Instruments*

a.   b.

c.

EXAMPLE 7. Marpurg, *Kritische Briefe*

However, if all the instruments attack simultaneously, the keyboardist does not anticipate, but signals with his head or body in good time so that all will enter together [example 6a]. In [example 6b], a six-four chord is required over the bass note, preferably with the octave on top. At the rest, the seventh and fifth of the same bass note are played.[13]

Friedrich Wilhelm Marpurg makes an unequivocal statement against the undelayed cadence in his *Kritische Briefe* (1760):

> Moreover, there are some [accompanists] accustomed to anticipating the penultimate bass note of the cadence, namely the dominant, without interpolating a rest, in the following manner [i.e., playing example 7a as seen at 7b, rather than as he implies at 7c]. . . . I know that the same errors have been committed by very great composers, but errors always remain errors, wherever they occur.[14]

Marpurg's rather pedantic reasoning is that the tonic chord must come on a strong beat and that tying a quarter note to a whole note is against the rules. Nevertheless, it is quite clear that he expects the performer to insert a rest before making his cadence.

Giannantonio Banner, a rather obscure *maestro di cappella* in Padua, has in his manuscript treatise *Compendio musicale* of 1745 a chapter on playing accompaniments for recitative. Illustrating his remarks with example 8, he writes that when coming to the period at the end of a recitative, "the bass must pass to the fourth degree, whereupon one stops with a rest until the upper part has made the proper cadence of the recitative . . . after which cadence the bass must enter immediately with the usual authentic cadence. . . ." [15] Banner gives a lengthy example of recitative from his own oratorio *S. Elena al Calvario*, in which all the cadences are delayed. Banner then states that there is another manner for theatrical recitatives, [16] and without further explanation gives an example in which there are two cadences as seen in example 9: the

EXAMPLE 8. Banner, *Compendio musicale*

EXAMPLE 9. Banner, *Compendio musicale*

first an interrupted cadence that is delayed, the second a final cadence in which the voice completes its cadence together with the bass. We cannot be certain, therefore, whether or not Banner reflects the later practice of delaying cadences in operatic recitatives.

As a matter of fact, some Italian composers occasionally wrote out delayed cadences, as example 10 illustrates with cadences from Legrenzi's *Totila* (1677), A. Scarlatti's *Massimo Puppieno* (1696), and Steffani's *Tassilone* (1708). The most revealing illustrations are to be found in *recitativo stromentato*, where the string parts are written out. Example 11 shows three cadences from Scarlatti's *Tigrane* (1715), two of them partially delayed, the third fully de-

a. Legrenzi, *Totila*   b. Scarlatti, *Massimo Puppieno*

c. Steffani, *Tassilone*

EXAMPLE 10.

EXAMPLE II. Scarlatti, *Tigrane*

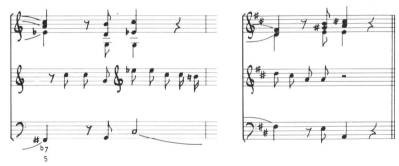

EXAMPLE I2. Scarlatti, *Marco Attilio Regolo*

EXAMPLE I3. Fux, *Costanza e fortezza*

a. Handel, *Giulio Cesare*   b. Handel, *Alcina*

EXAMPLE 14.

layed. There are two half-delayed cadences in Scarlatti's *Marco At-tilio Regolo* (1719) (example 12); one from Fux's *Costanza e for-tezza* (1723) that is not delayed (example 13); and finally two cadences from Handel, the first from *Giulio Cesare* (1724) that is not delayed and the second from *Alcina* (1735) that is delayed (example 14).

I have been using the terms "delayed" or "not delayed" rather than *cadenza tronca*, and there is reason for this: contrary to Sven Hansell I do not believe that *cadenza tronca* refers specifically to the undelayed cadence. Galliard, in his translation of Tosi, inter-prets the *cadenza tronca* (which he calls a "broken" cadence) and the final cadence as seen in example 15.[17] The broken cadence, as written at any rate, is not delayed, while the final cadence is the seventeenth-century cadence, which was no longer in use. Agri-cola, in 1757, may have been consulting Galliard as well as Tosi, for he uses the term *abgebrochene Cadenz*. But the example he gives (example 16)[18] is quite different from Galliard's, and is one which is literally "broken off" or "interrupted" by the first inver-sion of a chord other than the tonic. This is the same type of cadence that Rameau, in his *Traité* of 1722, calls a *cadence rom-pue*,[19] that is, a broken cadence, which we would call today "de-ceptive." That this is what Agricola had in mind is clear from his *Endigungscadenz*, or final cadence (example 16),[20] which, like his *abgebrochene Cadenz*, is delayed, unlike Galliard's broken cadence.

Cadenza tronca does not refer to the bass at all, but rather to the vocal part, which is "truncated" in that it does not complete the cadence with the bass, as in Galliard's final cadence. Furthermore, I cannot believe that Agricola is committed to the delayed cadence. His example of a church recitative is indeed delayed (example 17a),[21] but his two examples of *cadenze tronche* in theatrical recitative are not (example 17b).[22] Agricola seems to be making the same distinction as do Telemann and Quantz between church and theatrical recitative.

A rare example of the *cadenza tronca* with a written-out realization occurs in the *Biblische Historien* of Johann Kuhnau, published in 1700, in the movement entitled "Saul malinconico e trastullato per mezzo della Musica," which is entirely in recitative style.[23] Example 18 shows this undelayed cadence. I have duplicated what would be the vocal line of this cadence on a separate staff for the sake of clarity.

Another example, a true vocal recitative this time, appears in

a. Galliard, "broken" cadence

b. Final cadence

EXAMPLE 15.

a. Agricola, *abgebrochene Cadenz*   b. *Endigungscadenz*

EXAMPLE 16.

a.

b.

EXAMPLE 17.

EXAMPLE 18. Kuhnau, *Biblische Historien*

the *Reglas generales de accompañar* of Joseph de Torres Martinez Bravo, maestro of the Spanish Real Capilla.[24] The 1736 edition of the *Reglas* contains a supplementary treatise on accompanying recitatives in the Italian manner that is based largely on Francesco Gasparini's important *L'armonico pratico al cimbalo* of 1708. The difference is that Torres gives written-out realizations. Example 19 shows a *cadenza tronca* from one of his illustrations.[25] The keyboard cadence is not delayed, and the right hand doubles the vocal line until the singer truncates the cadence, whereupon the accompanist completes a final cadence of the type singers would have made in the common recitative cadence before the 1790s.

Before turning to the manner of realizing the accompaniment in

EXAMPLE 19. Torres, *Reglas generales de accompañar*

recitative, we may summarize the foregoing as first having shown that it is the vocal part that merits the term *cadenza tronca* and second having provided further substantiation for not delaying the dominant-to-tonic cadence in the accompaniment during at least the first half of the eighteenth century. Performers may, however, have had the option to delay the final cadences before arias and even intermediate full cadences in soliloquies where dialogue between characters does not press the action forward.

With regard to the style of accompanying recitatives in the early eighteenth century, Sven Hansell has again provided excellent information on Italian extravagances. My purpose will be to give additional documentation and to modify a few of his points.

We shall turn first to the manuscript treatise on accompaniment by Alessandro Scarlatti, *Per sonare il Cembalo*, written in 1715. Scalatti mentions that he has found by experience that wherever possible the third above the bass note should be played by the little finger of the right hand. He also provides rules for turning some root position and first-inversion chords into dominant sevenths in performance. Other incidental additions to the harmony that are required in his own style, he states, cannot be put into writing, but only shown at the keyboard.[26] These additions in what he calls the "most noble style of accompanying" (which he unfortunately does not describe) are, however, illustrated in some short preludes found just a few pages later in the manuscript. In the cadential passages from four of these preludes, shown in example 20, we find the handfuls of notes doubled in both hands and the sounding of dissonances together with their resolutions. These are explained by Francesco Gasparini, whom Scarlatti respected enough to send his

EXAMPLE 20. Scarlatti, *Per sonare il Cembalo*

son, Domenico, to study composition with, in his *L'armonico pratico al cimbalo* (1708). Gasparini recommends doubling the fourth
and sixth above the bass in the left hand, but the left hand should
retain the fourth and fifth sounding together while the right hand
resolves the fourth to the third. This, asserts Gasparini, produces a
most agreeable harmony on the harpsichord and is a type of *acciaccatura*.[27] Now this harmonic effect, which we see in the Scarlatti preludes, is precisely that combination of the cadential tonic
six-four with the dominant five-three in a single chord advocated
by Sven Hansell for the *cadenza tronca* (example 21).[28]

In his chapter 9, Gasparini elaborates on the harmonic *bizzarrie*
that may be added in accompanying recitative. His *mordenti* and
acciaccature, seen in figure 1 as black notes,[29] consist of adding
half steps to chord tones, the *mordente* a half step below a chord

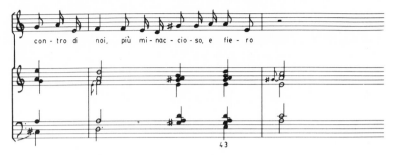

EXAMPLE 21. Scarlatti, *Per sonare il Cembalo*

tone, the *acciaccatura* a half step above a chord tone so as to fill in a third. These are not generally held down by the player. Professor Hansell has interpreted Gasparini's remark, "tutte le note poste tra le due linee servono, per un sol colpo, e si fanno tutte insieme," made in reference to figure 1, as meaning "all the notes placed between the barlines are played together at a single stroke."[30] I think however, that Gasparini is cautioning the reader not to take the semibreves of his examples literally, but to arpeggiate the chords rapidly in a single motion of the hand, especially since on the preceding page Gasparini admonishes the reader as follows:

> To introduce the accompaniments into recitatives with some sort of good taste, one must distend the consonances quasi arpeggiating them, but not continuously, because when one has caused the harmony to be heard, one must hold the keys down, and allow the singer to sing at his pleasure and according to the expression of the words, and not annoy or disturb him with continuous arpeggios and scale passages up and down, as do some [performers] (I don't know if I should call them *Sonatoronni* [show-offs] or *Sonatorelli* [incompetents]), who, in order to display their virtuosity, believing it to be stylish, just make confusion.[31]

To "distend the consonances quasi arpeggiating them" seems to leave no doubt, but the meaning is clarified by the previously mentioned treatise by Torres, which illustrates the *acciaccature* as seen in figure 2.[32] Citing Gasparini as his source, Torres quotes the paragraph about chords being played "quasi arpeando," and adds the illustration of the practice seen in figure 3.[33] Torres tells us that although the practice of adding dissonances seen in some Italian authors at first sight seems very extravagant, the ability, judgment,

FIGURE 1. Gasparini, *L'armonico pratico al cimbalo*

FIGURE 2. Torres, *Reglas generales de accompañar*

and dexterity with which the dissonances are executed make this rarified and strange harmony tolerable.[34]

Perhaps the clearest explanation of the manner of accompanying recitatives is given by Nicolo Pasquali in his *Thorough-bass made easy* (Edinburgh, 1757). In the section on "How to Accompany Recitatives," Pasquali writes:

> This Part of Thorough-Bass, to those that are not accustomed to it, is still more difficult than any of the rest; though, when once grown familiar, it becomes one of the easiest. It consists in filling up the Harmony as much as possible, and therefore the Left Hand strikes the Chords in it as well as the Right.
>
> Care must be taken not to strike abruptly, but in the *Harpeggio* Way, laying down the Fingers in the Chords *Harp-like*, *i.e.* one after another, sometimes *slow*, other times *quick*; according as the Words express either common, tender, or compassionate *Matters*.

FIGURE 3. Torres, *Reglas generales de accompañar*

For Example, for *common Speech*, a quick Harpeggio; for the tender a *slow* one; and, for any thing of *Passion*, where *Anger, Surprise, etc.* is expressed, little or no Harpeggio, but rather dry Strokes, playing with both Hands almost at once.

The abrupt Way is also used at a *Punctum* or full Stop, where the Sense is at an End.[35]

Pasquali's "Specimen how to accompany others" is seen in figure 4. That his illustration lacks the *stravaganze e bizzarrie* of Gasparini, Scarlatti, and Torres might be thought to result from a simplification of harmonic practice. Quite the contrary, however, for Pasquali cautions that the student should procure the assistance of an experienced Master, for, as he says, "There are several *Embellishments* used, in order to set off playing, which cannot be well expressed in Writing, and are only to be attained by carefully observing the *Method* of a good Performer."[36]

FIGURE 4. Pasquali, *Thorough-bass made easy*

When and where this extravagant practice of accompanying recitative originated and how long it persisted is difficult to ascer-
tain. A manuscript from the early years of the eighteenth century,
cited by Professor Hansell and found in the Biblioteca Corsiniana
in Rome, gives some pertinent information.[37] After describing the
full sound (*il suonar pieno*) of the harmonies, the parallel octaves,
fifths, and dissonant *acciaccature* in the inner parts as a style delightful to the ear, the anonymous author contrasts this style with
the old manner of playing with a dry sound (*il suonar secco*).[38]
One might hypothesize, since this manuscript apparently belongs
to the Roman circle of Gasparini and does not recommend the
"old manner," that the style emerged from the Roman-Neapolitan
axis of Gasparini and Scarlatti, who spoke of it as being his
own manner of accompaniment. And at least to the knowledge of

C. P. E. Bach, the style seems to have played out somewhat before 1762, for that author writes that until recently recitatives had been crammed with constantly changing harmonies, their resolutions, and enharmonic changes, a special beauty being sought in such harmonic extravagances. "Natural harmonies were thought too plain. Nowadays," he concludes, "thanks to our more intelligent taste, harmonic oddities are very rarely used, and then only with adequate justification."[39] And later, in speaking of how arpeggiation is not employed at the organ in accompanying recitatives, C. P. E. Bach states, "Other keyboard instruments do not use ornaments or refinements, aside from arpeggiation, in the accompaniments of recitatives."[40]

The practice may have lingered longer here and there, but certainly by the time we come to Mozart's recitatives, with their very long notes in the accompaniment, which, even though they are played very short, imply a much faster performance of the recitative itself, and with their infrequent cadences delayed in the continuo until after the vocal *cadenza tronca*, the *stravaganze e bizzarrie* are a thing of the past, a relic of a more impassioned and irrational era.

NOTES

1. The generalized statements in this introductory paragraph are not the product of exhaustive research, but are drawn primarily from examination of the facsimile scores edited by Howard Mayer Brown for the series *Italian Opera 1640–1770* (New York: Garland Publishing, Inc.).

2. Facsimile, ed. Erwin R. Jacobi (Celle: Hermann Moeck Verlag, 1966), p. 47.

3. Joanne Josepho Fux, *Gradus ad Parnassum* (Vienna: Typis Joannis Petri Van Ghelen, 1725), p. 278: "si autem alia prorsùs Oratio introduciture, clausula formalis, plerumque tamen truncata adhibenda est."

4. John Ernest Galliard, *Observations on the Florid Song* (London, 1743), pp. 74–75.

5. Johann Friedrich Agricola, *Anleitung zur Singkunst* (Berlin, 1757). Facsimile, ed. Erwin R. Jacobi (Celle: Hermann Moeck Verlag, 1966), p. 162.

6. See A. Scarlatti, *Tigrane* (Naples, 1715), ed. Michael Collins, Harvard Publications in Music 13 (Cambridge: Harvard University Press, 1983). See also Carlo Francesco Pollarolo, *Gl'inganni felici* (Venice,

1696), Francesco Mancini, *Gl'amanti generosi* (Naples, 1705), and Antonio Bononcini, *Griselda* (Milan, 1719), in *Italian Opera, 1640–1770*.

7. Sven Hostrup Hansell, "The Cadence in 18th-Century Recitative," *The Musical Quarterly* vol. 54 (1968): 229. For additional information see Jack Westrup, "The Cadence in Baroque Recitative," in *Natalicia Musicologica Knud Jeppesen*, ed. Bjørn Hjelmborg and Søren Sørensen (London: J. & W. Chester Ltd., 1962), pp. 243–252 and Winton Dean, "The Performance of Recitatives in Late Baroque Opera," *Music and Letters*, vol. 58 (1977): 389–402.

8. Heinichen, *Der General-Bass*, p. 791: "Giebet die Stimm die 4te an, worauff eine *Cadenz* in das *h moll* erfolget." Example 3 appears on p. 789.

9. *Per sonare il Gembalo, Pel Sr A. S., 1715* (British Library, Mus. Add. MSS 14244), fol. 39: "Cadenza si chiama la penultima consonanza, con cui si termina ogni compositione. . . ."

10. Heinichen, *Der General-Bass*, p. 674: "Natürlich solte diese *Recitativ-Cadenz* allzeit, ich sage allzeit auff folgende Arth *resolviren*, wie man dann und wann im Gebrauch hat: [example 3b] Weil aber dergleichen langweilige, und doch in *Theatrali*schen Sachen alle Augenblick vorkommende *Cadenz* endlich würde verdriesslich anzuhören, ja nicht selten den *agir*enden Sänger gleichsam unnüzter Weise auffzuhalten scheinen: so kan es seyn, dass man daher Gelegenheit genommen, die Sache abzukürtzen und nach dem [example 3c] . . . gerade zur *Cadenz* zu gehen."

11. Ed. Max Seiffert, 4th edition (Kassel: Bärenreiter Verlag, 1935), p. 40: "Die schlüsse werden in opern sofort angeschlagen, wann der sänger die letzten sylben spricht, in cantaten aber pfleget man sie nachzuschlagen."

12. Johann Joachim Quantz, *On Playing the Flute*, trans. Edward R. Reilly (London: Faber and Faber, 1966), p. 292.

13. Carl Philipp Emanuel Bach, *Essay on the True Art of Playing Keyboard Instruments*, trans. and ed. William J. Mitchell (New York: W. W. Norton & Company, 1949), pp. 421–422, 424–425.

14. Friedrich Wilhelm Marpurg, *Kritische Briefe über die Tonkunst* (Berlin: Friedrich Wilhelm Birnstiel, 1760), pp. 352–353: "Ferner sind einige gewohnt, die vorletzte Bassnote der Cadenz, nemlich die Dominante, ohne Einschiebung einer Pause, auf folgende Art, zu anticipiren: [example 7] . . . Ich weiss dass von sehr grossen Componisten dergleichen Fehler begangen werden, aber Fehler bleiben immer Fehler, sie finden sich wo sie wollen."

15. Banner, *Compendio musicale*, p. 211: "Bisogna che il Basso passi alla quarta Corda di quel Tuono ò maggior', ò minore, a cui vogliasi

passare, ed ivi fermarsi con una pausa finchè la parte superiore abbia fatta la Cadenze propria del Recitativo. . . ."

16. Ibid., p. 217. The example "Recitativo da Teatro" (example 9) is on p. 219.

17. Galliard, *Observations*, plate 5, no. 1.

18. Agricola, *Anleitung*, p. 162.

19. Jean-Philippe Rameau, *Treatise on Harmony*, trans. Philip Gossett (New York: Dover Publications, Inc., 1971), p. 289.

20. Agricola, *Anleitung*, p. 162.

21. Ibid., p. 151.

22. Ibid., p. 154.

23. Johann Kuhnau, *Musicalische Vostellung einiger biblischer Historien in 6 Sonaten*, ed. Karl Päsler, *DDT*, series 1, vol. 4 (Leipzig: Breitkopf & Härtel, 1901), p. 135, measures 13–14.

24. Madrid, 1736; first edition, 1702.

25. Ibid., p. 115.

26. Scarlatti, *Per sonare*, fol. 40: "Altre circostanze accidentali richieste dall'armonia dello stile di questo presente scrittore da Lui trovate nel più nobil modo di sonare, non ponno darsi in scritto, mà à voce, colle varie maniere de' movimenti della mano nel sonare; al che si riserba."

27. Francesco Gasparini, *L'armonico pratico al cimbalo* (Venezia: Antonio Bortoli, 1745), p. 27: "Alle volte il radoppiare la Quarta e Sesta con la mano sinistra fa buonissimo effetto, ma nel risolvere non si deve far sentire la Terza maggiore, e nel Cembalo lasciando la Quarta unita con la Quinta, mentre la destra risolve con la Terza maggiore, si riceve un'Armonia assai grata, ed è una specie (come molti Suonatori dicono) di Acciaccatura, di che ne faremo il suo Trattato."

28. Hansell, "The Cadence," p. 229.

29. Gasparini, *L'arminoco pratico*, p. 65.

30. Hansell, "The Cadence," p. 230.

31. Gasparini, *L'armonico pratico*, pp. 61–62: "Per introdur gli accompagnamenti ne' Recitativi con qualche sorte di buon gusto si deve distender le Consonanze quasi arpeggiando, ma non di continuo; perchè quando si è fatta sentire l'Armonia della nota, si deve tener fermi i tasti, e lasciar, che il Cantore si sodisfi, e canti col suo comodo, e secondo che porta l'espressiva delle parole, e non infastidirlo, o disturbarlo con un continuo arpeggio, o tirate di passagi, in su, e in giù, come fanno alcuni, non sò s'io dica Sonatoronni, o Sonatorelli, che per far pompa della loro velocità di mano, credendola bizzaria, fanno una confusione."

32. Torres, *Reglas generales*, p. 120.

33. Ibid., pp. 122–123.

34. Ibid., p. 120: ". . . me ha parecido forzoso poner aqui para mayor

complemento, varias posturas, quehe visto en algunos Autores Italianos, que aunque à la vista parecen muy estrabagantes, la habilidad, juycio, y destreza con que las executan las hace tolerables, y de muy rara, y estraña armonia. . . ."

35. Pasquali, *Thorough-bass*, pp. 47–48.

36. Ibid., p. 48. Figure 4 is Pasquali's plates 27 and 28.

37. Hansell, "The Cadence," p. 243: Musica R.I., entitled *Regole per accompagnare sopra la parte.*

38. Ibid., p. 245–246.

39. For the complete passage in translation see ibid., p. 245 or Bach, *Essay*, p. 420.

40. Bach, *Essay*, p. 422.

Declamation and Expressive Singing in Recitative *by Mary Cyr*

With the following account written in 1754, Giuseppe Tartini recalls a particularly moving scene from an opera performed some forty years earlier at Ancona. One passage at the beginning of act 3 "stirred such intense feeling, both in us orchestra players and in the listeners, that we all watched each other's faces to observe the change of color it caused in each of us. The affect was not one of sorrow (I remember very well that the words were angry) but a certain coldblooded grimness which really shook one's feelings."[1] At each of the thirteen performances, Tartini goes on to say, a silence fell in the theater when the scene approached, as the audience anticipated its effect. The history of eighteenth-century opera contains many such accounts, which stir our imagination, but the union of words and music that gripped the audience on the occasion Tartini described differs in one important way: the scene was set entirely in simple recitative.

Tartini was certainly not the first musician to isolate a passage of simple recitative as inspiring when well performed. Francesco Algarotti, Josse de Villeneuve, Jean-Jacques Rousseau, and others had also praised recitative's potential for powerful effect despite its simple resources. More frequently, however, eighteenth-century critics found that little dramatic effect usually resulted from the long stretches of dialogue set in simple recitative. Charles de Brosses complained of the monotony of recitative he heard in Rome during his visit in 1740, although other diversions at the opera pleased him, particularly the opportunity to play chess. The recitatives, he admits, allowed him to make progress in the game, while the arias prevented him from concentrating on the game for too long.[2] Jean d'Alembert found French recitative difficult to listen to largely because it moved at a "more fatiguing and odious pace" than Italian recitative.[3] Francesco Tosi also noted that recitative was frequently boring, and he attributed the fault to the performers. Among the "Defects and unsufferable Abuses which are heard in Recitatives,"[4] he mentions poor pronunciation, implying not only that diction must be excellent, but also that the singer must communicate inner thoughts and emotions to the audience through vivid actions and expressions. Mozart, too, lamented that the singers Raaf and Dal Prato lacked this skill, and he was thereby forced to cut two scenes from the beginning of act 2 in *Idomeneo.* They "spoil the recitative by singing it without any spirit or fire, and so monotonously."[5] Perhaps this frequently ineffective delivery of singers finally contributed to the pejorative designation of recitative as secco (dry); in any case, it seems that the term secco recitative was probably only applied sometime after 1800.[6]

The essential characteristics of French and Italian recitative are well known. Both were intended to imitate the natural accents of speech and to be delivered in a more or less rapid, declamatory manner. Both types of recitative harbored most of the action and furthered the plot. The arias then allowed for a momentary suspension of events so that the characters could indulge in their emotions.[7]

Differences in the notation of French and Italian recitative were well established by the mid seventeenth century. Nevertheless, most writers agreed that the metrical notation bore little relationship to actual performance. The notion that recitative should be freed from a strictly metrical delivery survived throughout the eighteenth century and beyond. Italian composers still continued to notate passages of simple recitative in common time, while French composers retained the frequent shifts in meter that underlined accents in the text. In both types of recitative, rests in the vocal part provided some clue for pacing, but decisions of speed, emphasis, and accent were left entirely to the performer.

Viewed in strictly musical terms based on the score alone, simple recitative has often appeared barren and uninteresting. In his study of the compositional changes in recitative between 1720 and 1780, Edward O. D. Downes identified certain stereotyped melodic formulas that recur,[8] and most scholars have been reluctant to view these progressions as anything but "hackneyed and conventional."[9] Yet Tartini's emphatic praise for the one passage of recitative quoted earlier suggests that composers also departed from conventional formulas when the occasion demanded it, sometimes with extraordinary effect. Marpurg, too, stressed that recitative "sets the listeners on fire" and prepares them for the aria to follow.[10] The composer's role was slight when compared with the performer's responsibility for creating a vivid declamation. Such matters as the speed and accentuation, the addition of expressive ornamentation, and a proper accompaniment in particular contributed to a fine delivery, and all of these must be considered if we are to achieve an authentic and moving performance of eighteenth-century opera.

The lack of precise indications in the score often represents a considerable obstacle to performers today. Despite the warnings of eighteenth-century writers, singers and conductors today are still often tempted to rely on a metrical performance of recitative, either by allowing the note values to dictate a speed or by maintaining a regular pulse throughout. Even when more freedom is attempted, conductors frequently demand excessive speed from singers at the expense of an expressive delivery. The results of recent research concerning the overlapping of final cadences in recitative have added significantly to the dramatic pacing of some performances,[11] but several other musical questions concerning the performance of recitative have never been discussed.

One of the critical points upon which an effective delivery depends is the appropriate speed for the declamation. On notational evidence alone, Downes has suggested that Italian recitative tends toward smaller note values in the period between 1680 and 1700, and that a faster performance tempo probably resulted. As we shall see, this conclusion warrants further consideration, for the same trend toward smaller note values in eighteenth-century French recitative actually produced the opposite effect, a slower overall pace. According to Downes, harmonies also grow simpler toward the middle of the eighteenth century, with the use of frequent dominant-tonic progressions.[12] Relying on theoretical and notational evidence as well, R. Peter Wolf has discussed the relative speed of half notes in the meters ¢ or 2 in French recitative, and has found them to be approximately equivalent to a quarter note in 3 or C.[13] Neither author attempts to relate these principles to the speed of actual performances except in the most general terms.[14]

A few additional clues concerning the speed of French and Italian recitative come from comments by eighteenth-century writers who compared the two types. French critics usually agree that Italian recitative during the first half of the eighteenth century was generally performed at a faster pace than French recitative. Rousseau praised the simplicity and expressive quality of Italian recitative, but he claimed that it often proceeded too quickly, owing to the singer's desire to hasten the declamation too much. Rousseau and others applied the French term *débiter* (to declaim) to the correct manner of delivering recitative with appropriate accents and stress; the too-rapid delivery he criticized as *débiter à l'italienne*.[15] According to Rousseau, French recitative had become "mannered" in performance and had slowed down since Lully's day. Note values in Rameau's recitative do tend to be consistently smaller than those in Lully's recitative,[16] but as Rousseau and others observed, this notational change did not necessarily result in a faster pace; in fact, the opposite effect was felt. Lully's recitative, according to Rousseau,

> . . . was performed by actors of that time entirely differently from the way we do it today. It was quicker and less dragging; one sang it less & declaimed it more. The trills and appoggiaturas [nowadays] are more languishing and one can find virtually nothing any more that distinguishes it from what we like to call air.[17]

Some evidence of the slower pace of recitative in the mid eighteenth century can be seen in the ornamented examples included in Jean-Antoine Bérard's treatise, *L'Art du chant* (Paris, 1755). A passage of recitative from Lully's *Atys*, for example, shows a number of ornaments and other nuances added by Bérard that did not figure in the original.[18] Thus the more concentrated dynamic and ornamental nuance that singers evidently applied to later recitative must have contributed to the slower pace. Even when these ornaments are notated by the composer himself, as is often the case in Rameau's music, Bérard's examples can be of considerable value in applying appropriate dynamic nuances to eighteenth-century recitative and in determining the length and stress of trills or appoggiaturas that might be appropriate in each circumstance.

In Estève's *L'Esprit des beaux arts*, published only two years before Bérard's treatise, the author must have referred to a similar variety of nuance and accent when he described the requirements of recitative performance:

> . . . in a word the simple recitative is a declamation in which one marks the intervals and tones forcefully and sometimes slowly in or-

der to make them felt more, [and] to which one adds ornaments on certain articulations of the voice and on the ends [of phrases] so that pronunciation will not be the least bit disagreeable.[19]

The choice of ornaments themselves often dictated the amount and type of stress on a syllable or word. For an accent, a quick, short trill gives stress and, according to Montéclair, is the one most often used in recitative, probably in order not to interfere with the flow of the declamation.[20] The *accent* on a long note, a rising inflection or "caressing" of the upper note, was frequently used by Bérard on accented words that carry an expressive meaning. The significance of these ornaments in eighteenth-century French recitative has frequently been overlooked in performance today, but when tastefully executed they enhance the delivery and add a dramatic dimension to the recitative.

By contrast with French recitative, that in the Italian style could proceed more rapidly, owing to its more restricted range, and a more limited application of ornaments in the voice. Italian recitative frequently remains within the compass of a fourth, and it features many more repeated notes than French recitative does. According to Scheibe, composers were expected to exhibit restraint in setting recitative with regard to the distance of melodic skips. Upward leaps may be larger than downward ones, he advises, and the latter should seldom exceed a fifth.[21] The recurrent melodic configurations also allowed for a rapid delivery. Composers chose the tessitura carefully for each part, confining it in general to the most comfortable register for each voice, called the *voce di petto* or chest voice. De Brosses described the characteristic registers of the voice, contrasting the two different qualities of sound: "The Italians nevertheless distinguish two kinds of voices: one they call *voce di testa*, which is quite light and suited to the charming little turns they can give to the musical ornaments; the other, the chest voice, or *voce di petto*, which has sounds more open, more natural, and fuller."[22] Tosi confirms similar characteristics, adding a third register to his descriptions, that of falsetto, and he emphasizes the expressive quality of the chest voice:

Voce di *Petto* is a full Voice, which comes from the Breast by Strength, and is the most sonorous and expressive. *Voce di Testa* comes more from the Throat, than from the Breast, and is capable of more Volubility. *Falsetto* is a feigned Voice, which is entirely formed in the Throat, has more Volubility than any, but of no Substance.[23]

Quantz advises that recitative must ordinarily not leave the range of the chest voice, since the latter is the usual speaking voice: "For this reason experienced composers have established a rule that you should not, except in cases of necessity or in other special situations, give the singer words to pronounce in arias—much less recitatives—outside the range of the chest voice, especially if the vowels u or i occur in them."[24] Tosi stresses the importance for sopranos to unite the natural voice with the falsetto in order to allow them to achieve a wider range, leaving "no Means untried, so to unite [them] . . . that they may not be distinguished."[25]

Quantz and Burney, among others, referred to this uniting of registers as the *portamento* or "carrying of the voice," a necessary quality for singing in the Italian style. The modern association of the word *portamento* with a "smooth and rapid 'sliding' between two pitches, executed continuously without distinguishing the intervening tones or semi-tones,"[26] was not present in the eighteenth-century usage of the word, but its meaning gradually altered after 1800. R. M. Bacon's treatise, *Elements of Vocal Science* (London, 1824), is one of the first to include the word with its modern meaning, that is, a smoothing of wide distances or leaps, thereby "lessening the effects of distant intervals." Bacon admits that this effect is "now (erroneously) called *portamento*."[27]

French composers generally demanded a wider range in their recitative, and French singers correspondingly made greater use of different registers of the voice. According to de Rochemont, French singers were more concerned with projecting the volume of their voices than Italian singers were, and the French, he says, also put greater emphasis upon articulation and a slower delivery.[28] Nevertheless, French singers and even actors in spoken drama were cautioned to avoid mixing the natural voice with the falsetto in recitative: "An actor must carefully avoid having two different tones of voice: that is to say, to pronounce in a natural tone in certain places and to jump into falsetto when he is obliged to go higher. This disfigurement is very shocking to the listener."[29] One of the harshest critics of the French manner of singing, Charles Burney, observed a lack of desire on the part of French singers to unite the registers of the voice. "The French voice never comes further than from the throat," he said. "There is no *voce di petto*, no true *portamento*, or direction of the voice."[30]

The opinion has been widely held that French recitative requires the addition of less ornamentation than Italian recitative. Bérard's examples illustrate that such was not the case, for numerous ornaments and dynamic inflections were applied in most eighteenth-century French recitative. Italian recitative, on the contrary, may have been more restrained, since ornaments were ordinarily limited to a few appoggiaturas. An exceptional case is documented by Charles Burney, who heard Luigi Marchese, a castrato who had "revived the primitive custom of gracing the recitative."[31] Although he does not elaborate on Marchese's specific manner of ornamenting the recitative, Burney's description of it as a "primitive custom" suggests the tantalizing possibility that more ornamentation had once been allowed, perhaps earlier in the eighteenth century.

The obligatory nature of appoggiaturas in Italian recitative during the first half of the eighteenth century is well known. At phrase endings, especially where the voice falls a third or fourth, an appoggiatura is always added, and the familiar melodic cadence of the falling fourth was usually notated merely by two repeated notes.[32] Equally important to eighteenth-century writers, but still frequently overlooked today, is the notion that these ornaments in recitative must be performed with different stress, accentuation, and dynamic nuance according to the words.

Mancini attached central importance to the correct placement of the appoggiatura, with proper stress, volume, and length. He mentions that a well-performed recitative has a variety of nuance in tone and rhythm, so that it does not sound continually "sung" and is always varied in its delivery: "Thus it would be a defect if the actor, instead of speaking the recitative with a free voice, should wish to sing it tying the voice continuously, and not thinking of ever distinguishing the periods and diverse sense of the words by holding back, reinforcing, and detaching and sweetening the voice, as a gifted man will do with he speaks or reads."[33]

One additional source must be included in our discussion of performance problems in recitative as an unusual, possibly even unique, discussion between two composers whose careers encompassed a long association with opera: Georg Philipp Telemann and Carl Heinrich Graun. In a group of letters written over a period of seventeen years, the two composers exchanged ideas on the relative merits of French and Italian opera. The correspondence has been cited by Gaudefroy-Demombynes for its historical interest as a critique by a German of French recitative,[34] but its importance for the performance of both French and Italian recitative has never been recognized. For the present discussion, their ideas about the dramatic impact of certain recitatives from Rameau's *Castor et Pollux* are of considerable interest.[35]

In two letters dated May 1 and November 9, 1751, Graun commences a discussion of French recitative, whose declamation he criticizes as "unnatural." Rameau's operas, he adds, offer many examples. He chooses a passage of recitative from act 1 of *Castor et Pollux* (example 1) to illustrate his claim that declamation is not carefully observed. According to Graun, Télaïre's attempt to persuade Pollux ought to have been given a more energetic setting by

EXAMPLE 1. "D'un frère infortuné," recitative from Rameau, *Castor et Pollux* (1.4)

EXAMPLE 2. "D'un frère infortuné," recitative from Rameau, *Castor et Pollux* (1.4), set by Carl Heinrich Graun

the composer. In another passage sung by Pollux ("Et c'est par lui que je respire," act 1, scene 4), he also criticizes Rameau for over-using the same progressions and for using too many changes of meter, which, he says, only increase the difficulty for both the singer and the accompanists. He then provides a musical setting for Télaïre's recitative as he would have preferred it. The text is the same, but otherwise the new setting resembles a passage of Italian recitative (example 2). Telemann's reply and critique of Graun's setting provide a valuable comparison between the two passages, and Telemann also adds some important observations about the performance of French recitative.

In his reply dated December 15, 1751, Telemann defends the setting by Rameau for its expressive qualities. He also cites several faults in Graun's setting: the rest in the voice in measure 2, which interrupts the sense of the line; a fault in prosody on *le rendre au jour*, in which *rendre* and *au* should have been elided; a mistake of accent at the first beat of measure 8, where *à* should not be lengthened or accented; and a fault of range of the vocal part of *Jupiter même*, which is set much too low. Apparently Telemann felt that the regal nature of the text demanded emphasis with a more dramatic, rising musical gesture. Graun attempts instead to create a musical setting that builds tension and dramatic effect by the frequent use of short, sequential rhythmic patterns in the voice (measures 2 to 5) and by the use of a chromatically rising bass line. Telemann finds the new setting by Graun conventional and ineffective, and he praises the expressive qualities of the ornaments in Rameau's setting. The appoggiatura in measures 1 to 2 (example 1) on *infortuné* should be rendered "tenderly," according to Telemann, and the succeeding trill on *ressusciter* should be a rolling trill (*un trill roulant*). This softly rolled trill probably corresponds to Bérard's *cadence molle*, a slowly beaten trill with a diminuendo. The phrase *l'arracher au tombeau* (measures 3 to 4) should be pompous, followed by a slower pace and a lofty sentiment (*hautin*) at *triumpher* (measure 5). Two additional directions concern mood rather than specific nuance: the phrase *à ce qu'il aime* should be tender, and *Jupiter même* elevated; the cadence at the end on the word *digne* should be prolonged (*élargi*) as the written-out ritardando indicates. Telemann's comments emphasize the importance of expressive shading of each phrase as essential in the delivery of French recitative.

The expression and emotional impact of the recitative does not depend solely upon the singer; the instruments that accompany it should also contribute to its effect. Their role has generally been overlooked since musical scores rarely indicate either the precise combination of instruments that should play or their appropriate sound. The following comments are intended merely to highlight certain trends in French and Italian practice; the subject deserves a more exhaustive study on its own.

In the French opera orchestra, the continuo section consisted of two parts: a *petit choeur* of harpsichord, one to three violoncellos, and one double bass, all of whom were responsible for the more delicate accompaniments, and a *grand choeur* of six to eight additional cellos, which joined the *petit choeur* when more sound was needed. Surviving manuscript parts from Rameau's works show that the double bass played as a member of the *petit choeur* in accompanied recitative, arias, and instrumental airs, but not in simple recitative.[36] Thus French recitative during the first half of the eighteenth century would have been accompanied by a single harpsichord joined by one or more cellos of the *petit choeur* (and possibly theorbo).

For Italian recitative of the same period, the question of which instruments played the simple recitative has never been satisfactorily resolved. Without mentioning a source, Downes surmised that "the *secco* in the opera house was performed by double bass as well as cello and harpsichord."[37] Scholars have tended to accept his conclusion, although there is little evidence to document it with certainty. Thus far, I have been able to discover only one reference to Italian recitative being accompanied by harpsichord, cello, and double bass in an eighteenth-century source. In his *Essay on Playing the Flute*, Quantz mentions this combination specifically, although he does not say how extensive the practice was.[38] As partial support for Quantz's assertion, one could also cite the shortage of cellos and relative abundance of double basses in most Italian opera houses.[39] However, if Burney was correct about the sound of most double basses, it seems unlikely that their participation was to be desired in the delicate accompaniments of simple recitative.[40]

In both French and Italian opera, theorbos were frequently added to the continuo section as well, either playing in addition to the harpsichord or substituting for it in certain places. Two theorbo players were included among the forty-three members of the *petit choeur* of the Paris opera orchestra in 1719,[41] although the use of the theorbo probably declined shortly thereafter. As early as 1715, Pierre Bonnet complains that performance of the basso continuo in Italian opera sounded complicated and somewhat confused owing to the use of more than one chordal instrument in the accompaniment:

> In general one hears in [Italian] music only a basso continuo always ornamented, which is often a kind of *batterie*, with chords and arpeggios, which casts dust in the eyes of those who are not connoisseurs, and which, reduced to its simplest form, is equivalent to ours.

FIGURE 1. *The Rehearsal of an Opera*, oil on canvas by Marco Ricci (1676–1729), 18¼ × 22¾ inches (Yale Center for British Art, Paul Mellon Collection)

> The B.C. are only good to show off the hand of those who accompany, either the clavecin or the viol. It is difficult for a clavecin, a viol, and a theorbo to be able to play together accurately.[42]

In many Italian orchestras theorbos were probably retained much longer, for they can be seen in numerous visual representations of operatic performances during the first half of the eighteenth century. For example, a painting by Marco Ricci, entitled *The Rehearsal of an Opera* (figure 1) shows several singers and a continuo group composed of theorbo and double bass as well as cello and harpsichord. Some arias may also have required the accompaniment of continuo only, but a scene such as that depicted by Ricci would very likely have been devoted principally to rehearsing the recitatives.

The actual nature of the continuo accompaniment, which must have varied considerably from one performance to another, remains largely unknown. According to de Rochemont, the lack of a conductor in Italian opera frequently meant that when faulty ensemble arose, the task of beating time was usually assumed by the first harpsichordist, often with unfortunate results. He recalls that Jomelli was known to have kept time so vigorously while playing the harpsichord that the instrument was in a state of disrepair after each performance. Three or four days of work were required before it would play again.[43] Even in more favorable circumstances than those described by de Rochemont, little is known about how the accompaniment actually sounded, since scores of the period usually preserve only a bass line and possibly a few figures. Max Schneider, citing German theoretical writings from Fux (1725) to Riepel (1776), concludes that the first rule of an accompaniment should be simplicity with little attempt on the player's part to be expressive.[44] Downes also concludes that "virtually all theorists of the 18th century insist on drastic simplicity in the harpsichord realization. Polyphony, moving parts, and all word painting, etc., are expressly forbidden. Aside from simple chords that are struck with each new note of the continuo part, only a rare arpeggio, generally at the beginning of a scene or during some lengthy pause between vocal phrases, is allowed."[45] While there is certainly evidence to support the exclusion of melodic and technical display on the part of the accompanist, it would be a mistake to assume that the boundaries of good accompaniment are so narrow. Like the singer, the keyboard player was expected to produce a varied sound and texture according to the demands of the text.

A few seventeenth-century sources deal with figured bass playing on the theorbo, but one of the earliest sources to include the harpsichord is Denis Delair's *Traité de l'accompagnement sur le théorbe et le clavecin* (Paris, 1690). Since his comments are intended for players of both instruments, they offer for the most part general advice rather than specific directions for performance. He suggests two important principles: (1) chords may be "filled in" with nonharmonic tones for greater sonority (see example 3) and (2) the texture should vary according to the tempo of individual passages.

> There are several ways of accompanying on the harpsichord: some play only the bass with the left hand, and the accompaniment with the right hand; others play chords with the left hand as well as the

"The eighth notes between the half notes, being only for ornament, are not absolutely necessary, thus one does not hold them at all, one only passes through them" (no page number, section titled "Principes d'accompagnement").

EXAMPLE 3. The manner of "filling in" chords, from Delair, *Traité de l'accompagnement sur le théorbe et le clavecin*

right; but in order to decide between the two ways, I shall say that they are both good, as long as one uses the first way only when the bass line moves quickly (*les basses de mouvement léger*) and the second way in pieces where the tempo is slow (*lent*).[46]

Jean Henri d'Anglebert probably implies the same variety of texture when he advises in his "Principes de l'accompagnement" (Paris, 1689) that "on peut remplir des deux mains sur le clavecin quand la mesure est lente."[47] He provides examples of several progressions notated as the harpsichordist might play them, with signs for arpeggiations and ornaments; they are remarkable in particular for their close spacing and sonority, with the left hand occasionally playing only one note but more frequently three or even four notes, while the right hand adds three or four additional notes to the harmony. His "Exemple général avec les agréments" (see example 4) illustrates the first principle mentioned by Delair,

EXAMPLE 4. "Exemple général avec les agréments," from d'Anglebert, *Pièces de clavecin*

that of filling in the harmony by arpeggiating the chord and adding appoggiaturas or nonharmonic tones, which would be quickly released while the chord is held.

Published a few years later, Michel de St. Lambert's *Les Principes du clavecin* (Paris, 1702) further supports these principles. He begins with a simple adage, that the player must "enter into the spirit of the words." He follows with instructions for producing a greater or lesser volume on the instrument according to the number of instruments and voices one accompanies. Thus he advises that the harpsichordist may repeat chords at will in choruses without interfering with the meter for greater rhythmic support and volume. In recitatives, where "there is no meter," the player should arpeggiate chords in general. In long recitatives, he advises striking a chord and, if the bass permits, dwelling on it for some time, and only then restriking it. Sometimes after a long chord, the player should repeat only a note or two, giving the impression that "the harpsichord did it all by itself." Of considerable interest to the modern player are his comments concerning the accompaniment with more or less sound according to the timbre and quality of the voice one accompanies.[48] His examples, like those of d'Anglebert, demonstrate this variety in texture, with thicker chords providing more support and accent on stressed words or syllables and only a few notes for less important chords that pass quickly. Although he advises that ornate melodic realization should always be avoided, he does stress a variety of timbre, which does not correspond with the "drastic simplicity" that is usually recommended for such accompaniments. At least one writer, Bonnot de Mably, suggests that French recitative gradually acquired a more elaborate style of accompaniment during the early eighteenth century, possibly in response to the gradual slowing of performance speed in recitative that we have already observed:

> Lulli . . . thought that accompaniment, as its name indicates, is added only to support the voice and to give it grace and force, and that an accompaniment is truly admirable only when the listener's attention is not drawn to it but because of it he is more aware of the charms of the voice. It is only in our day [ca. 1740] that one is advised to make these accompaniments tumultuous, which destroys the illusion on the stage, and that in spite of their harmony, one ought not even to suffer [to listen to them] in our concerts.[49]

An early source that may be taken as the foundation of Italian continuo playing is the treatise by Francesco Gasparini, *L'armonico pratico al cimbalo*, published in 1708. The author devotes a full chapter to the accompaniment of recitative, in which he describes many of the features we have observed in French treatises of the same period concerning the freedom of the singer "to take the lead, singing at his discretion and in accord with the expression of the words."[50] His general description of how chords ought to be played recalls d'Anglebert's examples in its emphasis upon arpeggiation, particularly of *consonant* chords. Gasparini nevertheless warns against too much arpeggiation, a criticism that de Brosses and others expressed about Italian continuo players. Gasparini writes:

> In order to perform the accompaniments of recitatives with some degree of good taste, the consonances must be deployed almost like an arpeggio, though not continuously so. . . . Do not annoy or disturb him with a continuous arpeggio, or with ascending and descending scale passages, as some do. I do not know whether I should call those performers grandiloquent [*Sonatoroni*] or trivial [*Sonatorelli*] who, in their desire to display their facility, create confusion, and imagine that it is inspiration.[51]

His description of filling in the notes of a triad with a dissonant tone may be compared with the advice of French players and theorists such as Delair and d'Anglebert. His use of the passing dissonance is restricted to filling in a third in a triad, particularly a minor one, and to adding a half step below the root of a chord in first inversion. This sort of filler he calls a "mordent [*mordente* means "biting"] because of its resemblance to the bite of a small animal that releases its hold as soon as it bites, and so does no harm." This decoration is best done on the minor third, octave, and sixth of a chord. A more complicated dissonance, the *acciaccatura*, consists of two, three, or four notes struck with a chord, an effect desirable especially "in recitatives or in serious songs." Although he stresses the importance of these devices for making the accompaniment "harmonious and delightful," he does not elaborate further upon their specific use or frequency in relation to the text of a recitative.

Francesco Geminiani also offers examples (see figure 2) of how an accompaniment may be arpeggiated and the manner of adding *acciaccature* in his *Treatise of Good Taste in the Art of Musick*

Examples

FIGURE 2. The manner of adding *acciaccature*, from Geminiani, *Treatise of Good Taste in the Art of Musick*

(London, 1749). Like Quantz, he marks notes that should be released immediately in black, sometimes including several dissonant notes within a single chord, as in measure 4.

Descriptive sources for the accompaniment of Italian recitative toward the middle of the eighteenth century show that the general principles of accompaniment remain unchanged. Quantz provides specific directions for accompanying a passage, which he illustrates (see example 5). He advises that the accompanist should guide the singer by anticipating his notes at each rest; he thereby "puts them ·into his mouth for him by striking the chord with a quick arpeggiation in such fashion that, where possible, the singer's first note lies in the upper part; immediately afterwards he should strike separately several of the following intervals that appear in the vocal part."[52] He then notates the accompaniment in full in order to illustrate the procedure. Although he does not describe the procedure further, we see from the accompaniment as written that three- or four-voice chords may be played with each hand. This is done by doubling the bass at the octave occasionally and by filling it with the notes of the chord. As in Geminiani's example, the added notes in the left hand (noted in black) are probably meant to be released quickly. The chord at measure 2 suggests

EXAMPLE 5. Recitative and accompaniment, from Quantz, *Essay on Playing the Flute*

that ties in the bass should not prevent the player from restriking the harmony if the occasion demands it. Quantz's advice for a quick arpeggiation of each chord would produce a rich sonority from the harpsichord and sufficient volume of sound to be easily heard by the singer.

C. P. E. Bach's comments on continuo playing also reflect practices current toward the middle of the eighteenth century.[53] Like Quantz, he stresses the player's role in directing the flow of the dialogue by the placement of his chords. He recommends using arpeggios as a means for sustaining harmonies and avoiding arpeggiation when one wants to press onward. He also mentions a useful direction concerning the accompaniment in an intermezzo or comic opera "with much noisy action, . . . constant or frequent arpeggiation must be resorted to, so that the singer and the accompanist will hear each other clearly at all times."[54] Additional support for the variety of arpeggiation described by Quantz and C. P. E. Bach comes a few years later from Nicolo Pasquali's *Thorough-bass made easy* (London, 1763). In his section on how to accompany recitatives, he advises "filling up the harmony as much as possible" with the left hand striking chords as well as the right hand:

> Care must be taken not to strike abruptly, but in the harpeggio [*sic*] way, laying down the fingers in the chords harp-like, i.e., one after another, sometimes slow, other times quick, according as the words express either common, tender, or passionate matters: For example, for common speech a quick harpeggio; for the tender a slow one; and, for anything of passion, where anger, surprise, &c is expressed,

little or no harpeggio, but rather dry strokes, playing with both hands almost at once. The abrupt way is also used at a *punctum* or full stop, where the sense is at an end.[55]

As late as 1775, Vincenzo Manfredini describes in his treatise on harmony the particular importance of the arpeggio as a "nice effect" in pathetic and serious recitative. He also stresses the necessity for adjusting the texture of the harpsichord part to the requirements of the solo part. The *acciaccatura*, or crushed dissonance, struck and quickly released, can be attractive, according to Manfredini, for "a sparkling and brisk harmony."[56] For more sound, he recommends playing chords in both hands, but for less sound, as in accompanying a single voice, one could play only one note, or an octave in the left hand.

Comments from observers who heard performances in Italy provide a few first-hand accounts of accompaniment in the opera house. De Brosses witnessed many performances there and described the accompaniment he heard in some detail. He found the performance of Italian recitative in general to be "highly displeasing," although he admits that it first provoked his curiosity as to how it could be both so "baroque and so monotonous."[57] The basso continuo accompaniment, too, he characterizes as "very simple, only providing one note during the rests between phrases to sustain the tone; the harpsichord plays in a rough way (*une manière rude*] and never plays arpeggios."[58] The observation that Italian players used arpeggiated chords to a lesser extent than the French in recitative was also repeated by other observers. Rameau may have alluded to the absence of arpeggiated chords when he referred to Italian continuo accompaniment in his *Code de musique pratique* (Paris, 1760) as "très regulier" and "à la mesure près."[59] It was probably this Italian type of accompaniment that Rousseau preferred, for in an autograph manuscript of his motet, *Ecce sedes hic tonantis*, he added the following direction for the recitative: "The accompaniment of the recitative should not be connected [*traîné*] at all or even sustained, but struck briskly at each change of note."[60] All of the foregoing evidence suggests the same conclusion, that in the accompaniment of simple recitative throughout the first half of the eighteenth century, the player should adopt a texturally varied approach, closely associated with the words and the singer's delivery.

The importance of the accompanist's role was not always fully recognized even in the eighteenth century, and a few attempts were made after 1760 to dispense with the keyboard accompaniment entirely, although most of these were judged to be unsatisfactory. At the 1770 revival of Rameau's *Zoroastre* in Paris, the absence of a harpsichord continuo caused so many intonation problems among the singers that the instrument was reinstated.[61] Charles Avison, writing in 1752, felt that the harpsichord should be used only in choruses or large instrumental works.[62] Berlioz recounts in his *Voyage musical* an early attempt at using the pianoforte in the opera house; in order to achieve more contrast between aria and recitative, Mozart "insisted that the recitative in *Don Giovanni* be accompanied on the piano, . . . In a vast hall like that of the great opera house in Paris, the effect of the piano is so feeble and so thin that this kind of accompaniment has been completely abandoned."[63] Despite such exceptional accounts, evidence from Koch and others suggests that the presence of the harpsichord continuo persisted throughout the eighteenth century and into the nineteenth century.[64]

One hardly need point out that the foregoing principles for achieving a rich texture and sonority from the harpsichord require an instrument of accurate historical design. Although little is known about the type of instrument regularly employed in French or Italian eighteenth-century performances, we do possess one account that mentions the fine harpsichord that was in the Paris Opéra when it burned on April 6, 1763. The harpsichord was the only item that could be saved, and according to Abbé Barbier, it was agreed by everyone to be "le plus parfait de tout l'Europe," rather ugly, but priceless and very old.[65]

Simple recitative has possibly suffered more critical scorn than any other aspect of eighteenth-century opera. We know from accounts such as Tartini's that it was capable on occasion of communicating great passion and depth of expression, but, until now, scholars have studied only its musical features and have ignored the crucial issue of its delivery. When Telemann praised Rameau's recitative as dramatically compelling, he stressed the performers' role in producing that effect so that to the listener the declamation merely "flows like so much champagne." Fine champagne, like a moving performance of recitative, is the result of considerable

Declamation and Expressive Singing 253

knowledge, artistic skill, and intuition on the part of those who create it.

NOTES

1. Giuseppe Tartini, *Tratado di musica* (Padua, 1754), p. 135: ". . . una riga di recitativo non accompagnato da altri strumenti, che dal Basso, per cui tanto in noi Professori, quanto negli Ascoltanti si destava un tal, e tanta commozione di animo, che tutti si guardavano in faccia l'un l'altro per la evidente mutazione di colore, che si faceva in ciascheduno di noi. L'effetto non era di pianto (mi ricordo benissimo, che le parole erano di sdegno) ma di un certo rigore, e freddo nel sangue, che di fatto turbava l'animo. Tredeci volte si recitò il dramma, e sempre seguì l'effetto stesso universalmente; di che era segno palpabile il sommo previo silenzio, con cui l'uditorio tutto si apparecchiava a goderne l'effetto." The passage was translated by Edward O. D. Downes in his article "*Secco* Recitative in Early Classical Opera Seria (1720–1780)," *JAMS* 14 (1961): 53. The performance very likely took place in the theater La Fenice, built at Ancona in 1711. According to Algarotti, who repeats Tartini's comment, the opera was by Gasparini and the passage of recitative was sung by a brother of the famous Senesino (Francesco Bernardi) who also called himself Senesino. See Pierluigi Petrobelli, *Giuseppe Tartini, Le fonti Biografiche* (Venice: Fondazione Giorgio Cini, n.d.), p. 55, note 3. The singer may have been an elder brother, since Francesco Bernardi's name appears for the first time on a cast list in 1714 and his last performance was in 1739 (see Angus Heriot, *The Castrati in Opera* [London, 1956], pp. 91–95).
2. Charles de Brosses, *Lettres familières écrites d'Italie en 1739 et 1740*, 2nd edition (Paris, 1836), vol. 2, p. 314.
3. Jean d'Alembert, *Mélanges de littérature* (Paris, 1759), p. 422.
4. Pier Francesco Tosi, *Observations on the Florid Song*, trans. Galliard, 2nd edition (London, 1743; original edition, Bologna, 1723), p. 69.
5. Emily Anderson, ed., *The Letters of Mozart and His Family*, 2nd edition (New York, 1966), letter from Wolfgang to his father, Munich, December 27, 1780, pp. 697–698.
6. Downes, "*Secco* Recitative," pp. 50–69.
7. Patrick J. Smith, *The Tenth Muse, a Historical Study of the Opera Libretto* (New York, 1970), p. 83.
8. Downes, "*Secco* Recitative, pp. 60ff.
9. See, for example, Michael F. Robinson, *Naples and Neapolitan Opera* (Oxford, 1972), p. 73.

10. Marpurg, *Historisch-kritische Beyträge* (Berlin, 1754), vol. 1, pp. 128–129, note bb.

11. Sven Hansell, "The Cadence in Eighteenth-Century Recitative," *MQ* 54 (1968): 228–248; Jack Allan Westrup, "The Cadence in Baroque Recitative," in *Natalicia Musicologica Knud Jeppesen* (Hafniae, 1957), pp. 243–252.

12. Downes, "*Secco* Recitative," p. 67.

13. R. Peter Wolf, "Metrical Relationships in French Recitative of the Seventeenth and Eighteenth Centuries," in *Recherches sur la musique française classique* 18 (1978): 29–49.

14. Wolf cites St. Lambert's *Le Principes du clavecin* (Paris, 1702) and concludes that the pulse in recitative "is measured, at least early in the eighteenth century, approximately by the step of St. Lambert's man who walks at the rate 5/4 league or approximately 3 miles per hour" (p. 48).

15. Jean-Jacques Rousseau, *Dictionnaire de musique* (Paris, 1768), article "Débiter," pp. 139–140. See also d'Alembert, *Mélanges de littérature* (Paris, 1759), pp. 430–431.

16. Paul-Marie Masson, *L'Opéra de Rameau* (Paris, 1930), p. 138.

17. Rousseau, *Lettre sur la musique française* (Paris, 1753), pp. 61–62: ". . . l'ancien récitatif étoit rendu par les acteurs de ce temps-là tout autrement que nous faisons aujourd'hui. Il étoit plus vif et moins traînant; on le chantoit moins, et on le déclamoit davantage. Les cadences, les ports-de-voix se sont plus languissant, et l'on n'y trouve presque plus rien qui le distingue de ce qu'il nous plaît d'appeler *air*."

18. For a discussion of the two versions of the passage from *Atys*, see my article, "French and Italian Styles of Singing: Rameau's Writing for the Voice," *Music and Letters* vol. 61, no. 3 (July/October 1980): 318–337.

19. [Estève], *L'Esprit des beaux arts* (Paris, 1753), vol. 2, pp. 25–26: ". . . en un mot le Récitatif simple est une déclamation dont on marque avec force & quelque fois avec lenteur les intervalles & les tons pour les rendre plus sensibles, où on répand des agrémens sur certaines articulations de la voix & sur les finales afin que la prononciation n'en soit point désagréable."

20. Michel Pignolet de Montéclair, *Principes de musique* (Paris, 1736), p. 82.

21. Scheibe, "Abhandlung über das Rezitativ," in *Bibliothek der schönon Wissenschaften* (Leipzig, 1765), vol. 12, pp. 9–10.

22. De Brosses, *Lettres familières*, vol. 2, p. 319: "Les Italiens distinguent néanmoins deux espéces de voix, qu'ils appellent *voce di testa*, qui sont tout à fait légères et propres aux petites tournures charmantes qu'ils savent donner à leurs agréments musicaux; les voix de

poitrine, *voce di petto*, ont des sons plus francs, plus naturels et plus pleins."

23. Tosi, *Observations*, p. 22, note 18.

24. Johann Joachim Quantz, *Essay on Playing the Flute*, trans. Edward R. Reilly (New York, ca. 1966; original edition, 1752), p. 56.

25. Tosi, *Observations*, p. 23.

26. David Boyden, "Portamento," in *The New Grove Dictionary of Music and Musicians* (London, 1980), vol. 15, p. 134.

27. Bacon, *Elements*, p. 55.

28. De Rochemont, *Réflexions d'un patriote sur l'opéra françois et sur l'opéra italien* (Lausanne, 1754), pp. 51–52.

29. De Grimarest, *Traîté du récitatif* (Paris, 1707), p. 133: "Un Acteur doit éviter avec soin d'avoir deux tons de voix différens: c'est à dire, de prononcer dans un ton naturel en de certains endroits, & de tomber dans le fausset, quand il est obligé de s'élever. Ce desagrément est très-choquant pour l'Auditeur."

30. Charles Burney, *The Present State of Music in France and Italy* (London, 1773), p. 19.

31. Charles Burney, *Memoirs of the Life and Writings of the Abate Metastasio* (London, 1796), vol. 3, p. 387, note.

32. Robert Donington, *The Interpretation of Early Music*, new version (London: Faber and Faber, 1977), pp. 210–211.

33. Giambattista Mancini, *Riflessioni pratiche sul canto figurato*, 3rd edition (Milan, 1777), p. 239 (trans. Edward Foreman, Pro Musica, 1967).

34. J. Gaudefroy-Demombynes, *Les Jugements allemands sur la musique française au XVIIIe siècle* (Paris, 1941), pp. 110–121.

35. Hans Grosse and Hans Rudolf Jung, *Georg Philipp Telemann Briefwechsel* (Leipzig, 1972), pp. 264–306.

36. See my article, "*Basses* and *Basse Continue* in the Orchestra of the Paris Opéra, 1700–1764," *Early Music* (April 1982): 155–170.

37. Downes, "*Secco* Recitative," p. 55.

38. Quantz, *On Playing*, p. 292.

39. Burney, *The Present State of Music*, p. 365. He describes the Naples San Carlo orchestra with eighteen first violins, eighteen second violins, two cellos, and five double basses. See also Hector Berlioz, *A travers chants* (Paris, 1862), p. 169 on the shortage of cellos in Gluck's day.

40. Burney complains of "the double bass being played so coarsely throughout Italy that it produces a sound no more musical than the stroke of a hammer" (*The Present State of Music*, p. 365).

41. [Nicholas Boindin], *Lettres historiques sur tous les spectacles de Paris* (Paris, 1719), pp. 115–118. The theorbo players were Campion and

Bernardeau. Among the eleven members of the *petit choeur* were one harpsichord, two violins, two *basses de violes*, two *basses de violons*, two theorbos, and two flutes.

42. Jacques Bonnet-Bourdelot, *Histoire de la musique et de ses effets* (Paris, 1715), vol. 1, pp. 297–298: "L'on entend en général dans la Musique qu'une basse continue toujours doublée, qui souvent est une espèce de batterie, d'accords, & un harpegement, qui jette de la poudre aux yeux de ceux qui ne s'y connoissent pas, & qui réduites au simple, reviendroient aux nôtres. Ces B,C, ne sont bonnes qu'à faire briller la vitesse de la main de ceux qui accompagnent ou du clavessin, ou de la viole; encore pour rencherir sur ces basses déla trop doublées d'elles-mêmes, ils les doublent, & c'est à qui doublera le plus; . . . il se trouve un inconvenient dans les basses en batteries & doublées sur le champ; c'est qu'il est difficile qu'un clavessin, une viole & un thuorbe, se puissent rencontrer juste dans la même maniere de doubler. . . ." This passage was translated by Carol MacClintock in *Readings in the History of Music in Performance* (Indiana University Press, 1979), pp. 243–244.

43. De Rochemont, *Réflexions*, pp. 54–55, note.

44. Max Schneider, "Die Begleitung des Secco-Rezitativs um 1750," in *Gluck Jahrbuch* 3 (1917), pp. 88–107. He writes, "Diminution jeder Art ist aber im Secco ganz gewiss Fehl am Ort. Schon die ersten Vertreter des stile recitativo haben Sie für den Begleiter ausdrücklich ausgeschlossen und sondern schlichtes Spiel" (p. 89).

45. Downes, "*Secco* Recitative," p. 55.

46. Delair, *Traité*, p. 57: "Il y a plusieurs manieres d'accompagner sur le Clavessin, les uns ne sonnent que la basse de la main gauche, faisant les accompagnemens de la main droite, les autres font des accords de la main gauche aussi bien que de la droite; mais pour décider entre ces deux manieres, je diray qu'elle sont toutes deux bonnes, pourvû qu'on ne se serve de la premiere maniere, que dans les basses du mouvement leger se servant de la seconde maniere, dans les pieces ou le mouvement est lent."

47. Jean Henri d'Anglebert, "Principes de l'accompagnement," in *Pièces de clavecin* (Paris, 1689), ed. Kenneth Gilbert (Paris, n.d.), p. 141.

48. St. Lambert, *Les Principes du clavecin* (Paris, 1702), p. 61.

49. [Bonnot de Mably], *Lettres à Madame la Marquise de P . . . sur l'opéra* (Paris, 1741), pp. 152–153: "Lulli . . . avoit pensé que l'Accompagnement, comme son non même l'indique n'est fait que pour soutenir la voix, pour lui donner de la grace & de la force, & qu'un Accompagnement n'est veritablement admirable que quand le Spectateur, ni faisant pour ainsi dire pas attention, en est cependant plus sensible aux charmes de la voix. Ce n'est que de nos jours qu'on s'est

avisé de faire de ces Accompagnemens tumultueux, qui detruisent l'illusion sur le Théâtre, & qui malgré leur harmonie, on ne devroit pas même souffrir dans nos Concerts."

50. Gasparini, *L'armonico pratico*, p. 97.

51. Ibid., p. 91: "Per introdur gli accompagnamenti ne' Recitativi con qualche sorte di buon gusto si deve distender le Consonanze quasi arpeggiando, ma non di continuo; perché quando si è fatta sentire l'Armonia della nota, si deve tener fermi i tasti, e lasciar, che il Cantore si sodisfi, e canti col suo comodo, e secondo, che porta l'espressiva delle parole, e non infastidirlo, o disturbarlo con un continuo arpeggio, o tirate di passaggi in sù, e in giù, come fanno alcuni, non sò s'io dica, Sonatoroni, o Sonatorelli, che per far pompa della loro velocità di mano, credendola bizzaria, fanno una confusione."

52. Quantz, *On Playing*, p. 265.

53. C. P. E. Bach, *Essay on the True Art of Playing Keyboard Instruments*, trans. William J. Mitchell (New York: Norton, 1949; original edition, Berlin, 1753), pp. 420–425.

54. Ibid., p. 422.

55. Nicolo Pasquali, *Thorough-bass made easy* (London, 1763), facsimile edition with an introduction by John Churchill (Oxford University Press, 1974), pp. 47–48.

56. Vincenzo Manfredini, *Regole armoniche* (Venice, 1775), pp. 62–63.

57. De Brosses, *Lettres familières*, vol. 2, p. 331.

58. Ibid., p. 331.

59. Rameau, *Code de musique pratique* (Paris, 1760), p. 28.

60. Paris, Bibliothèque Nationale, Cons. ms. 379, p. 4: "L'accompagnement du recitatif ne doit point être traîné ni même soutenu, mais frappé brusquement à chaque changement de note." The motet was written for the dedication of the Chapelle du Château de la Chevrette, 1757.

61. Friedrich Melchior Grimm, *Correspondance littéraire, philosophique et critique*, ed. M. Tourreux (Paris, 1877–1878), vol. 8, p. 451.

62. Charles Avison, *An Essay on Musical Expression*, 2nd edition (London, 1753), p. 132.

63. Berlioz, *Voyage musical en Allemagne et en Italie* (Paris, 1844), vol. 2, p. 273.

64. Neal Zaslaw, "Toward the Revival of the Classical Orchestra," *PRMA* 103 (1976–1977): 158–187.

65. Pierre Daval, *La Musique en France au XVIIIe siècle* (Paris, 1961), p. 87, note.

Embellishing Eighteenth-Century Arias:
On Cadenzas   *by Howard Mayer Brown*

Thoughtful musicians have often looked askance at the liberties performers take with composers' scores. At least as early as the sixteenth century, various composers and writers on music deplored the excesses of virtuoso singers, who distorted the madrigals and motets they performed by adding florid *passaggi*.[1] Indeed, Giulio Caccini's monodies in the early seventeenth century can be considered "new" at least in part because he wrote down most of the embellishments he wanted, as he explained in his preface to *Le nuove musiche*.[2] And in the eighteenth century, that old curmudgeon Pier Francesco Tosi took every opportunity in his observations on the florid song, published in 1723 when he was nearly seventy, to criticize the excessive and usually empty display of the modern singers, contrasting their frivolity unfavorably with the more sober, sensible, and imaginative attitudes of the ancients, by which he apparently meant the singers of his youth and, presumably, himself.[3]

But even Tosi never wrote that eighteenth-century singers should perform just the notes the composers gave them. On the contrary, he explicitly acknowledged that the da capo structures of eighteenth-century operatic arias offer a rational resolution of the ever-present tension between composers and performers. "If whoever introduced the Custom of repeating the first Part of the Air (which is called Da Capo) did it out of a Motive to show the Capacity of the Singer, in varying the Repetition," he wrote, "the Invention cannot be blam'd by Lovers of Musick; though in respect of the Words it is sometimes an Impropriety."[4] Tosi made clear that all arias, and not just fast ones, slow ones, or those that were assigned to the leading singers, should be performed with embellishments, and particularly with a varied repetition of the da capo.

"In the first [section]," he wrote, "they require nothing but the simplest Ornaments, of a Good Taste and few, that the Composition may remain simple, plain, and pure; in the second they expect, that to this Purity some artful Graces be added, by which the Judicious may hear, that the Ability of the Singers is greater; and, in repeating the Air, he that does not vary it for the better, is no great Master."[5] Indeed, Tosi went even further. He took sharply to task those singers who used the same ornaments night after night: "Let a Student . . . accustom himself to repeat [his ornaments] always differently . . . The most celebrated among the Ancients piqued themselves in varying every Night their Songs in the Opera's, not only the Pathetick, but also the Allegro . . . A Singer is lazy, who on the Stage, from Night to Night, teaches the Audience all his Songs; who, by hearing them always without the least Variation, have no Difficulty to learn them by Heart."[6]

Tosi's treatise was considered by musicians to be the standard and fundamental work on singing throughout much of the eighteenth century. It was translated into Dutch, English, French, and German, and it was mentioned with great respect by various writers of the time: by Quantz in 1752, for example, and by Giambattista Mancini in 1774 and Johann Adam Hiller in 1780.[7] In 1789, Charles Burney claimed that Johann Friedrich Agricola's translation of Tosi's *Observations on the Florid Song* was the best book on the subject in German, just as the original was the best in Italian.[8] So presumably we can trust Tosi to explain to us what eighteenth-century conventions and practices were like, so long as we remember that the work reflects an individual's prejudices, and so long as we take account of the cranky querulousness of an old man.

As it happens, Tosi was especially peevish on the subject of cadenzas, on which he took a very conservative position. His most scathing and most colorful pronouncement on the subject has often been quoted. "Generally speaking," he complained, "the Study of the Singers of the present Time consists in terminating the Cadence of the first Part [of each Aria] with an overflowing of Passages and Divisions at Pleasure, and the Orchestre waits; in that of the second the Dose is encreased, and the Orchestre grows tired; but on the last Cadence, the Throat is set a going, like a Weather-Cock in a Whirlwind, and the Orchestre yawns. But why must the World be thus continually deafened with so many Divisions?"[9] The passage teaches us, of course, slightly more than Tosi in-

tended; not only that he himself did not approve at all of long cadenzas, but, perhaps more important, that many singers in 1723
added cadenzas at all three of the final cadences in a da capo aria:
at the end of the first as well as the second A section and also at the
end of the B section. (Indeed, by 1752, Quantz explains that some
singers added five cadenzas to each aria, one at the end of each of
the vocal entries both in the first and in the repeated A section, as
well as a flourish at the end of the B section; Quantz considers the
practice a great abuse.)[10]

Tosi included in his treatise a long list of complaints against the
things modern singers did in their cadenzas. They sometimes made
a trill on the third rather than the second above the note of resolution; they sometimes descended from the fifth to the first scale degree, creating parallel octaves with the bass; they sometimes sang
their trill on the short syllable of the last word; they sometimes
omitted the trill altogether (a thing Tosi only allowed occasionally
in cantabile arias); they sometimes sang an appoggiatura on the
penultimate trilled note rather than on the final note of resolution;
they sometimes sang an anticipation of the note of resolution (a
practice he did not approve at all); and, worst of all, they sometimes sang the same cadenza on successive nights.[11] But after this
diatribe, Tosi did at least admit that the very final cadence in an
aria does allow "a modest Liberty to the Singer,"[12] even though its
abuse is insufferable. But what he appears to be saying is that the
embellishments at the final cadence ought to be performed in time
and not extended over a pedal point (or against a silence in the
orchestra). "Composers leave generally in every final Cadence," he
wrote, "some Note, sufficient to make a discreet Embellishment,
without seeking for it out of Time, without Taste, without Art,
and without Judgment."[13]

Tosi's attitude toward cadenzas marks him as irredeemably old-
fashioned, a man of the seventeenth rather than the eighteenth
century. And yet we can gain some impression of what he thought
of as good and bad taste by comparing the two sets of cadenzas
reproduced here as examples 1 and 2—they are among the very
few cadenzas that survive from the first half of the eighteenth century—although the "bad" example displays none of the faults Tosi
singled out in his detailed criticisms, and the "good" example vio-
lates the letter of Tosi's law. Example 1 shows the cadenzas the fa-

With cadenza

a. At the end of the A section

b. Alternatives for the end of the B section

EXAMPLE 1. Faustina's cadenzas for "Sciolta dal lido," from Vignati, *Ambleto*

At the first fermata

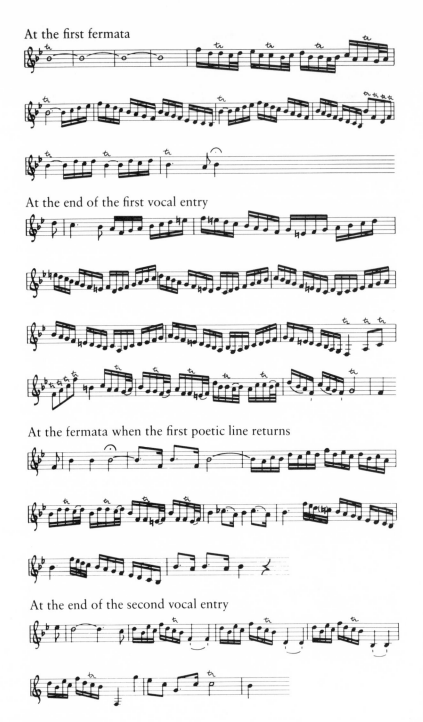

At the end of the first vocal entry

At the fermata when the first poetic line returns

At the end of the second vocal entry

a. In the A section

At the first fermata

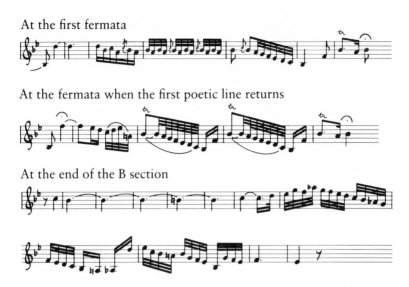

At the fermata when the first poetic line returns

At the end of the B section

b. In the B section

EXAMPLE 2. Farinelli's cadenzas for "Quell'usignolo che innamorato," from Giacomelli, *Merope*

mous mezzo-soprano Faustina Bordoni sang in the aria "Sciolta dal lido" from the opera *Ambleto* by Apostolo Zeno and Pietro Pariati, set to music by Giuseppe Vignati, when she performed it in Milan in 1719, close to the beginning of her incredibly successful career. The embellishments have recently been rediscovered and described in detail by George Buelow.[14] As we shall see, the cadenzas do not conform in every way to the guidelines set out by later writers on music. The alternatives given for the cadenza at the end of the B section require a certain amount of juggling of the orchestral parts, which is to say that the cadenza occurs neither on the I$^6_4$ chord nor on the V chord preceding the resolution. And while the cadenza that ends the repetition of the A section does involve an elaborated arpeggio, the triad outlined is that of the fourth degree of F major, not I or V. Moreover, Faustina violated one of Tosi's most pedantic rules and included anticipations to the note of resolution in all three cadenzas. Nevertheless, the most striking things about Faustina's cadenzas are their modest length—each of the three can be sung in one breath—and the fact that the cadenza at the end of the A section takes off from a figure (to be sure, one she added herself) heard just previously in the aria. I cite these as examples of what Tosi must have supposed to be good taste, because he singled out both Faustina and her great rival, Cuzzoni, as models of modern singers, as ideal performers that every young student should learn from, although never, Tosi hastened to add, imitate directly.[15]

Example 2 shows the cadenzas that Carlo Broschi (called Farinelli, perhaps the greatest soprano castrato of the age) added to Geminiano Giacomelli's aria "Quell'usignolo che innamorato" from the opera *Merope*, first performed in Venice in 1734.[16] Tosi objected to singers who added three cadenzas to every aria. But Farinelli added at least seven, and probably more, to "Quell'usignolo": four in the A section (at the end of each vocal entry and at the fermatas that occur in the middle of the first verse) and three in the B section (at the end of the first line of verse, when the first line recurs, and at the end of the section). Moreover, some of them seem too long to sing in one breath, and they certainly repeat the same figures more than any later writer said could be tolerated. Indeed, Farinelli's cadenzas—clearly an extreme case—seem to exemplify almost everything Tosi thought bad about modern singers and their inclination to show off. And Farinelli's cadenzas seem to break every guideline that later writers established. And yet, such was Farinelli's artistry that some of those writers also praised him to the sky as the greatest of all singers. But such paradoxes are the stuff of which operatic history is made.

In any case, Faustina's and Farinelli's cadenzas show two extremes of practice in the first half of the eighteenth century, and help us, therefore, to put Tosi's remarks in context. That his views on cadenzas were old-fashioned is confirmed by later writers, for that section of his observations on florid song is singled out for criticism by various later writers on the subject. Johann Friedrich Agricola, for example, appends a long footnote to his translation of Tosi, in which the German sets out his quite contradictory views on cadenzas and how they should be formed, views that borrow quite a lot from Quantz.[17] Similarly, Johann Adam Hiller in his *Anweisung zum musikalisch-zierlichen Gesange* of 1780 calls Tosi "no friend of cadenzas," while Giambattista Mancini in his treatise of 1774 does not explicitly cite the earlier writer, but offers sharply contradictory views.[18] In fact all of these writers—Agricola and Quantz in the 1750s, Mancini in the 1770s, and Hiller in the 1780s—present similar rules for singing cadenzas. Evidently the character of these improvised flourishes did not change much from about 1750 to 1780. The rules can easily be summarized:[19]

1. Cadenzas should neither be frequent nor long. By and large, they should be no longer than a singer can comfortably manage with one breath (leaving enough left over for a good trill and resolution). Cadenzas in two parts—that is, for voice and obbligato instrument or for two voices—can be somewhat longer.

2. Cadenzas should be metrically free.

3. Cadenzas ought to be appropriate to the main affect of the aria: florid for fast arias, more languid for slow arias.

4. Cadenzas can take place either on the I_4^6 chord or on the V chord preceding the tonic.

5. The final phrase of the text may have to be rearranged so that the main part of the cadenza falls on a long or accented syllable.

6. Cadenzas can involve no more than figuration patterns arranged to extend and vary an arpeggio or a scale, or else they can make reference to some earlier passage in the aria graced.

7. The same figures ought not to be repeated too often. Instead, new figures ought to be introduced. Ideally, cadenzas should present something unexpected, a final surprise for the listeners.

8. If a singer makes a modulation within a cadenza, it should not be very distant from the main key, and the singer must take care to make a smooth return to the tonic.

9. Cadenzas ought to be improvised, and they ought to change from performance to performance. Eighteenth-century musicians put a premium on the invention of the singer—after all, invention was one of the main justifications for the cadenza—and they had contempt for musicians who were not imaginative enough to invent their own cadenzas on the spot.

These rules correspond more closely with Faustina's relatively modest efforts than with Farinelli's gaudy display. And surely cadenzas improvised by the great eighteenth-century singers frequently deviated from the letter and even the spirit of these rules, according to the temperament of the individual performer. But before we accept these rules—compiled from writers working between about 1750 and 1780—as valid for operatic arias performed in the first half of the eighteenth century, we should try to find evidence that confirms the nature of embellished cadences from before 1750. Basing our conclusions on two isolated examples (even though by singers as distinguished as Faustina and Farinelli) may not be a sound guide for what thousands of singers did between 1700 and 1750. Unfortunately, though, few other examples of cadenzas from the first half of the eighteenth century have yet been described in print, although many more must certainly still exist.

Frederick the Great's own embellishments survive for an aria in Hasse's *Cleofide*, first performed in Dresden in 1731. They are written out in the king's own hand for the use of the castrato Porporino. The cadenza is not unlike those sung by Faustina, save that it does not refer to any previous figuration in the aria.[20] Handel's own embellishments for several arias are known and have been studied and published, but they are without cadenzas.[21] Two brief cadenzas do appear in Handel's score of *Samson*, but a longer cadenza in the copy of *Messiah* owned by St. Michael's College, Tenbury is now thought to have been added at some later time, long after the Dublin performance for which the manuscript was prepared.[22] The arrangements by William Babell of some of Handel's arias for solo harpsichord, complete with embellishments and cadenzas, cannot be directly transferred from keyboard to voice, especially since those cadenzas that do appear are invariably inserted at the end of the ritornellos and not at the ends of vocal entries.[23] All the other eighteenth-century cadences I have seen described in print—those illustrating Agricola's translation of Tosi's treatise, the pedagogical examples in the treatises of Quantz and Hiller, and those written into a copy of Gluck's *Tetide*—date from after the middle of the century.[24] It is, after all, possible that tastes changed drastically in the intervening time, and that what was appropriate for musicians of the second half of the century would not have been at all appropriate for the performers of Vivaldi's operas or, indeed, of any of those composed before 1750.[25]

Fortunately, one additional piece of evidence has recently come to light in an anthology of operatic arias lately acquired by the Joseph Regenstein Library of the University of Chicago (cataloged as MS 1267).[26] Among the arias excerpted from operas performed in Venice, Rome, and Bologna between about 1737 and 1741 appears a single leaf with a set of cadenzas, one for each diatonic key except E major. The manuscript consists of a series of fascicles in slightly different sizes, most of them presumably in the hands of various professional scribes. We can assume, I think, that such albums contained the favorite arias of their first owners, or at least a set of arias collected for the first owner by some friend, teacher, or other music lover. Two of the arias in Chicago 1267 are dated 1737 and four 1741. Presumably those dates fix, at least approximately, the time when the anthology was collected and bound. A checklist of the contents of the volume is given here as an appendix. The album includes operatic arias by Andrea Basili, Andrea Bernasconi, Giuseppe Carcano, Baldassare Galuppi, Johann Adolph Hasse, Nicolò Jommelli, Leonardo Leo, and Giovanni Battista Pergolesi, and there are as well a cantata by Nicola Porpora and a song by Gaetano Maria Schiassi. Some of the composers are among the most famous international stars of their day, and others had somewhat more local reputations.

Indeed, the presence of an aria by one of those lesser lights (Schiassi, who dedicated his "Romana" to Signora Catarina Fumagalli) made me wonder if the first owner of the album might not have been its dedicatee. But, as it turns out, Signora Fumagalli, called la Romanina, was a professional singer who took part in some of the productions excerpted in the Chicago anthology.[27] The selection of pieces by international and lesser composers, including examples by some of the best-known singers of the time (Lorenzino Gherardi, Carestini, Marianino, and Salimbeni),[28] and especially the informal note on folio 26ᵛ illustrating the resolution of an appoggiatura suggest to me that the first owner, whoever he or she was, was either an amateur singer or else a singer with rather limited experience.

Such albums are not particularly rare. Many of them languish on the shelves of libraries everywhere. Students of eighteenth-century music need to begin to use them more for what they can tell us about the music of the time, for they are gold mines of information, especially about operas that do not survive complete and about music by lesser composers. Chicago 1267, for example, includes arias from a setting of Metastasio's *Zenobia* by Andrea Basili, a composer not otherwise known to have written operas, and various arias from operas that do not survive complete.

The cadenzas on folios 58 and 58ᵛ, reproduced here as figure 1, follow quite closely some of the rules set out above as a compilation of later eighteenth-century views. In every case, these cadenzas extend and fill out the notes of the tonic triad, adding at the

FIGURE 1. Cadenzas in Chicago manuscript 1267

end of each a set of figures that leads to a trill (either indicated or implied) on the supertonic note before the resolution. The third cadenza, on B-flat, exemplifies the procedure as clearly as any. It consists of an extension of the B-flat-major triad, B-flat–D–F, with each note approached by an elaborate upbeat figure. This is followed by a decorated scale downward and finally the dominant seventh chord is outlined and leads directly to a trill on C. Moreover, all the cadenzas are short enough to be taken easily in one breath. In this they resemble Farinelli's extended virtuosity much less than Faustina's more modest efforts, partly because they do not repeat the same figures over and over again, an abuse signaled by a number of the writers on cadenzas.

Nevertheless, the set of cadenzas fails to meet the highest standards as set down in the synoptic rules. First and foremost, the very existence of a table of cadenzas presumably appropriate for any and all arias contradicts the assumption that singers should show their abilities by varying cadenzas at every performance. Moreover, since these cadenzas are presumably to be used indiscriminately over and over again they not only do not take off from the figurations of the arias to which they belong, but they also do not reflect the affect of a particular aria. They are useful rather than good.

Tosi has scathing things indeed to say about such sets of embellishments. "If, out of a particular Indulgence to the sex, so many female singers have the Graces set down in Writing, one that studies to become a good Singer should not follow the Example; whoever accustoms himself to have Things put in his Mouth, will have no Invention, and become a Slave to Memory." [29] And an even more scathing indictment of the practice comes from the pen of Benedetto Marcello in his well-known parody, *Il teatro alla moda*.[30] The ideal *cantatrice*, he writes,

> must demand that her part be sent to her as soon as possible. Maestro Crica will have to teach it to her, complete with variations, passage work, and other embellishments. She must ask Maestro Crica to write for her all embellishments in a book especially provided for that purpose, and she will carry that book with her no matter where she goes. . . . When the impresario . . . comes . . . to hear her, bringing the conductor with him, she will fuss around for hours, make a thousand excuses, and then finally oblige with an old warhorse such as the cantata *Impara a non dar fede*. Then, when she gets stuck in the middle because she forgot how one of the embellishments goes, she will turn to her mother, and out of the suitcase comes that book with the embellishments which she never manages to sing correctly. She will hasten to explain that she is sorry, "but I haven't sung this piece in ages, and furthermore this instrument is tuned somewhat higher than my own, and the recitative is too melancholy, and the aria just isn't in my style." She will go on in this fashion for awhile, though of course the real reason for her failure is that Maestro Crica is not there as usual to accompany her.

So the Chicago cadenzas do not, perhaps, exemplify the best models to follow in deciding how to perform cadenzas in operas by Vivaldi and others, but they do offer all-too-rare concrete examples of the sort of cadenza an eighteenth-century music master would write out for one of his charges.[31] As such, the manuscript is an important fragment of evidence, helping us to evaluate the personal memorials of the Faustinas and the Farinellis on the one hand and the pedagogical examples on the other. And though it is the first such set of cadenzas prepared for a particular singer in the first half of the eighteenth century to have been described in print, I have no doubt that many others will eventually be found once the rich treasures of eighteenth-century albums have been properly investigated.

APPENDIX. THE CONTENTS OF CHICAGO 1267

   1. FOLIO 1. "In te spero sposo amato." Del Sig. Andrea Bernasconi [sung by] Sig. Lorenzino Gherardi [at the Teatro] Alle Dame 1741. From *Demofoonte* (Metastasio): Rome, Dame, 1741. Libretto of 1741 production in Naples, Biblioteca Nazionale. Score of 1766 revival in Munich, Bayerische Staatsbibliothek.

   2. FOLIO 5. "La guerra la pace." Del Sig. Giuseppe Carcano [sung in] Venezia. From *Ambleto* (Apostolo Zeno and Pietro Pariati): Venice, Sant'Angelo, 1742. Libretto in Washington, Library of Congress, but no copies of the score are known.

   3. FOLIO 9. "La sorte mia tiranna." Del Sig. Gio. Adolfo Hasse detto il Sassone. From *Siroe* (Metastasio): Bologna, 1733. Libretto and score in *Italian Opera, 1640–1770*, ed. Howard Mayer Brown (New York, 1977), vols. 33, 59. For further information, see Reinhard Strohm, *Italienische Opernarien des frühen Settecento (1720–1730)*, 2 vols. (Cologne, 1976), vol. 2, p. 181.

   4. FOLIO 13. "Deh non tradirmi."

   5. FOLIO 17. "Parmi già che s'appressi il mio bene." Aria del Sig. [Nicolò] Jommelli. (On folio 26ᵛ is an informal note illustrating the resolution of an appoggiatura.) From *Eumene* (Apostolo Zeno): Bologna, 1742. Libretto for the 1742 production in Bologna, Civico Museo Bibliografico Musicale and elsewhere. Score of excerpts from a 1746 production (including "Parmi già") in London, British Library, MS Add. 24306; according to *New Grove*, autograph score of acts 1 and 2 in Stuttgart, Württembergische Landesbibliothek.

   6. FOLIO 27. [Cantata: *Amor timido*.] Del [Nicola] Porpora. Two arias, beginning "T'intendo si mio cor" and "Placido zeffiretto." Text by Metastasio. For further information, see Everett L. Sutton, "The Solo Vocal Works of Nicola Porpora: An Annotated Thematic Catalogue," Ph.D. dissertation (University of Minnesota, 1974), p. 238.

   7. FOLIO 29. "Risponderti vorrei." Del Sig. Leonardo Leo 1737 [sung

by] Sig. Carestini [in] Bologna. From *Siface* (Metastasio and others): Bologna, 1737. Libretto listed in Sartori, *Primo tentativo*, but no copies of the score are known.

8. FOLIO 33. "Se nò ti moro allato." From *Adriano in Siria* (Metastasio).

9. FOLIO 38. "Prigioniera abbandonata." Aria del Sig. [Giovanni Battista] Pergolesi. From *Adriano in Siria* (Metastasio): Naples, S. Bartolomeo, 1734. Modern edition in *Opera omnia di Giovanni Battista Pergolesi*, ed. Francesco Caffarelli (Rome, 1939–1942), vol. 14, pp. 38–41.

10. FOLIO 41. "Anima del cor mio." Del Sig. [Giovanni Battista] Lampugnani 1741. (On folios 43^v and 44^v are parts for first and second violin of an aria beginning "Ah figlio.")

11. FOLIO 49. "Se viver non poss'io." From *Alessandro nell'Indie* (Metastasio): possibly from the anonymous setting performed (according to Sartori, *Primo tentativo*) in Prato in 1734, at which Catarina Fumagalli sang Cleofide.

12. FOLIO 53. "Di rose spargerò." Del Sig. Lampugnani 1741 [sung by] Sig. Marianino.

13. FOLIO 58. Cadenzas in G, A, B-flat, C, D, and F.

14. FOLIO 59. "O tu che m'accendesti." Del Sig. Leonardo Leo 1737 [sung by] Sig. Salimbeni [in] Bologna. From *Siface* (Metastasio and others): Bologna, 1737. Libretto listed in Sartori, *Primo tentativo*, but no copies of the score are known.

15. FOLIO 63. "Oh che felice pianto." Aria di D. Andrea Basili. From *Zenobia* (Metastasio). Standard reference works (such as the *Enciclopedia dello spettacolo*, MGG, and *The New Grove*) do not list any operas by Basili.

16. FOLIO 67. "Se tu la reggi al volo" [sung by] Sig. Marianini. From *Ezio* (Metastasio).

17. FOLIO 77. Romana: "L'amante Paszorcha se al ruscelezzo." Aria del Sig. [Gaetano Maria] Schiassi per la S.^{ra} Catarina Fumagalli.

18. FOLIO 81. "Caro padre ancor tu vivi." Del Sig. [Baldassare] Galuppi 1741. From *Berenice* (Bartolomeo Vitturi): Venice, Sant'Angelo, 1741. Libretto for the 1741 production in Washington, Library of Congress, and elsewhere. Score in Berlin, Deutsche Staatsbibliothek.

19. FOLIO 85. "Vi conosco amate stelle." Aria di D. Andrea Basili. From *Zenobia* (Metastasio). See number 15.

20. FOLIO 89. "Sai che possiedi appieno." Aria.

NOTES

1. For further discussion of this point, see Howard Mayer Brown, *Embellishing Sixteenth-Century Music* (London, 1976), pp. 73–76.

2. See the English translation of his preface in Giulio Caccini, *Le nuove musiche*, ed. H. Wiley Hitchcock (Madison, Wis., 1970), pp. 44–45. On Caccini's indebtedness to earlier styles of embellishment, see Howard Mayer Brown, "The Geography of Florentine Monody: Caccini at Home and Abroad," *Early Music* vol. 9, no. 2 (April 1981): 147–168.

3. See Pier Francesco Tosi, *Opinioni de'cantori antichi e moderni, o sieno Osservazioni sopra il canto figurato* (Bologna, 1723). A facsimile of this edition appears as a supplement to Johann Friedrich Agricola, *Anleitung zur Singkunst (1757)*, ed. Erwin R. Jacobi (Celle, 1966). All references to Tosi's treatise are to the English translation by John Ernest Galliard, *Observations on the Florid Song* (London, 1743; reprinted London, 1967 and Geneva, 1978). Galliard adds a note at the beginning of his translation to explain that "by the Ancient, our Author means those who liv'd about thirty or forty Years ago; and by the Modern the late and present Singers."

Even some late seventeenth- and eighteenth-century composers refused to permit embellishments. Robert Donington, *The Interpretation of Early Music* (London, 1963), p. 92 quotes Sir John Hawkins as stating in his *Memoirs of the Life of A. S.* (London[?], ca. 1740), p. ii that Agostino Steffani (1654–1728) never allowed "any divisions, or graces, even on the most plain and simple passages, except what he wrote himself." Steffani seems to have been an exceptional case.

4. Tosi, *Observations*, p. 91.

5. Ibid., pp. 93–94.

6. Ibid., pp. 94, 162.

7. On the translations of Tosi's treatise, see Agricola, *Anleitung*, ed. Jacobi, pp. xxix–xxxiv. Johann Joachim Quantz, *Versuch einer Anweisung die Flöte traversiere zu spielen* (Berlin, 1752; 3rd edition, Breslau, 1789; facsimile by Hans-Peter Schmitz, Cassel and Basel, 1953; English translation by Edward R. Reilly, New York, 1966) provides much useful information about singing. Giambattista Mancini, *Pensieri e riflessioni pratiche sopra il canto figurato* (Vienna, 1774; 2nd edition, Milan, 1777; English translation of both editions by Edward Foreman, Champaign, Ill., 1967), Johann Adam Hiller, *Anweisung zum musikalisch-zierlichen Gesange* (Leipzig, 1780; facsimile, Leipzig, 1976), and the other writings on singing by Hiller are the principal sources of information about eighteenth-century singing styles and techniques.

8. See Charles Burney, *A General History of Music*, ed. Frank Mercer (New York, 1957), vol. 2, p. 950.

9. Tosi, *Observations*, "Of Cadences," pp. 126–139. The quotation

appears on pp. 128–129. Tosi's chapter deals with embellished cadences (those sung in time) as well as cadenzas proper, that is, extensions "of the embellishment outside the time of the movement," in the definition of Donington, *Interpretation*, p. 121.

10. See Quantz, *On Playing the Flute*, trans. Edward R. Reilly (New York, 1966), "Of Cadenzas," pp. 179–195 and especially pp. 180–181.

11. Tosi, *Observations*, pp. 127–137.

12. Ibid., p. 136.

13. Ibid., p. 137.

14. George J. Buelow, "A Lesson in Operatic Performance Practice by Madame Faustina Bordoni," in *A Musical Offering. Essays in Honor of Martin Bernstein*, ed. Edward H. Clinkscale and Claire Brook (New York, 1977), pp. 79–96. Buelow does not identify the opera from which the aria was taken. The manuscript anthology in which it appears (Washington, Library of Congress, Music Division, M1500 S28 G5) labels it merely as "Del S. Giuseppe Vignati di Milano—Cantata in detta Città da Faustina—con li suoi modi scritti come la cantava. Nel Carvenale [*sic*] 1720." Reference works, such as *The New Grove Dictionary*, "Vignati," by Sven Hansell, vol. 19, p. 756, state that all of Vignati's operatic music has been lost, and that the 1719 setting of Zeno's and Pariati's *Ambleto* was a first act composed by Vignati, a second act by Carlo Baliani, and a third act by Giacomo Cozzi. However, I own a manuscript copy of *Ambleto*, act 3, with three arias—among them the unembellished "Sciolta dal lido"—by Vignati (the others are presumably all by Cozzi, since the score is headed "Atto Terzo. Musica Del Sig.ʳ Giacomo Cozzi"). This manuscript, apparently the only surviving testimony to Cozzi's and Vignati's talents as operatic composers, includes, at the end of the volume, five substitute arias for the act, all without attribution (one is copied twice). According to Claudio Sartori, *Primo tentativo di catalogo unico dei libretti italianni a stampa fino all'anno 1800* (Milan, 1968–1980), copies of the libretto for the 1719 performance in Milan survive in Bologna, Civico Museo Bibliografico Musicale; Milan, Conservatorio di Musica Giuseppe Verdi; Milan, Biblioteca Ambrosiana; Milan, Biblioteca Nazionale Braidense; Parma, Conservatorio di Musica Arrigo Boito; and Rome, Conservatorio di Musica S. Cecilia.

The libretto (which lists Faustina in the role of Veremonda) does not mention any substitutions. The score follows the libretto even to omitting any musical setting for dialogue included within *virgolette*, except that it replaces the original aria in scene 10, "È pur dolce," with an aria by Vignati, "È troppo amabile," which in turn is re-

274 The Practice of Opera Seria

placed by one of the substitute arias at the end of the volume, "Rus-celletto ch'è lungi dal mare." Three of the five substitute arias are for the character Gerilda, sung in 1719 by Cuzzoni. Perhaps the substitutions can be explained as changes demanded by the singers at the last moment. Or perhaps the score reflects the version given at some later date for which no libretto survives.

15. At least Tosi's English translator, J. E. Galliard, supposed that the two female singers he cited as paragons among the moderns were Faustina and Cuzzoni. See Tosi, *Observations*, pp. 154, 169–172.

16. Printed, along with other examples of Farinelli's embellishment, in Franz Haböck, *Die Gesangskunst der Kastraten, Erster Notenband: A. Die Kunst des Cavaliere Carlo Broschi Farinelli, B. Farinellis berühmte Arien* (Vienna, 1923), pp. 140–152, after Vienna, Oester-reichische Nationalbibliothek, MS 19111, a manuscript dedicated to Maria Theresa by Farinelli in Madrid on March 30, 1753. For an aria embellished by Farinelli with a single, more modest cadenza, see Hans-Peter Schmitz, *Die Kunst der Verzierung im 18. Jahrhundert* (Cassel and Basel, 1955), pp. 76–93 (the cadenza appears on p. 90). On Farinelli's repertoire, see Robert Freeman, "Farinelli and his Repertory," in *Studies in Renaissance and Baroque Music in Honor of Arthur Mendel*, ed. Robert Marshall (Cassel and Basel, 1974), pp. 307–309. On p. 303, Freeman cites evidence to suggest that Farinelli's overuse of spectacular effects changed at some point during his career. For a brief summary of Farinelli's career, see Angus Heriot, *The Castrati in Opera* (London, 1956; reprinted New York, 1974), pp. 95–110.

17. Agricola, *Anleitung*, pp. 203–209.

18. Hiller, *Anweisung*, p. 109, and Mancini, *Practical Reflections*, pp. 54–57.

19. They are a synthesis of the advice given in Quantz, *On Playing the Flute*, "Of Cadenzas," pp. 179–195; Agricola, *Anleitung*, "Von den Cadenzen," pp. 194–209; Mancini, *Practical Reflections*, pp. 54–57; and Hiller, *Anweisung*, "Von den Cadenzen," pp. 108–128.

For further information on free vocal ornamentation in eighteenth-century Italian music, see Donington, *Interpretation*, and Frederick Neumann, *Ornamentation in Baroque and Post-Baroque Music* (Princeton, N.J., 1978), especially pp. 553–573. Neumann, p. 554, points out that Tosi recommended a nonlegato articulation for the performance of fast *passaggi* (see Tosi, *Observations*, p. 31).

20. The aria "Digli ch'io son fedele" is published in a modern edition in Schmitz, *Kunst der Verzierung*, pp. 121–125 and in Hellmuth Christian Wolff, *Original Vocal Improvisations from the 16th–18th Centuries* (Cologne, 1972), pp. 143–168.

21. Handel's own embellishments are described in James S. and Martin V. Hall, "Handel's Graces," *Handel-Jahrbuch* 3 (1957): 25–43 and Winton Dean, "Vocal Embellishment in a Handel Aria," in *Studies in Eighteenth-Century Music. A Tribute to Karl Geiringer,* ed. H. C. Robbins Landon and Roger E. Chapman (London, 1970), pp. 151–159. The three arias ornamented by Handel and published in G. F. Handel, *Three Ornamented Arias,* ed. Winton Dean (London, 1976) contain no cadenzas. The same three arias appear in a different reading from the same manuscript in Wolff, *Original Vocal Improvisations,* pp. 109–132, with the embellishments attributed to Gaetano Guadagni and dated ca. 1751.

22. The cadenzas in *Samson* are published in G. F. Handel, *Werke,* ed. Friedrich Chrysander (Leipzig, 1861), vol. 10, pp. v–vi. The *Messiah* cadenza and its date and provenance are discussed in Hall and Hall, "Handel's Graces," pp. 26–27. It is reproduced in facsimile in *Handel's Conducting Score of Messiah,* ed. Watkins Shaw (London, 1974), fol. 9.

23. Babell's arrangements are published, among other places, in Händel, *Werke,* ed. Friedrich Chrysander (Leipzig, 1894), vol. 42, pp. 210–243.

24. The examples from Agricola's, Quantz's, and Hiller's treatises all appear in the chapters on cadenzas cited in note 19 above. The cadenzas in Gluck's *Tetide* are published in a modern edition in Christoph Willibald Gluck, *Sämtliche Werke,* Abteilung III, vol. 22, *Tetide, Serenata teatrale in einem Akt von Gianambrogio Migliavacca,* ed. László Somfai (Cassel and Basel, 1978), pp. 78, 80, 121, 162, 206, 207, 215, 242.

25. On Vivaldi's own cadenzas for instrumental music, see Walter Kolneder, *Aufführungspraxis bei Vivaldi* (Leipzig, 1955), pp. 67–82. Eighteenth-century singers were sensitive to differences between vocal and instrumental styles. Tosi, for example, wrote in his *Observations,* p. 159: "the instrumental Performers of some Ability imagine that the beautiful Graces and Flourishes, with their nimble Fingers, will have the same Effect when executed with the voice; but it will not do," to which Tosi's English translator, J. E. Galliard, added, "It is a very great Error (too much in Practice) for the Voice, (which should serve as a Standard to be imitated by Instruments) to copy all the Tricks practised on the several Instruments, to its greatest Detriment."

26. The generous gift of Mr. John F. Fleming of New York. The only other collection of cadenzas arranged by keys known to me appears in Domenico Corri, *The Singers Preceptor* (London, 1810), pp. 75–76, reproduced in facsimile in *The Porpora Tradition,* ed. Edward

Foreman (Pro Musica Press, 1968). Corri also published a set of arias embellished and with cadenzas, as sung by renowned singers, in his *A Select Collection of the Most Admired Songs, Duetts, Etc.*, vol. 1 (Edinburgh, ca. 1779), which includes among others "Verdi prati" from Handel's *Alcina* as sung by Sig.ʳ Carestini, "Dove sei amato bene" from Handel's *Rodelinda* as sung by Sig.ʳ Senesino, and "Che farò senza Euridice" from Gluck's *Orfeo ed Euridice* as sung by Sig.ʳ Guadagni.

27. For example, Sartori, *Primo tentativo*, lists Fumagalli in productions of *Adriano in Siria* in Naples in 1734, *Demofoonte* in Naples in 1735, *Alessandro nell'Indie* in Prato in 1736, and *Siface* in Bologna in 1737. The 1736 libretto describes her as La Romanina.

28. For brief summaries of the careers of Carestini and Salimbeni, see *The New Grove*, vol. 3, pp. 778–779 ("Carestini") and Heriot, *Castrati*, pp. 181–183 (Selimbeni). Heriot mentions Marianino on p. 27.

29. Tosi, *Observations*, p. 88.

30. The translation is taken from Reinhard G. Pauly, "*Il teatro alla moda* by Benedetto Marcello," *Musical Quarterly* 34 (1948): 394. For the Italian, see Marcello, *Il teatro alla moda*, ed. Ariodante Marianni (Milan, 1959), pp. 45–47.

31. Lowell Lindgren has kindly pointed out to me that another single page containing embellishments (but no cadenzas) survives in the Yale University Library as Filmer MS 23. It is briefly described in Robert Ford, "The Filmer Manuscripts: A Handlist," *Notes* 34 (1978): 821–822. The page, presumably written by a teacher or coach for his student, offers a number of sets of embellishments for arias in Giovanni Bononcini's *Il trionfo di Camilla*.

PART IV
Vivaldi as Dramatic Composer

The Relationship between Text and Music in the Operas of Vivaldi   *by Eric Cross*

Opera seria has been labeled "undramatic" by many modern writers. The concept of a work comprising little else but alternating successions of recitatives and solo arias is so far removed from the average musician's concept of opera that even a scholar such as Michael Robinson, who has done much in recent years to increase our knowledge of eighteenth-century Neapolitan opera, can come out with a comment such as: "Alas, a concert-like succession of arias with intervening and sometimes very dull recitative builds neither a cogent nor very coherent music drama."[1] True, it *can* sometimes be dull and incoherent, but, as recent revivals of some of Handel's masterpieces have shown, once the conventions are accepted by the audience, good eighteenth-century opera seria can be as dramatic as anything written in the following two centuries. While perhaps not equaling Handel's undoubted genius for the stage, Vivaldi nevertheless reveals in the best of his operatic music an awareness of the theater that deserves recognition.

For the overall structure of his opera, Vivaldi was largely dependent on his libretto, its poetry differentiating between the freer verse of the recitatives and the more regular rhyme schemes of the arias and occasional ensembles or choruses, usually divided into two stanzas for a da capo setting. Vivaldi followed contemporary practice by resetting older librettos (his works include some of the most popular eighteenth-century texts such as Metastasio's *L'Olimpiade* and Zeno's *Griselda*), which were generally adapted for him by a local poet. This revision involved tailoring the number and scope of the roles to the singers available that particular season, but it could also give the composer the opportunity to suggest his own ideas on the reshaping of the drama, and we know of one case where Vivaldi certainly liaised very closely with his librettist.[2]

Often Vivaldi deliberately creates a sense of climax for the end of an act. In many of the later operas this is achieved through the use of an ensemble or chorus,[3] and while in some cases (such as *La fida ninfa*) it seems that this positioning is entirely due to the librettist,[4] in others it may well be Vivaldi's responsibility. Among the examples in the latter category is the final scene of act 2 of *Griselda*. The 1744 edition of Zeno's text[5] ends the second act with an aria for Griselda, yet Goldoni's adaptation, made under Vivaldi's supervision, ends the act with a trio for Griselda, Costanza, and Gualtiero. The pasticcio *Rosmira* ends act 1 with a chorus involving trumpets in praise of Partenope, although most other settings of this Stampiglia libretto (including Handel's *Partenope*) situate this battle scene at the beginning of act 2.[6] This work also shows a fascinating attempt to provide some kind of overall unity (even within that supposedly most "undramatic" of genres, the pasticcio): following the opera's final recitative Vivaldi wrote the direction "Coro primo dell'Opera" and copied out the bass line for a chorus, which appears in the work's very first scene.

Other ways in which Vivaldi increases tension in certain final scenes involve instrumentation, tonality, and vocal virtuosity. Some arias use unusual orchestral forces: act 1 of *Arsilda regina di Ponto* ends with a piece in which the voice is accompanied by muted five-part strings and a part for harpsichords written on two staves, while the final aria of act 2 of *Giustino* employs a psaltery obbligato. The aria from *Arsilda* also provides an example of Vivaldi's use of tonality, for it is in the relatively rare and extreme key of E major, which also appears at the end of acts 1 and 2 of *Teuzzone*[7] and, in the version containing the aria "Eccelso trono," at the end of act 2 of *L'Atenaide*. Emilia's aria at the close of act 2 of *Catone in Utica*, "Come in vano il mare irato," provides a virtuoso tour de force for its singer Maria Gasparini, with its wide compass of two octaves and a fourth $(g-c''')$ and its florid coloratura over nearly the whole of that range.

Vivaldi follows contemporary practice, especially in his later operas, by favoring the use of major keys for arias. Thus in some works the fact that the predominant mode is major increases the effectiveness when the composer does provide a minor-key aria. This can be seen, for example, in act 2 of *L'Olimpiade*, where the only two minor-key arias are "Se cerca, se dice" in scene 10, whose G-minor tonality emphasizes Megacle's great sorrow, and "Gemo

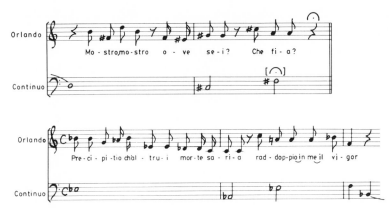

EXAMPLE 1. *Orlando* (2.8, 9)

in un punto, e fremo" at the end of the act, which is in C minor as Licida is left in despair and torment. Both these keys are, in fact, particularly associated with grief, and this can be seen again in *Griselda*, written in the following year (1735). At the end of act 1 Corrado's cheerful F-major aria "Alle minaccie di fiera belva," with its accompaniment including two horns, is followed by a recitative for Griselda alone, which opens in G minor and culminates in her C-minor aria "Hò il cor già lacero." This contrast of tonalities serves to underline Griselda's unhappiness compared with Corrado's optimism, and the juxtaposition of F major and G minor can be seen again in the second act.[8]

Tonal contrasts are also used to mark a change of set or an important entry of a new character. For example, in the version of *Farnace* in the Turin manuscript Giordano 36, following an aria for Selinda in E major, Tamiri begins the new scene, set outside the royal tomb, in E-flat major (act 1, scene 9). In act 3 of *L'Olimpiade* Aminta's B-minor aria in scene 5 ("Son qual per mare ignoto") is followed by a change of set from an overgrown ruin to the Temple of Jupiter for the entry of a chorus of priests with Licida, Alcandro, and Clistene, the last of whom opens the recitative in F major.[9] In act 2 of the 1727 setting of *Orlando*, the rocky scene suddenly changes to a "horrid cavern" without any apparent exit, and this transformation is mirrored by a sudden change from F-sharp minor to E-flat major (see example 1). Giustino's first appearance in the opera of that name, in a rustic setting complete with plough, is interrupted by the appearance of "La Fortuna in

Mac[c]hina," and an E-major symphony based on the ritornello from the first movement of *La primavera* RV269 follows directly on Giustino's C-major aria.

Vivaldi also uses tonality, along with other elements of the musical texture, to underline the drama in many places. Near the beginning of act 2 of *Giustino*, Arianna is left chained to a rock to await the arrival of a ferocious monster. This unfortunate situation leads her to begin act 2, scene 3 with a little eight-bar arioso accompanied by "Viol[on]e Solo p[ian]o, e Cembali Arpeggio" to express her despair, and its C-minor tonality contrasts strongly with the preceding B-flat aria of Polidarte.[10] In the fourth scene of the following act an unhappy Giustino and Leocasta affirm their love for each other, Giustino with an E-major aria with muted strings ("Il mio cor già più non sà") and Leocasta with her D-minor "Largo e staccato" aria "Senza l'amato ben," making use of the plaintive Neapolitan sixth. In the following scene, however, the mood changes as Amantio gloats over his good fortune, and he sings a bouncy gigue in A major to the text "Sì vuò à regnar." *L'incoronazione di Dario* act 2, scene 11 contains a discussion between Alinda and Oronte, in which the latter declares that he no longer loves her and, in a busy A-major aria, "Se fui contento della tua fede," tells her to find someone else. Alinda, however, cannot forget him so easily, and her recitative immediately moves to minor keys (hinting at B minor before cadencing in E minor and G minor) and, following a final cadence in E-flat, the scene ends with a gentle C-minor allegro in $\frac{12}{8}$ with pathetic chromatic inflections. At the opening of act 3 of the Mantuan opera *Tito Manlio*, Manlio is languishing in prison, and the act begins with a short through-composed aria (again in the significant key of C minor) as he attempts to sleep. Servilia, his fiancée, enters and at first sings a slow, sorrowful aria in D minor,[11] but then, after Manlio has awakened and suggested a more positive solution to his predicament, she cheers up and leaves him with an optimistic F-major allegro full of lively ♩♪♪ | ♪♪♩ | rhythms.

These examples reveal Vivaldi's dramatic use of tonality extending over two or more scenes, but he was also interested in reflecting aspects of the text on a smaller scale, within individual recitatives or single arias. The main function of recitative was to further the developments of the plot as quickly as possible, and it normally held little interest for the listener, yet even here Vivaldi often shows an unexpected degree of attention to detail. Although, as we have seen, it was often the librettist who decided various details of the opera's structure, it was entirely up to the composer to determine which parts of the recitative he set for continuo alone (the vast majority) and which portions he highlighted with an orchestral accompaniment. Accompanied recitative generally appears at a dramatic turning point in the opera when a character is under extreme emotional stress, but in several of the earlier operas Vivaldi uses it in the very first scene to provide a dramatic opening. *L'incoronazione di Dario* opens with the ghost of Ciro addressing his sleeping daughters; in *Teuzzone* the Emperor Troncone dies almost as soon as the curtain goes up; while the initial scene of *Tito Manlio* includes Tito's swearing of a patriotic Roman oath.

Vivaldi uses several different types of accompanied recitative, depending on the dramatic situation, The first basic type involves surrounding the vocal line in a halo of held string chords with slowly changing harmonies. This is particularly suitable for creating the mood of a ritual or magic incantation, as in *L'Olimpiade* act 3, scene 7, where Clistene prepares for Licida's sacrifice, or at several points in *Orlando*, whose libretto, with its strong supernatural element, provides numerous opportunities for accompanied recitative. It also serves to emphasize any strong emotional reaction, such as despair in *Griselda* as Ottone threatens Griselda's son (act 2, scene 5); jealousy in *Ottone in villa*, where Caio's desperation in act 2, scene 3 is portrayed by colorful harmonies (especially the augmented-sixth chord on *gelosia*; see example 2); or determination in *Orlando*, as Orlando affirms his duty to defeat Alcina (act 1, scene 5). A second type also involves the strings in four-part harmony, but this time with shorter quarter-note chords interspersed with rests, a texture suitable for more aggressive emotions (indeed, the section of *Griselda* already cited proceeds to this style of writing as Griselda takes a more positive attitude and dismisses Ottone). A mixture of the two styles can also be seen in the first scene of *Tito Manlio*. At the beginning of the oath the basic texture involves held chords, but at the words "Giuro l'odio, la guerra," the ideas of hatred and war bring a more aggressive setting, with not only sharp quarter-note chords but also vigorous ♩ ♫ ♬ rhythms (see example 3). A third style consists of similar sharp string quarter notes, but this time with all the strings in unison (a boon for the overworked eighteenth-century com-

EXAMPLE 2. *Ottone in villa* (2.3)

EXAMPLE 3. *Tito Manlio* (1.1)

poser, as it took no longer to write than ordinary simple recitative apart from the addition of the direction "Viol[in]i e Viol[et]te con il Basso"). This obviously also suits aggressive situations, such as in *L'Atenaide* act 3, scene 5 (scene 4 in the 1729 libretto), where Pulcheria can restrain herself no longer and bursts out in fury against Atenaide, and unison writing is frequently mixed in with fuller textures.

In act 2, scene 10 of the pasticcio *Tamerlano* (entitled *Il Bajazet* in Vivaldi's score), Bajazet believes that his daughter Asteria has betrayed him by accepting the hand of the tyrant Tamerlano. Initially, the basic texture is of four-part quarter-note chords, but, as Bajazet becomes more agitated, all the strings break out with unison triplet arpeggios, and the unexpected G-sharp in measure 5 and the A-sharp in measure 8 push the music forward (example 4).

EXAMPLE 4. *Tamerlano* (2.10)

EXAMPLE 5. *Orlando finto pazzo* (1.3)

His threat to return and haunt Asteria's dreams brings pulsating sixteenth-note tremolos, while, following a contrasting andante passage at the mention of her mother and brother, his final desperate attempts to make her change her mind return to unison arpeggios.

Although some of the most striking parallels between text and music can be seen in passages of *accompagnato* (something that is not surprising since these usually occur at key moments of the drama), there are also frequently close links within simple recitatives. There are several ways in which simple recitative can reflect the text: a judicious choice of harmonies can depict an overall mood or underline an individual word or phrase, an increase in the harmonic rhythm or a steadily rising bass line can increase tension, and melodic phrases can portray pictorial ideas in the text. The initial choice of tonality for a recitative can often seem arbitrary, simply one of the various related keys that can follow the preceding aria, but sometimes it appears to be chosen for a specific dramatic purpose. Some examples, such as the choice of G minor to contrast with F major in *Griselda*, have already been mentioned, and a similar instance can be seen in act 1 of Vivaldi's first opera, *Ottone in villa*. In scene 5 Caio dismisses the protestations of his former lover Tullia (who is in disguise as a man, Ostilio), saying that he now has eyes only for Cleonilla, and ends with a happy G-major aria. In the following scene Tullia reveals her true feelings of jealousy and despair, and so the recitative begins straight away with a strong cadence in C minor to the text "Ah! Traditor t'intendo."

When a character becomes particularly emotional, this anxiety is often paralleled by a speeding up of the harmonic rhythm, with the bass changing every half note. This can be seen at the end of *Orlando finto pazzo* act 1, scene 3, where Tigrinda can restrain herself no longer and bewails her fate over rapidly changing chro-

EXAMPLE 6. *Orlando finto pazzo* (3.7)

matic harmonies (example 5). The progression from a diminished-seventh chord to the last inversion of the dominant seventh via a falling semitone in the bass is a favorite of Vivaldi's at emotional moments. The diminished-seventh chord is frequently used to color any kind of dramatic outburst (it is an important aspect of the characterization of Griselda),[12] but elsewhere in *Orlando finto pazzo* harmony is used to convey more subtle meanings. In act 1, scene 4, Tigrinda claims that events can change suddenly ("Si cangia in un'istante la vicenda"), and at this phrase the bass undergoes an enharmonic change from E-flat to D-sharp, something very rare in Vivaldi's recitatives. Later in act 3, scene 7 of the same opera, Ersilla advances on Brandimarte and accuses him of betraying her, and here the word *ingannator* (deceiver) is highlighted by an unusual augmented-sixth chord (example 6), again involving a chromatic bass line.

A sense of mounting excitement is sometimes generated by a rising chromatic bass. In *L'Atenaide* act 3, scene 12 (scene 11 in the 1729 libretto) the Emperor Teodosio's almost neurotic behavior is underlined in this way (the bass line, which moves rapidly in half notes under a partly sequential vocal line, is marked "Presto"), and in *Tito Manlio* act 1, scene 13 Manlio declares his courage and determination with another sequential vocal line over an emphatic bass, which rises steadily in semitones from d-sharp to b before cadencing in F-sharp minor (example 7). This example reveals another tendency in Vivaldi's recitatives: to move toward the sharp

EXAMPLE 7. *Tito Manlio* (1.13)

EXAMPLE 8. *Il Tigrane* (2.14)

end of the tonal spectrum in order to heighten tension. The keys employed by Vivaldi in his recitatives fall largely between E major and C-sharp minor on one side and A-flat major and F minor on the other; whereas the extreme flat minor keys are generally associated with sorrow and despair, the sharp minor keys are often employed as a means of generating dramatic excitement. This occurs in *Orlando* act 1, scene 12 (scene 13 in the 1727 libretto) as Bradamante becomes agitated and accuses Ruggiero of infidelity, bringing the music round to C-sharp minor. In *Il Tigrane* act 2, scene 14[13] Cleopatra believes that Tigrane has killed her father Mitridate and becomes very excited, almost fainting as she imagines that she is being called to follow the ghost of her father. This is mirrored in the extreme tonality, the harmonies implying first D-sharp minor (a very rare key) and then G-sharp minor, before finally relaxing slightly to cadence in D minor (example 8).

A further feature to be found in some simple recitatives, mainly in Vivaldi's later operas, is a cadence comprising four quarter-note chords instead of the usual two. This provides a very emphatic cadence and so is ideal for underlining a firm decision, sometimes at the very end of a scene. In *L'Olimpiade* act 1, scene 2 Licori dismisses Megacle, telling him that all will be explained when he returns, and in *Griselda* act 2, scene 3 Roberto looks forward to the glory of hopeless love to a firm I-IV♭-V-I cadence in quarter notes.

Although the vocal line in recitative consists largely of stock figures,[14] it does sometimes contain pictorial ideas. In *La fida ninfa* act 3, scene 1 the word *discende* is depicted by a falling scale through nearly an octave, while in *Orlando* act 3, scene 4 the command *suonate*, as Orlando directs imaginary musicians to play while he dances, is set to trumpetlike patterns with the intervals of a fifth and a fourth. The word *piansi* (I wept) is highlighted in *Ottone in villa* act 1, scene 5 by a diminished third in the voice

EXAMPLE 9. *Ottone in villa* (1.5)

coupled with Neapolitan-sixth harmony, which helps to convey Tullia's unhappiness in this scene (example 9). Orlando's madness in *Orlando finto pazzo* provides the opportunity for unusual recitative writing in certain places, and in act 2, scene 10 Vivaldi sets the text in a very flexible way: he moves freely from accompanied to simple recitative; he suddenly varies the pace of harmonic movement; and he makes considerable use of special effects, from his vivid portrayal of Orlando's cries to his horse Brigliadoro, to his triplet setting at the words "danzava all'Italiana un ballo in aria."

Unusual dramatic touches can also be seen in the recitatives of other works. In one of his late operas, *Catone in Utica*, written for Verona in 1737, Vivaldi actually marks dynamics in a passage of simple recitative. In act 2, scene 1 every bass note is marked "F" as Catone reads out a letter from the Senate, but then "Piano sempre" as soon as the letter is finished. The direction "Forte" is used later in this scene as Catone angrily contradicts Fulvio, and an "a tempo" marking follows two asides by Marzia and Arbace, implying that these asides would have been sung in a freer tempo. On one occasion (in *Orlando* act 1, scene 6) the bass is marked "Arpeggio" to portray the violent sea from which Medoro has just escaped.

Apart from the recitatives, most of the opportunities for the early eighteenth-century musical dramatist are presented by the arias, the vast majority of which are in da capo form, and here Vivaldi's greatest interest is in depicting the general mood of his text or of the character concerned. This is not surprising when one considers the pictorial talents that he displays over and over again in his instrumental music, not only portraying natural phenomena and events, as in *Le quattro stagioni*, but also depicting abstract ideas such as rest (*Il riposo*), night (*La notte*) or pleasure (*Il piacere*). The type of dynamic instrumental writing that appears in the *Tempesta di mare* concertos is equally appropriate to an aria in which a character's thoughts are in turmoil, especially as one of the favorite forms of "simile aria" in eighteenth-century opera seria compares the singer's situation with that of a ship tossed around by stormy seas.

In most of Vivaldi's arias the mood is clearly apparent before the singer even enters as a result of the opening ritornello. Here orchestration plays an important part: trumpets (sometimes with timpani) provide a martial atmosphere (see *Tito Manlio* act 2, scene 11), horns are particularly appropriate for hunting arias (see *Tito Manlio* act 1, scene 5),[15] while recorders of various sizes give a bucolic flavor (*La verità in cimento* requires a sopranino and two tenor recorders, which are also called on in *Tito Manlio* in addition to the usual treble recorder). Vivaldi also, however, creates more individual sonorities. In *Orlando* act 1, scene 2 (scene 12 in the 1727 libretto), after Ruggiero has drunk from the magic spring and become enchanted with Alcina, he sings of his love for her in the aria "Sol dà te mio dolce amore" with a virtuoso obbligato part for transverse flute accompanied by muted violins in two parts and a bass line marked "1 Violone con Arco / Violette e Bassi / Pizzicatti [*sic*] / Senza Cembali"—a truly magical sonority. Giustino's aria from *Giustino* act 1, scene 4, "Bel riposo de' Mortali," portrays the "dolce sonno" of the text in a gentle $\frac{12}{8}$ andante with the pastoral tones of recorders, oboes, and muted strings, but also contains an extra bass line for the double basses comprising a drone C pedal throughout most of the aria. Unusual orchestration also serves to create the appropriate mood, this time of solemn expectancy, in the sinfonia from the final act of *Tito Manlio*. This is scored for two trumpets, two oboes, bassoon, timpani, and strings, all of which are muted. The music is, in fact, a version of the opening of the *Concerto funebre* RV 579.[16]

In *Catone in Utica* act 2, scene 11 Catone furiously disowns his daughter, asking Emilia and Arbace if they have ever seen a more faithless daughter or a more miserable father. His anger is reflected in the vigorous tremolo accompaniment of repeated sixteenth notes in the upper strings and eighths in the bass, and Vivaldi is very specific with his dynamic markings, repeating "f" each bar and later, after the vocal entry, using the rare direction "fp." An accompaniment of unison strings is obviously another suitable texture for an aria expressing anger or any other aggressive emotion, and in *La fida ninfa* act 3, scene 9 it appears in the B section of the da capo aria "Perdo ninfa." In this aria the pirate Oralto, who believes that his beloved Licori has committed suicide, laments her loss in a gentle larghetto in common time accompanied by four-part strings,[17] but after the end of the first section his thoughts turn to revenge. This change of mood is immediately apparent from the structure of the text, and the contrast is achieved musically by a change to a $\frac{3}{8}$ presto with the strings in unison with the voice.

Perdo ninfa, ch'era una dea,
e'l suo prezzo era un tesor.
Vendicarmi,
disfogarmi,
turba rea,
al ritorno io ben saprò.
Voi malnati allor farò
scopo e segno al mio furor.

[I lose a nymph who was a goddess, and who was worth a treasure. I shall have my revenge and rid myself of this wicked crowd on my return. Then I shall make you wretched ones the object of my fury.]

Another common method of creating a mood of agitation is by the repetition of certain string figurations, and here there is an obvious connection between Vivaldi the violinist and Vivaldi the dramatist. Arpeggio patterns in the violins in Licida's aria "Gemo in un punto, e fremo" (from *L'Olimpiade* act 2, scene 15) serve to convey his mental turmoil as he is torn apart by conflicting emotions, whereas repeated short sobbing figures ♪♪ in Narete's "Deh ti piega" (from *La fida ninfa* act 2, scene 3) provide a melancholy atmosphere as he pleads with Oralto. One of Vivaldi's favorite figures used to create unrest is the repeated pattern ♪♪♪, which often appears in the violins alone but can also be found on all the strings in unison, as in the middle section of "Sento, che l'alma teme" (*Griselda* act 3, scene 7) as Gualtiero describes his unsettled feelings.

Harmony can also play an important part in establishing the mood of an aria. In *L'Olimpiade* act 3, scene 6 King Clistene is strangely moved by Licida, who is being prepared for the sacrifice, but cannot understand why (Licida is in fact his long-lost son Filinto). The strength of these feelings is portrayed in the aria "Non sò donde viene" by extraordinarily rich harmonies (particularly ninth chords) in the rare key of F minor, against which the violin sixteenth notes often create strong dissonances with their angular intervals. A feeling of intensity is also created by constricting the usual da capo structure, despite the fact that the text falls into the customary two stanzas. The first part involves just one instead of two statements of the A text, and, instead of ending in the tonic it modulates to C minor. After just two measures of ritornello material the B text is presented (again just once), and this modulates to A-flat major before another two-measure intervention of ritornello material returns to the tonic. The A section is then repeated largely as before, but altered this time to remain in the tonic, where the aria is rounded off by a brief homophonic cadence in the orchestra.

On occasion Vivaldi's music stresses the light-hearted side of a particular character. Niceno is the old philosopher in *L'incoronazione di Dario*, and in his aria "Non lusinghi il core amante" in act 2, scene 19 the bass voice is accompanied by the comical texture of solo bassoon and solo double bass. In *Tito Manlio* the seventeenth-century libretto by Matteo Noris includes an old-fashioned comic servant, Lindo, whose music is distinguished from that of the other characters by its eccentric style. In act 1, scene 12 Lindo, confronted with Geminio's amorous problems, muses on the folly of love. The opening section of his aria uses short phrases for the contradictory statements "L'intendo, e non l'intendo, mi par, e non mi par" before changing to repeated sixteenth notes and a kind of "patter" singing reminiscent of the contemporary intermezzo. The middle section, in a contrasting $\frac{12}{8}$ time, again makes use of repeated notes and phrases, particularly on the word *matti* (mad), which is singled out for special emphasis. The unusual nature of this aria also extends to its form, for the usual da capo repeat is replaced by an abbreviated version of the first part, which uses only the first two lines of the stanza. In the second act Lindo contemplates Manlio's unfortunate position of being ill-treated not by just one woman, which is bad enough, but by two. The aria "Rabbia che accendasi" claims that woman's anger is worse than any poison from hell, and the mood is established in the opening unison string ritornello in B minor. The vocal line again involves short phrases—this time of two measures—repeated up to four times in the A section and as many as six times in B, as though portraying the relentless buildup of anger within the female heart. In the final act Lindo rather resents being instructed to collect information for Vitellia and complains that a spy has an unpleasant job ("Brutta cosa è il far la spia"). Once again there are rapid sixteenth notes, here connected with repetitions of the word *tutto* (an obvious form of word-painting), and in the middle section the concepts of the serious and the witty, which the servant can mix up in the course of his work, are represented by contrasting the pause on the word *serio* with the repeated phrase on *col facetto* (example 10).

As well as portraying the general sense of an aria text, Vivaldi

EXAMPLE 10. "Brutta cosa è il far la spia," from *Tito Manlio* (3.7)

often takes his cue from a particular phrase or word. In "Sento in seno ch'in pioggia di lagrime" (from *Giustino* act 2, scene 1), pizzicato strings are called on to represent falling raindrops in the same way as they are in the slow movement of *L'inverno* RV297.[18] The opening word of the aria "Gelido in ogni vena" from *Siroe rè di Persia* (which also appears in act 2 of the version of *Farnace* in the Turin manuscript Giordano 36) must have suggested the use of shuddering repeated notes in its introductory ritornello, which is paraphrased from the opening of the first movement of *L'inverno*.[19] This technique of building on a single word is varied slightly in *Ottone in villa* act 2, scene 3, for the first line of Caio's aria "L'ombre, l'aure e ancora il rio" contains three different ideas; Vivaldi treats it phrase by phrase in the voice, interspersing these adagio sections with pictorial orchestral writing. The shadows (*l'ombre*) are depicted by throbbing andante eighths with rich harmonies in the strings, the breezes (*l'aure*) by an allegro passage of thirds on two violins, and the brook (*il rio*) by similar patterns with trills, this time on two recorders. The aria "Qui mentre mormorando" from act 2 of *Il Tigrane* is dominated by the idea of murmuring waves, and all the strings except for the double basses, which are omitted, have repeated ♩♪♪ figures throughout.

Two further arias from *Il Tigrane* show how Vivaldi's music can be dependent on textual details. The opening lines of Tigrane's aria "Mi vedrai con lieta fronte" in act 2, scene 3 are directed at Mitridate as he looks forward confidently to meeting *l'ultimo fato* and are set in an optimistic D major. The text "sì, sì per te bel volto amato sì contento morirò," however, is spoken to Cleopatra, and the idea of dying for his beloved brings an echo of the initial phrase in D minor, and throughout the aria the actual key signature fluctuates from two sharps to one flat and back again as Tigrane turns from one character to the other. The following A-minor aria, "Squarciami pure il seno," opens almost like an accompanied recitative with quarter-note chords interspersed with rests as Cleopatra offers to die, but this is contrasted with slower sections as she turns to her own inner feelings ("eccoti ancora il cor"). After a short concluding presto ritornello, the B section continues these contrasts. The idea of death by sword or poison ("Ferro, ò veleno mi ponno uccidere") brings forth a change of time signature to $\frac{3}{8}$ and vigorous strings in unison with the voice in C major, yet once again her thoughts return to love, which cannot be extinguished even by death, and so "mà non dividere dell'alma un giusto ardor" moves to C minor and to a more lyrical vocal line accompanied by upper strings alone.

The use of a totally different texture for the middle part of a da capo aria for dramatic purposes is more common than the type of internal variety in the two arias from *Il Tigrane* described above. In *Catone in Utica* act 2, scene 9 the first half of Cesare's aria "Se in campo armato" concerns fighting and is given an extroverted $\frac{3}{8}$ allegro setting in D major for two trumpets and strings, with vigorous arpeggio figures and long triplet melismata. The B section of text, however, turns to grief, and is set as a $\frac{2}{4}$ larghetto, with gentle sobbing phrases in the voice accompanied by dissonant harmonies in the upper strings (example 11). In the pasticcio *Tamerlano* act 3, scene 14 the first part of Asteria's aria "Svena uccidi"[20] concerns her hatred for Tamerlano and is a $\frac{3}{8}$ presto in F minor with a violent unison string accompaniment. In the middle section the text turns to thoughts of her dead father, bringing a change to a $\frac{2}{4}$ andante with a gentle, throbbing quarter-note accompaniment, although the original mood eventually breaks through at one point with a unison dotted phrase marked "f."

So far Vivaldi's approaches to recitative and to arias have been discussed separately, reflecting the strict eighteenth-century distinction between the two genres. Vivaldi was generally content to accept contemporary operatic conventions and to seek dramatic

EXAMPLE 11. "Se in campo armato," from *Catone in Utica* (2.9)

possibilities within these limits, unlike a composer such as Handel, whose greatest dramatic masterstrokes frequently involve the flouting of convention. There are, nevertheless, occasional instances when Vivaldi, too, ignores normal practice for a particular effect.

Act 2, scene 6 of *Arsilda regina di Ponto* comprises a hunting scene, whose text deals with the various attractions of nature and hunting and in which sinfonia, chorus, recitative, and aria are all combined into a fluid structure. The opening sinfonia begins with ten measures for two onstage horns that, with their F-major arpeggios, establish the pastoral tone that is then taken up by the strings, producing an almost incessant ♩♪♪ galloping rhythm. This is followed by a chorus, again in F major, that leads directly, without any recitative, into a short binary-form aria for Lisea in G minor, accompanied by two onstage recorders and a bass line for the violins. This in turn leads into a C-major duet (though the two voices are in unison) for Mirinda and Nicandro, again in binary form with an introductory ritornello comprising an orchestral version of the first half of the duet. After only four measures of simple recitative comes another binary-form aria, this time in G major for Arsilda and accompanied by two onstage violins and recorders in thirds. This is followed by a twenty-five-measure ensemble in which the voices sing a line in turn, accompanied by a bass line for the strings in unison, and ending with a choral shout of "Viva Cintia, viva viva." A longer section of simple recitative is then rounded off by a repeat of part of the earlier chorus, thereby providing a degree of unity to a picturesque scene in which musical variety compensates for a basic irrelevance to the plot.

One of the most impressive moments in *L'Atenaide* is the solo scene for the heroine in act 3, scene 7 (scene 6 in the 1729 libretto). Atenaide (under the assumed name of Eudossa) has just been unjustly banished by the Emperor Teodosio, who is not prepared to listen to her side of the story. Unable to stop him from leaving in a brief simple recitative, she breaks into a short arioso, something suggested by the librettist, Zeno, through his provision of a rhyming couplet. Vivaldi, nevertheless, seizes the opportunity, taking *lamenti* as his key word and setting it to a long melisma with expressive appoggiaturas (example 12). Though only lasting six measures, this arioso, with its G-minor/C-minor tonality and affective intervals such as the rising minor sixths in measures 1 and 5 and rising minor seventh in measure 3, provides a clear picture of Atenaide's distress. Her reactions suddenly become more aggressive, however, and the key changes to E-flat with violent string sixteenth notes. After this brief outburst the accompaniment reverts to continuo alone as, in short phrases split by rests in both voice and bass, Atenaide reflects on the fact that everyone seems to be against her. The strings return with B-flat arpeggios but are suddenly interrupted by an unexpected diminished-seventh chord on G-sharp as Atenaide's thoughts turn to Teodosio's words of banishment ("Io ti dò bando, e ti dò bando eterno"). The vehemence of Teodosio's dismissal leads Vivaldi to start an allegro molto in C minor with sharp staccato chords, and at first it sounds as if this is a ritornello to a full-scale aria, but shortly after the voice enters Atenaide's thoughts again change. She pulls up with an adagio cadence at the words "lungi da me?" as though she can scarcely believe what is happening to her, and then decides that she must leave; the text "Fuggirò, volerò" is set as a furious presto with violent string scales, though this is twice contrasted with a gentle largo section as she considers her innocence ("Innocente amor mio povera fè"). In the second of these slower passages (example 13), the falling sevenths in the vocal line underline her feeling of despair. Although the rhyme scheme of the text falls into two stan-

EXAMPLE 12. *L'Atenaide* (3.7)

EXAMPLE 13. *L'Atenaide* (3.7)

zas, there is no da capo, and a further section of recitative follows, first simple over a four-measure pedal on G as Atenaide muses on her father's advice, which previously she had ignored, and then accompanied with sharp string quarter-note chords marked "Presto" as she finally resolves to leave. The whole scene, with its rapidly changing textures reflecting the various thoughts that are flashing through Atenaide's distraught mind, has generated a great deal of tension, which is now released in a full-scale da capo aria in the tragic key of F minor. This strange piece, with its insistent, almost hypnotic syncopation in the voice, its repeated rhythmic patterns in the accompaniment, and its bare harmonies, seems to suggest Atenaide's emotional exhaustion following her earlier violent reactions (example 14).

Apart from recitative and aria, the other main opportunity for dramatic writing in Vivaldi's operas is provided by the ensembles. Although these are infrequent (normally only one or possibly two per opera),[21] they generally appear at key moments in the drama. Where more than two characters are concerned, they often present conflicting feelings; thus the composer has the problem of conveying these feelings through his music. In the trio at the end of act 2 of *Griselda*, Costanza is sympathetic to Griselda and pleads with her against the stern Gualtiero; for much of the piece the two

EXAMPLE 14. *L'Atenaide*

women are paired together with similar, gentle music, while Gualtiero is set apart with angry, aggressive writing.[22]

The largest ensemble in any Vivaldi opera is the quintet from act 2 of *La verità in cimento*.[23] The plot of the opera centers around the typical Baroque device of mistaken identities: Rustena, the wife of the Sultan Mamud, whom he has married for political reasons, has a son, Zelim, but he is passed off as the son of Damira; Damira, who is Mamud's real love, also has a son by him, Melindo, but he in turn is passed off as belonging to Rustena. Thus the quintet, which is written for these five characters, involves Mamud, the two women in his life, and their sons, whose true identities are thoroughly confused throughout much of the opera.

The quintet opens with a short three-measure introduction,

EXAMPLE 15. *La verità in cimento* (2.9)

which creates an appropriately somber atmosphere with its slow falling chromatic bass and its key of G minor. First Damira and then Rustena enter with similar phrases, each in turn claiming her son, and they are answered by Zelim and Melindo who, being in similar positions, are given almost identical vocal lines. Initially they address their mothers, but then, as they turn to Mamud, the style of the vocal lines changes completely to emphatic falling sixteenth-note scales in thirds (example 15). Throughout the first section of the quintet the music reflects the dramatic situation of the characters; the pair of mothers, Damira and Rustena, and the two sons, Zelim and Melindo, imitate each other closely or sing together in thirds. After a concluding orchestral passage marked "Andante," the whole position is changed by the entry of Mamud (who up to now has been silent) with the B section of text. He is furious, and so the tempo changes to allegro and the orchestral texture to a unison string accompaniment, and his first line "Sei un empio, sei schernito" is set to a vigorous arpeggio figure in B-flat major (example 16). Now, however, the other four are united in their condemnation of the "crudel Padre spietato," and so the tex-

EXAMPLE 16. *La verità in cimento* (2.9)

ture rapidly thickens as they come together for the first time, Mamud's protestations eventually falling away when confronted by the insistent *no*'s in the upper parts and their cadence in C minor with "Tu non meriti pietà." Although the mood of the opening largo returns in G minor as one would expect, Vivaldi must have felt that the violent emotions of the B text were too strong to be forgotten, for after only four measures of slightly altered da capo with Damira's first couplet, the music returns to the allegro texture and another outburst from Mamud. Now, however, his anger is matched by Zelim, who follows his vocal line in canon after only two beats. This time the music remains in G minor, and again a full five-part texture is built up, with Zelim's repeated d'' *no*'s being screamed out at the top of the texture before the four-measure orchestral passage that closed the first section returns to round off the piece. Thus Vivaldi is prepared to sacrifice the normal da capo convention when he feels that this is justified by the emotional state of the characters concerned.

In discussing the link between music and drama in late Baroque opera, many writers have regarded the frequent transplantation of arias from one work to another, the success of the genre of the pasticcio, and the custom of making considerable alterations in works if they were to be revived as indications of the composer's lack of interest in opera seria as a legitimate dramatic form. Certainly there were times when the hard-pressed composer reached for the first successful aria from another opera that came to hand, perhaps simply transposing it into a suitable key, but there were others when he carefully considered the implications of the plot before choosing an appropriate piece that reflected precisely the emotional reaction required. The fact that the quintet from *La verità in cimento* is based on an earlier quartet from *La Candace* does not make it any less effective in its new setting: its dramatic implications are equally appropriate. There are occasions when Vivaldi's choice of tonalities in a recitative, of accompanimental texture in an aria, of melodic style in a vocal line, or of overall structure across several scenes may appear to be purely arbitrary, but there are undoubtedly others, as this study has attempted to demonstrate, that reveal him as a true man of the theater.

NOTES

1. M. F. Robinson, *Opera before Mozart* (London, 1966), p. 111.

2. This was the occasion of his meeting with the young Carlo Goldoni, who was instructed by the proprietor of the Teatro San Samuele in Venice, Michele Grimani, to rearrange Zeno's libretto *Griselda* for Vivaldi's setting in 1735. Goldoni recounts the meeting in his *Memoirs*, trans. J. Black (London, 1828), vol. 1, pp. 174–177, and in his *Commedie* (Venice, 1761), vol. 13, pp. 10–13.

3. All Vivaldi's surviving operas end with a generally perfunctory chorus, although *Giustino*, written for Rome in 1724, is rounded off by an unusually extended piece in the form of a chaconne. Peter Ryom has demonstrated by comparing librettos that this chorus was based on the closing movement of *La verità in cimento*, written for Venice in 1720, whose final number is missing from the autograph manuscript in Turin (Foà 33); see P. Ryom, *Les Manuscrits de Vivaldi* (Copenhagen, 1977), p. 115.

4. The setting of Scipione Maffei's libretto *La fida ninfa* was originally commissioned from G. M. Orlandini for the reopening of the Teatro Filarmonico in Verona in 1730, but it was not until 1732 that it was eventually performed with music by Vivaldi. Maffei's libretto was published, along with other works, in his *Teatro . . . cioè la tragedia, la comedia e il drama, non più stampato* (Verona, 1730); this edition is virtually identical with Vivaldi's text, so that the situating of the trio at the end of act 1 and the quartet at the end of act 2 must have been Maffei's idea.

5. A. Zeno, *Poesie drammatiche* (Venice, 1744), vol. 3.

6. See R. S. Freeman, "The Travels of Partenope," in *Studies in Music History: Essays for Oliver Strunk*, ed. H. S. Powers (Princeton, 1968), pp. 356–385.

7. Act 2 of *Teuzzone* ends with a setting of the text "Ritorna à lusingarmi," later reset by Vivaldi for his opera *Griselda*, which is probably by G. M. Orlandini; see R. Strohm, "Eine neuentdeckte Mantuaner Opernpartitur Vivaldis," *Vivaldi Informations* 2 (1973): 105.

8. See E. Cross, "Vivaldi as Opera Composer: 'Griselda,'" *Musical Times* 119 (1978): 415.

9. This may not, however, have been Vivaldi's original intention. The 1734 libretto of *L'Olimpiade* indicates that scene 6 should start with the opening two stanzas of Metastasio's chorus "I tuoi strali," the first of which Vivaldi actually sets in D major in the following scene of the autograph score (volume Foà 39 of the Turin manuscripts). The score's physical structure also suggests that some music may have been removed at this point.

10. There are two versions of this scene in the autograph score in Foà 34; the paper contains holes to show where fols. 79ᵛ and 80ʳ were tied up, leaving the new version on Fol. 80ᵛ. Both settings involve echo effects, the original going to the extreme of a triple echo, whereas the revised version requires a simpler double echo.

11. This aria, "Tu dormi in tante pene," appears in two different versions in the two Turin scores of *Tito Manlio*, one with an obbligato part for solo violin, and one written for a viola d'amore using scordatura; see E. Cross, "Vivaldi's Operatic Borrowings," *Music and Letters* 59 (1978): 434.

12. See Cross, "Vivaldi as Opera Composer," p. 413 and *The Late Operas of Antonio Vivaldi, 1728–1738* (Ann Arbor, 1981), vol. 1, pp. 172ff.

13. Only Vivaldi's setting of act 2 of *La virtù trionfante dell'amore, e dell'odio, overo Il Tigrane* survives in the Turin manuscripts (Giordano 37). Act 1 was set by B. Micheli and Act 3 by N. Romaldo.

14. For a discussion of eighteenth-century recitative techniques see E. O. D. Downes, "'Secco' Recitative in Early Classical Opera Seria (1720–1780)," *Journal of the American Musicological Society* 14 (1961): 50–69.

15. This aria from *Tito Manlio* act 1, scene 5, "Alla caccia d'un bell'adorato," also appears with the text "Alla caccia d'un cuore spietato" in the serenata *Mio cor povero cor* RV690.

16. For a comparison of the two versions see Ryom, *Les Manuscrits*, p. 158. From the paper on which the concerto is written, it seems likely that the operatic version may be the earlier of the two; see Cross, *The Late Operas*, vol. 1, p. 39. The sinfonia is marked "Tutti gl'Istromenti sordini" in the original autograph score of *Tito Manlio* in Giordano 39, but in the copy of the opera in Foà 37 Vivaldi has carefully added "sordini" directions for each part (including the wind), the drums being marked "Timpani scordati."

17. This aria is incorrectly marked "Allegretto" in Raffaello Monterosso's edition (Cremona, 1964).

18. Vivaldi is typically very careful with his orchestral texture here, for as well as the direction "Tutti pizzicatti," he asks for "Un P[ri]mo Un 2dō Viol[i]no, et un Violone con l'arco."

19. R. Strohm, "Italienische Opernarien des frühen Settecento (1720–1730)," *Analecta Musicologica* 16 (Cologne, 1976), part 2, pp. 96–100, quotes this aria from *Siroe* and, in part 1, pp. 51ff., points out similarities with a setting of the same text by Vinci.

20. Although *Tamerlano* is a pasticcio, the last three scenes of the opera, with their powerful dramatic climax, were set entirely by Vivaldi. Whereas for most of the work Vivaldi wrote just the recitatives on numbered sheets and then inserted arias by other composers taken from different scores in various hands, this final section is all in Vivaldi's hand and the numbering of its folio gatherings, including the aria "Svena uccidi," is continuous with those of the recitatives.

21. *La fida ninfa* has an unusually high proportion of ensembles with two duets, one trio, and one quartet.

22. See Cross, "Vivaldi as Opera Composer," p. 415 and *The Late Operas*, vol. 1, pp. 184–186.

23. This quintet was, in fact, based on an earlier quartet from the opera *La Candace o siano Li veri amici*. The score of the quartet appears in the Turin volume Foà 28, a collection of arias from various operas.

Vivaldi as Self-Borrower
by Klaus Kropfinger

Vivaldi's activity as an opera composer coincides with the widely spread practice of the time known as parody.[1] This well-known technique entails the transference of material from preexisting compositions to new ones, often involving a modification of the borrowed material. Even the most extreme examples of musical borrowing, the pasticci (operas consisting of arias and music borrowed from different works and composers),[2] can be found among the manifold activities of the *prete rosso*. Vivaldi even based an entire opera (the *Orlando furioso* production of 1714) on another composer's work.[3] Within this wide field of borrowings, the reuse of music from his own operas in newly formed operatic works was for Vivaldi and his contemporaries as customary as the implantation of foreign operatic material.[4]

The practice of borrowing and self-borrowing brings to mind the often-discussed problem of dramatic integrity in opera seria of the early eighteenth century. Aestheticians of that time such as Giuseppe Riva,[5] Pier Jacopo Martello,[6] and Francesco Algarotti[7] focused especially on the unity of text, music, and action. According to the ideal of dramatic integrity, a reused aria had to fit in with the new dramatic context, and in order to do so it had to be modified textually, musically, or both. The difficulties with these techniques of parody, however, increased with the quantity of reused music, which in turn had a direct relation to the pressures of time, public taste, money, and—last but not least—the whims of vocalists. Thus arias and their contexts often became mere functions of staging instead of dramatic integrity.[8]

This dissolution of dramatic coherence may have been caused by the practice of borrowing and self-borrowing. One wonders if Benedetto Marcello was also thinking of these techniques when he complained satirically about weakened dramatic unity: "Be advised then that the arias throughout the whole opera are to be alternately happy and pathetic, without any regard for the words, the keys, and the dramatic context."[9] In reality, however, the extent to which the dramatic integrity of an opera is impaired by borrowings and parody can be judged only from case to case, and it is often difficult to come to a clear-cut decision. While investigating the alterations that Goldoni made in *Griselda* for Vivaldi's ideal prima donna, Anna Giraud, John Walter Hill came to the following conclusion:

> Undoubtedly she [Anna Giraud] and Vivaldi were motivated by an understandable desire to save time and effort and to repeat success. But the result should be evaluated on its own terms in each case. In spite of reusing two arias, Giraud's role of Griselda was very well integrated with the plot and was remarkably effective.[10]

Reinhard Strohm, in reviewing the disparity between Zeno's original text and Goldoni's modified version set by Vivaldi, comes to a rather different evaluation. In his view, Goldoni's addition of simile arias—some set to music borrowed from other operas—causes a decided divergence between music and dramatic action. A similar problem arises in an aria like Ottone's "Vede orgogliosa l'onda," in which Vivaldi replaces the original text without modifying the music accordingly.[11] The sailor Ottone's optimism in the second text, for example, seems less well projected in the music than does the wanderer's despondency in the original text.[12] Here, however, the question arises as to which affection of the scene Vivaldi actually focused upon when composing his aria. Obviously his focus was on the general atmosphere of oppression that was affecting Ottone after his rejection by Griselda rather than on any specific affection. It is apparently this complex of affections that forms Vivaldi's aria, from which hope as well as despair may spring, feelings that are in themselves ambiguous. This mixture of conflicting negative and positive emotions and this uncertainty of feeling, which are inherent in *both* texts, may explain why Vivaldi kept the music while changing the text. This view is supported by taking into account the dramatic context, which reveals Ottone in a chaotic emotional state, torn by extremes of feeling.[13] It is this complex situation, the interlacement of hope and despair, which here pervades Vivaldi's compositional procedure.

The task of retaining dramatic integrity despite borrowings seems less problematical when instrumental music is adopted. In the case of borrowings from operatic works, the reused aria is at least semantically outlined by text and plot. Purely instrumental music, on the other hand, can be interpreted within a broader field of meaning, and thus its affects are less determined than those of operatic pieces.[14] Consequently they are open to the expression of a variety of affects within the operatic text and context. It is obvious that borrowing from instrumental music, in contradistinction to operatic borrowing, cannot occur without some modification. Since the reused instrumental music must fit its new operatic context with regard both to affect and structure, some recomposition is often necessary for it to suit a coherent unit of text, a specific affect, and the musical structure of an aria. Kolneder indicated this point when he described the adoption of the ritornello of the Concerto in C Major for bassoon RV471[15] in Vivaldi's *Griselda* as considerably condensed in comparison with the original version.[16]

In the light of this observation, then, it is necessary to investigate not only additional self-borrowings from Vivaldi's instrumental music, but also the dramatic suitability of such adoptions, focusing in greater detail on the compositional procedures. This will prove especially interesting when two movements of the same instrumental composition have been adopted, a good example of this being the reuse of the first and third movements of the Concerto in A Major RV159 in scenes three and four of the first act of *La verità in cimento.*[17]

Questions arise as to Vivaldi's compositional intentions particularly when he reuses sections of the famous *Quattro stagioni* concertos. The borrowing from the first movement of the "Inverno" concerto for the aria "Gelido in ogni vena" in the opera *Siroe re di Persia* (1727) presents an example of adoption that intensifies the scenic expression by condensing the programmatically fixed musical structure.[18] By retaining the tremolos in all instruments throughout the aria, Vivaldi intensifies the meanings of "cold" and "icy" to "extreme coldness." By confining himself primarily to the adoption of the opening ritornello of the concerto's first movement, Vivaldi evolves a basic musical meaning that encompasses both the first verse of the concerto's programmatic *sonetto* ("Agghiacciato tremar tra nevi algenti") and that of the aria "Gelido in ogni vena." This partial reuse of the first movement of "L'inverno" shows an important aspect of Vivaldi's compositional procedure. Obviously, he prefers to base his setting on a broader field of meaning, which gains its specific features and affects by text and context of the plot; the descriptive elements of "L'inverno" are given specific meaning by the operatic text.[19]

The "Inverno" ritornello is not the only example of self-borrowing from the *Quattro stagioni* concertos, but as far as is known they all come from the first concerto, "La primavera." Probably the earliest of these is found in Vivaldi's opera *Il Giustino* of 1724.[20] The appearance of Fortuna ("La Fortuna in Mac-[c]hina") in the first act presents music from the first movement of "La primavera" in its original key of E major. As in "L'inverno," however, only the opening ritornello appears. Vivaldi has even shortened the first eight measures by crossing out the repetition in measures 4 through 6 and the second half of measure 8, which are, however, still visible in the manuscript. In this way, the first seven measures—turning to the supertonic chromatic triad and accentuating the half cadence more clearly than in the concerto—form a unit of their own. They prepare for the elaboration in the following measures, which include F-sharp major once more and end with the modified version of the ritornello's measures 8 to 9 (or 11 to 13).[21] These alterations underline the origin of the borrowing; they show Vivaldi at work and that this was not merely a chance borrowing. The ritornello of the "Primavera" concerto, with its atmosphere of nature and landscape in expectation of growth and new life, fits the operatic scene extremely well. The appearance of the goddess Fortuna is described as follows: "Mac[c]hina maestosa con la Fortuna assisa su la rota che gira, accompagnata da' suoi Genii."[22] If we look at the iconography of Fortuna in the visual arts, in association with other figures and seated on the wheel of fortune, we see her with a landscape in the background.[23] Not only are the music and the scenic depiction compatible, but the context itself—the preceding fourth scene with "Giustino coll'aratro cantando"[24]—frames, so to speak, the music and iconography of "La Fortuna in Mac[c]hina": the working farmer in his pastoral environment. Here we clearly have a dramatic constellation that surpasses the boundaries of aria and scene. Giustino, with his recitative and aria "Bel riposo de' mortali" (example 1), is not only the mediator between the surrounding landscape and its center of

EXAMPLE 1. "Bel riposo de' mortali," from *Il Giustino* (1.4)

EXAMPLE 2. "La Fortuna in Mac[c]hina," from *Il Giustino* (1.5)

EXAMPLE 3. "Da tuoi begl'occhi," from *Il Giustino* (1.3)

EXAMPLE 4. "Della tua sorte con destra forte," from *Il Giustino* (1.5)

attraction, the "Fortuna in Mac[c]hina" (example 2), but his humble being and the exciting event of the *macchina* are harmonically linked (C major to E major).[25] A flash of harmony, in other words, underlines the "Fortuna in Mac[c]hina" as an apparition of fate, causing a decisive dramatic configuration. And it is apparently this dramatic impact that—consciously or unconsciously—made the composer aware of the dramatic possibilities of the "Primavera" ritornello. We can find its musical imprint melodically or rhythmically not only in Arianna's aria "Da tuoi begl'occhi" (example 3), which ends the third scene, but also in some other passages, such as Fortuna's aria "Della tua sorte con destra forte" (example 4), if we take into account the additional parts that Vivaldi crossed out. This practice of borrowing within the context corresponds to Giustino's new destiny offered by Fortuna: it is Giustino, changed from peasant to warrior, who defeats Vitaliano and saves the empire. It is he who rescues Arianna, in particular, from being given to Vitaliano as the price for peace.

In his opera *Dorilla in Tempe* of 1726, Vivaldi borrowed again from the "Primavera" concerto. Here the context fits the program and meaning of the ritornello particularly well. Even if we take into account that the preserved score[26] pertains to the production of 1734,[27] the Sinfonia and its connection with the first act may be considered as representing the version of the first production in 1726, a supposition that is supported by the description of the stage setting at the beginning of the first act. In both cases (1726 as well as 1734)[28] it reveals a "deliziosa veduta di colline e campagne fiorite,"[29] a surrounding that ideally fits the "Primavera" ritornello, especially in combination with the text of the chorus, which consists of Dorilla, Elmiro, nymphs, and shepherds.

Dell'aura al sussurar	Of the whispering breezes
Dell'onda mormorar	Of the murmuring waves
Cantiamo con piacer	We sing with pleasure
Fra il dolce e bel goder,	Amid sweet and lovely enjoyment.
Della nuova stagion	Of the new season
L'onore è il vanto,	Honor is the vaunt,
E sia di primavera,	And of the spring,
D'ogni gioir foriera	Harbinger of all joy,
Il nostro canto.[30]	May our song be.

Here again the borrowing accords with a broader context. This becomes clearer when we present a summary of the beginning of the first scene and include the third part of the Sinfonia.

The entire first scene with its emphasis on spring is prefigured by the third part of the Sinfonia. This portion of the Sinfonia (example 5) presents the first thirteen measures of the ritornello in C major, as does the following *coro* (example 6), which opens the first scene. Here we have one of the rare cases in which the Sinfonia and the beginning of the dramatic action are related. But the scene as a whole includes both a broader adaptation from the "Primavera" concerto than occurred in *Il Giustino* and modifications as well. For example, Vivaldi extends the first six measures to seven (because of the amplified turn to the dominant) and he does not write out the reused measures 7 to 13 of the ritornello but employs a repeat sign. Thus are excluded the changed metrical order of motifs within measures 10 to 13 of the concerto. The following

EXAMPLE 5. Sinfonia (third part), from *Dorilla in Tempe*

EXAMPLE 6. "Dell'aura al sussurar," from *Dorilla in Tempe* (1.1)

Allegro of the nymphs (example 7) clearly replaces that part in the concerto where Vivaldi had added the explanation "La salutan gl'augei con lieto canto." It is the first "interlude," the "singing of the birds,"[31] which is now specified as the song of the nightingale in a pastoral surrounding. But Vivaldi's adoption is based upon an art of adaptation that in this case means specifically the close relationship between the dominating section (example 6) and the parts preceding and following it. Thus, just as the Sinfonia (example 5) is connected thematically with the first scene, the *coro* (example 8), which follows the Allegro (example 7) and brings back the shortened ritornello, leads into the following dance of the shepherds (example 9). After this the last *coro* (example 10) of the scene prepares for the atmosphere of the following action.

In *Dorilla in Tempe* Vivaldi reused the first movement of the "Primavera" concerto in a more extended form than in *Il Giustino*, and the whole complex of borrowed material gives an idea of the semantic implications—nature, landscape, singing birds, love, and so forth—to which the aura of spring is open.

At this point we might ask if other relationships with Vivaldi's "Primavera" concerto might be identified as self-borrowings, even if complete melodic identity does not exist. In such cases, we must proceed with caution when attempting to identify motivic and melodic affinities. However, the implications of meaning that Vivaldi's

EXAMPLE 7. "Senti gl'usignuolo," from *Dorilla in Tempe* (1.1)

EXAMPLE 8. "E in noi di primavera," from *Dorilla in Tempe* (1.1)

EXAMPLE 9. "Ride il colle e ride il prato," from *Dorilla in Tempe* (1.1)

EXAMPLE 10. "Quest e la bella stagion novella," from *Dorilla in Tempe* (1.1)

Quattro stationi and unquestionable examples of self-borrowing present must also be considered. Thus other melodies, which only partially correspond to the arias or instrumental pieces to which they might possibly relate, are open for discussion, as in the following example from Vivaldi's opera *Orlando furioso*.

Although the melody of Alcina's aria "Vorresti amor da me?" in the third scene of act 2 is not identical with the "Primavera" ritornello, it clearly has a melodic affinity with it. Here, the dramatic context of the scene—a "boschetto delizioso con ritiri di verdure"—presents the environment for a love scene that has a clear connection with the "Primavera" movement. Alcina's haughty taunting of Astolfo, moreover, corresponds to the modification and shortening of the melodic line (example 11). The approximation of Alcina's melody to the "Primavera" ritornello can be seen with particular clarity in the first measure with the characteristic

EXAMPLE 11. "Vorresti amor da me?" from *Orlando furioso* (2.3)

combination of major third and fifth—the third here playfully doubled and allied to the following fifth by two sixteenth notes—and in the cadential line ending the first ritornello of the aria. The playful sixteenths might be connected with Alcina's capriciousness, while the melodic line of the first ritornello in the following part of the "Primavera" melody is extended precisely at those words that prove her inconstant and cruelly mocking character. Here, possibly, we have traits of sharp emotion that Vivaldi himself, when speaking with Goldoni about alterations in *Griselda*,[32] declared to belong to "a piece with expression, with agitation, an aria that expresses passion by different means, by separated words. . . ."[33] These "different means" and "separated words" can be found here, when the mood of nature and love to which the "Primavera" motifs allude are distorted by Alcina's exclamations. It is noteworthy that Vivaldi had in mind, when speaking with Goldoni, the special character of his favorite prima donna, Anna Giraud, who sang Alcina's aria when *Orlando* was first staged at Teatro Sant'Angelo in 1727.[34]

When reusing his music, Vivaldi was undoubtedly influenced by the desire to capitalize on previous successes. We can be certain that this aim, which guided his operatic borrowings, also motivated his adoption of instrumental music. This may well have been the case with the *Quattro stagioni* and especially with "La primavera." Vivaldi may have felt that these compositions represented a special quality of his art. Even his dedication of opus 8 (which comprises the *Quattro stagioni* concertos) to Count Venzeslav von Morzin shows that Vivaldi was convinced he had achieved something new. Recalling that the *Quattro stagioni* had been known by Count Morzin for some time, Vivaldi points out in his dedication that these concertos had now been amplified, not only by programmatic sonnets, but also musically, by all that is expressed in those poems. And he closes by saying, "I am therefore certain that, although they are the same concertos, they will seem new to Your Highness."[35] It may indeed be the intertwining of concerto form, programmatic annotations, and musical "scenes" that made the *Quattro stagioni* concertos a profound success even after Vivaldi's disappearance from the stage of musical life. But it was one concerto above all, "La primavera," that endured after Vivaldi's death when all of his other works were forgotten.[36] This did not happen fortuitously. Vivaldi's borrowings from his *Quattro stagioni*, and especially from the "Primavera" concerto, reflect his success in this genre, a success that incited his ambitions as a composer. It was very natural for him to borrow from these famous pieces and take advantage of their popularity in his operas.

Vivaldi's fame as an instrumental composer was in fact far greater than his reputation as a composer of operas. In this regard, Tartini had a very pronounced opinion:

> I have been asked to write operas for Venice but I never consented, knowing full well that a throat and a violin fingerboard are two different things. Vivaldi, who tried his hand at writing for both, was always hissed in one of the fields though he was very successful in the other.[37]

Tartini criticized Vivaldi for being an instrumental and an operatic composer at the same time, and in doing so he may have alluded to Vivaldi's borrowings from instrumental compositions. Undoubtedly, the adaptation of Vivaldi's instrumental music in his operas could only enhance Tartini's accusation that the singer's throat was treated like a "violin fingerboard." It may be that Marcello also alluded to Vivaldi when he wrote:

On the other hand, it might be quite useful for a composer to have spent many years playing the violin or viola, or copying music for some famous composer. From the latter, he might have appropriated some manuscripts of opera or serenades, and he can steal from these and other compositions themes for use in *ritornelli*, overtures, arias, recitatives, variations on *La follia*, and choruses.[38]

Surely Vivaldi, as an acknowledged and highly productive instrumental composer, was not in need of another composer's products, but we may suppose that simple borrowing, rather than "stealing," offended Marcello's aesthetic sense as well. And when we recall the passage previously quoted from *Il teatro alla moda*, which points out satirically that arias should alternate throughout the opera, from beginning to end, regardless of any meaning of text or stage action,[39] Marcello must have been concerned about the practice of borrowing, which could greatly jeopardize the integrity of the drama. However, Vivaldi's borrowings from "Inverno" and especially from "Primavera" stand as proof to the contrary. He was well aware of the artistic possibilities of instrumental borrowing offered by the mutual signification of music, text, and scene. As we noted in *Dorilla in Tempe*, the structure of the first movement of "La primavera"—the alternation of the ritornello with its atmosphere of spring and the interludes with more specific musical meaning[40]—supports the succession of singing and acting at the beginning of the opera.

But in his opera *Il Giustino*, the integrative function of the "Primavera" quotation seems to be extended in an even broader sense. This becomes clear when we remind ourselves of the structure of acts as underlined by Martello:

Custom demands that your *melodramma* be divided into three acts. . . . In the first act it will be your job to prepare the auditors for the unfolding of the plot, giving them the necessary information about the heroes that tread the stage, about the antecedent events suitable for the understanding of the fable or story, and introducing the characters, at least of the principals, who will take part in the action. . . . In the second act you must think about the complication of actions as well as passions. . . . In the third act think about the unraveling or dénouement of the plot, and also about the machine, if the impresario will permit it, which certainly will be the most acceptable for a marvelous apparition, even though the plot for some reason does not really call for a god to descend from heaven to unravel it.[41]

In *Il Giustino*, Vivaldi's "Primavera" borrowing accords with Martello's principles.[42] In accentuating the appearance of Fortuna with the ritornello, Vivaldi musically underlines this prediction of dramatic development: he not only uses the ritornello as the structural basis of the Fortuna apparition within the first act, but it also, as the ritornello of the concerto's first movement, corresponds to the function of the first act within the drama as a whole. This means that the dramatic development in the second and third acts, not only dramatically but also musically, can be foreseen in the ritornello's appearance in the first act. In Vivaldi's time this does not yet indicate a consciously developed sense of musical unification in the work, but rather a relationship between the ritornello and certain arias or groupings of arias with respect to their function within the drama.

Another point to consider involves the placement and function of the rare slow-movement arias, with their special evocative color and expression. A very important example related to the "Primavera" borrowing occurs in the first act of *Il Giustino*, with Leocasta's aria "Senti, senti l'aura che leggiera và scuotendo e ramo, e fronda e con dolce mormorio và spiegando il suo piacer."[43] This aria is placed in the eighth scene of the second act, after the liberation of Arianna from Vitaliano's grasp. The tyrant and aggressor, Vitaliano has been defeated by Giustino's might. The aria has the function of repose, and it is not just by chance that it appears approximately at the middle of the drama, that is, after Arianna's liberation and Vitaliano's defeat, but preceding Amantio's intrigue. Amantio is the emperor's general, and he envies Giustino's success. Leocasta's aria, which presents an affecting picture of landscape in repose, is really very much like the slow movement of "La primavera," for which the text of the *sonetto* includes the words "caro mormorio di fronde e piante" to accompany the shepherd's slumber. Finally, the aria's setting itself reflects that of the concerto. Despite a difference in tonality (A major instead of C-sharp minor), the configuration of musical structure and melody is very similar. Both have a continuously flowing accompaniment and a melodic line that encircles the descending tonic triad, supported by a steady combination of eight dotted-sixteenth and thirty-second notes.

Among the many correspondences between this aria and others in the opera, the associations with Leocasta's aria "Sventurata navicella se mai giunge à navigar" in the last scene of the second act is important.[44] This aria reveals Leocasta in a rather desperate mood. She is reluctant to accept Andronico's love, and she desires Giustino, who has just driven away Andronico. Giustino's aria "Ho nel petto un cor si forte," which follows, closes the second act and presents a firm response to her despair.[45] His encouraging outlook, moreover, links the developing love-affair of the subordinate plot with his own destiny, as the warrior who rescues the emperor Anastasio and his wife Arianna, into a single line of dramatic development.

These two arias by Leocasta and Giustino, which conclude the second act, point to a dramatic development leading to the fourth scene of the third act, in which both Leocasta and Giustino are struck by fate. Anastasio is outraged by Amantio's whispers of intrigue. He has rejected his wife Arianna, who appears overly grateful to Giustino, and has condemned Giustino to death. Exactly at this point Giustino's aria, "Il mio cor già più non sa,"[46] which has a certain melodic affinity with the "Primavera" ritornello in its combination of three eighth and two sixteenth notes, brings another aspect to mind: that of the dramatic interrelationship of keys. Giustino's aria is the only one in the entire opera to be in E major, and this key relates to that of "Fortuna in Mac[c]hina" in the first act, which is also in E major.[47] This correspondence undoubtedly is motivated by dramatic considerations. It presents the prediction of future glory in contrast to crises at the threshold of peripeteia: the apparent ruin of glory and love. This threat of destruction is underlined by Leocasta's aria "Senza l'amato ben vivere questo sen non può," which follows Giustino's aria marked "Largo e staccato."[48] Thus Vivaldi's borrowing of the "Primavera" ritornello in the first act of *Il Giustino* reveals clear dramatic consequences with musical interrelationships throughout the opera—consequences that sustain the development of plot as well as give a certain musical coherence to the drama.

On the other hand, not even the slightest dramatic consequences can be detected in *La Dorilla in Tempe*. This opera consists primarily of a loosely connected story: in brief, a monster threatens Tempe; Dorilla, chosen by her father Admeto to be a placating sacrifice, is saved by Nomio, a shepherd, who solves all problems concerning Dorilla's love of Elmiro and at the end reveals his identity as Apollo. This story, comprising a variety of legends, has no dramatic concept nor any real development. Thus, Vivaldi works in accord with the plot when he borrows and integrates parts of the "Primavera" ritornello only at the very beginning of the opera. In this way the background, the atmosphere of pastoral landscape and life, is presented.

Oddly the influence of Vivaldi's "Primavera" concerto on his operas is not limited to the composer's lifetime. In 1939, *L'Olimpiade*, which was first staged in 1734 at Teatro Sant'Angelo in Venice, was performed in an arrangement by Virgilio Mortari. As artistic adviser, Alfredo Casella commented on the production as follows:

> The opera has required patience in the work of adaptation, mainly because of the necessity of reducing as much as possible the very long recitatives, to which most certainly the theater goers of that time would not have paid attention. Then, lacking some important pieces, these were taken from another opera of Vivaldi—*La Dorilla*—which was performed the same year (1734) in the same Teatro Sant'Angelo in Venice. *La Dorilla* is an opera, which in the Turin manuscript bears the wording, "act three, with sinfonia and choruses which contain singing and dancing," and whose ensembles are much richer than those in *L'Olimpiade*, especially in the choruses and dances. Thus the decision to extract from this opera what was lacking in *L'Olimpiade*, secure in the knowledge of not doing anything other than what was practiced by the maestros of that epoch. . . .[49]

An investigation of Vivaldi's self-borrowings in *Dorilla*, comparing Mortari's version of *L'Olimpiade*[50] with the original score,[51] shows that the reuse of parts from *Dorilla in Tempe* concerns specifically the beginning of the opera, i.e., the "Primavera" borrowings.[52] Thus, after Aminta's aria "Il fidarsi della speme" in the third scene of the first act of *L'Olimpiade*, the short choral pieces in that score are replaced with almost the complete "Primavera" complex from *Dorilla*.[53] The choral pieces also begin with the third part of the Sinfonia, but they exclude the last *coro* (example 10), which apparently for Mortari eliminated too much of the ritornello melody, the first part of which reappears at this point in the Mortari arrangement.

The replacement of the original choruses in the score of *L'Olimpiade* seems acceptable if we look at the relative simplicity of the "Primavera" borrowings and the pastoral atmosphere of these *Dorilla* sections, which suit the atmosphere of the replaced choruses. In a story of Olympic competition, however, the text and substitute music indulge too much in the pleasures of nature and love. Moreover, the prominent emphasis on the "Primavera" complex seems inappropriate for the development of the action. The association, which is inherent in the "Primavera" ritornello and supports the borrowing and its elaboration at the beginning of *Dorilla*, here seems to overload the scene.

This "borrowing of a borrowing" is an interesting example of the way in which Vivaldi is perceived. Mortari's arrangement is governed by his having to select popular music from among Vivaldi's works. However, the reference to the "maestros of that epoch" only sharpens our sense of distinction. The way in which Martori reused Vivaldi's borrowings is quite different from the way in which Vivaldi himself worked as a self-borrower.

NOTES

1. Parody may also include aspects of *contrafactum*. Reinhard Strohm, for whose help (along with that of Antonio Fanna and Peter Ryom) I am grateful, has focused on this technique in more detail in "Italienische Opernarien des frühen Settecento (1720–1730)," *Analecta Musicologica* 16 (Cologne, 1976), part 1, pp. 245–260 passim. I am indebted to Sally Katz for help with my English and to my wife, Helga von Kügelgen, for her advice and criticism.

2. Ibid., part 2, pp. 266–285. Concerning the special situation in Vivaldi's *Griselda*, see John Walter Hill, "Vivaldi's Griselda," *Journal of the American Musicological Society* (Spring 1978): 67ff.

3. Ibid., p. 247.

4. This paper can give only a very small part of this highly important chapter in the history of musical style and practice, a chapter that needs further investigation.

5. Giuseppe Riva, *Avviso ai compositori ed ai cantanti* (London, 1727), in Francesco Degrada, "Giuseppe Riva e il suo 'Avviso ai compositori ed ai cantanti,'" *Analecta Musicologica* 4 (1967): 112–123.

6. Pier Jacopo Martello, *Della tragedia antica e moderna* (Rome, 1714), in *Pier Jacopo Martello, Scritti critici e satirici*, ed. H. S. Noce, Scrittori d'Italia no. 225 (Bari, 1963).

7. Francesco Algarotti, "Saggio sopra l'opera in musica," (Venezia, 1754) in *F. Algarotti, Saggi*, ed. G. de Pozzo, Scrittori d'Italia no. 226 (Bari, 1963).

8. Helmut Hucke, "Die Neapolitanische Tradition in der Oper," in *International Musicological Society Congress Report* (New York, 1961), vol. 1, p. 261.

9. Benedetto Marcello, *Il teatro alla moda* (Venezia, 1720), Biblioteca Universale (Milano, 1959), p. 32: "Avverta poi, che l'Arie sino al fine dell'Opera siano a vicenda una allegra ed una patetica, senza aver riguardo veruno a Parole, a Tuoni, a Convenienze di Scena."

10. Hill, "Vivaldi's Griselda," p. 70.

11. Reinhard Strohm, *Die italienische Oper im 18. Jahrhundert*, in Taschenbücher zur Musikwissenschaft 25 (Wilhelmshaven, 1979), p. 229.

12. Concerning both versions see the facsimile of Vivaldi's *Griselda*, in *Italian Opera 1640–1770*, ed. Howard Mayer Brown, no. 35 (New York/London, 1978), fols. 144ᵛ–146ᵛ.

13. Ibid., fols. 142ff. See Griselda's aria "Brami le mie catene" (act 1, scene 4) preceding Ottone's recitative and his following aria "Vede orgogliosa l'onda."

14. It is clear that this determination of affects can be understood only relatively.

15. There also exists an arrangement for oboe RV 450. Cf. Walter Kolneder, "Vivaldis Aria-Concerto," *Deutsches Jahrbuch der Musikwissenschaft* 9 (1965): 20.

16. Walter Kolneder, *Antonio Vivaldi* (Wiesbaden, 1965), p. 232.

17. Peter Ryom, *Les Manuscrits de Vivaldi* (Copenhagen, 1977), pp. 266–274. Concerning further relationship between operas and instrumental works in Vivaldi's works, see Ryom, "Les Relations entre les opéras et la musique instrumentale," in *Il melodramma nel Settecento* (Venice, 1978).

18. Strohm, "Italienische Opernarien," part 1, p. 53.

19. Ibid. Strohm has pointed out convincingly that two influences are intertwined here: that of Leonardo Vinci's aria "Gelido in ogni vena" (1726) and that of Vivaldi's "Inverno" concerto, the last of the *Quattro stagioni*. The effect of these corresponding influences is that Vivaldi's ritornello, from the first movement of the concerto, permeates the setting, giving a semantic base, while Vinci's aria adds certain specifying melodic features.

20. Ryom, "Les Relations," p. 260.

21. See the score of *Il Giustino* (Turin, Biblioteca Nazionale Universitaria, Fondo Foà, no. 34), fols. 23ᵛ–24ʳ.

22. Francesco Degrada and Maria Teresa Muraro, *Antonio Vivaldi dal Venezia all'Europa* (Milan, 1978), p. 127.

23. A. Doren, "Fortuna im Mittelalter und in der Renaissance," *Vorträge der Bibliothek Warburg* II, Vorträge 1922–1923, 1. Teil (reprint 1967), pp. 132ff., figs. 7, 11–13, 18. It is noteworthy that Fortuna also can be combined with the idea of the *Quattro stagioni*, as indicated by Doren, "Fortuna im mittelalter," pp. 103, 141. The aspects

presented by the visual arts should be included in investigations concerning the broad field of musical meaning in opera, also in the case of (self-)borrowings, where the context of the scene can help to identify the source of borrowed yet modified material.

24. See the score of *Il Giustino*, fols. 20ff.

25. E major belongs to the "extreme keys" (cf. Strohm, "Italienische Opernarien," part 1, p. 235).

26. The score has the title *La Dorilla* (Turin, Biblioteca Nazionale Universitaria, Fondo Foà, no. 39).

27. There were other productions of *Dorilla* in 1728 (Venice) and 1732 (Prague).

28. In 1726, as well as in 1734, the stage setting was created by Antonio Mauro (cf. Degrada and Muraro, *Antonio Vivaldi*, pp. 132ff.).

29. Ibid.

30. See the score of *Dorilla*, fols. 147ʳ–147ᵛ.

31. Werner Braun, ed., Vivaldi, Concerti grossi, Op. 8, No. 104, *Die Jahreszeiten* (Munich, 1975) in *Meisterwerke der Musik* 9, p. 18.

32. Goldoni's report of his meeting with Vivaldi, presented in his memoirs, exists in two versions. Regarding a comparison of both versions, see Hill, "Vivaldi's Griselda," p. 54.

33. The translation follows ibid., p. 53.

34. Ibid., p. 79.

35. Braun, Vivaldi, p. 38.

36. W. Kolneder, *Antonio Vivaldi. Dokumente seines Lebens und Schaffens*, in Taschenbücher zur Musikwissenschaft 25 (Wilhelmshaven, 1979), p. 207.

37. Charles de Brosses, *Lettres familières sur l'Italie*, ed. Yvonne Bézard, 2 vols. (Paris, 1931), vol. 2, p. 341.

38. The translation follows Reinhard G. Pauly's English edition of Marcello's *Il teatro alla moda* in *The Musical Quarterly* 34 (1948): 381.

39. Ibid.

40. Despite the fact that the sonnet "denotes" Vivaldi's "La primavera" in the sense of Umberto Eco's "semiotics" (cf. Umberto Eco, *Einführung in die Semiotik* [Munich, 1972], p. 22), the interrelationship of ritornello and interludes—considered until recently as aspects of form *or* program music, but not as form and *semiotic structure* of mutual meaning—represents the interlacement of connotation and denotation (concerning these terms see Eco, *Einführung*, pp. 101, 108 passim). The ritornello, presenting the basic meaning of the whole piece, is nevertheless more vaguely described and signified than the interludes. Thus, the ritornello is more open to "association" than the interludes, which may be viewed as fixed connotation, making the meaning of "spring" more precise. It is precisely this rela-

tive vagueness that makes the ritornello appropriate for its integration into opera, in that the dramatic context denotes the reused music more distinctively, while the music itself unfolds in accordance with the plot.

41. Noce, *Martello*, pp. 282ff.:

L'uso commanda che il tuo melodramma sia diviso in tre atti. . . .
Nell'atto primo sarà tua cura il preparar gli ascoltanti all'intreccio, dando loro la necessaria notizia degli eroi che battono il palco, degli antefatti opportuni alla cognizione, sia della favola sia della storia, e facendo la prima mostra de' caratteri, almeno de' principali, che dovranno intervenire all'azione. . . . Nel secondo atto tu dei pensare al viluppo tanto delle azioni quanto delle passioni. . . . Nel terzo atto pensisi allo sviluppo, o sia scioglimento, e sia pur anche per macchina, se lo permetterà l'impressario; che certamente sarà più accetto per la maraviglia dell'apparenza, ancorchè il nodo per avventura non meritasse più che tanto d'incomodar un nume a scender dal cielo per scioglierlo.

42. Here we must focus on some of the main aspects, primarily on the function of acts. The fact that Vivaldi uses his "machine" not in the third but in the first act of *Il Giustino* is not important in this connection.

43. See the score, fols. 95ᵛ–97ᵛ.

44. Ibid., fols. 127ʳ–128ᵛ.

45. Ibid., fols. 129ᵛ–132ʳ.

46. Ibid., fols. 147ʳ–149ᵛ.

47. From case to case, not only the key characteristics but also the interrelationship of keys should be investigated.

48. See the score, fols. 150ʳ–151ᵛ. The dramatic knot, however, is untied: an apparition ("Voce di dentro") detects the secret, which is that Giustino, Vitaliano, and Andronico are brothers, and by their united action matters take a new turn; Amantio, who tried to usurp the empire, is defeated. Thus Giustino is finally acknowledged for his merits and virtue, and he gains Leocasta and the empire.

49. *Antonio Vivaldi, Note e documenti sulla vita e sulle opere* (Rome, 1939), pp. 11ff.:

L'opera ha tuttavia richiesto un paziente lavoro di adattamento, anzitutto per le necessità di dover ridurre allo stretto necessario i lunghissimi *recitativi* ai quali certamente il pubblico teatrale dell'epoca non dava nessun ascolto. Mancando poi alcuni pezzi importanti, questi sono stati tolti da un'altra opera vivaldiana: "La Dorilla," la quale fu rappresentata lo stesso anno (1734) sullo stesso teatro di S. Angelo a Venezia. La "Dorilla" è un'opera di cui il manoscritto torinese porta la dicitura: "atti tre, con sinfonia e cori che cantano e ballan," e che è assai più ricca dell'*Olimpiade* in pezzi di insieme e sopratutto di cori e danze. Donde la decisione di togliere da questa quanto mancava all'*Olimpiade*, avendo per sè la coscienza di non fare altro che quante praticavano correntemente i maestri di quell'epoca. . . .

50. Antonio Vivaldi, *L'Olimpiade* (HUNGAROTON SLPX 11901-03, 1978).
51. Turin, Biblioteca Nazionale Universitaria, Fondo Foà no. 39.
52. See the score of *Dorilla*, fols. 146^v–151^r.
53. See the score of *L'Olimpiade*, fols. 24^r–25^r.

Vivaldi's *Orlando*: Sources and Contributing Factors   *by John Walter Hill*

Many components of Vivaldi's *Orlando* had already been in existence before the opera was first performed in 1727. This paper will distinguish some of what was old from what was new in the 1727 production. It will compare Vivaldi's earlier use of old material with his reuse of it in *Orlando*. It will examine some of Vivaldi's choices and his manipulation of components. And from all of this it will suggest something of what Vivaldi seems to have been aiming for in the opera, especially with respect to the relationship between music, text, and drama.

Vivaldi seems always to have been a busy person. After 1713, he was actively putting together opera productions as composer, arranger, impresario, music director, and violinist in the orchestra. By the beginning of 1739, two years before his death, he claimed to have put together ninety-four operas, and his claim is worthy of belief. Through librettos, we know of about sixty opera productions in which Vivaldi certainly had a part. To be sure, twelve of these are known to have contained music by other composers, and thirteen were repetitions of earlier works.[1] But the repetitions were rarely done without changes in the music. And some operas thought to have been composed entirely by Vivaldi may eventually turn out to have borrowed music by other composers. *Orlando* is one of these.

In any case, ninety-four opera productions place Vivaldi among the most prolific opera composers in history, just after Alessandro Scarlatti with 114 and Reinhard Keiser with one hundred, but ahead of Tommaso Albinoni, Antonio Caldara, George Frideric Handel, Leonardo Leo, Leonardo Vinci, Johann Adolf Hasse, and Niccolo Porpora, to name his principal contemporaries. By any measure, Vivaldi was a major opera composer, and he was busy.

He often had to put together several operas for a single season. The score to *Tito Manlio* says it was written in five days. How could Vivaldi do this? As every stage composer of his day, Vivaldi assembled his operas out of standard features and stereotyped components. And as most of his contemporaries, perhaps even more than most, he borrowed heavily from his own earlier operas and from those of others.

Admittedly this practice of borrowing goes against our present-day notions of an opera as an original musical composition in which the music, text, and drama have a close, even a unique relationship. And, it must be admitted also, this practice went against ideals held by some of Vivaldi's contemporaries such as Benedetto Marcello, Pier Martello, and Carlo Goldoni.[2] These and other writers refer scornfully to the routine and insensitive way in which many operas were assembled, the standardization and predictability of so many aspects of an opera at that time, the practice of borrowing arias from roles previously sung by the various performers in the production, and the composer's demand that the poet fit new words to old music. All of their remarks apply to Vivaldi's operas, but the results seem often quite good if taken on their own terms. In fact, Vivaldi's operas were usually successful. While his critics wrote pamphlets, opera lovers went to the theater. Enhancing our understanding of the success of Vivaldi's *Orlando*, or at least finding a way of judging its success from a point of view consonant with Vivaldi's, is the aim of this study of the sources.

Now the sources that we have for the opera are neither unusual nor especially problematic. The libretto, printed in the autumn of 1727, evidently preserves the text that was sung in that production, at least at the beginning of or just before its run of performances. The score (I: Tn, Giordano 39 bis) corresponds with the 1727 libretto except for one aria substitution, one chorus substitution, two eliminations of arias, and three abbreviations of arias.[3] There is no evidence that these changes were made for a revival of the opera in some later year. In general the score still corresponds with the 1727 libretto as closely as do most of Vivaldi's opera scores with their respective librettos.

But the sources that Vivaldi used in creating the 1727 *Orlando* are a bit more interesting and problematic. To begin with, he was setting a libretto that he had dealt with thirteen years before. In December 1714 Vivaldi revised a setting of *Orlando furioso* that had been composed the previous year by Giovanni Alberto Ristori. For this revision in 1714, Vivaldi replaced twenty-two of Ristori's arias and ensembles with numbers, probably his own, that had different texts from those set by Ristori. There is no evidence that Vivaldi replaced any of Ristori's recitatives. Nevertheless, the revised opera was mostly Vivaldi's.

This 1714 production of the Ristori-Vivaldi *Orlando furioso* became one of Vivaldi's sources of music when he reset the opera in 1727, for he took at least two arias and two choruses from the 1714 version, possibly three arias, one duet, and two choruses.[4]

The two choruses taken from the 1713/1714 score (I: Tn, Giordano 37) of *Orlando furioso* into Vivaldi's 1727 *Orlando* are mentioned in a recent article by Eric Cross, who, however, remains silent about the evidence of the sources that touch upon the question of authorship.[5] This evidence is furnished by the state of the score relating to Vivaldi's 1714 revision of *Orlando furioso*. Originally it had been Ristori's score for his 1713 setting, but it contains some of the revisions that Vivaldi made in 1714. In act 1, Vivaldi crossed out or ripped out all the arias that he replaced in his 1714 revision. Only one of Vivaldi's substituted arias is fully written in, however. Most of the others are represented only by the bass part for the accompanying continuo group, with or without a vocal cue at the beginning. But act 2 of Ristori's score has been left virtually untouched. All of Ristori's arias of 1713 have been left in the score, and none of Vivaldi's substitute texts, as shown in the 1714 libretto, are present in any form. It seems reasonable to conclude, therefore, that all the music in act 2 of this score is from Ristori's setting of 1713. But this includes the two choruses that were mentioned earlier. This means that the music with its onstage instruments in Vivaldi's 1727 *Orlando* for the two very effective choruses in the wedding scene of act 2 ("Al fragor de' corni audacci" and "Gran madre Venere," with its later repetition to the words "Diva dell'Espero") is not by Vivaldi, but by Giovanni Alberto Ristori. Likewise much of the recitative toward the end of act 2, including the very dramatic mad scene for Orlando, which Cross has traced to the 1713/1714 score of *Orlando furioso*, is based on music that must be Ristori's. The rest of Vivaldi's 1727 act 2 is different from Ristori's of 1713, as a comparison of the scores shows.

Still other items in the 1727 *Orlando* were taken from the 1714

Orlando furioso, but we cannot be sure how many. Beyond any doubt, Vivaldi took two arias—"Come l'onda" and "Anderò, chiamerò dal profondo"—from his 1714 revision of *Orlando furioso* and reused them in his 1727 *Orlando*. These texts are not found in Ristori's 1713 *Orlando furioso*, but were added to the opera by Vivaldi in 1714. Surviving music shows that Vivaldi reused them in 1727, but both were actually composed before 1714, as I will show later. Six other aria or ensemble texts were taken from the 1714 libretto into the 1727 *Orlando*, not in every case with their music. The settings of two of these survive in the 1713/1714 Ristori-Vivaldi score of *Orlando furioso* ("Nel profondo cieco mondo" and "Tacci non ti lagnar"), where it seems that the music is Ristori's, since in both cases the same singer performed them in 1713 and in 1714. In Vivaldi's 1727 score of *Orlando* they are both set to new music. Another two aria texts taken into the 1727 libretto were new in 1714 (they did not appear in Ristori's 1713 libretto), but were also set to new music for Vivaldi's 1727 *Orlando*: "Tu sei degl'occhi miei," which is in the 1714 score but is set to different music in the 1727 score, and "Dove il valor combatte," which is not among the arias preserved in the incomplete 1714 score but was sung by a soprano in 1714, by a bass in 1727. The duet "Sei mia fiamma, e sei mio bene" for Angelica and Medoro (act 2, scene 12) has different music in the 1713/1714 and 1727 scores. But Vivaldi did not make his changes in act 2 of the score he inherited from Ristori in 1714. If he reset this duet, the score would not show it. Now Margherita Gualandi, who sang Angelica in the 1714 *Orlando*, received all new arias, as is shown by comparing the librettos of 1713 and 1714. This circumstance makes it seem possible that her duet, "Sei mia fiamma," was reset in 1714 and that Vivaldi used his setting again in 1727. Again, we cannot know because none of Vivaldi's new music for act 2 of the 1714 *Orlando* is known to survive.

The last possible borrowing from the 1714 *Orlando furioso* that I will discuss is "L'arco vuò frangerti," sung by Alcina in act 3, scene 3. The text was in Ristori's 1713 *Orlando furioso*, sung by a soprano. In 1714 the role was sung by an alto who received six new aria texts out of the eight she sang. This text, too, might have received a new setting by Vivaldi in 1714, and if so he may have used it again in 1727 when Anna Giraud, also an alto, sang the role. Since the 1713/1714 score is lacking the third act, this hypothesis cannot be tested.

The remaining borrowed numbers came out of other earlier operas by Vivaldi or from those of other composers. Only Vivaldi's self-borrowings can be dealt with here; there are probably five but possibly seven of them. Yet the fact that the texts for twenty of the thirty-one numbers in Vivaldi's 1727 *Orlando* differ from those in either the 1713 or 1714 settings of *Orlando furioso* suggests a larger number of as yet undetected borrowings. Not to be included among the self-borrowings are three arias that *Orlando* shares with Vivaldi's *Farnace*, also of 1727, because evidence suggests that *Farnace* was produced later in the 1727 season.[6]

Of the five arias in *Orlando* that probably came from Vivaldi's earlier operas, only one has been mentioned by other writers.[7] The evident reason for this is that the remaining four borrowings are not to be discovered by the usual methods of comparison between musical sources or librettos. As a consequence, it will be best to begin by examining the borrowing that is easiest to demonstrate and conclude with the more difficult cases.

Ruggiero's aria "Come l'onda," found in the 1727 libretto (act 3, scene 8), was used in Vivaldi's revised *Orlando furioso* of 1714, as mentioned above. Actually it goes back at least to *Ottone in Villa* of 1713, Vivaldi's first known opera. When he brought the aria into *Orlando furioso*, Vivaldi or his poet changed half of the text in order to accommodate a new dramatic context. In *Ottone in Villa*, act 2, scene 1, Emperor Ottone is finally told that Cleonilla, his mistress, whom he has everyone treat as if she were the empress, is actually unfaithful to him. Ottone justifiably explodes into a rage of jealousy:

Come l'onda	As a wave
Con voragine orrenda, e profonda	with a horrid, deep whirlpool,
Aggitata da vento, ò procella	agitated by wind or storm
Fremendo,	roaring,
Stridendo	shrieking,
Là nel seno del mare sen và.	rolls there in the middle of the sea,
Così il core	so my heart,
Assalito da fiero timore	assailed by violent fear,
Turbato, Aggitato	troubled, agitated
Sospira, S'aggira	sighs, is confused
E geloso	and, jealous,
Ritrova più riposo non sà.	knows not how to find rest.

But in the 1714 and 1727 *Orlando* librettos the situation is quite different. Medoro berates Ruggiero for abandoning Alcina and returning to Bradamante after Alcina's spell over Ruggiero was broken. Ruggiero, quite rightly, objects to Medoro's criticism, and they eventually draw swords over the argument. Here Angelica rushes in to shield her beloved Medoro. Ruggiero, in just a few lines, accuses Angelica of driving his friend Orlando insane by playing false with his affections. The aria "Come l'onda" given to Ruggiero at this point elaborates on his accusation of Angelica, which, however, was not the main point of the scene. The words of the second stanza had to be changed:

Il tuo core	So your heart
Combattuto da fiero timore	embattled by violent fear,
Turbato, agitato	troubled, agitated,
Sospira, s'adira,	sighs, is confused,
E sdegnoso	and, angered,
Ritrova più riposo non sà.	knows not how to find rest.

The reference to jealousy in the singer's heart, appropriate to the situation in *Ottone*, had to be changed to anger in Angelica's heart, which is all right for this scene in *Orlando*. The change was accomplished even while retaining much of the original text. But since there is really little preparation for these thoughts and feelings in the preceding scenes, this fierce and furious bravura aria seems an overreaction. Perhaps Vivaldi thought so, too, in the end. For although he used it in the 1714 *Orlando furioso* and kept it in the 1727 production at least until the libretto was printed, he eventually removed it from the score. In doing so he revealed good dramatic judgment, in my view.

The aria "Come l'onda" was borrowed with the text of its first stanza intact. More often, Vivaldi fit new text to old music when reusing his arias. Such a case is the aria, "Anderò, chiamerò dal profondo," which Alcina sings near the end of the opera, vowing revenge for her defeat at the hands of Orlando and his friends. It is a very effective aria in this context, but it was originally composed for Vivaldi's *Orlando finto pazzo* in 1714. In that opera, Origille believes that Grifone has been betrayed, and she vows to gather an army of thousands of Christian warriors, Charlemagne's vassals, from the banks of the Tiber, the Seine, and the Rhine.

Anderò,	I shall go,
Volerò,	I shall fly,
Griderò.	I shall cry,
Su la Senna, su il Tebro, su il Reno,	upon the Seine, the Tiber, the Rhine,
Animando a battaglia a vendetta	arousing to battle for revenge
Ogni cuore, che vanti valor.	every heart that boasts valor.
Empio duol, che me serpi nel seno	Pitiless sorrow, which hides in my breast,
Scaglia pur la fatale saetta	hurl at last the fatal dart
A finire il mio acerbo dolor.	to finish my harsh pain.

The aria was taken into Vivaldi's revision of *Orlando furioso* later in the autumn of 1714 without any change of text. It was given to Alcina, who, by the way, was sung by Anna Maria Fabbri, the very singer who, as Origille, had performed this aria in *Orlando finto pazzo*. The words of the aria, however, do not suit Alcina in *Orlando furioso*. It would be unlikely that Alcina, as enemy of Orlando and the Christians, would find allies all over Europe. Hers are in the underworld, where in the revised 1727 text she expects to seek them:

Anderò, chiamerò dal profondo	I shall go, I shall call from the depths
L'empie furie del baratro immondo.	the wicked Furies of the foul underworld.
Chiederò negl'abissi vendetta	From the abysses I shall ask revenge
Dell'offeso, e tradito mio amor.	for my offended and betrayed love.

The second stanza of this aria had been copied unchanged into the 1727 score and had been printed in the libretto, but it was eventually crossed out in order to achieve an accelerated pacing at the end of the opera, I would guess.

Example 1 shows how the new 1727 text and the original words fit the music. Of course both texts have the same underlying affection: fury. Also the pattern of accentuation and inflection is the same in both texts. Notice, too, that in retexting the aria, Vivaldi, or his poet acting on his instructions, has managed to keep the correspondence between the three-note motive and the individual words at the beginning: "Anderò, / Volerò, / Griderò" becomes "Anderò, chiamerò dal profondo." But the parallelism in the list of rivers in the second phrase is lost: "Su la Senna, su il Tebro, su il

EXAMPLE 1. "Anderò, chiamerò dal profondo," from *Orlando* (1727, 3.13) and "Anderò, / Volerò, / Griderò," from *Orlando finto pazzo* (1714, 3.12)

Reno," becomes "L'empie furie del baratro immondo." The key word, *vendetta*, is kept in the revised text, however, and an important word, *offeso*, has been found to replace *cuore* at the top of the D-minor scale. The octave leap in the first measure was added when Vivaldi decided to change the text of this aria after having begun to copy it into the score with the original words, which he then crossed out. In retexting this aria, Vivaldi managed to preserve, then, the basic affection, the declamation, the correspondence between motive and word, and some of the key words that are given special emphasis by the music.

The aria just examined is preserved in the surviving scores of both *Ottone in Villa* and *Orlando*. But at least three other arias in *Orlando* seem to be retextings of older arias from operas for which no score survives. In general this is the most common situation encountered in Vivaldi's operatic self-borrowing and one that has not been explored very much by other researchers.

By matching verse scannings, possible sources of arias can be found using only librettos. Probable cases of borrowing with text parody emerge when the older and newer texts match not only in scanning pattern and number of lines, but also in some key words or phrases, type of feeling expressed, and imagery, if the imagery seems to be of the sort often reflected in music.[8] These requisites are fulfilled in cases of the two arias already discussed, "Come l'onda" and "Anderò, chiamerò dal profondo," for which the earlier setting survives in score. In the cases remaining to be examined, these similarities of text provide the only evidence of borrowing.

The aria "Se cresce un torrente," which Bradamante sings in *Orlando* act 2, scene 10, expresses her boundless joy at having regained the love of Ruggiero, freed from Alcina's enchantment. The text of her aria compares her boundless joy to a stream that breaks its banks:

Se cresce un tòrrente	If a stream grows
Con torbida piena,	with a turbulent flood
E rompe la sponda,	and breaks its banks,
Altera si spande	proudly that water
Nei campi quell'onda,	is poured into the fields
E freno non ha.	and it has no restraint.
La gioia è si grande,	The joy is so great
Che l'anima sente,	that my soul feels,
Che il cor si risente,	that my heart is affected,
E dentro se stesso	and within it
L'estremo piacere	knows not how to
Racchiuder non sa.	contain its extreme pleasure.

The imagery of the turbulent flood water is certainly reflected in the rumbling split-octave figure played by the bass instruments that accompany Vivaldi's setting of this text in *Orlando*.

It seems very likely that this aria was borrowed from Vivaldi's *Siroe re di Persia*, which was performed in Reggio Emilia during the preceding April, although no score of that opera is known to survive. The text of the aria sung by Medarse in act 3, scene 13 of *Siroe* is a very close match to "Se cresce un torrente" in *Orlando*. The scanning and number of lines are the same, except that the second stanza of the *Siroe* aria would require the repetition of one line, a common adjustment in Vivaldi's retexted arias. Instead of "Se cresce un torrente," it begins "Torrente cresciuto." The second line is almost the same, as are the last two words in the first stanza. And the image of the rampaging stream, overflowing its banks, is found in both.

If the texts are so similar, why did Vivaldi bother to change the words when he took the music from *Siroe* into *Orlando*? The answer is that the original text uses the image of the flood in a different way:

Torrente cresciuto	A stream swelled
Per torbida piena,	by a turbulent flood,
Se perde il tributo	if it loses the contribution
Del giel, che si scioglie,	of the melting ice,
Fra l'aride sponde	within dry banks,
Più l'onde non ha.	has no more water.

Ma il fiume, che naque	But the river that is born
Da limpida vena,	from a clear spring,
Se privo è dell'acque,	if deprived of water
Che il verno raccoglie,	collected by the winter,
Più chiaro si fa.	becomes even clearer.

These words are very appropriate for the repentant Medarse, who has just been defeated and forgiven by Siroe. His recitative leading into this aria says, "Ah, I learn from my defeat that innocence is the more certain guide. Whoever trusts wickedness makes an enemy of destiny and loses everything. Whoever places his faith in virtue, even if dismally fated, at least retains the peace of his soul." But these ideas would make no sense in the mouth of Bradamante, who rejoices at Ruggiero's release from Alcina's enchantment. Hence the retexting shown in "Se cresce un torrente" (example 2).

In the case of "Se cresce un torrente," the substitution of new text and music was not a matter of working in an aria from the singer's repertoire, as was the case with Anna Fabbri's aria "Come l'onda." Possibly Vivaldi and his collaborators wanted in this place in *Orlando* a far more energetic aria than the 1714 text would have implied. The image of boundless joy may have suggested Medarse's metaphor aria to Vivaldi. Unity of scene complex comes into question here, too. This subject will be taken up later.

A similar case of borrowing with text parody, also from Vivaldi's *Siroe*, is "Benchè nasconda," which Astolfo sings in *Orlando* act 2, scene 2:

Benchè nasconda	Although it is hidden,
La serpe in seno	the snake at your breast,
Spietata, e immonda	cruel and unclean,
Il rio veleno,	its wicked poison
È men crudele	is less cruel
Dell'infedele,	than a faithless lover
Che t'ingannò.	who deceives you.
È pien di frodi	It is full of deceptions,
Il Regno infido,	this faithless realm,
E in altro lido	and to another shore
Io fuggirò.	I shall flee.

Evidently Vivaldi had already used the music for this aria in his *Siroe re di Persia*, Reggio, 1727, act 2, scene 5, where Emira, disguised as Idaspe, sings these words:

EXAMPLE 2. "Se cresce un torrente," from *Orlando* (1727, 2.10) and "Torrente cresciuto," from *Siroe re di Persia* (1727, 3.13)

Benchè s'asconda	Although it stays hidden,
La serpe antica	the ancient serpent,
Tra fronda, e fronda,	from bush to bush
Tra spica, e spica,	and stalk to stalk,
Pur dalla cura	still
Non è sicura	it is not safe from the diligence
Del pastorello	of the shepherd
Che l'osservò.	who watches.
Al par di quello	Just like him,
Sol per te fido	devoted only to you,
Fin dentro il nido	even to its nest
L'assalirò.	I shall pursue it.

Although no score for *Siroe* is known, there are several strong reasons for believing that the same music served to set both texts. First of all, both texts have the same number of syllables per line and the same accent pattern. The first stanza of the *Orlando* text is one line shorter, but in fact the sixth line of that stanza is invariably repeated in Vivaldi's score, a repetition that would not have been necessary with the *Siroe* text. Both texts have elisions forming the third of the theoretical five syllables (lines 2 and 3), which Vivaldi separates in his setting, making them into caesuras. Then, of course, there is the metaphor of the serpent common to both. The first lines of the two aria texts are practically the same. Indeed, Vivaldi, when putting the text under the vocal line in his score for *Orlando*, began by writing "Benchè s'asconda," corresponding to the *Siroe* text. He subsequently corrected the mis-

taken by writing an *n* over the erroneous letter *s*'. Finally, the *Siroe*
text fits the vocal line better than the substituted text in *Orlando*.
The double ploce of the *Siroe* text at lines 3 and 4 ("Tra fronda, e
fronda, / Tra spica, e spica") matches the repetitions of the rhythmic motive in measures 8 to 11 of the first vocal period (example
3) and in parallel places. The fourth line of the *Siroe* text continues
the pattern of poetic elisions treated as caesuras by Vivaldi, whereas
the same line in the *Orlando* text breaks the pattern and therefore
requires the slur in measure 10 of example 3. Again, the *Siroe* text
could accommodate the slurs in the *Orlando* score as shown in
measures 21 to 23 and 60 to 62 of example 3, slurs that would
have been superfluous in the melisma that resulted when the *Orlando* text was set under the vocal line. And in a similar way, the
Siroe text could have been set under measures 56 to 59 of example
3 so as to preserve the pattern of syllable setting established with
that rhythmic motive in measures 6 to 10 and 45 to 49.

Given the need to change the meaning of this text from one expressing militant loyalty in *Siroe* to one projecting resentment and
defiance in *Orlando*, Vivaldi or his poet managed to retain several
features of the poem. The pattern of versification has been mentioned, and it has an obvious relationship with the rhythm and
phrasing of Vivaldi's setting. The metaphor of the hidden serpent
was retained, possibly because precisely at the word *serpe* the sec-

EXAMPLE 3. "Benchè nasconda," from *Orlando* (1727, 2.2) and "Benchè s'asconda," from *Siroe re di Persia* (1727, 2.5)

EXAMPLE 4. "Qual candido fiore," from *Orlando* (2.5) as first written

ond violins begin a wriggling, broken-figure accompaniment. But with greater security we can point to the melismatic painting of the word *fuggirò* in the *Siroe* text (example 3, measures 84 to 88 and 97 to 98), which is suitably replaced by *l'assalirò* in *Orlando*. It may even have been for reasons of expressive sound qualities that the shrill vowel of the word *infido* (example 3, measures 83 and 94) was retained by the substitution of *nido* at the same cadences.

Vivaldi's concern for the relationship between music and text extended even further when he borrowed the music for "Qual candido fiore," sung by Medoro in *Orlando* act 2, scene 5:

Qual candido fiore   That bright flower
Che sorge nel prato   that grows in the meadow
Rinasce nel core   revives in my heart
La bella mia spene;   my beautiful hope;
Poi torna à perir.   but then it dies.

Son troppo felice,	I am too happy
Se amarti mi lice;	when you let me love you.
Mà l'anima amante	But the loving soul,
Fedele, e costante	faithful and constant,
Lontan dal suo bene	far from his beloved,
Si sente languir.	feels itself die.

In the score of the 1727 *Orlando*, Vivaldi wrote out the last repetition of this aria's first stanza, which closes the second vocal period, in the way shown in example 4. Then he crossed out the portions enclosed within the two dotted brackets. Above the first of these phrases, he wrote in a revision that only affects the vocal line, not the bass or the harmony, as shown in example 5. The second of these phrases he cut. Why the revision? Melodically it is far less interesting than the first version, and the cut makes the bass line awkward. I believe the answer may be that Vivaldi borrowed the music, reclothed it in new text, then decided that the music had to be adjusted to the new words.

In general, the 1727 text works well enough with the music. Medoro's mixture of hope and sorrow, expressed in the metaphor of a wilting flower, is sufficiently supported by the continuously coaxing syncopated figure and the generally cantabile style of the whole aria. But just at the phrase that Vivaldi altered in 1727, the original version of the music seems to express sorrow and pain rather too strongly for the words "revives in my heart my beautiful hope." The musical symbolism of the original descending line with

EXAMPLE 5. "Qual candido fiore," from *Orlando* (2.5) as rewritten

appoggiaturas and shift to the parallel minor suggests just the opposite of revival and hope. Vivaldi must have noticed that after writing out the whole aria. His sense of appropriate music and text relationship was evidently offended. Given the text and the dramatic situation to which it is connected, he changed the music in the simplest way he could: he replaced the expressive descending line with rather neutral repetitions of the first and fifth degrees of the scale.

The original text for this music, I would suggest, was the aria "Le vaghe pupille" from Vivaldi's *Tieteberga* (1717) act 1, scene 2:

Le vaghe pupille	The charming eyes
Del caro mio sposo	of my beloved spouse,
Non so se sdegnose	I do not know if they are scornful,
Se meste, o ritrose	if mournful, or bashful;
Io debba temer.	I must be afraid.
Sò ben ch'il timore	I know well that fear
Mi toglie il riposo,	robs me of repose,
E che del mio bene,	and that my beloved's
Incerta la spene	uncertain hope
Mi turba il piacer.	disturbs my pleasure.

The score to *Tieteberga* is lost. Only the libretto is known. But in form and declamation the words of "Le vaghe pupille" in *Tieteberga* fit the music to "Qual candido fiore" in *Orlando* hand in glove. The overall sense of the words suggests a mixture of love and delicate sorrow, not unlike the *Orlando* text that apparently replaced it. But at the expressive descending phrase in example 6, the *Tieteberga* text says of the eyes of the heroine's beloved, "I do not know if they are scornful, if mournful, or bashful." These sorrowful, painful, and unexpansive words would have been well expressed by Vivaldi's original descending phrase, and might easily have borne the more emphatic repetition that Vivaldi cut out of this revision for *Orlando*.

From these examples of Vivaldi's borrowing in *Orlando* alone nothing very general can be proven. They are offered only as samples of what we find when examining the sources—ours and Vivaldi's. On the basis of my continuing research on Vivaldi's self-borrowing, I would offer the following provisional generalizations. According to the standard practice of his time, Vivaldi fitted his opera roles to his singers. He rarely revived an opera without mak-

EXAMPLE 6. "Qual candido fiore," from *Orlando* (2.5) with corresponding text from "Le vaghe pupille," from *Tieteberga* (1.2)

ing changes in it. Sometimes he accommodated his singers by inserting into their roles arias that they had sung with success in other operas, whether by him or by other composers. Other times he found in the growing stock of his own arias an item that suited the context and the singer quite well. In a few cases Vivaldi was able to use the text that originally went with the borrowed music. More often he required new text to fit the old music. But he was quite particular about the way the new text fit. Numbers of lines, scanning, and meaning had to be similar. Elisions, caesuras, repetitions, and emphases of words and phrases had to coincide. The musical symbolism evoked by the original text had to be worked into the new text, or else the expressive symbolism had to be removed from the music. And I would say that the new text and borrowed music usually had to be fitted well to the character and to the shape of the whole opera. On this last point I would like to add a brief epilogue.

In my article on Vivaldi's *Griselda* (see note 8) I dealt with the question of character shaping and redefining by means of substituted and borrowed arias. In *Orlando*, Alcina is the central figure. Through Vivaldi's aria substitutions and cuts, the character of the 1713 Braccioli-Ristori Alcina becomes focused and strengthened. With far greater clarity and forcefulness, her development is traced in Vivaldi's six arias, which express, in turn, hope mixed with fear, satisfaction mixed with worry, haughty betrayal, sorrow, bitterness, and finally fury. The substituted arias trace a tragic downfall that the original arias hint at, but also obscure.

Likewise, by replacing arias of one type with arias of another character, Vivaldi gives unity to his scene complexes. In the 1727 *Orlando* there are eight changes of scenery that divide the opera into nine scene complexes: act 1, scenes 1 to 5, 6 to 13; act 2, scenes 1 to 4, 5 to 8, 9 to 10, 11 to 13; act 3, scenes 1 to 3, 4 to 10, 11 to 13. As a result of aria substitutions, all five arias in the first complex are of the bravura type, like "Se cresce un torrente," expressing hope, fear, or anger. In the second complex, they are all but one of the cantabile sort, like "Qual candido fiore," and express love. In the third complex they are parlante bravura arias, like "Anderò, chiamerò dal profondo." In the fourth, they are cantabile love arias again; in the fifth, dance arias expressing joy; in the sixth, cantabile love arias; in the seventh, parlante bravura arias expressing anger; in the eighth, two cantabile arias and one dance aria, all expressing love; and in the last the only aria is parlante and expresses fury.

I have never noticed such a pattern of unity in any other serious opera of this time, by Vivaldi or by any other composer. The pattern certainly contradicts Carlo Goldoni's report that opera seria composers of that time were expected to alternate aria types, not bunch them together.[9] Vivaldi's grouping seems far too consistent and deliberate to be dismissed as accidental. Only further study will determine whether or not Vivaldi's *Orlando* is unusual in this respect.

It is hoped that this kind of examination of sources, of the composer's borrowing, of his choices, and of his manipulation of material will give us a clearer view of his aims. Too often when we see only one setting of a text, or only one text for an aria, we are inclined to assume that between the poetry and the music it was a marriage made in heaven. But when we see the same text set differently, or the same music reclothed in new text, we have the opportunity to view the relationship from two or more different angles, and, like a surveyor, to judge more precisely the moment that we are just beginning to explore: the operas of Antonio Vivaldi.

NOTES

1. These estimates are offered by Reinhard Strohm, "Zu Vivaldi's Opernschaffen," in *Venezia e il melodramma nel settecento*, ed. Maria Teresa Muraro, Studi di musica veneta 6 (Florence, 1978), pp. 237–248.

2. Reinhard G. Pauly, "Benedetto Marcello's Satire on Early 18th-Century Opera," *Musical Quarterly* 34 (1948): 222–233; Benedetto Marcello, "Il teatro alla moda," trans. Reinhard G. Pauly, *Musical Quarterly* 34 (1948): 371–403 and 35 (1949): 85–105; Piero Weiss, "Pier Jacopo Martello on Opera (1715): An Annotated Translation," *Musical Quarterly* 66 (1980): 378–403; Carlo Goldoni, "Mémoires [1787]" and "Prefazione dell'edizione Pasquali," *Tutte le opere di Carlo Goldoni*, ed. Giuseppe Ortolani, 4th edition, I classici Mondadori (Verona, 1949), vol. 1; Piero Weiss, "Carlo Goldoni, Librettist: The Early Years," Ph.D. dissertation (Columbia University, 1970).

3. The score, Turin, Biblioteca Nazionale Universitaria, Giordano 39 bis, fols. 1–151, contains "Rompo i ceppi e in lacci" (fols. 40^r–42^v) in place of "Se tacendo, se soffrendo," found in the libretto, act 1, scene 10. The final chorus given in the libretto is "Vien dal cielo in noi l'amore," while the score (fols. 151^r–152^r) contains "Con mirti, e fiori volate amore," which was taken from Vivaldi's *Orlando finto pazzo* (1714). The arias "Non è felice un'alma" (Alcina), act 3, scene 6, and "Come l'onda" (Ruggiero), act 3, scene 8, found in the 1727 libretto are not in the score. In fact, most of act 3, scenes 6–9 of the libretto are not in the score. But the numbering of scenes is continuous in act 3 of the score, where scene 6 corresponds to scene 10 of the libretto. In the score, three arias appear with the setting of the second stanza (i.e., the middle section of the da capo scheme, and, hence, the repeat of the first section) crossed out: "Dove il valor combatte" (Astolfo), act 3, scene 1 (fols. 113^r–115^v); "Poveri affeti miei, siete innocenti" (Angelica), act 3, scene 5 (fols. 127^r–129^v); and "Anderò, chiamerò dal profondo" (Alcina), act 3, scene 13 (act 3, scene 9 in the score, fols. 148^r–150^r). The cancellations look very much like cancellations in many of Vivaldi's scores.

4. Reinhard Strohm, "Italienische Opernarien des frühen Settecento (1720–1730)," *Analecta Musicologica* 16 (Cologne, 1976), part 2, p. 248, is evidently referring to the incomplete score of 1713/1714, not to the evidence presented below, when he writes, "Vivaldis Musik von 1714 hat in den erhaltenen Teilen nichts gemeinsam mit der 2. Vertonung des *Orlando furioso* von 1727."

5. Eric Cross, "Vivaldi's Operatic Borrowings," *Music and Letters* 59 (1978): 429–439.

6. The music of "Un raggio di speme," *Orlando*, act 1, scene 1, was given the text "Pensando allo sposo" in *Farnace*, act 2, scene 3, and was sung by Benedetta Serosina in both operas in the same season. The music of "Benchè nasconda," *Orlando*, act 2, scene 2, was given the text "Se si nasconda" in *Farnace*, act 1, scene 13, sung by Gaetano Pinetti in both. And "Sorge l'irato nembo," *Orlando*, act 2, scene 4, was taken into *Farnace*, act 3, scene 3, both text and music, sung by Lucia Lancetti in both. Cross, "Vivaldi's Operatic Borrowings," pp. 435–437 discusses the first and last of these borrowings, but he refers to a score of *Farnace* (I:Tn, Giordano 36), for which he suggests the date 1731. The three texts do appear in the libretto for the 1727 production of Vivaldi's *Farnace*, however. Claudio Scimone, in his notes, translated by Edward Houghton, for the 1977 Erato-RCA recording of *Orlando*, implies that Vivaldi took these three arias from *Farnace* into *Orlando*. My reason for believing that the reverse is true is that none of the arias was in the first production of Vivaldi's *Farnace* of 1726; each of them was added to *Farnace* for the first time in the 1727 production. Furthermore it seems more likely that the autumn 1727 opera season would have begun with the premiere of *Orlando* than with a revival of *Farnace*, which had been sung in the same theater during the previous Carnival season.

7. The borrowing of "Anderò, chiamerò dal profondo," *Orlando*, act 3, scene 3, from *Orlando finto pazzo*, act 3, scene 12, where it carries the text "Anderò, / Volerò, / Guiderò," has been discussed by Peter Ryom, *Les Manuscrits de Vivaldi* (Copenhagen, 1977), pp. 325–327 and by Cross, "Vivaldi's Operatic Borrowings," p. 437.

8. I first used this method for my study "Vivaldi's Griselda," *Journal of the American Musicological Society* 31 (1978): 53–82, which concerns the relationship between musical-dramatic type-casting and the use of borrowed arias in operatic roles sung by Anna Giraud from 1723 to 1747.

9. For context and evaluation of Goldoni's classification of arias and his report concerning alternation of types, see Strohm, "Italienische Opernarien," part 1, pp. 239–245.

PART V

Baroque Opera Today

Preparing the Critical Edition: An Interview with Alan Curtis *by Marita P. McClymonds*

With the advent of a new generation of scholar-performers and an increasing interest on the part of major opera houses in giving authentic performances of early operas, it no longer makes sense to differentiate between the scholarly critical edition and the heavily edited performing edition. Knowledgeable modern performers are no longer willing to let an editor make decisions on the addition of ornamentation, articulations, and dynamics or dictate how the continuo should be realized since they have been trained to make these decisions for themselves. Even performers or opera companies lacking such expertise are better advised to seek the counsel of a specialist in performance practice than to base a production on a performing edition that may already be hopelessly out of date.

Both performers and musical directors are increasingly demanding editions that faithfully represent the original manuscripts of the work, be they scholarly critical editions or facsimiles. While the lengthy critical apparatus may well be published in a separate volume, no edition should be without at least a brief scholarly introduction reviewing the sources, outlining the general state of knowledge about the work, and concluding with a bibliography. A facsimile edition will also need instructions on how the facsimile should be read.

The few dramatic works by Vivaldi that have been published recently make a good starting point for a discussion of what constitutes a sound, useful, modern edition: one that is both scholarly and practical and that will not go out of style as our understanding of eighteenth-century performance practice evolves. Presently on library shelves, one finds Vito Frazzi's edition of the oratorio *Juditha triumphans*,[1] Raffaello Monterosso's edition of *La fida ninfa*,[2] Luciano Bettarini's edition of *Eurilla e Alcindo*,[3] and a facsimile of *La Griselda* with a preface by Howard Brown.[4]

Of the four, the Bettarini and Frazzi editions are the least valuable, and unfortunately they are typical of much Italian publication. The score consists of vocal parts in modern clefs and a piano reduction. The editors give no indications either of editorial cuts or additions or any inkling of the original instrumentation. One cannot even distinguish continuo arias from those having additional accompanying instruments, and one is presumably supposed to rent parts in order to try to learn more. Since a facsimile edition of *Juditha triumphans* exists,[5] one can easily see how much was added or altered. Vivaldi's articulations and bowings were changed, dynamics improperly added, and an unnecessarily pianistic continuo realization thrown in. The whole score is thoroughly "modernized" and therefore already completely out of date.

Since a fair evaluation of Vivaldi's operas can be made only through study and performance, our primary and immediate objective should be to make Vivaldi's operas as widely available as possible. This can best be done through inexpensive, paperback, facsimile editions. Even the greatly welcome Garland facsimile editions are beyond the means of most private individuals to acquire as a series.

Making facsimile editions available to a large number of people will most certainly increase the chances of having Vivaldi's operas selected for performance. Looking at the score of *La Griselda*, one can see that it would be possible to put on a performance of a Vivaldi opera from a facsimile. Vivaldi's autographs are neat and legible. Even his corrections are nicely done so that one can read both the original notation and the corrected version. It would present no problems to a copyist extracting instrumental parts or making a keyboard reduction for rehearsals, with vocal parts in modern clefs to accommodate singers lacking experience in reading C clefs. A few peculiarities of Vivaldi's hand should be pointed out in the preface. For example, the trill sign might be mistaken for a piano marking due to a pronounced right hook. Still the two markings are easily distinguishable once the reader has been warned. The preface should also point out that C.B. stands for Col Basso, meaning that the viola should not drop out, but should continue to play in octaves (or unison) with the bass line.[6]

Howard Brown's edition gives a synopsis, which is excellent, but there should also be a list of the cast, giving the vocal category of each part. In fact, any edition should include detailed information about the kinds of singers required. Does the role demand acting ability, and if so, what type? Any information about the original singers can be extremely helpful in proper casting. For example, we know a good deal about Anna Giraud, who sang in *La Griselda*, including information both about her acting ability and about her vocal credits and debits. The editor should go through each part, taking note of the extremes of the range, sections requiring unusual agility, and long sustained notes, wide leaps, and any other special vocal demands that will assist in selecting the appropriate singer for each role.

Opera managements need to become aware of the importance of hiring a specialist with a wide knowledge of the repertoire when choosing an early opera for production. Such an expert would be able to recommend operas that have strong plots acceptable to the modern audience, that will work well in the theater, and that suit the facilities and the singers of the company. Why is it that opera managements always seek a specialist to make a certain kind of wig, to coach fencing, or to provide laser-beam lighting, yet when they choose a Baroque opera, they often ask advice of someone who has little real knowledge, interest, or experience in opera before Mozart—or before Verdi for that matter! As a result the same few successful works are repeated over and over again while equally worthy scores languish on library shelves or in archives awaiting first the notice of a specialist and then the years of persistent promotional effort required to see a fresh work into production.

By the same token, specialists in the performance of early opera should be consulted when choosing an opera for a modern edition. Too often published works are not performable because of a plot unappealing to the modern audience, demands of excessive vocal prowess, extensive spectacular effects, or any number of other reasons. *La Griselda* is a case in point. It is of interest to scholars because Goldoni, who revised Zeno's libretto for Vivaldi, wrote charmingly about it in his memoirs.[7] But in this era of profound concern for women's rights, the plot, which revolves around Griselda's unfaltering fidelity in the face of persistent cruelty, degradation, and repudiation on the part of her husband, is likely to arouse antagonism rather than sympathy from a modern audience.

After a number of Vivaldi's operas have been performed and

proven popular, we will want more accessible editions than the facsimiles, giving preference to works that have proven most successful in the theater. In discussing what form the printed editions should take, Monterosso's edition of *La fida ninfa* must be considered. Although in some ways it is a great improvement over the two Italian editions mentioned earlier, it still has been made unnecessarily expensive. The oversized format makes it unwieldy both to use and to store. Furthermore, it was printed in a limited edition of only five hundred copies. It does not take advantage of any of the eighteenth-century short cuts, such as placing doubled parts on one line. In addition, it gives both a continuo realization and a keyboard reduction, one above the other and often, absurdly, almost identical. Nearly anyone can be taught to play a good realization from a reduction, but in any case no one should play a realization like the one given. While a reduction is preferable to a realization, neither is essential in a modern edition since our musical world is again becoming filled with players who can realize a continuo part from a figured bass. This is done without writing out the right hand, which makes the blank treble staff above the bass redundant and old-fashioned.

A good modern edition should certainly not omit a completely figured bass. Most composers in the eighteenth century, at least outside of France, thought only "nincompoops" needed an abundance of figures (Vivaldi himself called them *coglioni*).[8] Still, presumably the editor has more time to think about what the figures should be than does the continuo player on a minimal rehearsal schedule. When the composer gives only a few figures, some way must be devised for setting them apart without putting all of the editor's figures in brackets. One might put them in boxes, for example. Using different sizes of type can produce an impossible proofreading job.

If the editor is forced to include a realization, Monterosso's practice of putting in small passing notes without stems is a good way of indicating *acciaccature* without continually writing out arpeggiated chords. It also gives the player some idea of what can be done with the basic part. But a capable person should not waste time (nor an incapable person the reader's time and money) on an elaborate realization that will most certainly go out of style. Indicating the basic harmonies is quite sufficient.

In general the editor should plan to do a minimum of editing.

Monterosso's additions to the score are much more accurately done than those in the other two Italian editions. The dynamics he adds are in parentheses. For example, when a forte marking is found in only one part, he puts it in brackets in all of the others, a generally safe though often unnecessary practice. On the other hand, he adds crescendo and decrescendo markings that are mostly either obvious to any sensitive performer or else quite incorrect. The concept of terraced dynamics having—thank goodness—become passè, the best rule is to confine dynamic markings to those given in the original score. The same is true of suggested appoggiaturas placed in small staves above the part. Many of the appoggiaturas suggested in the score would be performed differently today. It would be far better to go over the places where appoggiaturas are appropriate and give a selection of alternative styles in the preface.

Problems of inconsistencies in the original manuscript inevitably arise. Generally, attempts at consistency are dangerous but may be done with editorial indications. Many times the best solution is not obvious. For example, should one regularize inconsistencies in ornamentation between the usually more meticulously marked violin parts and the often undecorated vocal parts? Again, it may simply have been a matter of pointing out to the players what the singer would have known to do without special markings. On the other hand, the heterophony produced by an appoggiatura in one part against its resolution in another may have been intended, and the effect will be lost if one regularizes the parts. In many cases the final decision is best left to the musical director, the principal violinist, and their expert advisers in rehearsal. Certainly the addition of bowings should remain the province of the principal violinist in collaboration with the conductor.

Knotty problems can also arise in dealing with the very casual way that both composers and copyists marked articulations in their scores. The same figure may be marked several different ways, and then not at all. The editor must ultimately decide what was most likely intended, preferably with the aid of a specialist in Baroque violin. In the preface and the critical notes, the performer can be made aware of the problems and be given to understand to what extent the editorial markings are based on vague indications and to what extent the original sources were lacking in clarity and consistency. If articulations are indicated only in the first few measures, follow them with a bracketed [etc.] rather than filling the score with hundreds of bracketed markings.

Metronome markings are unnecessary, but the editor might include in the preface a scale of tempo markings drawn from the composer's works. Editorial comment on gradations in tempo including possible metronome equivalents based on the composer's usage would also be helpful.

Suggestions for orchestration should be made in brackets, even such obvious ones as [violins]. The question often arises as to when the oboe and bassoon should play, and when they should drop out. There are no hard and fast rules in this regard, and it is impossible to be certain without part books. Parts for Handel scores in Manchester, England, for example, give an entirely different picture of oboe and bassoon doubling than one gets from the Chrysander edition. Often in the eighteenth-century "tutti" means the winds should play, while "piano" may mean that they should drop out and even that there should be a thinning of the strings, particularly if the change in dynamics coincides with a vocal entry. This means that the full band would play the tutti sections and a scaled-down group the vocal sections, a not uncommon scoring in many manuscripts of the period. Everything ultimately depends on the size and acoustics of the hall where the opera is to be performed.

The same uncertainty holds true for differentiations in the treatment of the various members of the continuo. It is not at all certain, for example, that a change from bass to tenor clef indicated that the contrabasses should drop out, unless, of course, the composer so specified. The tenor clef may have been used simply to avoid ledger lines. In identical scores of Jommelli operas done by different copyists, one can find the same passages written in tenor clef in one score and in bass clef in another. The editor should in general simply retain the tenor clef without comment, if it appears in the principal source. The basses should drop out or simplify the part if it goes too high, requires exceptional agility, or does not work acoustically. One will run into contrabass players who will insist that they can play all of the notes. But this is not the point. For acoustical reasons they must, in most cases, simplify the part. On the other hand, sometimes the harpsichord should play the fastest notes in an Alberti bass, and both the cellos and basses the slower notes. Indications of such differentiations are almost never given in the score, but again part books, when there are any, will show that such practices were followed.

Suggestions for methods of adding improvised ornamentation should be included in the preface. One might even print one slow and one fast aria showing the kinds of ornamentation that could be added in a da capo. Along with this, one might also provide several internal and final cadenzas and a sampling of other types of ornamentation to guide the initiate.

Since textual variations in printed librettos for subsequent productions of the same opera reflect the revisions made for each, they are an indispensable aid in dating manuscript scores. Lacking an autograph score they can help identify what revisions are likely to be the work of the original composer and what should be attributed to others. Revisions traced to a libretto for Esterhaza, for example, would have to be attributed to Haydn, while revisions made for the Portuguese court in the latter half of the eighteenth century would have been the work of João Cordeiro da Silva, regardless of the original composer.

When several entirely different authentic versions of the same opera survive for a single composer, the editor will have to decide which version his edition will represent. Similarly, decisions may have to be made as to which revisions, whether authenticated or of unknown origin, will appear in the main text and which will be relegated to the appendix or to critical notes. Since such choices are often simply a matter of personal taste or preference, all such decisions should be meticulously documented and the variants, whether in the main text or in the appendix, clearly identified. The circumstances leading to the revisions, if known, should be outlined in the preface so that the performers understand clearly what their options are in choosing one over another.

A printed text in proper literary form makes an excellent accompaniment to any edition. The editor should go through all of the librettos for the opera, including those of subsequent productions, recording in the critical notes all variants in the text and inconsistencies with the score. Mistakes in the score should be pointed out and corrected in the edition. Italian spellings should be modernized if the change will not affect the sound. For instance, *ò* as a verb must be changed to *ho*, etc. Capitalization and syllabification should also conform to modern usage. After the text has been carefully underlaid, even a native Italian editor should have an expert go over both the syllabification and the textual underlay. Baroque underlay is not a simple matter even in one's native language, and an error can become frozen in common practice and be repeated for years thereafter.

The editor can do one final important service by suggesting cuts that, alas, often must be made. The editor is presumably in a better position to do this than is a harried producer, who may have to decide on cuts before having had a chance to get to know the score or its background at all well, and who may be under pressure by the most prestigious of the singers hired for the production. The editor, on the other hand, can view the work as a whole rather than through the eyes of a singer anxious to enhance his or her role, and is therefore better able to make sensible decisions as to what will improve and tighten the action and thereby increase the dramatic force. There must necessarily be some compromises with modern taste. What seemed exotic and strange and therefore exciting to the eighteenth-century audience sometimes no longer seems so and may become tedious. Handel and Rameau often cut pieces in subsequent performances because they did not meet with success. These are sometimes among the best pieces written for the opera and perhaps should be restored to their original places in the modern production. These and many other considerations can aid in achieving a production of maximum effectiveness.

In conclusion, the first priority should be to make all of Vivaldi's operas generally available. This might most easily be done by publishing them in inexpensive facsimile editions, which can and will be used for performance. Second, experts in early opera should be called upon to assist in the selection of the operas both to be performed and to be published in minimally but responsibly edited full scores. Appropriate specialists should also be consulted during the preparation of both performances and editions. In this way Vivaldi's operas have some hope of receiving the exposure and the fair evaluation long overdue them.

NOTES

This article is based on a telephone conversation with Alan Curtis, who approved its contents as a summation of his views on the editing of Vivaldi's operatic scores.

1.   Antonio Vivaldi, *Juditha triumphans*, ed. Vito Frazzi, Musiche vocali e strumentali, sacre e profane, sec. xvii, xviii, xix, no. 10 (Roma: De Santis, 1949).

2. Antonio Vivaldi, *La fida ninfa*, ed. Raffaello Monterosso, Instituta et Monumenta, ser. 1, no. 3 (Cremona: Athenaeum Cremonense, 1964).

3. Antonio Vivaldi, *Eurilla e Alcindo*, ed. Luciano Bettarini, Collezione Settecentesca Bettarini, no. 11 (Milano: Nazionalmusic, 1976).

4. Antonio Vivaldi, *La Griselda*, ed. Howard M. Brown (New York: Garland, 1978).

5. Antonio Vivaldi, *Juditha triumphans* (Siena: Accademia Musicale Chigiana, 1948).

6. See *La Griselda*, fol. 154ʳ for examples of these notational peculiarities.

7. Carlo Goldoni, *Memorie del Sig. Carlo Goldoni scritte da lui medesimo* (Venezia, 1788), vol. 1, pp. 261–264.

8. Olga Rudge, revised, "Vivaldi, Antonio," in *Grove's Dictionary of Music and Musicians*, 5th edition, ed. Eric Blom (1954), vol. 9, p. 29.

Opera Seria Today: A Credo
by Andrew Porter

Seated on the platform at the Dallas Opera symposium was a mixture of the scholars who had been taking part in it and the performers and management who had made possible the production of Vivaldi's *Orlando furioso*, around which the symposium came into being. It was rather like one of those eighteenth-century cast lists where the characters are divided into *personaggi nobili* and *genti plebei*; I won't suggest which was which. As "presenter" for the panel "Baroque Opera Today" I endeavored to play a *mezzo-carattere* role. In recent years, I have been at several of these performance-cum-conference events, and toward the end of them there has usually been a session like this one: a "confrontation" between the performers and the scholars, and at some of them there have been low growls on the one side of "these musicologists have no idea of the practical realities of putting on an opera" and murmurs on the scholarly side of "now if only they had listened to us. . . ."

But those days, I trust, are passing. At the Verdi Congress in Chicago in 1974, at a session rather like this one, I said gently, "What a pity that the Lyric Opera's production of *Simon Boccanegra* has so little to do with the opera that we have been discussing." And there was a minor ruckus. But in the end some good did come of it: the American Institute for Verdi Studies, which, among other things, makes available to performing companies the kind of information and the kind of scholarship that opera companies need—and the more serious opera companies seek—if they are going to give stylish performances. I would go so far as to say that at the next Verdi Congress, held at the University of California at Irvine in 1980, the performance of *La forza del destino* was in matters of style and execution actually a few steps ahead of some of the ideas held by the *congressisti*—at any rate when they first arrived.

Several of the scholars who participated in the Dallas Opera symposium are actively concerned with contemporary performances, scholar-performers who are helping to change the state of affairs: Alan Curtis, who has conducted opera seria at La Scala; Shirley Wynne, who shows modern singers how to move both stylishly and eloquently in eighteenth-century dramas; Philip Gossett, who provides accurate scores for so many *Ottocento* performances and stands at conductors' right hands while they are preparing their material; William Holmes, who edited the *Forza* we used at Irvine; Mary Cyr, who has played continuo string bass for many opere serie. I needn't go on. I merely want to make the point—in case any of the performers in Dallas doubted it—that we are all on the same side, the side of the composer. At the worst, the performers may just have felt, "If only this symposium could have been held six months ago, so that we could have taken its findings into our production!"

A music critic is a mixture in varying parts of musicologist, historian, chronicler, enthusiast, and other things. (In my case, those "other things" include translating, editing, and occasional episodes of coaching, directing, and conducting to keep me in touch with the realities of actual performance.) As a critic, I try to span a bridge between, on the one hand, scholarship and research and, on the other, the performers who bring the results of scholarship and research to life in the theater. As I've not got three hands, let me change the image and suggest also a Triborough Bridge that leads also to the public at the receiving (and also, for that matter, the paying) end.

Our aim was to weave together some of the many threads that had been pursued both during the symposium and in the performances of *Orlando furioso*. I found the performances full of good things: brilliant singing, spectacular decor, and conducting that was sensitive to the affecting and exciting score. But some aspects of it were in conflict on points of detail with a sort of credo in linked clauses that I presented as a simple affirmation of belief in the value of opera seria. This credo was followed by statements of practical ways in which that value—both as an entertainment and as an inspiration—could be manifest to contemporary audiences.

I believe in opera seria both as an entertainment and an inspiration for modern audiences. No one who saw and heard the Dallas *Orlando* is likely to dispute that belief. And now straight into practicalities. On the first day of the symposium, Gary Schmidgall voiced some doubts whether the performance of an opera seria was possible at all today. He raised questions that have long troubled me, questions that both theorists and performers need to answer. During a life that has been pretty well devoted to the study of opera, both on the page and in the theater, I have seen about a hundred different productions of opere serie. For one thing, most of Handel's operas have been revived in England, some of them several times over. My friend Daniel Heartz might well say that because of this Handelian core my position (like Handel's) is off center, London-provincial; in the *New Grove Dictionary*, Heartz writes a long entry on opera seria without once mentioning Handel. But there have also been frequent opportunities in Europe for seeing operas by, among others, Vinci, Scarlatti, Caldara, Keiser, Bononcini, Arne, and Traetta. This Dallas *Orlando*, however, was my first full-scale Vivaldi. I mention these things not as a collector's boast, but to provide a background for the summary, perhaps overconfident assertions and prescriptions that follow. By trial and error, we have found a way of presenting opera seria today. After making just about all the mistakes that can be made, we have found some of the answers. As a critic, I now grow impatient when watching or hearing unnecessary mistakes being made all over again.

Let us suppose, then, that we are going to put on an opera seria, one whose worth we believe in. The remarks that follow are proposed as a series of possible ground rules, or statements of an ideal. In practice, there will nearly always have to be some compromise. And what forms the compromise takes will depend on the nature of the company concerned. But it should never be more than an adjustment between the ideal and the practicable. As Winton Dean writes in his *Handel and the Opera Seria*, "A compromise between what a great composer desired and what we happen to be accustomed to is not a valid artistic operation. It is a piece of intellectual slovenliness, and its fruit is a stunted mediocrity."

So, first, the edition, which is where we have to begin. Conductor and director must start with a complete knowledge of the work that the composer wrote, not someone else's *Bearbeitung* thereof. Their first aim should be to do the work complete. That will seldom be practicable. There is likely to be cutting. But the cutting must be done with care and scrupulousness. To be frank, although I enjoyed and admired the Dallas *Orlando*, I had serious objections to an edition by which the dramaturgical and musical shape of Vivaldi's opera was deformed by the cutting to a text that showed little feeling for the form and build of opera seria in general and of this exceptional opera in particular. (There was a practical reason: the production, the orchestral parts, the decor, and the prima donna came to Dallas from Verona as a package deal, its elements interdependent. But the criticism of Claudio Scimone's edition stands.) The opera seria performances I have attended have generally grown longer and longer. Here, we heard something over two and a half hours of music—between two-thirds and one-half of Vivaldi's score. In England, Handel's *Giulio Cesare*, one of his longest operas, was recently staged quite uncut.

Second, the casting. All parts must be sung in their original vocal registers. (The New York City Opera's recent *Giulio Cesare* was an abomination in this as in just about every other respect.) I do not understand why in the Dallas *Orlando* the role of Ruggiero was transposed down an octave. The only compromise that can be countenanced under this head—*must* be countenanced unless we resume the practice of gelding our promising boy sopranos—is to employ either women or male altos (countertenors) in the castrato roles. But it is not really a problem, or at any rate not a new one: when Handel did not have a castrato at hand, he used a woman. On the whole, I have found that in big theaters women in *primo uomo* heroic roles are generally more audible, more even of register, more effective, in a word more *heroic* than countertenors are. In Dallas, the castrato title role was sung—brilliantly—by a woman, Marilyn Horne.

Singers should be chosen who are both expressive and clean, flexible, accurate; not those with rich, wobbly voices vague of pitch and ripe with vibrato. Train them, if need be, in the refinements and stylistic accuracy of decoration, variation, and cadenza such as we discussed at this symposium. Teach them to utter recitative as exciting dramatic dialogue, not as something sung out in full voice at a snail's pace, in measured $\frac{4}{4}$, with every rest observed and every cadence emphasized and protracted.

Third, the orchestra. The ideal, of course, is an orchestra of Baroque players versed in the style, sure in intonation, eloquent in timbre. If that cannot be achieved, make sure that the modern players have at least a Baroque sound ideal in their minds if not under their fingers. Teach them, if necessary, something about Baroque bowing, phrasing, articulation, timbre. Use the right sort of continuo instruments. (What was that organ doing in *Orlando*?) Make sure the continuo players and the coaches have read and understood what Sven Hansell and others have written about continuo practice. Bring the orchestra up to the level of the theater floor, or as close to it as the sight lines of the theater allow. The deep pit is a modern invention. (The Italian term for it is *golfo mistico*; it was unknown in Italy until Wagner's idea of the "mystic gulf" spread southward.) A pit disturbs Baroque balances. And incidentally, when the orchestra is out in the open, sounding directly into the audience's ears, the manager may well be able to save on orchestral salaries. Seat the players in such a way that as many of them as possible can see the singers and dancers they are accompanying.

Fourth, the language of the performance. It is, as Addison remarked long ago, "an absurdity that reveals itself at first sight" for a musical drama to be performed in a language that the audience does not understand. What is the answer? The best answer would be to perform operas in the original and to provide compulsory Italian classes for all your subscribers, not to allow anyone to buy a ticket unless he had shown at the box office a certificate of minimum proficiency in that language. Maybe that is not practical. There are two ways out, two compromises possible. One is to perform the opera in translation. Inevitably there are losses of sense and of sound, but against them can be set the gain in dramatic communicativeness. That is probably the best thing to do when the cast itself does not have a command of Italian. But when it does and when—as in Dallas—an international cast is assembled, then the sensible thing, it seems to me, is not only to provide an Italian-English libretto but also to leave the house lights up during the performance. Darkness in the auditorium is another modern convention that has no place in Baroque or, for that matter, in most nineteenth-century opera. As late as 1875, when Verdi visited Vienna, he remarked with surprise that the house lights were turned down. He fell asleep, he said, and so did most of the audience.

This brings us to the matter of lighting and, linked to it and even more important, of decor. Banish follow spots. Light with foot-lights and from battens behind the proscenium arch; light from the sides as well as from above. A singer's chief medium of expression after the voice is the eyes, while the libretto is read off the lips. With lighting angled solely from above, you see neither eyes nor lips, just forehead, nose, and chin. The old critics wrote often about the flash and fire or the mournful tears that filled a great singer's eyes. Can anyone here tell me (I asked) what color Marilyn Horne's eyes are? And don't let your prima donna gum on those enormous modern false lashes, jutting marquees that shadow the expression of her eyes still further.

There has been much experiment lately with decor, and in my experience the best results have been achieved with sliding painted panels in the eighteenth-century manner, not with heavy built sce-nery, and above all not the modish "unit" sets. Painted flats not only suit the works better, they are also cheaper in the long run and are far more portable. So revive the art of perspective design-ing and perspective painting and, just as you strive to sing and play so far as possible in the eighteenth-century manner, design in that manner as well.

On the question of acting, movement, and gesture, my confident tone falters just a little. Because, I think, singers and audiences still have a lot more to learn about them. I have seen some striking re-sults achieved by the adoption of eighteenth-century attitudes, but also some that were rather ridiculous. Unless singers are them-selves convinced, what comes out is often unconvincing. Perhaps this is the field where most of all we still need more research and more experiment. What I prescribe, I think, is a basis of authentic gesture tempered with a shade of realism, the kind of thing that we read Guadagni learned from Garrick. I am sorry not to sound quite so hard-line about this as about everything else. I am wait-ing, and hoping, to be utterly convinced.

A word to designers: Use a flat floor, or at most just the gentle, regular rake built into some eighteenth-century stages, for most of the set. Singers have quite enough hard work to do without being required to perch and sing on a steep slope or negotiate perilous steps or bridges. (Note that one of the singers in *Orlando* sprained her ankle, which had to be bound for subsequent performances, on the severely raked stage.) And a word to directors: Preserve the original form and organization of the scenes. Shift the scenery only where the opera calls for changes. Bring characters on and take them off exactly where the composer specifies. Do not shuffle the arias around. These things are all part of the dramatic and musical shape. In the Dallas *Orlando*, I think that Pierluigi Pizzi, who was at once designer and director, sometimes treated both Vivaldi and his librettist, Braccioli, with a high-handedness that amounted to contempt for their carefully and unusually fashioned work.

The conventional thing to say last would be that I am not advocating a strict, so-called museum, authentic reconstruction of an eighteenth-century performance (as close as we can hope to get to one), but only a performance that takes such a reconstruction into account. Thirty years ago I would have said that, but I am not quite prepared to say it today. On the purely musical side, we have all heard now how authentic performing practice (as close as we can get to it) on the right instruments makes anything else—however accomplished it may be on its own terms—seem no more than second best. The same sort of thinking now needs to be applied to *all* aspects of an operatic presentation. Whenever it has been applied with knowledge, imagination, and skill, its results have been totally convincing.

It cannot always be achieved, not in our huge theaters. And in any case *some* compromise is inevitable. We use modern voices, modern materials, modern lighting equipment. And we listen with modern ears, conditioned inevitably by 250 years of later musical developments. But we do try to get the notes right, and we should try to get everything else as right as possible. A compromise must be admitted as such, as a regrettable necessity, not something to boast of. Do not listen to any more of that nonsense about reworking or adapting masterpieces of the past to match twentieth-century susceptibilities. One does not repaint the Duccio *Maestà* to accord with twentieth-century susceptibilities or to "bring out its relevance." Of course, I am not denying that modern glosses, commentaries, and reworkings can be instructive, illuminating, and enjoyable and even considerable works of art in their own right. I want twentieth-century painters and twentieth-century composers to go on treating the old important themes in twentieth-century works. But I am prepared to take the basic idea very far, even to claim that a woman playing Shakespeare's Juliet, Lady Macbeth, or Cleopatra is only second best (wonderful second best though she may be), a compromise made necessary today by our lack of superb boy actors. The masterpieces of any age speak to a modern audience most freshly, most directly, most clearly—and most entertainingly—in the tones, with the accents, and in the visual dress that their creators intended them to have.

So I am not going to advocate jollying people along gently, at first applying just a few touches of "authenticity" in a cosmetic way. I think that whenever possible we should go *all* the way, plunge audiences straight in at the deep end. Performances conceived in that spirit have provided revelations. I very much enjoyed and admired the Dallas *Orlando* and learned a lot from it. I know we all did. But perhaps I have managed to suggest some ways— some readily achievable ways—in which it could perhaps have been more enjoyable and more instructive still.

Postscript: In February 1983 a thoroughgoing Baroque revival of Handel's *Orlando* at the University of Washington, St. Louis, directed scenically and musically by Nicholas McGegan, effectively demonstrated most of the points I make above. It was given uncut, staged in painted scenery, lit by simulated candlelight, enacted with Baroque gestures and demeanor, accompanied by period instruments disposed at theater-floor level, and directed from the harpsichord. I described it in the *New Yorker* of March 14, 1983.

APPENDIX
Grazio Braccioli's *Orlando furioso*:
A History and Synopsis of the Libretto
by Michael Collins

The libretto *Orlando furioso* by Grazio Braccioli, a young lawyer from Ferrara who at the time was pursuing a literary career in Venice, was originally set to music by Giovanni Alberto Ristori in 1713 for Teatro Sant'Angelo, where Vivaldi was impresario. The work was a great success, and Vivaldi asked Braccioli for another libretto on the same subject, the music to be composed by himself, for the 1714 season. Vivaldi's new work, *Orlando finto pazzo*, was a dismal failure, and he was obliged to replace it with the Ristori opera, composing much new music for the revival. When Vivaldi returned to the subject in 1727, again for Teatro Sant'Angelo, much of the libretto of the 1714 revival was used again, but as Braccioli had long since returned to practice law in Ferrara, he was not responsible for any of the new aria texts and his name does not appear on the printed libretto. The 1727 libretto is titled simply *Orlando*, the original title, *Orlando furioso*, having been restored for the revivals in Verona and Dallas in 1978 and 1980, respectively.

Braccioli turned to one of the most popular sources for librettos in the seventeenth and eighteenth centuries: Lodovico Ariosto's epic romance *Orlando furioso*, dedicated to the illustrious Cardinal Ippolito d'Este in 1516. Ariosto's masterwork is a mélange of the Carolingian epic (which chronicles the exploits of Charlemagne's champion Roland [Orlando] against the encroaching Moors), themes from the Arthurian romances, and the Vergilian *Aeneid*. Interwoven are romantically erotic interludes for the pleasure of sophisticated Italian courtiers. Among these is the story of Ruggiero and Bradamante, whose union marked the beginning of the Este family, Ariosto's patrons in Ferrara.

In his preface of 1713, Braccioli writes,

> Only the [Mediterranean] island of Alcina . . . is the setting where
> the action takes place, although the numerous exploits of the vast
> epic [of Ariosto] involve half the world, so to speak. Such actions
> have been limited by us in this drama to one. At its beginning, mid-
> dle, and end are the love, madness, and recovery of Orlando. The
> loves of Bradamante and Ruggiero, Angelica and Medoro, the vari-
> ous inclinations of Alcina, and diverse passions of Astolfo serve to
> accompany this action and lead to its end.

Braccioli thus unites widely separated episodes on Alcina's isle and
choreographs the action like some intricate eighteenth-century
minuet. To appreciate this satire and whimsy, it is necessary to
have some familiarity with Ariosto's epic, as did the Italian audiences of Vivaldi's day, who knew the legend as English-speaking
audiences knew Shakespeare. A brief summation of the Ariostan
episodes involved will help close the gap for non-Italian readers.

The knight Orlando has fallen in love with Angelica, daughter
of the king of Cathay, whom he seeks throughout the world.
Meanwhile Angelica has angered the God of Love with her incon-
stancy in love, and in revenge he wills that she will fall in love with
a totally unsuited person, the young and beautiful but lowborn
Moor Medoro, whom she discovers mortally wounded and cures
with Oriental potions. The pair retire to a shepherd's hut, where
they are married, and ecstatically carve their names in the bark of
surrounding trees (canto XIX). After their departure, Orlando
comes upon the carved trees, hears their story from the shepherd,
and goes mad, tearing off his clothes and uprooting trees (canto
XXIII). In canto XXIX Orlando overtakes the lovers and pursues Angelica. He is then pursued by Medoro, who bests the hero in combat, while Angelica puts her magic ring into her mouth, causing
her to become invisible. In the meantime Astolfo, cousin to Orlando, rides to the moon astride the fabulous hippogriff to reclaim
Orlando's lost senses, which he finds there in an urn (canto XXIV).
They are restored to Orlando when Astolfo causes him to inhale
them from the urn (canto XXXIX).

The love of Ruggiero and Bradamante is recounted elsewhere.
Ruggiero is carried by the same unruly hippogriff to the idyllic isle
of the evil sorceress Alcina, where he is warned by Astolfo, who
speaks to him enclosed in a myrtle tree (canto VI), that she transforms her erstwhile lovers into objects of natural beauty. Although
he desires to overthrow her power, Ruggiero is enchanted by her

beauty and falls under her spell (canto VII). Seeking her beloved, Bradamante entreats the aid of the enchantress Melissa, who reveals Ruggiero's ensnarement and, armed with Angelica's magic ring (at this time in Bradamante's possession), magically disguises herself as Ruggiero's old tutor, the sorceror Atlantes. Melissa then translates herself to Alcina's island, where she manages to slip the ring (which has the power to break all magic spells) on Ruggiero's finger (canto VII). Ruggiero seeks help from the forces of Alcina's sister, the fairy Logistilla, in canto VIII, and in canto X Alcina is defeated in a great battle and her kingdom returned to her good sister Morgana.

These are the diverse elements that Braccioli juxtaposed in his *Orlando furioso*, attempting an Aristotelian unity of time, place, and action by bringing all the characters together on Alcina's isle and embellishing the action with the sort of amorous dalliance appreciated by contemporary Venetian audiences. His first scenes take place in a court of Alcina's palace, where in scene 1 Alcina's guest Angelica recounts how the God of Love took revenge on her by bringing before her eyes the handsome, lovable Medoro, for whom she immediately burned and sighed with love, how Orlando came upon them, and how she lost Medoro when she fled. Alcina instills hope, saying that Medoro will find her and they will marry and enjoy happiness on her island.

In scene 2 Astolfo and Orlando enter engaged in combat, not recognizing one another until they raise their visors, at which point they embrace. Alcina immediately begins to beguile Orlando, saying, "O renowned and valorous champion, permit me humbly to kiss thy invincible hand." "No, great goddess, which I believe thou must be, since no mortal woman would have such rare beauty, it is for me to kiss thy white hand in vowing my heart," he replies. She begs him to tarry awhile in her kingdom, while Astolfo, her suffering lover, complains of not receiving a single glance from her. Alcina exhorts the god to awaken love in Orlando's heart. Left together in scene 3, Astolfo warns Orlando of Alcina's power, telling him she has the urn containing Merlin's ashes (the source of her invincible power), which are guarded by the invulnerable Aronte. (Merlin's tomb indeed figures in Ariosto, but it is there Bradamante hears that she and Ruggiero will spawn the Este family; there is no connection with Alcina.) Left alone, Orlando hopes the God of Love will pierce the breast of Angelica, whom he serves in sweet bondage. Bradamante enters in scene 4 seeking Ruggiero, whom Melissa has told her would succumb to Alcina's magic. (We note that here, just as in Handel's *Alcina* of 1735, it is Bradamante herself, not Melissa, who comes to save Ruggiero.) We hear that she possesses the magic ring, which when worn on the finger breaks spells and when held in the mouth causes invisibility. Orlando, again alone in scene 5, receives a message from Merlin by some sort of extrasensory perception to the effect that if he regains Merlin's ashes (which Alcina has stolen), Alcina's power will be destroyed and heaven will dispose for him the fortunes of love. He is optimistic that he will be victorious and win love with the help of valor.

With scene 6 we see a delightful garden with two fountains, one of which extinguishes love, the other arousing it. (These fountains have no place on Alcina's isle, for in Ariosto they appear in canto I in the Forest of Arden, where Rinaldo and Angelica drink, causing Rinaldo to love Angelica and her to forget her love for him.) In the distance is seen a tempestuous sea. Angelica is in the garden, and hearing a cry for help sees a small boat about to capsize in the storm. To their mutual delight, Medoro is cast from the boat upon the shore, but he is mortally wounded and tells her, "My soul issues from my open side, but it will be sweet to die in thy arms." Scene 7 brings Alcina to heal Medoro with magic incantations. Their delight is interrupted by the arrival of Orlando in scene 8, and this is one of the humorous moments in the libretto. Orlando is about to attack Medoro when Alcina tells him that this boy of whom he is jealous is Angelica's brother. (This motif is borrowed from canto XXXVII, in a scene involving Martano, Grifone, and Orrigille.) The cowardly Medoro breathes more easily, while Angelica berates Orlando for insulting the sincere and faithful love she bears him. "How cunningly she dissembles," murmurs Alcina, and in a series of exchanges, aloud and aside, Angelica feigns weeping at how Orlando rewards her love, tells Medoro she is pretending, offers her hand in pledge of chaste love to Orlando, and keeps telling the jealous Medoro to be silent. After Angelica's departure, Orlando begs Medoro's pardon, saying that love is too wild when poisoned by jealousy. In scene 10 Alcina gives Medoro a lesson on love: does he not know the arts of a lover's heart? Both to suffer and to be silent is true love. Medoro decides that it is lovely to suffer.

Scene 11 finds Alcina alone in the garden musing on Medoro's naiveté: "Innocent boy, thou dost not know yet with what arrows love wounds the heart. The day will yet come when thou wilt change thy notions. If I had but a single lover, I would be a common woman among women. But what is this? I see an armed cavalier descending on a flying steed!" Ruggiero alights, and Alcina tells him that here, where she is queen, valorous Ruggiero is lord, for she owes as much to his name (and to his good looks). Ruggiero, in an aside, declares that only Bradamante's beauty compares with that of Alcina, and she decides that he will be her newest prey. Inviting him to sit beside her and refresh himself at her fountains, she informs us, as he drinks from the first, that his ardor for anyone else will be extinguished as she draws him into her net. Offering him waters from the other, she tells us that he has fallen into the trap, for a passion for her will be aroused. Immediately Ruggiero says, "How courteous thou art, gentle lady; mine eyes have ne'er seen anyone with more grace and loveliness," and Alcina gloats that he is already sighing with love, as Bradamante enters to hear him continue, "Lovely one, the power of thine eyes constrains my heart to adore thee." Bradamante reveals herself, reviling Ruggiero as a traitor, but as he seems not to know her, she says that she is Olimpia and he, perfidious Bireno, has abandoned her. (The real Olimpia is in fact abandoned by Bireno in Ariosto's canto XI.) After some confusion, Ruggiero leaves Alcina to try to convince "Olimpia" that he is not Bireno in scene 13, after which Bradamante leaves in a rage, while Alcina exults that Ruggiero is already hers.

Act 2 opens in a delightful grove where in scene 1 Alcina tells Astolfo, "To vary love's object makes sweeter the joy of new affection," to which the suffering Astolfo rejoins, "An inconstant woman is a great torment," and that although he no longer wishes to suffer her artifices, his chains are too tenacious. If he must stay, she tells him, he must be silent, for his suffering is the way to her affections, but he must not expect that his will be the only fire to burn her heart, for she is not content with but one lover. Alcina departs, and in scene 2 Bradamante enters to chide Astolfo for allowing a perfidious, deceiving woman to hold him in love's snares. Together they plan revenge on Alcina. In scene 3 Ruggiero, glowing with love for Alcina, meets Bradamante, whom he still believes to be the delirious Olimpia. She asks him if he does not recognize the heart of his Bradamante, and at his lack of recognition forces the ring into his hand. As if a veil is lifted from his eyes, he knows Bradamante, who tells him to go with the ring to observe the beauty of Alcina. Not in a forgiving mood, she tells him he may as well disperse his tears and prayers to the winds. In scene 4 Orlando assures the chagrined Ruggiero that an involuntary error will not stain his heart and that his shame indicates the high virtue of a noble soul, which, blushing in shame, will soon see an end to dishonor.

With scene 5 the stage reveals a mountainous place with rocky cliffs where Angelica awaits Orlando. She tells Medoro that he must leave her if she is to rid them of Orlando. Vacillating between hope and fear, he sadly departs. In scene 6 Braccioli continues his fanciful fabrications, as Angelica plans to use Alcina's enchanted cliffs to her own advantage. Orlando arrives in hope that some quest may gain Angelica's favor: "Are there perils? Monsters or giants? I have heart, arm, and sword to overcome them for thee!" Cunningly she demurs, and Orlando asks if she would deny him the sweet glory of dying for her. Pretending at last to give in, she tells him that high on one of the cliffs there is a silver vase containing the magic liquor with which Medea restored the youth of declining Jason. She would have it so they might always remain in the flower of youth to make eternal their affection. Undaunted by the horrid monster she says guards the vase, he begins his ascent as Astolfo appears to warn that certain death awaits him. If Orlando's heart knows no fear, he should know that fear is a virtue if death is certain. Orlando answers that his joy is in trying new feats and new monsters whereby he can demonstrate his great valor. Astolfo does not know what he is talking about, and Angelica tells him she has tried to dissuade Orlando from his insane undertaking. Astolfo leaves, secure that Angelica's powers of persuasion will win, but she immediately begins to goad Orlando, who ascends the cliff crying, "Love lends me his wings!" Angelica departs murmuring, "How credulous he is! I counted on that," as Orlando challenges, "Monster, where art thou?"

Stage machinery transforms the cliff into a horrid cavern from which there is no exit, and Orlando challenges the monster to confront him, for he expects to make trophies of its horrid head and hairy hide. A hidden voice informs him that he is a prisoner of Alcina. "Who speaks?" he cries. "I have my sword at my side . . .

your insane words do not daunt Orlando," but peering around he realizes there is no way out and that he has been betrayed. The thought of ungrateful Angelica redoubles his energy, and as the stones fall he swears he will escape and trample her new love with scorn and wrath. At last, opening a passage, Orlando cries, "Orlando escapes thy prison, Alcina, of thy infamous kingdom to make a merciless and unforgettable example!"

In scene 10 we are with Bradamante and Ruggiero, who has just returned from confronting Alcina with the ring in his hand and seeing her true deformed and ugly aspect, which the witch had made seem beautiful by force of magic. He has regained his soul from shameful servitude, but must now endure the taunts of Bradamante. Even as he tells her he owes everything to her love and devotion, she orders him to return to his Alcina. When he offers her his sword and his breast that death might come from her hand, she relents, saying, "Die, cruel one, but in this embrace." Ruggiero finds it lovely to die on the breast of his sweet beloved, and Bradamante's pleasure knows no bounds.

Scene 11 brings the wedding of Angelica and Medoro, complete with nuptial choirs invoking a host of pagan deities in the pastoral tradition. Alcina arrives to present the wedding cup with its inscription "May they live always in love, Angelica and Medoro, lovers and spouses" and expresses the desire to share a like happiness with Ruggiero. In scene 12 the newlyweds carve their names on laurels and myrtles to celebrate their joy. As the couple departs, Orlando comes upon the scene, reviling the faithlessness of Angelica. Maddened with rage as he reads the arboreal carvings, he flings down helmet, shield, armor, and mail and uproots the offending trees.

Act 3, scene 1 finds Astolfo and Ruggiero before the Temple of Infernal Hecate, which is surrounded by a wall of steel. Believing Orlando to have perished within the cliff, Ruggiero offers Astolfo his winged steed to reclaim the body, and they prepare for revenge against Alcina with the aid of the warriors of Logistilla. In scene 2 Bradamante enters in male attire to tell Ruggiero that she wants the honor of striking the first blow to Alcina, but that even Melissa cannot penetrate the steel wall to obtain Merlin's ashes from their fierce and immortal guardian. They withdraw as Alcina approaches in a rage against the God of Love, against whom she will raise the Gods of Hell. But she is frustrated in her attempts to raise them, calling them lazy and threatening to plunder their realm if they do not appear. The impotency of her incantations is humorous. At length she decides to consult the ashes of Merlin for advice, and the wall opens at her command to reveal the temple, within which is seen the statue of Merlin upon the urn containing his ashes, enclosed by bars of iron and guarded by the invincible Arontes, who grips a mace. Alcina is imploring Merlin to take pity on her saddened heart when the disguised Bradamante steps forth to tell her that Ruggiero has escaped upon his winged steed. Remarking at once on the handsome face before her, Alcina says, "Gracious warrior, tell me thy name?" and Bradamante identifies herself as Aldarico, her brother. Alcina tells the knight that she does not despair the loss of Ruggiero, for a beautiful woman never lacks an obliging lover. Aldarico says that Ruggiero must have been blind to her beauty, and Alcina rejoices at having found a new lover.

At this point (scene 4) Orlando appears before them naked and completely mad. Spouting phrases in French in the 1713 and 1714 librettos and 1727 score (the 1727 libretto has the lines in Italian), he tells them that Madame Cruelty and Monsieur Severity thwarted his desire to dance with Beauty, but perhaps the lovely lady present will dance with him, and he sings a fa-la refrain to the strains of the famous "Folies d'Espagne," which heard in this situation is very humorous. Angelica enters and Orlando, believing her to be Madame Cruelty, holds her fast, accusing her of laughing at him. The others express pity for him and accuse Angelica of treating him shamefully, but she departs, still falsely avowing her faithfulness to him. Orlando follows her to destroy the lizards, serpents, and dragons he believes accompany her. In scene 6 Alcina, beguiled by her new cavalier, explains to him that the guardian of Merlin's ashes, Aronte, is invulnerable as long as the mace he is holding is attached to his arm by a chain. The chain itself, tempered in the fires of Hell, gives her eternal power as long as it remains unbroken. As Aldarico leaves, Alcina expresses her joy at the good looks and brilliance of her new love, more handsome than Ruggiero. "A heart is indeed fortunate in changing lovers often."

In scene 7 Ruggiero comes forth from hiding, feeling that Glory and Honor invite him to challenge Aronte, but when he thinks of Bradamante's peril, he opts for the invitation of Love and Mercy. His pursuit of Bradamante is interrupted by the arrival of Medoro, who challenges him for deserting the amorous Alcina. Ruggiero feels it would be unworthy to defend his honor against Medoro's soft breast, so he easily disarms him by hand, and when Angelica appears in scene 7 he tells her to begone with her lover, for she has driven insane the flower of chivalry. She retorts that it is not her fault if her lovely face allures hearts. He departs in fury, leaving Medoro in scene 9 to whimper to Angelica about his loss of honor in the face of Ruggiero's insults. Angelica tells him that sword and fury are denied his soft and and tender heart; beauty and love are his weapons and her breast is the field where he will receive sweet rebuffs ending in conjugal embrace. Together they will find happiness in her kingdom.

In scene 10 Orlando comes upon the empty stage still senselessly ranting about his lost Angelica. Suddenly he sees the statue of Merlin and takes it for Angelica imprisoned by Aronte, whom he kills after a struggle. He then breaks the iron bars with Aronte's mace. He embraces the statue, believing Angelica to be frozen with fear when he feels the cold stone. When he removes the statue from its pedestal there is great tumult, and the island transforms into barren, craggy cliffs, with a lone tree in which Orlando's arms are hung as a trophy. He has unwittingly broken the power of Alcina, but feeling tired from his efforts at rescuing his beloved, he lies upon the ground in the statue's embrace and falls asleep.

Scene 11 brings Alcina, complaining that though immortal she must now live in eternal pain without her magic powers. Spying the sleeping Orlando and drawing a dagger for revenge, she is stopped by the arrival of Ruggiero and Bradamante, who now reveals her identity just as the fleeing Angelica and Medoro arrive in scene 12. Their flight is arrested by Bradamante, who accuses Angelica of deception and responsibility for Orlando's madness. At this point (scene 13) Astolfo arrives with soldiers of Logistilla, one of whom bears a lighted torch. He tells the assembly that he was taken aloft by the disobedient winged steed, which, not fearing his hand or the bit, carried him through regions of air to the moon, where from the sphere a celestial voice told him, "Take in this torch the lost light of Orlando's mind. It is the divine will of the region of light that thou take it back to the Paladin." They awaken Orlando, who still believes himself to be in the arms of Angelica, but when he sees the torch his sanity is restored and he is ashamed to find himself lying naked upon the earth. Astolfo tells him to don his arms, and Alcina explodes in fury against the unjust gods, Fates, and adverse stars. She announces that she will summon the merciless Furies from the depths of the foul abyss to avenge her and storms from the stage. Bradamante points out that Orlando's triumph has been the destruction of Alcina, and he now understands a prophecy (not in Ariosto) that after this feat heaven would take the fortunes of love from his heart. He forgives Angelica and wishes her and Medoro eternal happiness. Astolfo intones that a wise man is one who learns wisdom from his errors.

We can easily see that Braccioli's libretto is not informed by rationalistic and neo-Aristotelian principles of the age concerning genre. Rather it is a late addition to those satiric-comic extravaganzas set by Vivaldi's Venetian predecessors of the seventeenth century, as the 1727 libretto dubs it, a *drammatico divertimento,* an operatic diversion, about the foibles of love. Not certainly to be taken seriously, *Orlando* impudently mixes the genres: pastoral in its love entanglements and magic spells, yet including too many satiric and heroic elements; heroic, yet with its great paladin rendered comical in his boasting and madness; comic, or at least witty and amusing, yet involving characters too highborn for that genre. True comedy was supplied by the already-famous intermezzo, *Il marito giocatore e la moglie bacchettona,* written in 1719 by A. Salvi with music by G. M. Orlandini, which played between the acts of *Orlando.*

The moral lesson drawn in the final chorus is not for princes but for lovers. Actually there are two final choruses. The musical score of 1727, perhaps completed after the printing of the libretto, borrows the rather superficial closing chorus from Vivaldi's *Orlando finto pazzo* of 1714:

Con mirti e fiori	With myrtle and flowers
Volate amori	Take flight, cupids,
A coronare	To crown
Costanza e fè.	Constancy and faith.
S'ama costante	The faithful lover
Fedele amante,	Whose love is constant
Gode in amare	Enjoys in loving
Per fin mercè.	The final reward.

The 1727 libretto, however, has a deeper, more Platonic final chorus, taken from Ristori's *Orlando furioso* of 1713 and used again in Vivaldi's 1714 revision:

Vien dal cielo in noi l'amore	Love comes to us from heaven,
Ma il desio del nostro core	But the desire of our hearts at times
Spirto reo tallor lo fá.	Turns it into an evil spirit.
S'ami sì, ma s'ami il bello,	One loves, yes, but one should love beauty
Perchè imagine de quello,	Because it is the image of Him
Ch'è l'autor della beltà.	Who is the author of beauty.

Both morals are pastoral in nature. The proper princely and heroic moral would point up Orlando's renunciation of love for the virtues of duty and honor. As they stand, the closing choruses reveal the opera as a diverting entertainment about the pitfalls in blindly serving the God of Love.

Contributors

William L. Barcham Professor of art history at the New York Fashion Institute of Technology, specialist in painting of the Italian Baroque and author of articles on Canaletto and Giambattista Tiepolo.

C. Peter Brand Professor of Italian and dean of the arts at the University of Edinburgh, Scotland, author of *Ariosto: A Preface to Orlando Furioso* (1975).

Howard Mayer Brown Ferdinand Schevill Distinguished Service Professor at the University of Chicago, author of *Music and the French Secular Theater* (1963), *Music in the Renaissance* (1976), and editor of the Garland Press facsimile series, *Italian Opera, 1640–1770*.

Michael Collins Professor of musicology at North Texas State University, author of articles on Baroque performance practice and opera, editor of *Tigrane* (1983) in the Harvard Publications in Music Series: The Operas of Alessandro Scarlatti, and deputy chairman of the symposium "Opera and Vivaldi."

Roger Covell Musicologist, critic, conductor, professor at the University of New South Wales, member of the Australian Council for the Arts, and music critic with the *Sydney Morning Herald*.

Eric Cross Professor of music at the University of Newcastle-upon-Tyne, England, specialist in the operas of Vivaldi and author of *The Late Operas of Antonio Vivaldi (1727–1738)* (1981).

Alan Curtis Harpsichordist, conductor, and musicologist at the University of California, Berkeley, whose recordings include Monteverdi's *L'incoronazione di Poppea* and the harpsichord works of Louis Couperin.

Mary Cyr   Professor of music at McGill University, specialist in French and Italian opera of the eighteenth century, and editor of Rameau's opera-ballet *Les Fêtes d'Hebe.*

Sven Hansell   Professor of music and harpsichordist at the University of Iowa, editor of eighteenth-century vocal works, and author of articles on Baroque performance practice.

Ellen T. Harris   Professor of musicology at the University of Chicago, author of articles on Baroque opera and *Handel and the Pastoral Tradition* (1980).

John Walter Hill   Professor of music at the University of Illinois and author of articles on Vivaldi's dramatic music and on Muzio Clementi.

William C. Holmes   Professor of music at the University of California at Irvine, chairman of the International Verdi Congress at Irvine (1980), editor of Scarlatti's *Statira* in the Harvard Publications in Music Series: The Operas of Alessandro Scarlatti, and editor of Cesti's *Orontea.*

Elise K. Kirk   Chairman and program director of the symposium "Opera and Vivaldi," editor of *The Dallas Opera Magazine,* professor of music at Southern Methodist University, author of several articles on opera and a forthcoming book, a historical study of musical activities at the White House.

Klaus Kropfinger   Professor of music at the Free University of Berlin, author of *Wagner und Beethoven* (1975), *Klassik-Rezeption in Berlin 1800–1830,* and contributor to Beethoven's *Werke* (1970).

Marita P. McClymonds   Professor of music at the University of Virginia, editor of Jomelli's *La schiava liberata,* conducted by Alan Curtis in Amsterdam, 1982.

Andrew Porter   Music critic with the *New Yorker* and author of singing translations of Wagner's *The Ring,* Handel's *Ottone,* Mozart's *Lucio Silla,* and several Verdi works.

Ellen Rosand   Professor of musicology at Rutgers University, author of publications in the field of Venetian opera, especially those of Francesco Cavalli, former editor-in-chief of the *Journal of the American Musicological Society*.

Gary Schmidgall Professor of English literature at the University of Pennsylvania, author of *Literature as Opera* (1977) and *Shakespeare and the Courtly Aesthetic* (1981).

Eleanor Selfridge-Field Editor of the North American Vivaldi Association newsletter and author of *Venetian Instrumental Music from Gabrieli to Vivaldi* (1975), specialist in music criticism as social history in seventeenth- and eighteenth-century Venice.

Shirley Wynne Professor of theater arts at the University of California at Santa Cruz, director of the Baroque Dance Ensemble, which has performed in major cities throughout the world.

Index

Accademia degli Incogniti, 25
Addison, Joseph, 84, 362
Adolfati, Andrea, *Didone abbandonata* (1747), 52
Aeschylus, 17, 34
Agnelli, Giuseppe, 102
Agricola, Johann Friedrich, 211, 220f.; *Anleitung zur Singkunst* (1757), 229, 231, 259, 264, 266, 272, 274f.
Albinoni, Tomaso, 327; *Didone abbandonata* (1725), 52; *Le due rivali in amore* (1728), 52; *Elena* (1730), 52; *Meleagro* (1718), 52
Alembert, Jean d', 233, 253f.
Algarotti, Francesco, *Saggio sopra l'opera in musica* (1754), 165, 167, 169, 196, 207, 233, 253, 308, 322
Allacci, Lione, 166
Anderson, Emily, 253
Andreozzi, Gaetano, *Giasone e Medea* (1793), 51
Anglebert, Jean Henri d', 246–248, 256
Anguillara, Giovanni Andrea dell', 23
Antonelli, Margherita, 166
Arcadian Academy, 15f., 95f., 100
Ardoin, John, 7
Ariosti, Attilio, *Vespasiano* (1724), 209
Ariosto, Lodovico, 1, 23, 44, 55–63, 65–69, 71, 76, 78–80, 84, 88f., 91, 94f., 102, 104; *Orlando furioso*, 44, 46–48, 50, 52–55, 62–69, 72–80, 82f., 87, 88, 90–95, 97, 105, 106f., 124f., 150, 153, 367f., 368–369
Aristotle, 15f., 18–20, 24, 27, 30, 32, 45, 69, 71, 92; *Poetics* of, 18, 31, 35; on Unities, 18f.
Arne, Thomas, 117, 360
Arróniz, Othón, 36
Aubignac, Abbé d', *Pratique du Théâtre* (1657), 32
Auden, W. H., 67, 82
Aureli, Aurelio, 30, 92, 94; *Claudio Cesare* (1672), 29; *Medoro* (1658), 30, 87, 91, 93, 101; *Olimpia vendicata* (1681), 87, 93, 102
Avison, Charles, 252, 257

Babell, William, 266, 275
Bach, Carl Philipp Emanuel, *Essay on the True Art* (1753), 215f., 229f., 232, 250, 257
Bacon, R. M., *Elements of Vocal Science* (1824), 238, 254
Badoaro, Giacomo, 26; *Le nozze di Enea con Lavinia* (1641), 28; *Il ritorno d'Ulisse* (1640), 26; *Ulisse errante* (1644), 29, 31
Baker, Stewart A., 125
Baliani, Carlo, 273
Ball, William, 7
Balzac, Honoré de, 16, 32, 34
Banner, Giannantonio, 217f., 230

Barbier, Abbé, 252
Barcham, William L., 7, 379
Barnett, Dene, 170, 178
Bartolini, Niccolò Enea, *Venere gelosa* (1643), 28
Basili, Andrea, *Zenobia* (n.d.), 267, 271
Bassani, Girolamo, *Cimene* (1721), 199
Basso, Alberto, 38 f.
Bauer, Anton, 51
Beattie, James, 75, 85
Beauchamps, Pierre, 172
Belloni, Antonio, 36, 38
Bérard, Jean-Antoine, *L'Art du chant* (1755), 236 f., 239, 242
Berg, Alban, 193
Berlioz, Hector, 86; *Voyage musical* (1844), 252, 257
Bermúdez, Jerónimo, 23, 35
Bernasconi, Andrea, 267; *Demofoonte* (1741), 270; *Didone abbandonata* (1741), 52
Bertoni, Ferdinando, *Didone abbandonata* (1748), 52
Bettagno, A., 168 f.
Bettarini, Luciano, 128; editor of Vivaldi's *Eurilla e Alcindo*, 350, 357
Bianconi, Lorenzo, 11
Bidney, David, 52
Biego, Paolo, *La Fortuna tra le disgratie* (1688), 185
Binni, Walter, 46
Bissacioni, Maiolino, *Ercole in Lidia* (1645), 100
Bissari, Pietro Paolo, 87, 90, 97; *Angelica in India* (1656), 87, 91–93, 97, 100 f.; *Bradamante* (1650), 99
Bjurström, P., 146–148, 167
Blunt, A., 168 f.
Boileau, Nicholas, 85
Boindin, Nicholas, 255
Boniventi, Giuseppe, *Arianna abbandonata* (1719), 52; *Circe delusa* (1711), 51
Bonnet-Bourdelot, Jacques, 243, 255

Bononcini, Antonio, *Griselda* (1719), 230, 360
Bononcini, Giovanni, 211; *Il trionfo di Camilla* (1696), 276
Bordoni [Hasse], Faustina, 158, 166, 168, 199, 208, 261, 263–266, 268, 270, 273 f.
Boretti, Giovanni Antonio, 211; *Claudio Cesare* (1672), 207
Bouquet, Marie-Thérèse, 169
Bowman, James, 1, 3, 7, 193
Boyden, David, 254
Braccioli, Grazio, 1 f., 46–48, 50, 56, 61–63, 77, 88, 94–96, 99, 103 f.; *Orlando finto pazzo* (1714), 88; *Orlando furioso* (1727), 98, 102, 107, 109–111, 119 f., 124, 126 f., 344, 367 f., 369–376; *Rodomonte sdegnato* (1714), 88, 99
Brand, C. Peter, 63, 379
Braun, Werner, 324
Brewster, William T., 36
Britten, Benjamin, *Death in Venice*, 193; *A Midsummer Night's Dream*, 193
Brook, Barry S., 7
Brook, Claire, 273
Broschi, Carlo. *See* Farinelli
Brosses, Charles de, 49, 168, 233, 237, 248, 251, 254, 257, 324
Brown, Howard Mayer, 4, 53, 229, 270–272, 323, 350, 379
Brunelli, Bruno, 51 f.
Brusa, Giovanni Francesco, *Medea e Giasone* (1726), 52
Buelow, George J., 273
Buina, Giuseppe Maria, *Il filindo* (1720), 52
Bulgarelli, Marianna, 127
Bunker, L. A. C., 210
Burney, Charles, 238 f., 243, 255, 259, 272
Burney, Edward, 168
Burt, Nathaniel, 33
Busenello, Francesco, *La Didone* (1641), 26, 100; *L'incoronazione*

di Poppea (1642), 26; *Prosperità infelice di Giulio Cesare* (1644), 26; *Statira* (1655), 30

Caccini, Francesca, *La liberazione di Ruggiero dall'isola di Alcina* (1626), 99
Caccini, Giulio, 37; *Le nuove musiche* (1602), 37, 175, 194, 258, 271
Cafaro, Pasquale, *Il natale d'Apollo* (1775), 51
Caffarelli, Francesco, 271
Cahusac, Louis de, *La Danse ancienne et moderne* (1754), 176
Cairns, David, 86
Caldara, Antonio, 201 f., 210, 327, 360; *Adriano in Siria* (1732), 202; *L'Olimpiade* (1733), 202
Calderón de la Barca, Pedro, 25
Caloprese, Gregorio, 102
Calzabigi, Raniero, 49
Campanini, Barbara [La Barbarina], 172
Campra, André, *L'Europe galante* (1704), 170 f.
Canal, Bernardo, 137
Canaletto, Antonio, 137
Canzini, Natal, 156
Capeci, Carlo Sigismondo, *Orlando* (1711), 96, 103 f., 110 f., 118, 124, 126–128
Capelli, Giammaria, *Giulio Flavio Crispo* (1722), 199; *Mitridate re di Ponto* (1723), 199
Carcano, Giuseppe, 267, 270
Carestini, Giovanni, 208, 267, 276
Casella, Alfredo, 321
Castelvetro, Lodovico, commentaries on Aristotle, 19 f., 35
Castiglione, Baldassare, *Il cortegiano* (1516), 175
Castro, Don Pietro Fernando de, 25
Catalano, M., 63
Cavalieri, Emilio de', 22, 27 f.; *La rappresentazione di Animo e di Corpo* (1600), 28, 35

Cavalli, Francesco, 89, 205 f.; *La Calisto* (1651), 29; composer(?) of *Bradamante* (1650), 97, 99; *Giasone* (1649), 90, 93, 207
Caylus, Count de, 49, 167
Celletti, Rolando, 207, 210
Cesti, Antonio, *Alessandro vincitor di se stesso* (1651), 29; *L'Argia* (1655), 207; *La Dori* (1657), 207
Chamant, Joseph, 145
Chapelain, Jean, 16 f., 34
Chapman, Roger E., 275
Charlton, H. B., 35
Chedel, Pierre-Quentin, 162 f.
Chelleri, Fortunato, *Penelope la casta* (1716), 51
Chevalier, M., 63
Chiabrera, Gabriello, 28, 37
Christina, Queen of Sweden, 15
Chrysander, Friedrich, 126, 275, 354
Cicero, Marcus Tullius, 17
Cicognini, Giacinto, 26, 28; *Giasone* (1649), 29; *Orontea* (1649), 28, 37
Cicognini, Jacopo, 23, 25; *Amor pudico* (1614), 23; *Il convitato di pietra* (n.d.), 25; *Il trionfo di David* (1633), 36
Cimarosa, Domenico, 210; *Oreste* (1783), 51
Cinzio, Giraldi, 19, 20, 23; *Altile* (ca. 1541), 20; *Discorsi* (1554), 34; *Orbecche* (1541), 20, 35
Cioranescu, A., 63
Cipolla, Francesco, *Polifemo* (1786), 51
Clark, Barret H., 34, 40
Clinkscale, Edward H., 273
Clubb, Louise George, 104, 126
Coli, Francesco, 181
Collins, Michael, 10, 229, 379
Comini, Alessandra, 3, 7, 9, 11
Commedia dell'arte, 23, 26
Conti, Antonio, 53
Conti, Gioacchino, detto Gizziello, 127
Cordans, B., *La Sylvia* (1730), 52

Corneille, Pierre, *Le Cid* (1636), 16, 32

Corri, Domenico, *A Select Collection* (ca. 1779), 276; *The Singers Preceptor* (1810), 275

Courcelle [Corselli], Francesco, *Venere placata* (1731), 52

Covell, Roger, 379

Cowan, Louise, 7

Cozzi, Giacomo, 273

Crescimbeni, Giovanni Maria, 15, 33, 95 f., 103 f.

Croft-Murray, Edward, 168 f.

Crosato, Giambattista, 162

Cross, Eric, 7, 11, 305–307, 329, 346, 379

Cueva, Juan de la, 23, 36

Curtis, Alan, 7, 356, 359, 379

Cuzzoni, Francesca, 264, 274

Cyr, Mary, 254, 359, 380

Dallas Opera, *Orlando furioso* production, 1 f., 8 f., 80 f., 358 f., 360–365; symposium, 4–7, 10 f., 358 f.

Dante Alighieri, 23

Daval, Pierre, 257

Davis, Peter F., review of Dallas *Orlando*, 11

Dean, Winton, 125, 208 f., 230, 275, 360

Degrada, Francesco, 2, 146–148, 322–324

Delair, Denis, *Traité de l'accompagnement* (1690), 245 f., 248

Dennis, John, 84

DePure, Michel, *Idée des spectacles* (1668), 176

De Rochement, *Réflexions* (1754), 238, 245, 254, 256

Donatus, Aelius, 17 f., 34

Doni, Giovanni Battista, on prosody, 27, 37; *Trattato della musica sceneca* (1633–1635), 27

Donington, Robert, 255, 272–274

Doren, A., 323

Döring, Renate, 52

Downes, Edward O. D., 234 f., 243, 245, 253, 306

Dufort, Jean-Baptiste, *Trattato del ballo nobile*, 172

Dumont, J. Gabriel Martin, 136

Eco, Umberto, 324

Este, Ippolito d', 56, 367

[Estève], *L'Espirit des beaux arts*, 236, 254

Euripides, 17, 34, 162

Evanthius, 34

Fabbri, Anna Maria, sings in Vivaldi's *Orlando finto pazzo* (1714) and *Orlando* (1727), 333, 336

Falco, Simone de, 207

Fanna, Antonio, 322

Farina, Edoardo, 7

Farinelli [Broschi, Carlo], 127, 263–266, 268, 270, 274

Fassini, Sesto, 209

Faustini, Giovanni, 28; *La Calisto* (1651), 29; *Doriclea* (1645), 11; *Egisto* (1643), 101; *Il Titone* (1645), 28; *La virtù de' strali d'Amore* (1642), 100

Feo, Francesco, *Arsace* (1740), 157

Ferrari, Benedetto, *La ninfa avara* (1643), 101

Ferrero, Mercedes Vide, 168 f.

Feuillet, Raoul-Auger, 170–172, 178

Filippis, Felice de, 51

Fischietti, Domenico, *Arianna e Teseo* (1777), 51

Fleming, John F., 275

Foffano, F., 63

Fontana, Giacinto, detto Farfallino, 208

Ford, Robert, 276

Foreman, Edward, 272, 276

Frazzi, Vito, editor of Vivaldi's *Juditha triumphans*, 349, 356

Frederick the Great, embellishments of aria from Hasse's *Cleofide* (1731), 266

Freeman, Robert, 33, 39, 84, 86, 104, 274, 305
Frere, J. H., 63
Freschi, Domenico, *Olimpia vendicata* (1681), 97; *Sardanapolo* (1679), 207
Frugoni, Carlo, 49
Frugoni, Francesco Fulvio, 15
Fumagalli, Catarina [La Romanina], 267, 271, 276
Fusconi, Giovanni Battista, *Amore innamorato* (1642), 30
Fux, Johann Joseph, 109, 211; *Angelica vincitrice di Alcina* (1716), 109; *Costanza e fortezza* (1723), 219 f.; *Gradus ad Parnassum* (1725), 211, 229, 245

Gabrielli, Domenico, 182; Maurizio (1687), 188
Gagliano, Marco da, *Medoro* (1619), 99
Galliard, John Ernest, *Observations on Florid Song* (1743), 211, 220 f., 229, 231, 253, 272, 274 f.
Galliari, Bernardino, 162
Galli-Bibiena, Ferdinando, 141 f.
Galli-Bibiena, Francesco, 143, 145 f.
Galli-Bibiena, Giovanni Carlo, 151 f.
Galli-Bibiena, Giuseppe, 142 f.
Galuppi, Baldassare, 267; *Berenice* (1741), 271; *Dorinda* (with Pescetti, 1729), 52; *La ninfa Apollo* (1734), 52; *Gli odi delusi dal sangue* (with Pescetti, 1728), 52
Garbero, E., 11, 147
Garrick, David, 363
Gasparini, Francesco, 52, 211, 253; *L'armonico pratico al cimbalo* (1708), 222–228, 231, 247 f., 256; *La ninfa Apollo* (with Lotti, 1709), 52
Gasparini, Maria, 280
Gaudefroy-Demombynes, J., 239, 255
Gay, John, *Acis and Galatea* (1718), 117
Geiringer, Karl, 126

Geminiani, Francesco, *Treatise of Good Taste* (1749), 248 f.
Gherardi, Lorenzino, 267, 270
Giacomelli, Geminiano, *Merope* (1734), 263
Giamatti, A. Bartlett, 125 f.
Gianettini, Antonio, *Artaserse* (1705), 185, 190; *Virginio consolo* (1704), 185.
Gielig, Franz, 2
Gilbert, Kenneth, 256
Giraud [Girò], Anna, 47, 309, 330, 346, 351
Gluck, Christoph Willibald, 49; *Alceste* (1785), 51; *Orfeo ed Euridice* (1774), 51, 118, 276; *Tetide* (1760), 266, 275
Goldoni, Carlo, 305, 324, 328, 345 f., 357; adapter of Zeno's *Griselda* for Vivaldi (1735), 280, 309, 316, 351
Gossett, Philip, 7, 231, 359
Graun, Carl Heinrich, 159, 239–242; *Iphigenie in Aulis* (1749), 159
Gravina, Gian Vincenzo, 95, 103 f.
Grimarest, de, *Traité du récitatif* (1707), 255
Grimm, Friedrich Melchior, 257
Grosse, Hans, 255
Guadagni, Gaetano, 275 f., 363
Gualandi, Margherita, sings in *Orlando furioso* (1714) of Vivaldi, 330
Guarini, Giambattista, *Il pastor fido* (ca. 1585), 21 f., 26, 35, 107, 109
Guglielmi, Pietro Alessandro, *Enea e Lavinia* (1785), 51

Haböck, Franz, 274
Hall, James A. and Martin V., 275
Handel, George Frideric, 65, 117 f., 124, 194, 209, 211, 266, 275, 279, 327, 354, 356, 360; *Acis and Galatea* (1718), 108, 117; Acis legend (1708), 108; *Alcina* (1735), 65, 117, 220, 276; *Ariodante* (1735), 117; *Giulio Cesare* (1724), 127, 220, 361; *Messiah* (1742), 266,

275; *Orlando* (1733), 79, 84 f.,
110 f., 117–120, 124, 126–128,
193 f., 197, 203 f., 365; *Partenope*
(1707), 280; *Radamisto* (1720),
209; *Rodelinda* (1725), 276; *Samson* (1743), 266, 275
Hanning, Barbara R., 37
Hansell, Kathleen Kuzmick, 53
Hansell, Sven, 126 f., 212, 220, 223–
225, 228, 230–232, 253, 262, 273,
388
Hardy, Alexandre, 15
Harris, Ellen, 127, 380
Harris, Ernest, 125
Haskell, Francis, 166
Hasse, Johann Adolph, 168, 201, 210,
267, 327; *Alessandro in Persia*
(with Leo and D. Scarlatti, 1741),
209; *Cleofide* (1731), 266; *Demofoonte* (1748), 208; *Didone abbandonata* (1744, 1748), 52, 209;
Partenope (1767), 51; *Semiramide*
(1748), 209; *Siroe* (1736), 209, 270
Hawkins, Sir John, 272
Haydn, Franz Joseph, 107 f., 124,
355; *Orlando paladino* (1782), 206
Heartz, Daniel, 360
Heinichen, Johann David, *Der General-Bass* (1728), 212 f., 230
Heriot, Angus, 206, 253, 274, 276
Herrick, Marvin T., 34 f., 40
Hill, John Walter, 128, 309, 322–
324, 346, 380
Hiller, Johann Adam, *Anweisung zum
musikalisch-zierlichen Gesange*
(1780), 259, 264–266, 272, 274 f.
Hilton, Wendy, 178
Hitchcock, H. Wiley, 272
Hjelmborg, Bjørn, 230
Holmes, William, 37 f., 168, 359, 380
Homer, *Iliad* illustrated by Tiepolo,
150 f.
Hook, John, 68, 83
Hooker, Edward, 84
Horace, 17 f.
Horne, Marilyn, 1 f., 4, 9, 361, 363
Houghton, Edward, 126

Howard, Donald, 83
Howard, Henry, Earl of Surrey, 34
Hucke, Helmut, 322
Hume, David, 49

Insanguine, Giacomo, *Arianna e
Teseo* (1773), 51; *Calipso* (1782),
51
Ivanovich, Cristoforo, 97

Jacobi, Erwin R., 229, 272
Jaucourt, Louis chevalier de, 41 f., 50
Jenkins, Newell, 2
Johnson, Samuel, 75
Jommelli, Nicolò, 267; *Eumene*
(1742), 270
Jung, Hans Rudolf, 255
Jusserand, J. J., 34, 39
Juvarra, Filippo, 152

Karayanis, Plato, 7, 9 f.
Keiser, Reinhard, 327, 360
Killebrew, Gwendolyn, 1, 3
Kindermann, H., 168
Kirk, Elise K., 380
Knox, G., 166
Kolneder, Walter, 275, 323 f.
Kropfinger, Klaus, 380
Kuhnau, Johann, 221 f., 231

Lampugnani, Giovanni Battista, 271;
Didone abbandonata (1753), 52;
Siroe (1755), 209
Lancetti, Lucia, 47, 205, 346
Landi, Stefano, *La morte d'Orfeo*
(1620), 28
Landon, H. C. Robbins, 275
Lanfranchi, Ariella, 38
Latilla, Gaetano, 48, 124; *Alceste*
(1740), 51; *Angelica ed Orlando*
(1735), 48, 111, 204; *Olimpia
nell'isola di Ebuda* (1741), 51
LeBrun, Charles, *Conférence sur l'expression* (1698), 176, 178
Legrenzi, Giovanni, 211; *Totila*
(1677), 218
Leo, Leonardo, 267, 327; *Alessandro*

in Persia (with Hasse and D. Scarlatti, 1741), 209; *Arianna e Teseo* (1721), 51; *Le nozze di Amore e Psiche* (1738), 51; *Siface* (1737), 270 f.
Levey, Michael, 150, 166 f.
Lincoln, Stoddard, review of Dallas *Orlando*, 11
Lindgren, Lowell, 276
Livy, 93
Lombardus, Bartholomaeus, 35
Loredan, Gian Francesco, 25
Luccio, Francesco, *Medoro* (1658), 97
Lully, Jean-Baptiste, *Atys* (1676), 236, 254; recitative in, 236; *Roland* (1685), 104
Mably, Bonnot de, 247, 256
MacClintock, Carol, 256
Madius, V., commentary on Aristotle, 19, 35
Maffei, Scipione, 15, 33, 169; *La fida ninfa* (1732), 280, 291–293, 305; *La Merope* (1713), 162 f.
Magri, Gennaro, *Trattato teorico-pratico di ballo* (1779), 172
Majo, Giuseppe de, *Arianna e Teseo* (1747), 51; *Erminia* (1729), 51
Mancini, Francesco, 211; *Gl'amanti generosi* (1705), 230
Mancini, Franco, 51
Mancini, Giambattista, *Edimione* (1721), 51; *Riflessioni pratiche* (1774, 1777), 239, 255, 259, 264 f., 272, 274
Manelli, Francesco, *L'Andromeda* (1637), 206
Manfredini, Vincenzo, *Regole armoniche* (1775), 250 f., 257
Mangini, N., 147
Manna, Gennaro, *Didone abbandonata* (1751), 52
Manuel, Frank E., 52
Marcello, Benedetto, *La Morte d'Adone* (1719), 52 f.; *Teatro alla moda*, 53, 70, 142, 156 f., 160, 168 f., 209, 269, 276, 308, 317 f., 322, 324, 328, 345

Marchese, Luigi, 239
Marchi, Antonio, *Avenimenti di Ruggiero* (1732), 99
Marianino, 267, 271, 276
Marianni, Ariodante, 276
Marini, Leonardo, 164 f., 169
Marpurg, Friedrich Wilhelm, 216; *Historisch-kritische Beyträge* (1754), 235, 253; *Kritische Briefe* (1760), 230
Marshall, Robert, 274
Martello, Pier Jacopo, 70–75, 77, 78, 81, 83 f., 308, 318, 322, 325, 328, 345
Masson, Paul-Marie, 254
Mattheson, Johann, 105, 111 f., 125
Mauro, Alessandro, 47
Mauro, Antonio, 137, 324
Mayor, A. H., 147
Mazzocchi, Domenico, *La catena d'Adone* (1626), 27
Mazzoni, Antonio Maria, *Arianna e Teseo* (1758), 43; *Clemenza di Tito* (1755), 152
Mazzuchelli, Giovanni Maria, 103
McClymonds, Marita, 7, 380
McGegan, Nicholas, 365
Melani, Jacopo, 211
Meleager, 28
Mercer, Frank, 272
Meredith, William, 64–67, 69 f., 82, 86
Metastasio, Pietro, 32, 40, 42–47, 50–52, 199, 201, 205; *Adriano in Siria* (1732), 202, 206, 271, 276; *Alessandro nell'Indie* (1734), 271, 276; *Amor timido* (cantata, n.d.), 270; *Angelica e Medoro* (serenata, 1720), 46, 107, 111, 118, 127; *Artaserse* (1730), 201; *Demofoonte* (1733), 270; *Didone abbandonata* (1724), 46 f., 52, 206, 209; *Endimione* (1720), 43; *Ezio* (1728), 271; *Galatea* (1722), 43; *Olimpiade* (1733), 47, 202, 205, 279; *Gli orti esperidi* (1721), 43; *Ruggiero* (1771), 46 f; *Siface* (1737),

271, 276; *Siroe* (1733), 270;
Zenobia (1740), 271, 267
Micheli, Benedetto, 306; *La virtù tri-
onfante dell'amore e dell'odio,
overo Tigrane* (with Vivaldi and N.
Romaldo, 1724), 306
Minturno, Antonio, commentary on
Aristotle, 19, 35
Mitchell, William J., 230
Molière, Jean-Baptiste, 17, 34; *Le
Bourgeois Gentilhomme*, 35
Molina, Tirso de, 25, 33, 40; *El bur-
lador de Sevilla* (n.d.), 25; *Cigar-
rales de Toledo* (1624), 40
Molinaro, Julius A., 104, 126
Molmenti, P., 166
Montagnana, Antonio, 203
Montaigne, Michel de, 69
Montéclair, Michel Pignolet de, *Prin-
cipes de musique* (1736), 237, 254
Monterosso, Raffaello, 128, 306, 349,
352 f., 357
Monterosso-Vacchelli, Anna Maria,
38
Monteverdi, Claudio, 194; *L'in-
coronazione di Poppea* (1642), 26,
90, 93, 195 f., 207; *Le nozze di
Enea con Lavinia* (1641), 28; *Or-
feo* (1607), 16, 26, 28; *Il ritorno
d'Ulisse* (1640), 26, 195; *Scherzi
musicali* (1607), 37; *Tirsi e Clori*
(1619), 28
Morassi, A., 166
Morelli, Giovanni, 11
Moretti, L., 147
Mortari, Virgilio, 321 f.
Morzin, Count Venzeslav von, 317
Mozart, Wolfgang Amadeus, 234,
351; *Idomeneo* (1781), 234;
pianoforte for recitative in *Don
Giovanni* (1787), 252; recitative in,
229; *Die Zauberflöte* (1791), 79
Muraro, Maria Teresa, 5, 98 f., 136,
145–148, 166, 168, 323 f., 345
Muratori, Judovico, 16, 33
Muret, Marc-Antonio, 37

Mysliveček, Josef, *Adriano in Siria*
(1776), 210

Naseli, Alberto [Ganassa], 23
Natali, Giulio, 53
Neumann, Frederick, 274
Newton, Sir Isaac, response to Han-
del's *Radamisto* (1720), 80
Noce, H. S., 322
Nolfi, Vincenzo, *Bellerofonte* (1642),
30

Olivero, D., 157, 166
Opera composers, Adolfati, Andrea,
52; Albinoni, Tomaso, 52, 327; Andreozzi, Gaetano, 51; Ariosti, Attilio, 209; Arne, Thomas, 117, 360;
Baliani, Carlo, 273; Basili, Andrea,
276, 271; Bassani, Girolamo, 199;
Bernasconi, Andrea, 267; Bertoni,
Ferdinando, 52; Biego, Paolo, 185;
Bissacioni, Maiolino, 100; Boniventi, Giuseppe, 51 f.; Bononcini,
Antonio, 230, 360; Bononcini, Giovanni, 211, 276; Boretti, Giovanni
Antonio, 207, 211; Britten, Benjamin, 193; Brusa, Giovanni Francesco, 52; Buina, Giuseppe Maria,
52; Cafaro, Pasquale, 51; Caldara,
Antonio, 201 f., 210, 327, 360;
Campra, André, 170 f.; Cannin,
Giulio, 37, 175, 194, 258, 271;
Cannini, Francesca, 99; Capelli,
Giammaria, 199; Carcano, Giuseppe, 267, 270; Cavalieri, Emilio
de', 22, 27 f., 35; Cavalli, Francesco, 29, 89, 90, 93, 97, 99, 205–
207; Cesti, Antonio, 29, 207; Chelleri, Fortunato, 51; Cimarosa,
Domenico, 51, 210; Cipolla, Francesco, 51; Cordans, B., 52; Courcelle [Corselli], Francesco, 52;
Cozzi, Giacomo, 273; Feo, Francesco, 157; Ferrari, Benedetto, 101;
Fischietti, Domenico, 51; Freschi,
Domenico, 97, 207; Fusconi, Gio-

vanni Battista, 30; Fux, Johann Joseph, 109, 211, 219, 220, 229, 245; Gabrielli, Domenico, 182, 188; Gagliano, Marco da, 99; Galuppi, Baldassare, 52, 267, 271; Gasparini, Francesco, *see* Gasparini; Giacomelli, Geminiano, 263; Gianettini, Antonio, 185, 190; Gluck, Christoph Willibald, 49, 51, 118, 266, 275 f.; Graun, Carl Heinrich, 159, 239–242; Guglielmi, Pietro Alessandro, 51; Handel, George Frideric, *see* Handel; Hasse, Johann Adolph, 168, 201, 208–210, 266 f., 270, 327; Haydn, Franz Joseph, 107 f., 124, 206, 355; Insanguine, Giacomo, 51; Jommelli, Nicolò, 267, 270; Keiser, Reinhard, 327, 360; Lampugnani, Giovanni Battista, 52, 209, 271; Landi, Stefano, 28; Latilla, Gaetano, 48, 51, 124, 204; Legrenzi, Giovanni, 211, 218; Leo, Leonardo, 51, 209, 267, 270 f., 327; Luccio, Francesco, 97; Lully, Jean-Baptiste, 104, 236, 254; Majo, Giuseppe de, 51; Mancini, Francesco, 211, 230; Mancini, Giambattista, 51, 239, 255, 259, 264 f., 272, 274; Manelli, Gennaro, 52; Manna, Gennaro, 52; Marcello, Benedetto, *see* Marcello; Mazzocchi, Domenico, 27; Mazzoni, Antonio Maria, 43, 152; Melani, Jacapo, 211; Micheli, Benedetto, 306; Monteverdi, Claudio, 16, 26, 28, 37, 90, 93, 195 f., 207; Mozart, W. A., 79, 229, 234, 251 f.; Mysleveček, Josef, 210; Nolfi, Vincenao, 30; Orefice, Antonio, 43, 51; Orgiani, Teofilo, 185; Orlandini, Giuseppe Maria, 8, 145, 305, 376; Paer, Ferdinando, 51; Paisiello, Giovanni, 51; Pallavicini, Carlo, 181–183, 211; Pasquini, Bernardo, 211; Perez, David, 210; Pergolesi, Giovanni Battista, 210, 267, 271; Peri, Jacopo, 99, 194 f.; Pescetti, Giovanni Battista, 52, 117 f., 204, 209; Piccinni, Niccolò, 51; Piticchio, Francesco, 51; Platania, I., 51; Pollarolo, Antonio, 52, 88; Pollarolo, Carlo Francesco, 52, 113, 168, 211, 229; Porpora, Nicola, 52, 111–118, 120, 123 f., 127, 205, 267, 270 327; Porsile, Giuseppe, 211; Porta, Giovanni, 52; Priati, A., 51; Provenzale, Francesco, 207, 211; Pugnani, Gaetano, 51; Rameau, Jean-Philippe, 172, 220, 236, 240–243, 251 f., 257, 356; Rampini, Giovanni, 51; Reimann, Aribert, 193; Ristori, Giovanni Alberto, *see* Ristori; Romaldi, N., 306; Sarri, Domenico, 51 f.; Sartorio, Antonio, 207, 211; Scarlatti, Alessandro, *see* Scarlatti; Scarlatti, Domenico, 95 f., 103, 110, 209; Scarlatti, Giuseppe, 209 f.; Schiassi, Gaetano Maria, 267; Schuster, Joseph, 51; Sigismondi, G., 51; Steffani, Agostino, 211, 272; Stradella, Alessandro, 207, 211; Strauss, Richard, 79; Traetta, Tommaso, 49, 51 f., 209 f., 360; Verdi, Giuseppe, 69, 351, 358 f., 362; Vignati, Giuseppe, 261, 263, 273; Vinci, Leonardo, 43, 52, 208, 210, 323, 327, 360; Vivaldi, Antonio, *see* Vivaldi; Wagner, Richard, 79, 194, 362; Zanettini, Antonio, 207; Ziani, Pietro Andrea, 207, 211; Zucchini, Marco, 199
Opera houses, Königliche Oper (Berlin), 159; Teatro Barberini (Rome), 25 f.; Teatro alle Dame (Rome), 270; Teatro la Fenice (Ancona), 253; Teatro Filarmonico (Verona), 1, 143, 145, 305; Teatro de' Fiorentini (Naples), 43, 48; Teatro Novissimo (Venice), 146; Teatro della Pergola (Florence), 210; Teatro Regio (Turin), 152 f., 157, 165; Teatro Regio Ducal (Milan), 53; Teatro

San Bartolomeo (Naples), 43, 271; Teatro San Carlo (Naples), 43; Teatro San Cassiano (Venice), 26, 131, 167; Teatro San Giovanni Grisostomo (Venice), 131–133, 158, 168, 181; Teatro San Moisè (Venice), 131, 135–137, 186, 190; Teatro San Salvador (Venice), 131; Teatro San Samuele (Venice), 131, 305; Teatro Sant'Angelo (Venice), 1, 47, 88, 98, 131 f., 136 f., 147, 185 f., 190, 271, 316, 321, 325, 367; Teatro Santissimi Giovanni e Paolo (Venice), 89, 134–137; Teatro Stabile (Rome), 54; Teatro del Tejo (Lisbon), 152

Opera librettists, Aureli, Aurelio, 29 f., 87, 91–94, 101 f.; Badoaro, Giacomo, 26, 28 f., 31; Bartolini, Niccolò Enea, 28; Bissari, Pietro Paolo, 87, 89–93, 97, 100 f.; Braccioli, Grazio, *see* Braccioli; Busenello, Francesco, 26, 30, 100; Calzabigi, Raniero, 49; Capece, Carlo Sigismondo, 96, 103 f., 110 f., 118, 124, 126–128; Chiabrera, Gabriello, 28, 37; Cicognini, Giacinto, 26, 28 f., 37; Faustini, Giovanni, 28 f., 100 f.; Frugoni, Carlo, 49; Gay, John, 117; Goldoni, Carlo, 280, 305, 309, 316, 324, 328, 345 f., 357; Maffei, Scipione, 15, 33, 162 f., 169, 280, 291–293, 305; Marchi, Antonio, 99; Metastasio, Pietro, *see* Metastasio; Pariarti, Pietro, 109 f., 190, 263, 270, 273; Pasqualigo, Benedetto, 199 f., 208 f.; Porta, Nunziato, 107; Quinault, Philippe, 104; Rinuccini, Ottavio, 21 f.; Rospigliosi, Giulio (Pope Clement IX), 25 f., 48, 53, 99; Rossi, Luigi, 48, 99; Sabadini, B., 141; Sacrati, Francesco, 140; Salvadori, Andrea, 25, 29, 99; Salvi, Antonio, 99, 168; Saracinelli, Ferdinando, 99; Sbarra, Francesco, 27, 29, 196, 207; Stampiglia, Silvio, 280; Striggio, Alessandro, 22, 28; Strozzi, Giulio, 29, 91, 100; Tronsarelli, Ottavio, 27; Tullio, Francesco Antonio, 48 f.; Vedova, Carlo, 99; Zeno, Apostolo, 32, 200, 263, 270, 273, 280, 305, 351

Opera singers, Bordoni [Hasse], Faustini, 158, 166, 168, 199, 208, 261, 263–266, 268, 270, 273 f.; Bowman, James, 1, 3, 7, 193; Broschi, Carlo, *see* Farinelli; Bulgarelli, Marianna, 127; Campanini, Barbara [La Barbarina], 172; Carestini, Giovanni, 208, 267, 276; Cuzzoni, Francesca, 264, 274; Fabbri, Anna Maria, 333, 336; Falco, Simone de, 207; Farinelli [Broschi, Carlo], 127, 263 f., 265 f., 268, 270, 274; Fontana, Giacinto, detto Farfallino, 208; Fumagalli, Catarina [La Romanina], 267, 271, 276; Gherardi, Lorenzino, 267; Giraud [Girò], Anna, 47, 309, 330, 346, 351; Guadagni, Gaetano, 275 f., 363; Gualandi, Margherita, 330; Horne, Marilyn, 1 f., 4, 9, 361, 363; Killebrew, Gwendolyn, 1, 3; Lancetti, Lucia, 47, 205, 346; Marchese, Luigi, 239; Marianino, 267, 271, 276; Montagnana, Antonio, 203; Paris, Nicolin, 185; Pasi, Antonio, 161 f., 165, 169; Pinetti, Gaetano, 346; Raffanti, Dano, 1, 6; Riccioni, Barbara, 182 f.; Rimini, Bernardda, 186; Salimbeni, Felice, 267, 271, 276; Senesino [Bernardi, Francesco], 204, 253, 276; Serosina, Benedetta, 346; Shade, Ellen, 1, 7; Taylor, Rose, 1; Tosi, Pier Francesco, *see* Tosi; Valletta, Gaetano, 160, 165 f., 169; Vittaloni, Angelica, 185; Volsechi, Signora, 185, 190; Zaccaria, Nicola, 1

Orefice, Antonio, *Circe delusa* (1713), 43, 51

Orgiani, Teofilo, *Il Dioclete* (1687), 185

Orlandini, Giuseppe Maria, 8, 145; *Il marito giocatore* (1719), 305, 376
Orlando furioso librettos, *Alcina* adapted for Handel (1735), 65, 117, 220, 276; *Angelica ed Orlando* (Tullio, 1735) set by Latilla, 48, 111, 204, 124; *Angelica e Medoro* (Metastasio, 1720) set by Porpora, 46, 107, 111–118, 120, 123 f.; *Angelica e Medoro* (Vedova, 1739) set by Pescetti, 117 f., 204, 209; *Angelica in India* (Bissari, 1656), 87, 91–93, 97, 100 f.; *Angelica vincitrice di Alcina* (Pariarti, 1718) set by Fux, 109; *Ariodante* (Salvi, 1716) set by C. F. Pollarolo, 168, set by Handel (1735), 99; *Avenimenti di Ruggiero* (Marchi, 1732), 99; *Bradamante* (Bissari, 1650) set by Cavalli(?), 87, 89, 91, 99; *Ginevra* (adaptation of Salvi's *Ariodante*, 1736) set by Vivaldi, 99; *La liberazione di Ruggiero dall'isola di Alcina* (Saracinelli, 1625) set by F. Caccini, 99; *Medoro* (Aureli, 1658) set by Luccio, 30, 87, 91, 93, 97, 101; *Olimpia nell'isola di Ebuda* (Trabucco, 1741) set by Pescetti, 117, set by Latilla, 51; *Olimpia vendicata* (Aureli, 1681) set by Freschi, 87, 93, 102; *Orlando* (Capeci, 1711) adapted by Handel (1733), 96, 103 f., 110 f., 118, 124, 126–128; *Orlando* (1727) adaptation of Braccioli's *Orlando furioso* (1713) set by Vivaldi, see Braccioli and Vivaldi; *Orlando finto pazzo* (Braccioli, 1714) set by Vivaldi, see Braccioli and Vivaldi; *Orlando furioso* (Braccioli, 1713) set by Ristori, see Braccioli and Ristori; *Orlando paladino* (Porta, 1782) set by Haydn, 107, 206; *Il palazzo incantato di Atlanta* (Rospigliosi, 1642) set by Luigi Rossi, 48, 99; *Rodomonte sdegnato* (Braccioli, 1714), 88, 99; *Roland* (Quinault, 1685)

set by Lully, 104; *Ruggiero ovvero l'eroica gratitudine* (Metastasio, 1771) set by Hasse, 468; *La sposalizio di Medoro et Angelica* (Salvadori, 1619) set by Gagliano and Peri, 22, 99
Ortolani, Giuseppe, 345
Ovid, *Metamorphoses*, 41; in opera, 93

Pace-Sanfelice, F., 34
Paer, Ferdinando, *Ero e Leandro* (1794), 51
Paisiello, Giovanni, *Apollo e Dafne* (1791), 51; *Fedra* (1788), 51; *Giunone e Lucina* (1787), 51; *Le nozze di Peleo e Tetide* (1768), 51; *Pirro* (1790), 51
Palladio, Andrea, Teatro Olimpico (Vicenza), 20
Pallavicino, Carlo, *Elmiro* (1687), 181 f., 211; *Galieno* (1675), 207; *Gierusalemme liberata* (1687), 182 f.
Pallucchini, R., 166
Pariarti, Pietro, 109 f., 127; *Ambleto* (with Zeno, 1719), 263, 270, 273; *Angelica vincitrice di Alcina* (1718), 190
Paris, Nicolin, 185, 190
Pasi, Antonio, 161 f., 165, 169
Pasquali, Nicolo, *Thorough-bass made easy* (1757), 226–228, 232, 250, 257
Pasqualigo, Benedetto, *Cimene* (1721), 199 f., 208; *Giulio Flavio Crispo* (1722), 199 f.; *Ifigenia in Tauride* (1719), 208 f.; *Mitridate, re di Ponto* (1723), 199 f., 209
Pasquini, Bernardo, 211
Pauly, Reinhard G., 276, 324, 345
Pazzi, Alessandro, commentary on Aristotle, 18, 34
Pécour, Louis, 170, 172
Perez, David, *L'Olimpiade* (1753), 210
Pergolesi, Giovanni Battista, 210, 267; *Adriano in Siria* (1734), 210, 271

Peri, Jacopo, 99, 194; *Euridice* (1600), 195
Pescetti, Giovanni Battista, *Angelica e Medoro* (1739), 117 f., 204, 209; *Dorinda* (with Galuppi, 1729), 52; *Gli odi delusi dal sangue* (1768), 52; *Olimpia in Ebuda* (1740), 117
Petrarch [Petrarca, Francesco], 18, 23
Petrobelli, Pierluigi, 253
Philip II, 23
Piccinni, Niccolò, *Ercole al Termedonte* (1793), 51
Pinetti, Gaetano, sings in Vivaldi's *Orlando*, 346
Pirrotta, Nino, 36, 102
Piticchio, Francesco, *La vendetta di Medea* (1798), 51
Pitré, G., 63
Pizzi, Pier Luigi, 1, 3 f., 364
Platania, I., *Bellerofonte* (1778), 51
Plautus, Titus Maccius, 24
Pléiade, 28, 58
Pollarolo, Antonio, 88; *L'abbandono di Armida* (1729), 52; *Nerina* (1728), 52
Pollarolo, Carlo Francesco, 211; *La fede riconosciuta*, 113; *Ariodante* (1716), 168; *Gl'inganni felici* (1696), 229; *Marsia delusa* (1714), 52
Pope, Alexander, on Shakespeare, 31
Porpora, Nicola, 127, 205, 267, 327; *Amor timido* (n.d.), 270; *Angelica e Medoro* (1720), 111, 113–118, 120, 123 f.; *Arianna e Teseo* (1727), 52; *Imeneo in Atene* (1726), 52; *Polifemo* (1735), 109, 117
Porsile, Giuseppe, 211
Porta, Giovanni, *Ulisse* (1725), 52
Porta, Nunziato, *Orlando paladino* (1775), 107
Porter, Andrew, 4, 380
Povoledo, Elena, 145, 147 f.
Powers, H. S., 305
Pozzo, G. de, 322
Prato, G., 168

Priati, A., *Olimpia* (1786), 51
Provenzale, Francesco, 211; *Lo schiavo di sua moglie* (1671), 207
Pugnani, Gaetano, *Adone e Venere* (1784), 51
Pulci, Luigi, *Il Morgante* (1483), 55

Quantz, Johann Joachim, *Versuch einer Anweisung die Flöte traversiere zu spielen* (1752), 214 f., 221, 238, 243, 248–250, 254, 257, 259 f., 264–266, 272–275
Quinault, Philippe, *Roland* (1685), 104

Racine, Jean, 32 f.
Raffanti, Dano, 1, 6
Ramat, Raffaello, 102
Rameau, Jean-Philippe, 236, 243, 252, 356; *Castor et Pollux* (1737), 242; *Code de musique pratique* (1760), 251, 257; *Fêtes d'Hébé* (1739), 172; *Traité d'harmonie* (1722), 220, 240 f.; *Zorastre* (1770), 252
Rampini, Giovanni, *La gloria trionfante d'amore* (1712), 51
Reilly, Edward R., 254, 272 f.
Reimann, Aribert, *Lear* (1978), 193
Rennert, Hugo Albert, 39
Rescigno, Nicola, 1, 3, 7 f., 10
Revegnan, Giuseppe, 102
Reynolds, Barbara, 75, 82, 85
Ricci, Marco, 169, 244
Riccioni, Barbara, 182 f.
Richelieu, Cardinal, 16, 32
Riemann, Margarete, 125
Riepel, Joseph, 245
Rigoli, P., 145, 148
Rimini, Bernardo da, 186
Rinuccini, Ottavio, *Dafne* (1597), 21 f.; *Euridice* (1600), 21 f.
Ristori, Giovanni Alberto, 1, 88; *Orlando furioso* (1713, 1714, 1727), 1, 328, 331, 367, 376; *La Pallade trionfante in Arcadia* (1714), 52
Riva, Giuseppe, *Avviso ai compositori ed ai cantanti* (1727), 308, 322

Robinson, Michael, 207, 253, 279, 305
Robortellus, Franciscus, commentary on Aristotle, 19, 34
Roland, Chanson de, 1, 54, 63, 367
Rolandi, Ulderico, 35, 37f.
Romaldi, N., *La virtù trionfante dell'amore e dell'odio, overo Il Tigrane* (with Vivaldi and B. Micheli, 1724), 306
Romano, Giulio, 165
Ronsard, Pierre de, 28, 37
Rosand, Ellen, 38f., 100, 102, 125, 380
Rose, William Steward, 125
Rospigliosi, Giulio (Pope Clement IX), 25f., 53; *Chi soffre speri* (1637), 25f.; *Dal male il bene* (1624), 25; *Il palazzo incantato* (1642), 48, 99; *Sant'Alessio* (1632), 26
Rossi, Luigi, *Il palazzo incantato* (1642), 48, 99
Rousseau, Jean-Jacques, 233, 236, 251, 254
Rudge, Olga, 357
Ryom, Peter, 11, 98, 147, 305f., 322f., 346

Sabadini, B., *Didio Giuliano* (1687), 141
Sacrati, Francesco, *Il Bellerofonte* (1642), 140
Saint Augustine, 83
St. Lambert, Michel de, *Les Principes du clavecin* (1702), 247, 254, 256
Salimbeni, Felice, 267, 271, 276
Salvadori, Andrea, *Medoro* (1619, 1623), 29, 99; *Regina e Sant'Orsola* (1625), 25
Salvi, Antonio, *Ariodante* (1716, 1718), 99, 168
Sanguineti, 54, 58
Sannazzaro, Jacopo, 23
Saracinelli, Ferdinando, *La liberazione di Ruggiero dall'isola di Alcina* (1625), 99

Sarri, Domenico, *Adone in Cipro* (1724), 51; *Didone abbandonata* (1730), 52; *Le nozze de Teti e Pelio* (1738), 51; *La Partenope* (1739), 51
Sartori, Claudio, 99, 271, 273, 276
Sartorio, Antonio, *Seleuca* (1666), 207, 211
Sbarra, Francesco, *Alessandro vincitor di se stesso* (1651), 27, 29, 196, 207
Scaliger, Julius Caesar, commentary on Aristotle, 19, 35
Scarlatti, Alessandro, 197, 207, 211, 212, 327, 360; *Marco Attilio Regolo* (1719), 219, 220; *Massimo Puppieno* (1696), 218; *Pompeo* (1683), 207; *Per sonare il cembalo* (1715), 212, 223–225, 227f., 231; *Tigrane* (1715), 218f., 229
Scarlatti, Domenico, 95f., 103; *Alessandro in Persia* (with Leo and Hasse, 1741), 209; *Orlando* (1711), 110
Scarlatti, Giuseppe, 210; *Adriano in Siria* (1752), 209; *Alessandro nell'Indie* (1753), 209
Scheibe, Johann Adolph, 237, 254
Schiassi, Gaetano Maria, 267, 271
Schmidgall, Gary, 360, 381
Schmitz, Hans-Peter, 272, 274
Schneider, Max, 245, 256
Schuster, Joseph, *Amore e Psiche* (1780), 51
Schwartz, Delmore, 68, 70
Scimone, Claudio, 1, 10f., 126, 346, 361
Segni, Bernardo, commentary on Aristotle, 19, 34
Selfridge-Field, Eleanor, 53, 188, 381
Seneca, Lucius Annaeus, 20, 23
Senesino [Bernardi, Francesco], 204, 253, 276
Serimen, Zaccaria, 132, 147
Serosina, Benedetta, sings in Vivaldi's *Orlando*, 346

Shade, Ellen, 1, 7
Shakespeare, William, 15, 32 f., 81, 364, 368; *Hamlet*, 79; *Midsummer Night's Dream*, 38; *The Rape of Lucrece*, 31; *Venus and Adonis*, 31
Shaw, Watkins, 275
Sigismondi, G., *Endimione* (1764), 51
Silva, João Cordeiro da, 355
Smith, Patrick J., 36, 39, 253
Solerti, Angelo, 35, 37 f.
Somfai, László, 275
Sonneck, Oscar G. T., 51
Sophocles, 17, 34
Spenser, Edmund, *The Faerie Queene*, 68
Stampiglia, Silvio, *Rosmira* (1738), 280
Steele, Richard, 85
Steffani, Agostino, 211, 272; *Tassilone* (1708), 218
Stendhal [Beyle, Henri], 209
Stieger, Franz, 51, 209
Stradella, Alessandro, 211; *Corispero*, 207
Strauss, Richard, *Die Frau ohne Schatten*, 79
Striggio, Alessandro, *Orfeo* (1607), 22; *Tirsi e Clori* (1615), 28
Strohm, Reinhard, 11, 99, 126, 270, 305, 307, 309, 322–324, 345 f.
Strozzi, Giulio, 29; *La finta pazza* (1641), 91, 100
Sutton, Everett L., 270

Tagliacozzo, G., 52
Tartini, Giuseppe, 317; *Tratado di musica* (1754), 233 f., 252 f.
Tasso, Torquato, 55, 63, 107; *Aminta* (1573), 21–23, 26, 44, 56, 63; *Gerusalemme liberata* (1581) illustrated by Tiepolo, 150, 165
Taylor, Rose, 1
Telemann, Georg Philipp, 214, 221, 239, 241 f., 252
Tentelnot, Hans, 168
Terence [Publious Terentius Afer], 17, 24

Tessin, Nicodemus, 137
Tiepolo, Giambattista, 4, 149, 160, 162, 166 f., 169; illustrates Ariosto's *Orlando furioso*, 150, 153 f.; illustrates Homer's *Iliad*, 150 f., 164; illustrates Tasso's *Gerusalemme liberata*, 150, 153 f.
Torelli, Giacomo, 131, 140, 146, 167
Torres, Joseph Martinez Bravo de, *Reglas generales* (1736 edition), 222 f., 225–227, 231
Tosi, Pier Francesco, *Opinioni de' cantori antichi e moderni* (1723), 208, 211, 220, 235, 237 f., 253 f., 258–260, 263 f., 266, 272–275
Traetta, Tommaso, 49, 360; *Armida* (1673), 51; *Didone abbandonata* (1757), 52; *L'Olimpiade* (1768), 209 f.
Tribolo, Niccolò, 165
Trissino, Giangiorgio, 17, 20; *Sofonisba* (1515), 17 f., 22
Tronsarelli, Ottavio, *La catena d'Adone* (1626), 27
Troy, Charles E., 178
Tullio, Francesco Antonio, *Angelica ed Orlando* (1735), 48 f., 111

Valla, Giorgio, 34
Valletta, Gaetano, 160, 165 f., 169
Valmarana, Gaetano, Villa Valmarana frescoes by Tiepolo, 150, 153, 161, 164, 166 f.
Vedova, Carlo, *Angelica e Medoro* (1738), 99
Vega Carpio, Lope de, 15, 23–26, 31–33; *Arte nuevo de hacer comedias*, 24, 32, 36
Verdi, Giuseppe, 69, 351, 362; *La forza del destino*, 358 f.; *Simon Boccanegra*, 358
Verene, Donald, 52
Vergil [Publius Vergilius Maro], 66, 93; *Aeneid*, 34, 367; illustrated by Tiepolo, 150
Verués, Cristóbal, *La gran Semiramis*, 36

Vico, Giambattista, *Scienza nuova*
(1725), 44 f., 52
Vignati, Giuseppe, 273; *Ambleto*
(1719), 261, 263
Villeneuve, Josse de, 233
Vinci, Leonardo, 323, 327, 360; *Artaserse* (1730), 208, 210; *Didone abbandonata* (1726), 210; *La festa
di Bacco* (1722), 52; *Peleo* (1729),
43, 52
Vitruvius [Lucius Vitruvius Ma-
murra], 20
Vittaloni, Angelica, 185
Vivaldi, Antonio, 44, 46 f., 50, 56, 58,
62–64, 66, 68, 70, 74 f., 88, 131 f.,
136 f., 145–147, 156, 166, 177,
179, 181, 185–187, 194, 269, 275,
279 f., 324, 351, 356, 358–361,
376; *Arsilda regina di Ponto*
(1716), 280, 298; *L'Atenaide*
(1728), 280, 287, 289, 299, 300–
302; *La Candace* (1720), 304, 307;
Catone in Utica (1737), 280, 287,
292 f., 297 f.; *Dorilla in Tempe*
(1726 and 1734), 52, 313–315,
318, 320–322, 324–326; *Eurilla e
Alcindo* (n.d.), 120, 357; *Farnace*
(1727), 2, 281, 296, 331, 346; *La
fida ninfa* (1732), 2, 120, 124, 143,
145 f., 280, 291, 293 f., 307, 350,
352, 357; *Ginevra* (1736), 99; *Il
Giustino* (1724), 280, 282, 293,
296, 305, 311, 314, 318–320, 323,
325; *Griselda* (1735), 2, 280 f.,
283, 288, 291, 294, 301, 305,
309 f., 322 f., 343, 346, 350 f., 357;
L'incoronazione di Dario (1717), 2,
137, 186, 190, 282 f., 295; *Juditha
triumphans* (1716), 349 f., 356 f.;
Mio cor povero cor (serenata, n.d.),
306; *L'Olimpiade* (1734), 2, 280 f.,
283, 291, 294, 306, 321, 326 f.;
Orlando (1727), 1–10, 56, 58, 62,
65, 68, 70, 72–74, 79, 80 f., 85,
99, 107, 111, 119–124, 149, 165,
193, 197, 205 f., 281, 283, 291–
293, 315 f., 327–334, 346, 358 f.,

367, 360–365, 376; *Orlando finto
pazzo* (1714), 1, 88, 99, 288 f., 292,
332–346, 367, 376; *Orlando
furioso* (pasticcio with Ristori,
1714), 308, 315, 328, 330–333;
Ottone in Villa (1713), 283 f., 288,
291, 296, 331 f., 334; *Rosmira*
(pasticcio compiled by Vivaldi in
1738), 280; *Siroe re di Persia*
(1727), 296, 310, 335–337, 339 f.;
Tamerlano [also called *Bajazet*]
(1735), 286 f., 297, 307; *Teuzzone*
(1719), 280, 283, 305; *Tieteberga*
(1717), 186, 190, 342 f.; *Il Tigrane*
(pasticcio, 1724), 290 f., 296 f.,
306; *Tito Manlio* (1720), 282 f.,
285, 289 f., 292 f., 295 f., 306, 328;
La verità in cimento (1720), 293,
302–305, 310; *Il vinto trionfante
del vincitore* (1717), 137
———, instrumental music, Concerti
Grossi, Op. 8 No. 104, 324; *Concerto funebre*, 293; Concerto in A
Major (RV 159), 310; Concerto in
C Major (RV 471), 310; "Inverno,"
296, 310 f., 318, 323; "Primavera,"
282, 311–322, 324; *Quattro stagioni*, 292, 310 f., 315, 317, 323
Volsechi, Signora, 185, 190
Voltaire, Jean-François, 17

Wagner, Richard, 362; *Parsifal*, 194;
Der Ring des Nibelungen, 79
Walker, Thomas, 11, 98
Watteau, Antoine, *Les Bergers* (1717),
174, 178; *L'Indifferent* (1707),
173–175, 178; *La vraie Gaieté* (ca.
1702), 175, 178
Weaver, John, 176, 178
Weil-Garris, Kathleen, 167
Weinberg, Bernard, 102
Weiss, Piero, 39, 70 f., 83, 345
Weisstein, Ulrich, 82
Westrup, Jack, 230
White, H. V., 52
Wiel, Taddeo, 199–201, 208 f.
Winckelmann, Johann Joachim, 49, 53

Wolf, R. Peter, 235, 253 f.
Wolff, Hellmuth Christian, 39, 274 f.
Worsthorne, Simon Towneley, 33, 36, 38, 40, 147
Wynne, Shirley, 359, 381

Zaccaria, Nicola, 1
Zanetti, Anton Maria, 158, 160–162, 168
Zanettini, Antonio, *Medea in Atene* (1675), 207
Zaslaw, Neal, 257

Zeno, Apostolo, 32, 200, 305; *Ambleto* (with Pariarti, 1705), 263, 270, 273; *Eumene* (1697), 270; *Griselda* (1701), 279 f., 305; *Griselda*, revised by Goldoni (1735), 309, 351
Ziani, Pietro Andrea, 207, 211; *L'Heraclio* (1671), 207; *La Semiramide* (1670), 207
Zorzi, L., 168
Zucchini, Marco, *Cimene* (1721), 199
Zytowski, Carl, 126